SPORTS LAW

By

George W. Schubert
Dean of University College and
Institutional Representative for Athletics
University of North Dakota

Rodney K. Smith
formerly
Associate Professor of Law
University of North Dakota
currently
Visiting Associate Professor
Delaware Law School
Widener University

and

Jesse C. Trentadue
Associate Professor of Law
University of North Dakota

WEST PUBLISHING CO.
ST. PAUL, MINN., 1986

COPYRIGHT © 1986 By WEST PUBLISHING CO.
610 Opperman Drive
P.O. Box 64526
St. Paul, MN 55164–0526

Library of Congress Cataloging-in-Publication Data

Schubert, George W.
   Sports law.

   Includes index.
   1. Sports—Laws and legislation—United States.
2. Liability for sports accidents—United States.
I. Smith, Rodney K. II. Trentadue, Jesse C.
III. Title.
KF3989.S38   1986   344.73'099   86–10996
                          347.30499

ISBN 0–314–99967–1

 TEXT IS PRINTED ON 10% POST
CONSUMER RECYCLED PAPER

 Printed with Printwise
Environmentally Advanced Water Washable Ink

Sports Law (S, S & T)
1st Reprint—1995

Preface

Recently, one of the authors of this book was accosted by his seven year old daughter, Mary, while he was watching a program dealing with the professional sports industry. It seems that Mary was a bit disgusted to find that her desired program was being pre-empted by yet another sporting "event." In an effort to persuade his daughter that she should forego her program, our intrepid author, who fancies himself a better-than-average advocate, stressed that he was "doing his homework." After he explained that he taught a class in and was writing a book about sports law, Mary reluctantly left the room mumbling something to the effect that, "another ball game—homework?—you've got to be kidding."

There is, however, a bit of truth in this otherwise humorous experience. Legal issues have increasingly found their way into the domain of the world of sport. One need look no further than the morning sports section to realize that law now has a rather profound influence on the world of sport. With labor law issues, contract issues, issues regarding the regulation of amateur athletics, antitrust issues, issues regarding compensation for injuries, and many other legal issues arising in the sports context, attorneys and judges are more than idle spectators at sporting events. Sport revenues run into the billions of dollars each year. It is little wonder, therefore, that many commentators refer to the world of sport as the "sports industry". Like other industries, it is regulated by a body of laws and rules. Anyone who takes an active role in sports, from coaches and administrators to players, is in need of some understanding of the role that law plays in the sporting world. This book is intended to give such an understanding by serving as an introduction to sports law. While West's law books are familiar to law students, we are convinced that many nonlaw students will benefit from this book. Although the terms used are often legal—how could it be otherwise in a book about sports law—we have endeavored to make them understandable to the nonlawyer.

One need look no further than the background of the co-authors of this book to realize that it is our intent to reach a

iii

broader audience than law students and lawyers. This book is designed to satisfy the interest of law students, lawyers, and laypersons who desire a basic introduction to the legal principles which have come to permeate the world of sport. Two of the authors, Professors Smith and Trentadue, are law professors, and former collegiate athletes. Both Professors Smith and Trentadue have been involved in teaching sports law to nonlawyers, law students, and lawyers alike. The other author, Professor Schubert, is a nonlawyer. Professor Schubert is Dean of University College and has served the University of North Dakota as its Faculty Athletic Representative for many years. He has also served as the President of two major collegiate athletic conferences. Professor Schubert's interest in sports law, as a layman, provided much of the impetus for this book. He recognizes, as do the co-authors, that even participation in amateur athletics is fraught with legal implications.

Despite the fact that legal issues arise in amateur as well as professional sports, when most individuals think of sports law they think of the professional sports contract. A discussion of the dynamics of negotiating a sports contract for the professional athlete should be a part of any course or general book regarding sports law, but it hardly reflects the broad scope of the law of sport. Very few lawyers or would-be agents ever get the opportunity to represent a professional athlete. On the other hand, many lawyers and athletic or administrative personnel do find themselves involved in legal matters arising in amateur or recreational sports. There are many sports or recreational personal injury cases, and there are an increasing number of cases in which an amateur athlete argues that his or her rights have been violated. Given the willingness of individuals to seek to redress their grievances or to vindicate their rights through litigation or the legal process, it seems clear that the interaction between law and sport is on the rise.

Therefore, while we have tried to provide a basic introduction to sports law issues involving professional athletes, the emphasis in this book is clearly on issues arising in amateur athletics. We feel this reflects reality—the vast majority of legal issues related to sports involve participation in amateur athletics. Thus, while many law students may dream of representing professional athletes, it is much more likely that they will be involved in handling an amateur athletic matter. The supposed glamour of the professional contracting process will never directly touch as many lives as will the day-to-day resolution of legal issues in amateur sports.

It is our hope that this book will provide students, lawyers, administrators, coaches, trainers, and other sports personnel, as well as participants and spectators, with a sense of the relationship between law and sport. In the past, courts and other regulatory entities largely tended to take a "hands off" approach to matters arising in amateur sports. Although this tendency persists to some extent, courts and regulatory entities are becoming more active in the field of sports law. For example, as our society becomes more sensitive to issues of gender or sex discrimination, both legislatures and courts have become increasingly sensitive to sports law issues. We trust, therefore, that this book will give its readers a sense of the momentum influencing the law of sport as well as an understanding of the basic legal principles related to sport.

It must be remembered that this book presents an overview of sports law. It is not intended to be exhaustive in its treatment of legal issues arising in sports. This book should give its reader a feel for this area of law without presuming to be the final word on any issue. There are lengthy treatises—most notably *The Law of Sports* by Professors Weistart and Lowell, that cover specific issues in much greater detail. We trust, nevertheless, that even a general introduction to this subject will make the reader more sensitive to the interplay between law and sport.

GEORGE W. SCHUBERT
RODNEY K. SMITH
JESSE C. TRENTADUE

*

Acknowledgments

In writing a book, one incurs many debts. Having multiple authors has only increased our indebtedness. We are certainly indebted to our students, colleagues, administrators, and family members without whom this book would never have been written. Of course, any errors or oversights in the text remain our responsibility.

No acknowledgment for a book on sports law could justly fail to thank Professors Weistart and Lowell for the massive influence their seminal work, *The Law of Sport*, has had on this area of the law. We are also particularly grateful to Dean W. Jeremy Davis of the University of North Dakota School of Law for his continuing support. Whenever we needed extra assistance, Dean Davis was quick to see that it was provided. We are also grateful to Dean Anthony J. Santoro of the Delaware Law School of Widener University for his support after Professor Smith threatened to disrupt this project by moving from North Dakota to Delaware.

As to the manuscript itself, we are greatly indebted to Marcia O'Kelly and Barry Vickrey of the University of North Dakota School of Law. Professor O'Kelly read and offered helpful comments as to the content of much of this book. For his part, Professor Vickrey willingly offered his expertise in the area of professional responsibility by preparing the section dealing with ethics and the representation of professional athletes. Also, a thank you must be forwarded to Arline Schubert, an attorney and an instructor in Business Law at the University of North Dakota, for her assistance in writing, proof reading and suggestions regarding organization.

In addition to assistance received from our colleagues, we received invaluable assistance from our students and research assistants. One always risks the sin of omission in including a list of those who assisted in this fashion. Nevertheless, we feel it necessary to mention the contributions of the following students: Kathryn Apostal, Scott Brehm, Michael Bulzomi, Mark Chipman, Gary Euren, Mary Farrington, Allison Myrha, Cheryl Schubert and Robert Stroup. We are also very grateful to Colleen Reinke for her editorial work on the manuscript. Colleen had the difficult job of trying to make three separate writing styles seem as one, and she performed the task very effectively, even though she was under a rather severe deadline. We are especially grateful to Susan St. Aubyn, Jane Clement, Mickey Kemper, Bonnie Longshore, and Bernice Mullins, our secretaries who were both patient and competent in their processing of our numerous drafts. We have told them many times how very much we appreciate their efforts, but we are pleased to do so once again.

A special thank you is likewise extended to the agents, coaches and educators who reviewed our manuscript and offered many helpful suggestions on content. Of this number, Mal Scanlan, Gordon Cooper, and Paul Kerry are singularly thanked for sharing with us their many helpful comments and years of experience in athletics.

Finally, we acknowledge the support and thoughtfulness of the people at West Publishing Company.

GEORGE W. SCHUBERT
RODNEY K. SMITH
JESSE C. TRENTADUE

Summary of Contents

*

Table of Contents

CHAPTER 1. REGULATION OF COLLEGE AND UNIVERSITY ATHLETICS

CHAPTER 4. AVOIDING A DECLARATION OF INELIGIBILITY (Page 117)

CHAPTER 5. REPRESENTATION OF THE PROFESSIONAL ATHLETE

CHAPTER 6. LABOR LAW: DEVELOPMENTS IN PROFESSIONAL SPORTS

CHAPTER 7. TORT LIABILITY

*

TABLE OF CASES

*

SPORTS LAW

*

Chapter One

REGULATION OF COLLEGE AND UNIVERSITY ATHLETICS

At the college or post high school level, modern sports have developed into a highly specialized industry. When one thinks of athletics as a labor exploitive industry, the existence of some form of governmental regulation to safeguard employee welfare seems perfectly natural. But as with all regulation of industry, there exists considerable debate about how intrusive it should be. At each level there are rules governing both play and participation. Regulation of sports has evolved as the issues have compelled, and this development is far from complete. With contemporary issues such as violence and drug use as major driving forces, regulation of both amateur and professional sports will continue to grow. This growth will likewise unavoidably intrude upon the rights of athletes, coaches, and spectators, and in most instances the courts will be the final arbiter of how far regulation should go.

1.1 COLLEGE ATHLETIC ASSOCIATIONS

In the case of amateur sports, the regulating bodies are a hierarchical combination of national and regional associations, comprised of member institutions. The following are among the more powerful and commonly encountered regulators of amateur sports beyond the high school level.

A. NCAA

President Theodore Roosevelt is given credit for establishing the National Collegiate Athletic Association (NCAA) when, in December 1905, he called a White House conference with Henry MacCrachen, chancellor of New York University. Mr. Roosevelt

1

called this conference for the purpose of reforming football rules. A second meeting was held in New York City later that same year, at which time the Intercollegiate Athletic Association of the United States (IAAUS) was established with sixty-two members. In 1910, the IAAUS was officially changed to the NCAA.

The NCAA was initially only a rule-making body and a stage for sport discussion groups. However, in 1921 the Association sponsored its first men's collegiate championship event, and by 1941 the NCAA was offering championships in ten events. In the early 1950s the Association obtained its first football television contract, which was valued at over one million dollars. Control over sports telecasts of its member institutions has provided the NCAA with the revenues and power to become the most significant regulatory body in amateur sports.

Today the NCAA is composed of almost 1,000 member institutions. Any school that is accredited by a recognized academic accrediting agency and meets NCAA standards may become a member. Membership is presently divided into three legislative and competitive divisions, Division I, Division II and Division III. Division I is comprised of the larger schools with major sports programs. With respect to football, Division I has been further divided into Division I–A and I–AA. Division II consists of institutions with smaller student enrollments and modest athletic programs. Division II schools offer fewer athletic scholarships than their Division I counterparts. Division III schools have no athletic scholarships.

Women's athletics became part of the NCAA agenda in 1980 when ten women's championships were scheduled for the 1981–82 competitive year. The number of women's championship events increased by nineteen in 1982–83 and they have remained at twenty-nine.

In addition to sponsoring national championships in men's and women's events, the NCAA also maintains intercollegiate athletic records. But the most significant aspect of the Association's authority has to do with its rule-making and enforcement powers.

The prime purpose of the NCAA is to formulate policies pertaining to intercollegiate athletics. Through numerous committees, the NCAA supervises the conduct and needs of its member institutions and, via legislation, implements and enforces safety, administrative, athletic, and educational regulations affecting college athletics. A full-time executive director heads the NCAA. Its national headquarters are in Mission, Kansas.

B. NAIA

The National Association of Intercollegiate Athletics (NAIA) is an intercollegiate athletics governing organization composed of four-year institutions. This organization was initially formed in 1940 as the National Association of Intercollegiate Basketball. In 1952 it changed its name to the NAIA and expanded into sports other than basketball. By the early 1980s the NAIA had grown from a small organization to one with over 500 member institutions.

Membership in the NAIA is open to any four-year, degree-granting college or university in the United States or Canada that is fully accredited by accrediting agencies or commissions of the Council on Postsecondary Accreditation. Member institutions must conduct their intercollegiate athletic programs according to Association regulations and standards, but NAIA member institutions can establish rules and regulations that are stricter than the Association's. Numerous similarities exist between NCAA and NAIA eligibility regulations. One important difference, however, is that eligibility rules within the NAIA govern all play in sports recognized by the Association, whereas the NCAA has special post-season tournament rules.

Like the NCAA, the NAIA has specific regulations related to transfer student eligibility and hardship regulations. Typical of the NAIA general eligibility rules are the following: (1) the athlete must be making normal progress toward a recognized degree and maintain the grade-point average required to remain a student in good standing (as defined by the institution); (2) the student-athlete must be enrolled in a minimum of twelve credit hours (or equivalent) at the time of participation, or, if participation takes place between terms, the athlete must have been enrolled during the term immediately preceding the date of athletic participation; (3) an athlete must pass a minimum of twenty-four credit hours between the term of competition and the earlier of the two immediate previous terms of attendance; (4) a student may not count more than twelve credit hours of summer school or nonterm courses toward the twenty-four credit-hour rule for athletic eligibility; (5) a second term freshman must pass nine credit hours between the beginning of the first term of attendance and the start of the second term of attendance; (6) repeated courses previously passed in any term cannot count toward the twenty-four credit-hour rule; (7) student-athletes must be eligible according to their own conference regulations; (8) an athlete may not participate for more than four seasons in any one sport; (9) a student may not compete in intercollegiate athletics upon completing all requirements for graduating from a four-year institution; (10) an athlete must be an amateur (as defined by the NAIA) in the sports in which he or she participates. *See 1985–86 NAIA Handbook.*

C. NLCAA, NCCAA, NJCAA, USOC, And Other Regulatory Authorities

In addition to the NCAA and the NAIA, there are several other organizations governing amateur sports participation. The first is the National Little College Athletic Association (NLCAA), which offers championships for both sexes at four-year colleges with enrollments of less than 500 male undergraduate students. A second organization, which also offers championships to both sexes and governs athletics in four-year institutions, is the National Christian College Athletic Association (NCCAA). The NCCAA is only open to four-year Christian institutions willing to subscribe to a "Statement of Faith." The NCCAA has approximately 100 active members. The National Junior College Athletic Association (NJCAA) governs both men's and women's junior college athletics.

The United States Olympic Committee (USOC) establishes the national goals for, and coordinates both men's and women's noncollegiate athletics. Approximately 200 athletic associations are represented by the USOC, whose major role is coordinating and promoting amateur athletic activity involving the United States and foreign nations.

The world governing body for track and field is known as the International Amateur Athletic Federation (IAAF). The IAAF regulates not only track and field, but also sets the standards for long distance running and race walking. The Athletics Congress/USA (TAC) is the United States' member of the IAAF. Pursuant to the Amateur Sports Act of 1978, 36 U.S.C. § 391 (1982), TAC was designated a national governing body for athletics in the United States. Moreover, TAC has been instrumental in establishing a trust program that enables its member athletes to receive athletic funds and sponsorship payments without losing their Olympic and international eligibility. This Trust Fund Program of The Athletics Congress/USA (TACTRUST) is discussed *infra* at § 1.2A.

D. Women's Athletic Associations

In 1967 the Division for Girl's and Women's Sports (DGWS) established the Commission on Intercollegiate Athletics for Women (CIAW). Prior to this time there was little opportunity for women in competitive sports. The purpose of the CIAW was to establish intercollegiate athletic programs for women that would lead to national championships. The first women's national championship was held in 1969 in gymnastics.

An Association for Intercollegiate Athletics for Women (AIAW) was formed in 1971. The AIAW replaced the Commission on Intercollegiate Athletics for Women. In its first year, 1971–72, the AIAW offered a program of seven national championships. Thereafter the AIAW affiliated with the American Alliance for Health, Physical Education, Recreation, and Dance, and went from an institutional membership of 280 junior colleges and universities to almost 1,000 active member institutions by 1980–81.

Between the years of 1972 and 1980, the AIAW was the only major national intercollegiate athletic governing organization for women's sports. But in the early 1980's the NCAA expanded to include women's national championships in all three of its divisions. With the NCAA's entrance into intercollegiate athletics for women, the AIAW began to lose member institutions. There was a corresponding loss of revenue as the National Broadcasting Company (NBC) and the Entertainment and Sports Programming Network (ESPN) abandoned their coverage of AIAW athletic contests in favor of the more prestigious NCAA. AIAW sponsors, such as Kodak Company, sponsor of the All-Star Basketball Team, and Broderick Company, which presented an award to the single outstanding female collegiate athlete in the nation, also elected to withdraw their support of the AIAW. The AIAW ceased operations in June of 1982.

The AIAW sued the NCAA for alleged violations of the Sherman Antitrust Act. Concluding that the market for women's sports was open to competition, the United States District Court for the District of Columbia ruled in favor of the NCAA. *See Association for Intercollegiate Athletics for Women v. National*

Collegiate Athletic Association, 558 F.Supp. 487 (D.D.C. 1983). The AIAW appealed the district court's finding, but the appellate court determined that there were no antitrust violations. *See Association for Intercollegiate Athletics for Women v. NCAA,* 735 F.2d 577 (D.C. Cir. 1984).

E. Regional Associations

The NCAA, NAIA, and other regulatory bodies previously mentioned function at a national level, but there are other associations that govern amateur athletics at a regional level. Typical of these regional governing bodies are the various leagues and conferences to which universities and colleges belong. Regional associations are permitted to make and enforce their own rules and regulations for the governance of sports activities among themselves, but they must likewise comply with the standards established by the NCAA or other national association to which they belong. The natural effect of this relationship is that a national association such as the NCAA sets a minimum standard that its members must adhere to, but the members themselves are free to impose stricter standards within their own conferences. See *infra* § 1.2B for more discussion of the relationship between conferences and the NCAA.

1.2 REGULATIONS GOVERNING ELIGIBILITY

A discussion of the eligibility rules from the various governing bodies is clearly beyond the scope of this book. There are simply too many athletic associations with rule-making and enforcement powers, and too many rules to be considered in the space allowed. It is possible, however, to consider the main NCAA rules and regulations governing eligibility. Reference is made to the NCAA rules because the NCAA is the principal governing body for amateur athletics. Other associations and organizations with the same purpose, that of protecting college and amateur athletes, have rules and regulations similar to those promulgated by the NCAA. Legal concepts and standards applicable to the NCAA rules and regulations will, therefore, have relevance to the rules promulgated by other national and regional athletic associations.

The following information is based on the *1985–86 NCAA Manual* and related materials. Emphasis has been placed on Division I and Division II rules and cases pertaining to them. This information is not meant to be a substitute for the *NCAA*

Manual, nor should it be used as such. It is imperative that the *NCAA Manual* or other official documents be used when examining specific eligibility questions and in making decisions based upon an interpretation of the Association rules and regulations.

A. Amateurism and the Student-Athlete

One of the NCAA's declared goals is to promote and preserve amateurism in college athletics. In order to advance this goal, the NCAA Constitution contains a definition of amateurism that distinguishes between an amateur athlete and professional with several rules. One rule states that if an athlete has signed a professional contract, he or she is no longer an amateur and cannot participate in that collegiate sport. The athlete loses his or her amateur status even if the professional contract proves unenforceable. *See* NCAA Const. art. 3–1–(b).

This particular rule was challenged in federal court by a student athlete, Lonnie Shelton, who had allegedly been induced to sign a professional contract by the use of fraud and undue influence on the part of an agent. Shelton was declared ineligible and he sued the NCAA, contending that the rule should not be enforced against him because the agent's misconduct rendered the contract voidable. But the court disagreed.

After examining the rule, the court concluded that its goals to protect and to promote amateurism were legitimate. Thus, even though application of this rule might produce unreasonable results in certain situations, it did not violate the United States Constitution because the rule was both rational and reasonably related to the goal of promoting and preserving amateurism among college student-athletes. *See Shelton v. National Collegiate Athletic Association*, 539 F.2d 1197 (9th Cir. 1976). The constitutional limitations upon an athletic association's rule-making and enforcement power is more thoroughly discussed *infra* at § 3.3.

NCAA regulations define the "student-athlete" as someone who is solicited by a representative of an institution to enroll and participate in intercollegiate athletics. Students who attend a college or university without being recruited by a representative of that institution are not considered student-athletes until they report for an intercollegiate squad under the direction and supervision of the athletic department. *See* NCAA Const. art. 3–1, 0.I.1.

The NCAA also views the amateur student-athlete as one who is involved in a particular sport or sports for the educational, physical, mental, and social benefits derived from the activity. One cannot receive either payment or promise of payment for participation in sports at the collegiate level. Nor can a student-athlete enter into an agreement to receive a delayed payment for any intercollegiate sports activity. Payment in any form or the right to receive compensation for participation in college athletics makes the athlete a professional. *See* NCAA Const. art. 3–1–(a)–(1).

Student-athletes are not allowed to participate on a professional team in that sport. According to NCAA regulations, an amateur who knowingly participates with professional athletes becomes a professional in that particular sport. *See* NCAA Const. art. 3–1–(d). There are, however, major exceptions to this policy in golf and tennis.

According to the NCAA Constitution, article 3–1–(d), O.I.5., individuals may compete against golf or tennis professionals provided they do not receive any kind of payment for participation. An athlete who participates in special events in tennis or golf, such as invitational tournaments, may accept awards if the awards do not exceed $300 in value *and* if the awards received are properly personalized. NCAA Const. art. 3–1–(i)–(1)–(ii). The athlete must not accept merchandise that cannot be personalized by permanently inscribing the identification of the event or the identity of the recipient on it. A student-athlete who accepts an award that exceeds the $300 limit, is not properly personalized, or is an award of merchandise from a pro-shop, becomes ineligible for all intercollegiate competition, not just for the sport involved.

Contracts with equipment companies are another impermissible source of money for the student-athlete. Funding from event promoters and contracts from marketing firms for product endorsements are also potential eligibility hazards for college athletes, especially in track and field, which has experienced a burgeoning of public interest in recent years due in large part to the jogging and fitness trends. This funding problem is further compounded by the relaxation of amateur standards by some organizations.

The governing bodies for track and field, for example, the International Amateur Athletic Federation (IAAF) and The Athletics Congress/USA (TAC), have altered their rules controlling amateurism. A Trust Fund Program of The Athletics Congress/ USA (TACTRUST) has been established to enable athletes to receive certain sponsorship moneys without losing their amateur eligibility for purposes of Olympic and international competition. Participation in the TACTRUST is limited to athletes registered by TAC.

With the use of an approved trust, TAC-registered athletes may receive fees for product endorsements or expenses from event promoters and still maintain their amateur eligibility. A conflict exists in this area, however, because approval from TAC for receipt of moneys and products related to competition may not necessarily save the athlete's eligibility under NCAA or high school amateur regulations.

Student-athletes often have campus jobs or employment through alumni of the college, but they can be paid only for work actually performed. If athletes receive remuneration for work not performed, they are no longer eligible for participation in intercollegiate athletics. See NCAA Const. art. 3–1–(f). An exception to this rule exists when the individual receiving compensation is authorized to do so by the USOC and the funds are used to cover financial losses occurring as a result of absence from employment to prepare for or participate in the Olympic Games. NCAA Const. art. 3–1–(f).

If an athlete participates in practice sessions conducted by a professional team, chances for intercollegiate athletic eligibility may be jeopardized. In order to protect their amateur standing, the individuals cannot receive any compensation for participation; cannot enter into any contract or agreement with a professional team, sports organization, or agent; and cannot take part in any game or scrimmage involving any other team. Any participation must further meet the NCAA regulations governing try outs with professional athletic teams and the practice may not be arranged by any member of the institution's coaching staff. NCAA Const. art. 3–1–(a), (b) and (d); NCAA Bylaws 3–4–(a) and (b).

A student-athlete who wishes to continue eligibility in a particular sport cannot try out with a professional athletic team during the academic year or summer when enrolled as a full-time student. However, student-athletes may try out with a professional athletic team during the summer or academic year if they are enrolled as a part-time student and do not accept any expenses or other compensation from the professional organization. NCAA Const. art. 3–1–(b)–(2).

An individual may inquire as to eligibility for a professional league's player draft and not jeopardize his or her amateur standing, but if an athlete with college eligibility remaining asks to be placed on the professional draft, such action professionalizes the athlete in that sport. It is important to note that in order to professionalize one's position, the athlete must either place his or her name on the draft list, or agree to have their name placed on the draft list. It does not matter whether or not the athlete is eventually drafted. By allowing their name to be placed on the draft list, athletes have entered into an agreement to negotiate and this renders them ineligible for further college competition. NCAA Const. art. 3–1–(a)–(2).

One of the most difficult things for athletic directors, coaches and other responsible administrators to police is the contract between agents from professional organizations and the institution's student-athletes. Nevertheless, the NCAA regulations are strict regarding this matter. They provide, in essence, that a student-athlete who contracts (orally or in writing) to be represented by an agent in the marketing of his or her athletic skills or reputation in a particular sport is no longer eligible in that sport. Agreements with scouting services for the distribution of personal information to NCAA member institutions do not constitute marketing of the athlete's ability unless the agent is compensated for placing the athlete in an institution as a recipient of athletically related financial aid. NCAA Const. art. 3–1–(c). An agency contract not limited to a particular sport is considered applicable to all sports.

B. Conference and League Rules

According to the NCAA Constitution, article 4–2–(a), all member institutions agree "to administer their athletic programs in accordance with the constitution, the bylaws and other legislation of the Association." Most colleges and universities that belong to the NCAA also have affiliation with a conference or league. These organizations may, and usually do, establish and abide by rules and regulations that are in addition to NCAA regulations.

Member organizations may establish rules separate from the NCAA as long as they are not in conflict with NCAA regulations. In addition to the right to establish and create separate rules and regulations, these leagues and athletic conferences have enforcement authority. They, too, can sanction and reprimand member institutions. Probably the most noticeable difference between NCAA and conference or league rules is that conference or league rules are more restrictive.

C. Recruitment of Student-Athletes

It is no secret that successful recruitment is an essential element of progressive and thriving athletic programs. A major university or college that consistently wins athletic contests makes major efforts to locate and recruit the very best high school and junior college student-athletes. Because successful recruitment is the crux of a winning program, particularly at the Division I level, it should come as no surprise that the NCAA has established rigid and specific rules governing this activity.

A prospective student-athlete is one who is eligible for admission to an NCAA member institution or who has started classes in the senior year of high school. Junior college students are considered prospective student-athletes, too. *See* NCAA Bylaw 1-6-(b). NCAA rules and regulations state that an athletic candidate becomes a prospective student-athlete if and when someone from an NCAA member school's athletic staff or other institutional representative personally contacts the individual, his or her parents or guardian to encourage the athlete's attendance. An alumnus or interested student may mean well when personally contacting a prospective student-athlete, however, this contact may create a grave stituation in recruitment and in maintaining the athlete's amateur status.

The rules and regulations included in the NCAA Bylaws are clear. There can be no improper inducements to lure an athlete to a particular school. Among the more common illegal recruiting practices are the following: arrangement of employment for relatives of a prospective athlete; gifts of clothing, equipment or merchandise; co-signing of loans; cash, clothing or merchandise offered at a discount; and services or housing at reduced costs. Engaging in the foregoing recruiting practices may render an athlete ineligible as well as direct sanctions to the school. *See* NCAA Bylaw 1-1-(b)-(1). A violation occurs and sanctions may be applied when these recruiting practices are undertaken by alumnus acting without the institution's knowledge or consent.

The NCAA has determined that newspaper advertisements, bumper stickers, or message buttons are improper recruitment aids if they provide publicity for a prospective student-athlete or encourage enrollment at a particular institution. Media coverage is a particularly difficult recruitment problem to control and presents great potential for violating NCAA rules and regulations.

A typical problem that occurs with some regularity involves the pre-game, half-time, or post-game interview. NCAA Bylaw 1–4–(c) provides that neither a prospective recruit nor the recruit's coach can appear on a radio or television program conducted by a coach from the recruiting college, or a program in which the college coach is participating, or any program in which the college's athletic staff has been instrumental in arranging. In other words, neither a recruit nor his or her coach can appear on a radio or television program in which the recruiting institution's athletic staff is participating. If the athlete or coach does so, the athlete may not be eligible to compete for the recruiting college. This rule applies to in-person as well as film or video-tape interviews.

Giving of gifts to a high school or junior college athlete, or coach is also contrary to NCAA recruitment provisions. A member institution may entertain coaches, but only on the institutional campus. Entertainment may include two complimentary tickets to home athletic contests, but must not include food and refreshments, room cost, or transportation to and from the campus. *See* NCAA Bylaw 1–8–(m). The coach cannot be reimbursed for transportation expenses when accompanying a student-athlete on a campus visit. NCAA Bylaw 1–8–(m)–(1).

Another complex area of recruitment is that involving contact by a recruiting college's official representative with the prospective athlete, the athlete's relatives, or legal guardian. College recruiters are limited to three contacts at sites other than the student-athlete's school. Three additional off-campus contacts with the athlete are allowed when approved by his school principal or the school's executive officer or designee. *See* NCAA Bylaw 1–2–(a)–(1)–(i). Once the recruited student-athlete signs a National Letter of Intent, though, there are no further restrictions on contacts by the signing college. NCAA Bylaw 1–2–(a)–(1).

By signing a National Letter of Intent, the athlete indicates a commitment to one college or university. Even though the athlete may not attend the school that signed him or her, the athlete's signature on the Letter of Intent means that the individual cannot be contacted by other schools, and the athlete will not be permitted to compete for any other college or university during the upcoming sports season.

NCAA regulations restrict the publicity regarding the signing of a letter of intent to communications in media forms normally used by the school. Using press conferences, receptions, and dinners to call attention to the fact that an athlete has signed a Letter of Intent is expressly prohibited. NCAA Bylaws 1–4–(a)–(1) and (2).

The NCAA defines "contact" as follows: A face-to-face situation where dialogue (which is more than a greeting) takes place; a face-to-face meeting that is prearranged; a meeting that takes place at the prospect's school, or meeting at a practice or game site. NCAA Bylaw 1–2–(a)–(2). All off-campus recruitment contact is to be made by the institution's staff members. Contact with an athlete, his or her relatives or guardian may not take place until the athlete has completed the junior year in high school. See NCAA Bylaw 1–2–(a)–(3).

A student-athlete who is transferring from one four-year institution to another is also covered by recruitment regulations. The institution to which the student is transferring must have permission from the original school before it can actively recruit the athlete. NCAA Bylaw 1–2–(g). If the original institution will not grant its permission, the receiving school may not encourage the transfer, nor can it offer or provide athletically related financial assistance to that student.

Recruitment funds must be maintained by the NCAA member institution. The institution is responsible for the disbursement of those moneys. See NCAA Bylaw 1–5–(a). The school may not use recruitment moneys to pay the expenses of outside representatives who study or recruit prospective student-athletes. Of course, the college's alumni association may be considered a bona fide recruiting organization when it is certified by the school's chief executive officer, has its records inspected by the school, and files the reports required by NCAA legislation. If the alumni association has bona fide standing, it may sponsor luncheons and dinners at which prospective student-athletes from the local area are guests. Under these conditions, the alumni association becomes subject to institutional legislation of the NCAA. NCAA Bylaw 1–5–(g).

Visitations by prospective student-athletes to college and university campuses are common occurrences. Recruiting schools are allowed to finance one campus visit, limited to forty-eight hours, for each prospect. Expense-paid visits may not take place until the opening day of classes of the athlete's senior year in high school. Transportation expenses are limited to actual round-trip costs from the student's home to the college's campus. If the prospective student-athlete uses commercial air travel, the cost is limited to round-trip tourist air fare. It is permissible to pay the recruit's transportation costs from the site of a high school athletic event to the college as long as only actual expenses are paid *and* the total cost does not exceed the cost of transportation between the athlete's home and the college campus. The visiting athlete may likewise receive reasonable and actual cost of meals consumed during the visit to and from the college campus. NCAA Bylaw 1–8–(d).

Prospective student-athletes are limited to a maximum of five expense-paid visits to campuses and only one expense-paid visit per campus. Consequently, Division I and II institutions are required to notify each prospect in writing of this five-institution limit rule. This notification must be made a minimum of five days in advance of the scheduled visit. Once the prospect has made the maximum number of visitations allowed by the NCAA, the athlete may still visit other college campuses at his or her own expense. During these nonpaid visits the athlete may still receive three complimentary tickets to a campus athletic event, and may be provided with a meal. *See* NCAA Bylaws 1–8–(e) and (f).

Recruitment violations discovered by the NCAA Infractions Committee typically include cash inducements to prospects, cash and other benefits to enrolled student-athletes, complimentary ticket sales for enrolled student-athletes, outside funds that are maintained and administered contrary to NCAA rules, arrangement of cost-free room and board for "unaided" student-athletes, secret scouting of football opponents, out-of-season practices, and an excessive number of coaches for recruiting. In some instances, gifts are given to the prospective student-athlete's family. Alumni and boosters may entice the athlete with gifts and promises of future employment. All of these examples provide ample inducement to encourage a candidate's violation of the recruitment rules. Unfortunately, recruited athletes are often ignorant of the NCAA rules that ultimately lead to their ineligibility. Yet ignorance of the rules alone will not deter the NCAA from sanctioning the athletes because to do so would give the offending school a recruitment advantage over other institutions who were obeying the rules. While the athletes may not recover their eligible status, they may have breach of contract or tort causes of action against the offending parties. Contract and tort liability for recruitment violations are discussed *infra* at, respectively, §§ 3.1 and 7.4A–8–(e).

D. Financial Aid for Student-Athletes

In order to qualify for financial aid, a student-athlete must meet eligibility requirements for participation in intercollegiate sports. Financial aid may include commonly accepted educational expenses, such as tuition and fees, room and board, and required course-related books. NCAA Const. art. 3–1–(g)–(1). Benefits from the G.I. Bill of Rights, payments from participation in military reserve, and Social Security Insurance payments do not count as financial aid.

Aid may be awarded for any term during which the student-athlete is in regular attendance with athletic eligibility remaining. To receive financial aid during a summer session, the athlete must have been in residence for a minimum of one term during the regular academic year or be attending a summer orientation program. Participation in the orientation program must be required for both athletes and nonathletes, with financial aid being administered on the same basis for all participants in the program. NCAA Const. art. 3–4–(b)–(1).

Financial assistance may not be awarded to a prospective student-athlete on the condition that he or she report for practice in satisfactory physical condition. When a student's athletic ability is taken into consideration in awarding financial aid, the period of the award may not exceed one academic year. An athlete's aid may not be granted or cancelled during the period of the award due to the student-athlete's ability, contribution to a team's success, or because of an injury that prevents the student-athlete from participating in athletics. But financial aid may be decreased or cancelled when the student makes fraudulent misrepresentations, engages in serious misconduct, or voluntarily withdraws from a sport for personal reasons. *See* NCAA Const. art. 3–4–(c).

Institutions should exercise caution in terminating a student's scholarship aid. Notice and other due process requirements may be needed before an athlete's financial aid can be terminated. See *infra* § 3.3A. Termination of an athlete's scholarship may likewise give rise to a breach of contract suit on behalf of the athlete. See *infra* 3.1. Moreover, the existence of an athletic scholarship may entitle the student-athlete to certain workmen's compensation benefits. See *infra* chapter 8.

E. Eligibility for In-Season Competition and NCAA Championships

The NCAA has established a limited number of regulations related to in-season competition, that are of broad concern to coaches and athletes in general. These regulations establish, among other things, a minimum grade-point average for eligibility and limits on the duration of an athlete's college career.

1. Minimum Grade-Point Average and Proposal Number 48

A student directly out of high school must have graduated with a minimum grade-point average (GPA) of 2.000 on a 4.000 scale in order to participate in regular-season competition and to receive athletically related financial aid during the first academic year at a Division I institution. NCAA regulations specifically require a minimum 2.000 grade-point average for an entering student to be eligible for practice, participation and athletically related financial aid. The NCAA regulation provides that a student's cumulative high school record at the end of the sixth, seventh, or eighth semester shall be used in determining eligibility under the 2.000 rule. *See* NCAA Bylaw 5–6–(b).

The high school may compute the GPA of a student-athlete in its own manner. The NCAA does not determine the method or the subjects to be considered in the computation. The NCAA does specify, however, that the high school shall consider the grades in only those courses that it considers for all students in computing the GPA. If more than one method is used to compute scores, it is permissible to employ the method most beneficial to the student-athlete, but it is not permissible to round out a student's high school GPA. If the GPA is 1.999, it is not rounded out to equal 2.000, and the high school graduate with a 1.999 average is ineligible.

A problem might arise when a high school computes a student-athlete's GPA in an atypical manner. For example, a high school may normally compute GPA's by omitting physical education grades. If this method is used, the student-athlete's GPA in high school might be less than the minimum GPA required for participation in collegiate athletics, whereas, if the student-athlete's grades from the physical education courses were included in the computation, the GPA would be greater than the minimum 2.000. Consequently, if the high school furnishes the college with a GPA score computed by including the athlete's physical education grades, it has furnished a GPA that has been calculated in an atypical manner. According to NCAA regulations, the student-athlete would be ineligible for one year from the date ineligibility is determined. *See* NCAA Bylaws 5–1–(j)–(2) and 5–6–(b).

Generally, the student's high school GPA is computed from high school courses only. If a student-athlete does not graduate from high school before enrolling in a junior college, the courses at the junior college cannot be calculated in the student's high school GPA even though the courses taken at the junior college transfer to the student's high school record and the student then graduates from high school. The NCAA considers the student a transfer student from a junior college. To be eligible at a Division I member institution, the prospective student-athlete must satisfy the transfer provisions that apply to junior college students who do not graduate from high school with a minimum 2.000 GPA. That is, the prospective athlete is not eligible for athletically related financial aid, practice, regular-season competition, and the NCAA Championships during the first academic year in residence at a four-year institution unless he or she has graduated from the junior college. NCAA Bylaw 5–1–(j)–(9).

An exception to the general rule that only high school grades can be computed arises when a student does not graduate from high school but subsequently completes the General Educational Development (GED) test and obtains a state high school equivalency diploma. The NCAA then specifies that a prospective student-athlete's high school GPA may be determined through the use of an NCAA-approved table that converts the average of the five GED scores to the high school GPA. GED scores may be used only if obtained more than one calendar year from the date the athlete would have graduated had he or she remained in high school. It is not permissible to use GED scores if the student-athlete has graduated from high school. *See* NCAA Bylaw 5–6–(b).

If a student practices or participates in intercollegiate competition while ineligible, the athlete is charged with the loss of one year of eligibility for each year gained improperly. An athlete will be declared ineligible at the time the NCAA determines eligibility was gained improperly.

According to the NCAA Bylaws, a student who reports for practice or competition before a high school GPA has been certified may practice but may not compete for a maximum of two weeks. If the student, after the two-week period, has not established the minimum high school grade-point average of 2.000, he or she is barred from continued practice or competition. If a high school or preparatory school notifies the institution in writing that it will not provide a student's grade-point average or convert the grade-point average to a 4.000 scale, an NCAA member institution may submit the individual's high school or preparatory school transcript to the NCAA Academic Testing and Requirements Committee for certification or conversion. NCAA Bylaws 5–6–(b)–(1) and (2).

Opponents of the NCAA GPA regulation argue that the student-athlete who enters college with a high school GPA lower than 2.000, but who achieves satisfactory progress during the first semester, should be eligible to participate in collegiate athletics as soon as it is demonstrated that satisfactory grades can be achieved. What many opponents of the regulation fail to acknowledge, however, is that the student-athlete who enters an institution with less than the 2.000 GPA is not prevented from attending college. An athlete with less than a 2.000 GPA can enroll and attend college classes, but cannot participate in practices or scrimmages or receive athletically related financial aid. Upon satisfactory academic progress at the completion of the freshman year, the student-athlete becomes eligible for participation in collegiate athletics.

Courts have determined that the NCAA regulations (and other similar rules promulgated by institutions and conferences) which establish minimum entry-level GPA's for freshmen and transfer students are constitutional. *See, e.g., Jones v. Wichita State University*, 698 F.2d 1082 (10th Cir. 1983) (upholding NCAA's 2.000 GPA rule for freshmen). These decisions are generally based upon the determination that the regulations are reasonably related to the purpose for which they were enacted, and that the NCAA has a recognized right to pass legislation to promote the legitimate goals and objectives of the Association, to reduce exploitation of young athletes, and to insure the academic standing of all student-athletes. *See, e.g., Associated Students, Inc. v. NCAA*, 493 F.2d 1251 (9th Cir. 1974) (upholding NCAA's 1.600 rule).

In 1983 the NCAA took a major step when Division I schools approved a proposal that significantly strengthened the academic requirements for incoming freshmen. The proposal, commonly referred to as Proposal Number 48, stated that effective August 1, 1986, entering freshmen must meet certain standards in order to compete in intercollegiate athletics their first year. They must be a high school graduate and, at the time of graduation from high school, have an accumulative minimum grade-point average of 2.000 (based on a maximum of 4.000) in a core curriculum of at least eleven academic courses. Those courses must include a minimum of three years of English, two years of mathematics, two years in social science and two years in natural or physical science, including at least one laboratory class (if offered by the high school) as certified on the high school transcript or by official correspondence. In addition to this, the entering athlete must receive a 700 combined score on the Scholastic Aptitude Test (SAT) verbal and mathematics sections or a 15 composite score on the American College Test (ACT). NCAA Bylaw 5–1–(j).

Much has been said and written about the implications of this rule on admissions policies, including its adverse impact upon minorities and other similarly disadvantaged high school athletes. The NCAA has also been under considerable pressure to amend Proposal Number 48 to permit a higher grade-point average to counterbalance a low test score or vice versa, and to phase in application of the rule. The NCAA may very well temporarily retreat from the modest academic standards it originally set in Proposal Number 48, but regardless of the final form it takes, Proposal Number 48 will not interfere with the admissions policy of an institution. Furthermore, if a student-athlete does not immediately qualify for athletic participation under this proposed rule, he or she may still be admitted and attend classes. Students may also participate in varsity athletics as a sophomore if they satisfy the "satisfactory progress rules" promulgated by their league and individual institutions. See *infra* § 1.2E–5, for a discussion of this rule. Thus, so long as the individual makes satisfactory academic progress, the student-athlete has four years of eligibility in varsity sports, notwithstanding not having met the requirements of Proposal Number 48 upon graduation from high school.

2. Five-Year Rule

The NCAA grants athletes four years of eligibility at the college level. Bylaws 4–1–(a) and (b) prescribe the length of time that a student-athlete has to complete his or her eligibility. Division I student-athletes have five calendar years from the beginning of their first semester or quarter in college to complete their eligibility. In Divisions II and III, the student-athletes have the first ten semesters or fifteen quarters in which they are enrolled in a collegiate institution to complete their eligibility. If an institution determines registration using a nontraditional semester or quarter system, the NCAA Eligibility Committee will calculate an equivalent enrollment period.

A student-athlete is considered registered when he or she enrolls for a regular term in a minimum full-time program of studies and attends the first day of classes for that term in an institution classified by the United States Department of Education. Common exceptions to the five year rule are those for an official church mission, duty in the armed forces, or service with the United States Foreign Service. If the student-athlete wants to extend eligibility based upon military service or church mission, that individual cannot attend any institution during the time spent on the church mission or in the military service.

3. Full-Time Student

Student-athletes must be eligible under the rules of their athletic conference and must meet all of the applicable rules of the NCAA constitution and bylaws before they may participate in a championship event. NCAA Bylaw 5–1–(a). Among those rules is the requirement that the athlete be registered in a full-time program of studies (as defined by the institution) at the time of competition. The athlete's college is also permitted to define what constitutes a full-time student, but it cannot be less than twelve semester hours or twelve quarter hours.

A special exception exists for a student who is in the final semester or quarter and has fewer than twelve hours remaining to complete a degree. In this situation, upon certification of the circumstances by the institution's registrar, the requirement of full-time study is waived. This procedure is administered by the conference members of the NCAA. When the institution does not belong to a conference, the NCAA Eligibility Committee is the decision-making body.

If the institution uses other than the traditional semester or quarter-hour system, the minimum academic load will be determined by the NCAA Eligibility Committee. Graduate students must be registered in a minimum full-time graduate program defined by the institution. If the student-athlete enrolls in fewer than twelve credit hours, he or she needs approval from the NCAA Eligibility Committee to be eligible for athletic competition. NCAA Bylaw 5–1–(c).

4. *Four-Year Rule*

Another common eligibility rule is one that relates to the number of seasons a student-athlete may compete. NCAA Bylaw 5–1–(d) provides that the student-athlete shall not have previously engaged in more than four seasons of intercollegiate competition. Participation during a season in an intercollegiate sport is counted as a season of competition in that sport. Any seasons spent competing at the junior college level likewise count toward this four year total. NCAA Bylaw 5–1–(d)–(4).

A student-athlete is considered a participant in a sport if (1) the athlete represented the institution in regularly scheduled, regular-season or post-season competition or in a scrimmage with outside competition; (2) participated in collegiate competition, regardless of the fact that his or her performance was not included in the scoring of the event or was otherwise considered an exhibition; (3) competed in a school uniform; (4) received from the college or university any expenses associated with the competition, including transportation, meals, room, or entry fees; or (5) received from the institution any type of equipment or clothing for the competition. NCAA Bylaw 5–1–(d)–(1).

In Division I, students may lose one year of intercollegiate athletic competition if they enroll after their twentieth birthday. This rule is established by NCAA Bylaw 5–1–(d)–(3), which reads as follows:

> Any participation by a student as an individual or as a representative of any team in organized competition in a sport during each 12-month period after the student's 20th birthday and prior to matriculation at a member institution shall count

as one year of varsity competition in that sport, provided, however, that in no event shall the student be charged with more than one year of competition in that sport in any 12-month period after the student's 20th birthday.

The twenty-year age rule has been challenged, but was upheld by a federal court. *See, e.g., Butts v. NCAA*, 751 F.2d 609 (3d Cir. 1984) (rule served legitimate purposes of promoting equality of competition by preventing college sports from being dominated by more mature and experienced athletes, and of discouraging high school students from delaying their entrance into college in order to develop their athletic skills).

5. *Good Academic Standing*

The NCAA has addressed the problem of academic standards for student-athletes. A student-athlete cannot represent an institution in intercollegiate athletic competition unless he or she has been admitted as a degree-seeking student in accordance with the regular published entrance requirements of that institution. *See* NCAA Const. art. 3–1–(i)–(3). The student must be in "good academic standing" as those academic standards are determined and applied to all other students by the faculty, and also must be making "satisfactory progress" pursuant to NCAA Bylaw 5–1–(j)–(6).

A student-athlete who has completed at least one academic year in residence or utilized one season of eligibility is required to satisfy certain minimum academic progress requirements for continuing athletically related financial aid and eligibility. After an initial year in residence or after having utilized one season of eligibility in a sport, the athlete's qualification for continuing financial aid and participation are based upon the rules of the institution and the conference in which that school is a member. Eligibility for regular-season competition depends upon the student-athlete satisfactorily completing either of the following academic progress requirements *prior* to each school term in which a season of competition begins: (1) accumulating academic credit equivalent to an average of twelve semester or quarter hours for each academic term one has been enrolled; or (2) earning twenty-four semester or thirty-six quarter hours of acceptable degree credit since the beginning of the last season of competition. Only those credit hours that are acceptable towards a specific baccalaureate degree program at the student-athlete's college are counted, but any hours earned in summer school may be utilized to satisfy NCAA academic credit requirements. Graduate students who are otherwise eligible for regular-season competition are exempt from the provisions of this regulation.

At the 1985 annual NCAA meeting, Divisions I and II institutions affirmed a resolution requiring the student-athlete to designate a program of study leading to a specific baccalaureate degree by the beginning of his or her third year of study. This designation is also required of a transfer student.

6. Other Rules

There are eligibility rules governing participation in NCAA championship play, and these too are contained in NCAA Bylaw 5–1. The following examples are typical of these championship rules. First, a student-athlete may not engage in athletic competition under an assumed name or with the intent to deceive. See NCAA Bylaw 5–1–(h). Second, unless prescribed by a physician in the course of medical treatment, athletes competing in NCAA championships may not use drugs which endanger their health or safety. The NCAA's Executive Committee is authorized to and has established testing procedures for drug use during championship events. See NCAA Bylaw 5–2. (Testing athletes for illegal drug use raises some interesting constitutional questions. See infra at § 3.3B.) Finally, the athlete who has not previously been enrolled in a four-year college is immediately eligible for play in an NCAA championship if he or she is admitted with a minimum of twenty-four semester or thirty-six quarter hours of advanced placement examination credit or concurrent high school-college credit. Credits the athlete earned in summer session courses or extension courses may not be counted towards this requirement. NCAA Bylaw 5–1–(f).

F. Transfer Eligibility Requirements

Bylaw 5–1–(j)–(7) defines the general rule of eligibility for a student transferring from a four-year institution. At a Division I or Division II institution, the transfer student is not eligible for any NCAA championship until two requirements are met. The student must first fulfill a residence requirement of one full academic year. Second, one full calendar year must have elapsed from the first regular registration and attendance date at the certifying institution. At a Division III institution, one calendar year must have elapsed from the date of the student's official withdrawal from the previous institution.

In addition to the basic requirements set forth in Bylaw 5–1–(j)–(7), Bylaw 5–2–(m) describes exceptions under which a transfer student from a four-year institution might be eligible without meeting a residence requirement. There are fourteen situations in which an exception exists. According to Bylaws 5–1–(m)–(1) and (m)–(4), an exception to the one year residence requirement exists when the student has been a participant of a formal or cooperative educational exchange program. Another exception exists, according to Bylaw 5–1–(m)–(7), when the student is returning from eighteen months of active service in the armed forces of the United States or an official church mission. If a sport in which the athlete wishes to participate has never been offered at the institution from which he or she transfers or if the college terminates its participation in that athlete's sport, the student may qualify for an exception to the residence requirement under Bylaw 5–1–(m)–(8).

A student-athlete who is enrolled at a collegiate institution and participates in a sport that is discontinued may transfer to another institution and be eligible to participate immediately. However, in order to qualify for a waiver of the one year residence requirement, the student-athlete must transfer from the original institution at the end of the academic year in which the sport was dropped or before the start of the next season of the sport. *See* Bylaws 5–1–(m)–(8) and (n)–(1). A student-athlete may qualify for a waiver of the one academic and calendar year residence requirements if the original collegiate institution discontinues the intercollegiate sport and establishes that sport on a club basis or as an intramural activity.

Bylaws 5–1–(j)–(8), (9), and (10) govern the student transferring from a junior college. A student who transfers from a junior college before graduating is not generally eligible for any NCAA championships during the first academic year at the four-year institution. Nevertheless, Bylaw 5–1–(n) provides that the residence requirement is waived if the student has a 2.000 GPA and satisfactorily completed an average of twelve semester or quarter hours of credit during each academic term of attendance at the junior college, and has a minimum of twenty-four semester or thirty-six quarter hours of transferable degree credit. Bylaw 5–1–(j)–(9) allows a student who is transferring to a Division I institution with a high school GPA under 2.000 to participate without waiting for the one academic year requirement to elapse if the athlete has graduated from the junior college and completed a minimum of forty-eight semester or seventy-two quarter hours of transferable credit toward a baccalaureate degree program.

Bylaw 5–1–(n) provides two additional situations in which the one academic year requirement can be waived for junior college transfers. To quality for this exception the athlete must meet all of the following requirements: the athlete must be transferring in order to participate in a sport that the junior college has dropped or never sponsored; the student must not have attended any other institution that offered competition in that sport; and the student-athlete must have at least a 2.000 GPA at the junior college. When the junior college student is transferring to a Division III institution and has not competed in the sport for one year immediately prior to the date on which he or she begins participation at the four year school, Bylaw 5–1–(n)–(2) waives the one academic year requirement.

As previously noted, the NCAA is not the only governing organization in intercollegiate athletics that has instituted a transfer rule. For example, the National Association of Intercollegiate Athletics (NAIA) requires that transfer students be in residence for either one term of attendance or sixteen weeks before they become eligible. Although students do have the opportunity to apply for an exception to the NCAA's residence requirement, few are granted. Moreover, because courts have generally declined to intervene in the internal affairs of a private athletic association, there are few cases challenging the NCAA and its transfer rules, and these have generally gone against the ineligible athlete. *See, e.g., English v. NCAA*, 439 So.2d 1218 (La.Ct.App.1983) (upholding college transfer rules because it prevented evils of recruiting by prohibiting an athlete from playing for two different major colleges in successive years).

G. Hardship Eligibility

Despite being injured and unable to compete during most of the season, an athlete might still be charged with the loss of a year's eligibility in that sport. The NCAA has, however, attempted to alleviate some of the injustice in these situations with passage of its hardship rule. The rule provides that when an athlete is unable to compete due to a hardship, the otherwise lost season of eligibility will be restored. NCAA Bylaw 5–1–(d)–(2).

"Hardship" is characterized as being unable to participate due to injury or illness. In order to qualify under the hardship rule, an injured athlete must meet several conditions. First, injury or illness must have occurred in one of the allotted seasons of intercollegiate competition at an NCAA member institution. Second and most important, the injured or ill athlete must not have participated in more than twenty percent of the school's competitive events in the sport *or* must not have competed in more than two of the institution's completed events in that sport, whichever number is greater. In calculating the percentage of contests in which a student-athlete has participated, fractions of numbers are rounded to the next highest number.

This hardship provision is based on the assumption that the injury or illness occurred in the first half of the season and the student-athlete was not able to compete for the remainder of the season. It is important to note that the injury or illness does not have to be athletically related in order for the student-athlete to be considered for the hardship exception, but the promptness with which the athlete and coaching staff act upon the hardship application is important.

Each conference is charged with the administration of the hardship regulation and may add additional conditions that must be met before the student-athlete is considered for a hardship exception. These conditions usually address timely notification and filing of an appropriate petition. The responsibility of filing the appropriate hardship petition most often rests with coaches and the athletic director.

If a problem arises under the hardship rule, courts look deferentially at the regulations promulgated by both the NCAA and the conferences. If it appears that the rules are not arbitrary or capricious, and that they are enforced equally as to all intercollegiate athletes within the conference, a court will not interfere with their application. *Fluitt v. University of Nebraska*, 489 F.Supp. 1194 (D.Neb.1980), is a good example of both the need for timely action in filing a hardship petition and a court's general reluctance to interfere in the NCAA's eligibility rule-making and enforcement process.

Mark Fluitt entered the University of Nebraska in the fall of 1975 on an athletic scholarship and competed in cross country that fall. In late September, after regular workouts and practices, Fluitt was injured and experienced intense pain whenever he ran. He was able to compete in one meet in September and three in October. The cross country season was over in November and Fluitt began to practice with the men's track team indoors. But the pain worsened so that he was only able to compete in one track meet that season, a triangular meet in January, 1976.

This was Fluitt's last meet as a freshman and he did not practice during the remainder of the season. Nevertheless he was able to overcome his injury and competed during the next three years. The first two years Fluitt had a full scholarship. During his third and fourth year Fluitt had a partial scholarship which amounted to eighty percent of a full scholarship.

In the spring of 1979, his fourth year of college, Fluitt asked the coach to request an additional year of eligibility from the Big Eight Conference. The coach told Fluitt that his request was untimely. The Big Eight Conference regulation required that any request for an additional year of eligibility must be made during the academic year in which the injury or hardship occurred. However, the Conference had, in the past, granted late applications.

Fluitt petitioned the Big Eight Conference for hardship treatment, but his request was denied. Thereafter he brought suit against the University of Nebraska, the Big Eight Conference, and the NCAA alleging that he had been denied due process and equal treatment of the laws regarding his hardship application.

Fluitt's due process argument hinged in part upon the assertion that he was unaware of the regulation. The court, however, determined that since the regulations were available, it was the student-athlete's responsibility to know them or to read them. The court found that Fluitt was personally at fault when he made no attempt to find out about the eligibility rules of the Big Eight Conference until three years after his injury had occurred; Fluitt was "inordinately naive" not to realize that he was participating under Big Eight rules and regulations.

The court in *Fluitt* further determined that the regulations were not discriminatory and due process had been accorded throughout the proceedings for several reasons. First, the regulations were enforced by a governing body composed of a faculty representative from each member institution. Big Eight Conference rules gave these faculty representatives full power to act on all special cases not covered in the rules. Second, Fluitt had ample opportunity to present his petition for hardship to the Conference governing body the year he was injured. Under these circumstances it was difficult for the court to conceive of any other procedures that might be required for due process.

1.3 ENFORCEMENT

Membership eligibility in the NCAA has a broad base. By the terms of the NCAA Constitution, not only can institutions of higher education be members, but membership may be extended to athletic conferences, associations, or any other groups related to intercollegiate athletics. More importantly, once a school or athletic organization becomes a member, it agrees to administer its athletic program in accordance with the constitution, bylaws, and other rules and regulations promulgated by the NCAA. *See* NCAA Const. art. 4–2–(a).

NCAA rules and regulations are strictly enforced, both by the Association and by individual athletic conferences. A Committee on Infractions is the NCAA's investigative and enforcement arm, and the Association employs full-time investigators to look into alleged violations of its rules.

Investigations are normally commenced following receipt of a complaint, from a responsible source, to the effect that a member institution is involved in a violation of Association rules. The Committee may, however, commence its own investigation when it has reasonable cause to believe a violation has occurred. The institution being investigated is notified of the allegations and requested to cooperate with the Committee on Infractions. NCAA Bylaw 9–5.

Violations are classified as either secondary or major. A "secondary" violation is of an isolated or inadvertent nature, *and* one which does not provide the offending institution a significant recruitment or competitive advantage. All other violations are considered major, including repeated secondary violations. *See* NCAA Enforcement Procedure § 2–(d). Although the Committee on Infractions has some discretion in imposing penalties upon major violators, with few exceptions, these penalties will include:

> (1) A two-year probationary period (including a periodic in-person monitoring system and written institutional reports);

(2) The elimination of all expense-paid recruiting visits to the institution in the involved sport for one recruiting year;

(3) A requirement that all coaching staff members in the sport be prohibited from engaging in any off-campus recruiting activities for one recruiting year;

(4) A requirement that all institutional staff members determined by the Committee on Infractions knowingly to have engaged in or condoned a major violation be subject either to termination of employment, to suspension without pay for at least one year or to reassignment of duties within the institution to a position that does not include contact with prospective or enrolled student-athletes or representatives of the institution's athletics interests for at least one year;

(5) One year of sanctions precluding postseason competition in the sport;

(6) One year of television sanctions in the sport; and

(7) Institutional recertification that the current athletics policies and practices conform to all requirements of NCAA regulations.

NCAA Enforcement Procedure § 7–(c). Because they are less serious, secondary violations are not as severely punished as major violations.

Those individuals or institutions guilty of a secondary violation may not be sanctioned if the assistant executive director for enforcement determines that no penalty is warranted. But if a penalty is imposed, it may consist of one or more of the following:

(1) Termination of the recruitment of the prospect by the institution or, if the prospect enrolls (or has enrolled) in the institution, permanent ineligibility to represent the institution in intercollegiate competition (unless eligibility is restored by the NCAA Eligibility Committee upon appeal);

(2) Forfeiture of contests in which an ineligible student-athlete participated;

(3) Prohibition of the head coach or other staff members in the involved sport from participating in any off-campus recruiting activities for one year;

(4) An institutional fine for each violation with the monetary penalty ranging in total from $500 to $5,000;

(5) A limited reduction in the number of either initial or total financial aid awards that may be awarded during a specified period in the sport involved to the maximum extent of 20 percent of the maximum number of awards normally permissible in that sport; and

(6) Institutional recertification that its current athletics policies and practices conform to all requirements of NCAA regulations.

NCAA Enforcement Procedure § 2–(e). It is even possible for the institution to avoid being penalized, or at least minimize any sanctions, by voluntarily disclosing the violation prior to a complaint being filed with the NCAA's Committee on Infractions. *See* NCAA Enforcement Procedure § 2–(f).

An institution being investigated is advised of the charges against it by the Committee on Infractions, and given an opportunity to participate in the proceedings. Schools accused of a secondary violation are permitted to file a written response to the charges. Those institutions suspected of a major violation may appear before the Committee and produce evidence in their defense. NCAA Bylaw 9–5. Afterwards the Committee makes its written findings and imposes a penalty, if necessary, when an infraction has occurred.

Once a violation has been established, the offending institution can appeal the adverse decision to the NCAA Council. If the appeal is unsuccessful, however, the school committing a major infraction can be sanctioned with loss of scholarships, and television revenues, forfeiture of games, and other severe penalties. With recent passage of its "death penalty" rule, the NCAA made it very clear that it plans to continue its policy of monitoring and severely punishing those institutions that repeatedly violate Association rules.

The death penalty provision is contained in § 7–(d) of the NCAA Enforcement Procedures and it reads, in pertinent part, as follows:

An institution shall be considered a repeat violator if any major violation is found within the five-year period following the starting date of a major penalty. The minimum penalty for a repeat violator, subject to exceptions authorized by the Committee on Infractions in unique cases on the basis of specifically stated reasons, shall include:

(1) The prohibition of some or all outside competition in the sport involved in the latest major violation for one or two sports seasons and the prohibition of all coaching staff members in that sport from involvement directly or indirectly in any coaching activities at the institution during a two-year period;

(2) The elimination of all initial grants-in-aid and all recruiting activities in the sport involved in the latest major violation in question for a two-year period;

(3) The requirement that all institutional staff members serving on the NCAA Presidents Commission, Council, Executive Committee or other committees of the Association resign those positions, it being understood that all institutional representatives shall be ineligible to serve on any NCAA committee for a period of four years, and

(4) The requirement that the institution relinquish its voting privilege in the Association for a four-year period.

NCAA Enforcement Procedure § 7–(d). This punishment is reserved for repeat offenders. It is referred to as the "death penalty" rule because imposition of these sanctions not only kill a schools athletic program in an offending sport for the term of the sanction, but it may have a lasting adverse impact on future recruitment and the institution's overall ability to compete in that sport.

The NCAA has also taken steps to sanction coaches who violate its rules. Member institutions must now include in their contractual agreements with coaches a provision which provides that any coach found in violation of NCAA regulations shall be subject to disciplinary action according to the NCAA Enforcement Procedures. *See* NCAA Const. art. 3–2–(d) and (e). Coaches guilty of an NCAA infraction may be sanctioned even after they have left the school where the violations occurred. *See* NCAA Bylaw 5–6–(d)–(3). Prior to enactment of these provisions, a coach could violate the NCAA rules and, once sanctions were imposed upon the institution, the coach would simply leave to work at another school. For a discussion of the tort liability associated with violation of athletic association rules see *infra* at § 7.4A–8–(e).

Chapter Two

HIGH SCHOOL ATHLETICS

School boards and athletic administrators have enjoyed a powerful position in the regulation of institutional athletics. Moreover, courts have generally refused to intervene in the internal affairs of high schools, school districts, and organizations that control or govern any aspect of a school's athletic program. But in the 1960s athletes began to test the actual authority that was delegated to athletic coaches and directors of athletic programs because these administrators had begun to regulate personal behavior, including marriage and physical appearances. Courts accepted jurisdiction over these cases and invalidated rules that interfered with the constitutional rights of individual participants.

This judicial activity signified that the courts were no longer willing to allow administrators and other decision-makers uncontroverted control over athletics. Once the courts asserted jurisdiction to review questions of legality in the institutions' athletic programs, other restrictions in addition to freedom of expression were tested. The changing social attitudes toward marriage created a demand on the courts to review the rules and regulations that schools and institutions enforced in this area. Included in the reviewed rules were those disqualifying married students from participating in school-sponsored athletic programs. These rules, which prevented a protected class from participation, were changed under the close scrutiny of the courts because school districts and administrators were unable to show that such rules had a reasonable basis related to the health and welfare of the community and state. *See infra* at § 3.3D–1–(c) (classifications based on marital status).

Associations should, therefore, be careful in drafting and updating their rules and regulations so that they will withstand judicial scrutiny. The rules must protect the health and welfare of athletes and they must serve to protect a justifiable public interest. The court will, ultimately, employ a balancing of interests as a test for reviewing the constitutionality of high school athletic association rules. The court generally shows great deference to the judgment of the specialists who created these rules and are best equipped to decide controversies concerning them. Unless there is evidence of fraud, collusion, or unreasonable, arbitrary, or capricious action, a court is unlikely to intervene on behalf of a student concerning the interpretation of a rule promulgated by an athletic organization or school.

2.1 REGULATIONS GOVERNING ELIGIBILITY

The eligibility rules discussed below are the ones most commonly encountered by high school athletes and coaches. Since they share common objectives (*e.g.*, protection of the student-athlete, and the promotion of amateur athletics), rules enacted by high school athletic associations are quite similar to those which govern college athletics. Hence, anyone with questions about the enforceability of a particular interscholastic association rule would certainly want to review the NCAA's counterpart *supra* at § 1.2E. A more detailed discussion of constitutional challenges to both college and high school association rules is contained *infra* at § 3.3D–1.

A. Right to Participate

By necessity, one of the first questions that arose concerning high school athletics and the eligibility of a high school student to compete in a high school's athletic program was whether the student had any "right" to participate, and if so, how much of a "right." Courts have been genuinely reluctant to recognize a right to participate. *See, e.g., Florida High School Activities Association, Inc. v. Thomas,* 409 So.2d 245 (Fla.1982), *rev'd on other grounds,* 434 So.2d 306 (although participation in interscholastic athletics was held to be an "essential part of the American educational mosaic", it did not attain the level of a constitutional right). A more thorough treatment of the right to participate can be found *infra* at § 3.3A–1–(c).

B. Grade-Point Average

Among the most frequently challenged regulations are those pertaining to academic eligibility requirements. Challenges concerning academic eligibility requirements recently arose in the combined cases of *Bailey v. Truby* and *Myles v. Board of Education of the County of Kanawha*, 321 S.E.2d 302 (W.Va.1984). The first issue before the court in these consolidated actions was whether the West Virginia State Board of Education had the legal authority to impose a requirement for students to maintain a grade-point average of 2.000 in order to participate in extracurricular activities (*Bailey*). The second issue was whether the Kanawha County Board of Education could require students to receive passing grades in all of their classes in order to participate in nonacademic extracurricular activities (*Myles*). Both rules were upheld.

The Supreme Court of West Virginia stated that the State Board of Education's rule requiring a 2.000 grade-point average for participation in nonacademic extracurricular activities was a legitimate exercise of its power of "general supervision" over the state's educational system. The court used similar reasoning in determining that the county board's restriction was valid. The Kanawha County Board of Education also had a legitimate concern in the encouragement of academic excellence, and regulation of nonacademic extracurricular activity was a common and accepted method of achieving that fundamental goal.

C. Four-Year Rule

High school athletic associations often employ a four-year eligibility rule. Under this rule a student-athlete has eight consecutive semesters in which to participate in athletic competition commencing at the time the student finishes eighth grade or begins ninth grade. The Georgia Supreme Court recently ruled on two cases concerning the four-year rule. In the first case the parents of a young athlete decided to have their son repeat the eighth grade. The high school athletic association contended that this repeat year counted as one of the boy's four years of eligibility. The athlete sued to regain the lost year of eligibility, but the court upheld the four-year rule. *See DeKalb Co. School System v. White*, 244 Ga. 454, 260 S.E.2d 853 (1979).

In a similar case a Georgia high school male athlete was forced to interrupt his high school education in order to care for his invalid mother. When the young man reentered high school one year later, he learned that the one-year's absence counted as a year of eligibility. This athlete filed suit to regain his lost year of eligibility, but the court again held that the four-year rule was constitutional. The rule was constitutionally permissible because it assisted in keeping high school athletics safe and competitive by allowing athletes of near equal maturity to compete against each other. *See Smith v. Crim,* 240 Ga. 385, 240 S.E.2d 884 (1977). *But see Florida High School Activities Association v. Bryant,* 313 So.2d 59 (Fla.App.1975) (boy forced to withdraw from school because of personal hardship should not lose such an important experience as competing in high school athletics).

D. Transfer Rule

Transfer rules have been similarly upheld as valid unless the athlete establishes a serious infringement of a constitutionally protected right. In *Walsh v. Louisiana High School Athletic Association,* 428 F.Supp. 1261 (D.La.1977), for example, it was argued that a transfer rule which restricted the eligibility of students to compete in interscholastic high school contests violated their right to religious freedom. Several male students wanted to attend a Lutheran school outside their home district, but enrollment in any high school other than a school in their home district would have rendered them ineligible. The young men sued, contending that this rule violated their constitutional rights.

The United States district court determined that the rule did not encroach on religious freedom because the student was allowed to attend any school, private or public, religious or nonreligious. Although there was a restriction placed upon participation in athletics, the court did not find that the right to participate in athletics was protected by the Constitution. *See also Cooper v. Oregon School Activities Association* and *Faherty v. Oregon School Activities Association,* 52 Or.App. 425, 629 P.2d 386 (1981) (Oregon Court of Appeals held that a transfer rule similar to the Louisiana rule was, for the same or similar reasons, not violative of the right to free exercise of religion).

E. Age Restrictions

Most state high school athletic associations have a rule prohibiting students who are nineteen years old or older from participating in interscholastic athletics. Such rules are promulgated for the following reasons:

    1. Older and mature athletes could constitute a danger to the health and safety of younger students;

    2. Individuals of that age are not the "usual high school athlete," since many college players are nineteen;

    3. The possibility of "redshirting" athletes through voluntary repetition of grades to gain advantage in competition is eliminated; and

    4. The older student is prevented from precluding the fourteen-year-old from competition.

Courts have consistently found these to be legitimate goals for a state high school athletic association. Therefore, age rules have generally been upheld. *See, e.g., State ex rel. Missouri State High School Activities Association v. Schoenlaub,* 507 S.W.2d 354 (Mo.1974) (age rule reasonable even though no hardship exception existed).

F. Physical Impairment

    Students with handicapping conditions, such as impaired vision or hearing, have begun to question rules that prohibit them from participating in high school activities. Some students have challenged these rules on the basis of the Rehabilitation Act of 1973, 29 U.S.C. § 794 (1982), which protects the rights of students with handicapping conditions. Others have attacked rules that restrict participation by the physically impaired on constitutional due process and equal protection grounds.

    Regardless of the approach taken, if the rule is found to be reasonably related to a legitimate purpose and otherwise grounded on medical evidence, it will usually be upheld. *See, e.g., Colombo v. Sewanhaka Central High School District No. 2,* 87 Misc.2d 48, 383 N.Y.S.2d 518 (1976) (prohibiting participation by deaf football player); *Spitaleri v. Nyquist,* 74 Misc.2d 811, 345 N.Y.S.2d 878 (1973) (student with only one eye not allowed to play high school football). However, recent decisions do indicate that courts are becoming more inclined to recognize the rights of disabled athletes. This trend is reviewed in more detail *infra* at § 3.5 dealing with sports and the disabled.

G. Personal Appearance

In the late 1960s and early 1970s a controversial issue in the regulation of high school athletics was the length of an athlete's hair. Courts determined that if a rule regulating either hair length or facial hair was reasonable and advanced an educational purpose, it should be obeyed. *See, e.g., Zeller v. Donegal School District,* 517 F.2d 600 (3d Cir.1975) (federal courts should defer to the judgment of school officials). *But see Dostert v. Berthold Public School District No. 54,* 391 F.Supp. 876 (D.N.D.1975) (rule regulating hair length not found to be related to school's educational mission). For a discussion of grooming rules and possible impact upon the athlete's freedom of religion, see *infra* § 3.3C–1.

H. Good Conduct

Many high schools and interscholastic athletic associations have "good conduct" rules. These rules are general in nature, usually requiring that the athlete adhere to some vague standard of conduct. This poses enforcement problems. So long as the rule extends to a legitimate sports-related purpose, it is likely to be upheld. On the other hand, if the rule is too broad and attempts to regulate an athlete's conduct during the off-season or conduct not otherwise related to athletic activities, it will probably be struck down by the courts on due process or equal protection grounds. *See, e.g., Bunger v. Iowa High School Athletic Association,* 197 N.W.2d 555 (Iowa 1972) (presence of athlete in a car with other person drinking beer during the off-season had no relation to the high school's athletic program, hence the student-athlete could not be declared ineligible under state athletic association's good conduct rule).

2.2 SCHEDULING OF SPORTING EVENTS

A more comprehensive treatment of Title IX of the Education Amendments of 1972 can be found *infra* at § 3.4A. Yet brief mention of the impact this law has had upon the scheduling of boys' and girls' athletic events should be made at this time. In most school districts, boys' and girls' teams in the same sport have separate seasons. This is usually necessitated by lack of facilities; access to tennis courts, basketball courts, and swimming pools is limited in many school districts. Nevertheless, Title IX now mandates that schools develop gender-neutral co-educational sports programs or provide equal sports programs for males and females. The requirement that equal programs be provided has led to claims of Title IX violations for separately scheduling boys' and girls' sports, and at least one law suit has challenged the practice of separate scheduling on constitutional grounds.

An action was brought against the Minnesota State High School League for establishing separate sport seasons for males and females. The complaint charged that the scheduling was unconstitutional because it denied equal protection of the law, but the Minnesota Supreme Court held that the limitation of suitable facilities was a valid reason for the separate seasons. The court added, however, that if facilities were available, a policy of separate scheduling might be unconstitutional. The court also stated that while it favored a co-educational sports program, the high school league was not compelled to sponsor a "gender-neutral two season format." *See Striebel v. Minnesota State High School League,* 321 N.W.2d 400 (Minn.1982) (the dissenting judges stated that "administrative ease and convenience are not sufficiently important objectives to justify gender-based classification," and that sex-based separate seasons served no important governmental interest).

2.3   FEES TO PARTICIPATE IN EXTRACURRICULAR ACTIVITIES

When faced with serious financial problems, some school boards attempt to levy a fee upon students participating in extracurricular activities. This solution to funding interscholastic athletics was successfully challenged by parents in Santa Barbara, California in the case of *Hartzell v. Connell,* 137 Cal.App.3d 196, 186 Cal.Rptr. 852 (1982).

Plaintiffs in *Hartzell* claimed this fee violated the California statutes and the equal protection clauses of both the California and United States Constitutions. The court determined that since the fees were not authorized by the California Constitution, they were unlawful (*i.e.,* unconstitutional). Once it had determined that the fees were unconstitutional, the court did not have to consider whether the fee was reasonable or necessary. Although it recognized the financial predicament of the school system, the court concluded that the school district could not levy a fee on extracurricular activities at will.

Chapter Three

LIMITATIONS ON REGULATORY AUTHORITY

Chapters 1 and 2 outline the pervasive nature of regulations formulated for the governance and administration of amateur athletics at all levels. Given the expansive nature of these regulations and the relative disparity in bargaining power between student-athletes and the large associations that promulgate the rules and regulations, the courts are occasionally called upon to protect student-athletes from regulatory excesses. However, an examination of relevant caselaw quickly brings one to the realization that judicial intervention on behalf of athletes has been sparse. While there has been some willingness on the part of courts to intervene on behalf of individual athletes during the past decade or two, that intervention has been restrained. Courts often decline to intervene on the grounds that they ought to defer to the expertise of educators and administrators in athletic associations and educational or academic institutions, or that they (courts) lack competence in matters related to educational policy-making and administration, or because public education and related matters have largely been committed to the control of local and state authorities.

Nevertheless, there have been inroads made on behalf of athletes. Generally, athletes have been afforded some recourse under the principles of contract and constitutional law. Member institutions have also enjoyed some success in challenging larger athletic associations based on antitrust law. This chapter examines developments in these areas.

3.1 CONTRACTUAL RIGHTS AND OBLIGATIONS

By the 1970s, a few courts had begun to recognize that a contractual relationship can exist between an athlete who accepts

39

an athletic scholarship and the college or university that awards the scholarship. While this "contractual relationship" has occasionally been acknowledged, serious disagreements remain as to the nature and extent of the relationship. These disagreements arise even in the case of express agreements, such as letters of intent and tenders of financial assistance. These agreements, although signed by the athlete, are normally quite general, particularly insofar as the rights of the athletes are concerned. The agreements are also painstakingly drafted to limit the liability of the academic institutions and the athletic conferences involved. Despite this care in drafting, contractual issues arise that are not clearly covered by the language of these documents. Additionally, oral promises extending well beyond the scope of the language of the signed agreements are often made by coaches, recruiters, and athletic directors. Since enforceable promises may be expressed in writing or orally, or may be implied-in-fact, the athlete may be afforded relief under traditional contract law when he or she establishes the existence of a legally enforceable promise (*i.e.,* contract).

A. Express Contracts

A contract that results from oral or written statements is usually referred to as an express contract. Contracts can also result from one's conduct and these are often referred to as implied-in-fact contracts. Technically, the distinction between implied and express contracts has little legal consequence, but as a practical matter it is easier to prove express contracts and courts are much less inclined to defer to the judgment of the institution or association once the existence of a contract is established.

The case that is considered the seminal judicial authority for the position that a contract exists between the student-athlete and the university is *Taylor v. Wake Forest University*, 16 N.C.App. 117, 191 S.E.2d 379 (1972), *cert. denied*, 192 S.E.2d 197 (1972). The court in *Taylor* construed written as well as oral promises made to a student-athlete to be a contract. However, since the athlete had failed to comply with his obligations under the contract, Wake Forest University's termination of his scholarship was justified. Although the court held against the student-athlete in *Taylor*, despite having recognized the existence of a contract right in the scholarship, the court's reasoning relative to the existence of a contractual relationship opened the door to future actions by student-athletes based on their agreements with their respective colleges or universities.

It should also be noted that in construing the contract in *Taylor*, the court was willing to look at oral as well as written evidence to determine the meaning of the terms of the contract. Thus, even though student-athletes rarely bring actions based on their scholarship agreements with their respective colleges or universities, it is clear from *Taylor* that a lawsuit based on an express written or oral contract may be brought in certain jurisdictions.

B. Implied-in-Fact Contracts

Courts do not distinguish between express and implied contracts. A contract is enforceable regardless of whether it is express or implied-in-fact, but because implied contracts are based on conduct rather than words, it is sometimes more difficult to prove their existence. Moreover, since the institution has played the determinative role in defining trade usage, custom, and other related factors that are often critical in assessing whether conduct gives rise to a contract, the burden on the student-athlete is compounded. Despite these difficulties in proving their existence, implied-in-fact contracts remain a viable theory for scholarship athletes to sue under.

Student-athletes have experienced some success during the last couple of years in bringing suits based on implied-in-fact contracts. *See, e.g.*, cases discussed in Note, *Educating Misguided Student Athletes: An Application of Contract Theory*, 85 Col.L. Rev. 96, 108–111 (1985). This success should encourage coaches and other personnel (*e.g.*, student advisors) to be very careful when they make promises or representations to a student-athlete. Although universities and colleges have generally sought to limit their liability to the amount of assistance expressly promised in the tender of financial aid, additional promises and representations may be made, permitting the student-athlete to recover for damages incurred as a result of the breach or nonperformance of those promises or representations.

C. Reliance or Promissory Estoppel

Even when all the formalities required for an express contract are not present, a party may be able to enforce a promise or representation made by another party on the basis of promissory estoppel or reliance. For example, § 90 of the Restatement, Second, of Contracts provides that justifiable reliance upon a promise establishes a distinct or additional basis for creating contractual rights and duties. Therefore, even if a court were to hold that some contract formality was missing in the student-athlete and college relationship, it might nevertheless find a contract on the basis of justifiable reliance. It should be noted, however, that § 90 of the Restatement, Second, of Contracts limits recovery "as justice requires." Consequently, it is not clear whether athletes are entitled to their expectation damages in suits based on a reliance theory.

D. Implied-in-Law or Quasi Contracts

Implied-in-law or quasi contracts arise when a claim for restitution is initiated to redress inequities caused by the conferring of some benefit by one party upon another. All the formalities of a contract need not be present to establish an action in quasi-contract; the crucial element is unjust enrichment. When one party has been unjustly enriched at the expense of the other, quasi contract provides a legal basis for the recovery of the value of that benefit.

In the athletic context, a student-athlete might argue that the university would be unjustly enriched if permitted to retain the benefit of his or her services or to keep other institutions from obtaining them. This is particularly true with regard to athletic programs that enjoy substantial economic benefits and are largely businesses. Thus, even if the athlete cannot establish the presence of all the elements of a contract, he or she might be able to bring an action based on quasi-contract for restitution of the benefits conferred by the athlete on the institution when the institution failed to perform its obligations (*e.g.*, to educate the student-athlete). Given the magnitude of the possible contribution of or benefit conferred by a prize athlete to a college or university (such as increased media revenues and increased alumni support attributable to a successful athletic program), the potential exists for a large recovery against an institution.

E. Defense of Academic Abstention

Courts have historically deferred to the judgment of the academic community on decisions related to the internal operations of academic institutions. This deference is known as the doctrine of "academic abstention." The doctrine and its recognition of academic autonomy is not without limit. Recently, courts have been willing to distinguish between purely academic matters and matters of an administrative or basically nonacademic nature. If the court finds that a contract exists between the student-athlete and the institution, it will generally not permit the institution to rely on the doctrine of academic abstention as a complete defense to a contract claim by the student-athlete.

Even though the doctrine of academic abstention will seldom serve as a complete defense, it retains vitality as a limitation on the extent to which courts feel competent to render decisions related to the educational process. Courts are still disinclined to interfere in educational matters. The closer the issues in a given case are to purely academic decision-making, the less likely a court will be to interfere in the academic operations in anything but a marginal way. The reverse is also true. The less "academic" the decision, the more likely the court will be to refuse to defer to the decision of the institution. Of course, all other available contract defenses may be invoked as a defense in an action based on contract or quasi-contract principles.

F. Remedies

Courts will try to protect the expectations of the parties to a contract, but they are reluctant to require specific performance in personal service contracts. Instead of ordering an athlete to participate, courts prefer to permit the nonbreaching party to recover monetary relief sufficient to place the athlete in the position he or she would have been in had the contract been performed. The monetary relief is referred to as the expectation or expectancy of the bargain damages, but there are other ways to measure damages besides measuring the expectation of the bargain. When appropriate, courts may choose to award the reliance or restitution measure of damages. Reliance damages are limited to an amount necessary to reimburse the innocent party for the loss caused by his or her reliance on the contract, thereby placing the relying party in the position he or she would have been in had the contract never been made. Restitution damages, on the other hand, consist of restoring the monetary value of any benefit conferred upon another party to the party conferring that benefit.

Traditional contract principles are applied to determine what, if any, measure of relief is appropriate. Proving damages also places limitations on recovery. The burden is on the innocent or nonbreaching party to establish the existence of the contract and the damages alleged. Proof of damages can often be a difficult matter for the plaintiff, because contract damages must be established with reasonable certainty. For example, damages arising from a loss of educational opportunity may be immensely difficult to prove because the monetary loss attributable to lost opportunities for future employment (whether in athletics or otherwise) tends to be speculative and very hard to establish. In addition to the difficulty of proving damages, whether in the form of the expectation, reliance, or restitution interest, the nonbreaching party must make reasonable efforts to mitigate or avoid the consequences of the breach and will be held accountable for his or her failure to do so.

These burdens relative to the recovery of damages, coupled with the tendency of courts to defer to administrators in academic matters, often make legal actions based on contract law in the amateur sports context difficult to win and impractical to initiate. The weak bargaining position of most student-athletes further contributes to the current state of affairs in which successful legal actions on the part of student-athletes are rare. Nevertheless, legal relief based on contract law may be available, and may in time even include the award of punitive damages.

Courts have been very reluctant to award punitive damages in contract actions, but this is changing, especially in areas like insurance law. The status relationship between an insured and the insurer and the disparity in bargaining power inherent in that relationship now permits an award of punitive damages in the event of a bad faith breach of contract by the insurance carrier. The student-athlete's relationship to the educational institution and the athletic associations that promulgate regulations governing their relationship is arguably analogous to that of an insured to the insurer and the insurance industry.

Courts have also occasionally been willing to award punitive damages for a breach of contract that is in some respect tortious, particularly when a consumer or a fiduciary relationship is involved. As was the case with the insured-insurer relationship, the student-athlete's relationship to the educational institution is not unlike the relationship between the consumer and a large commercial enterprise.

Adhesionary or standardized form contracts are offered by the institution to the student-athlete on a take-it-or-leave-it basis. A student-athlete is encouraged to trust the coach as a sort of parental figure, only to discover that economic and employment considerations occasionally compromise or otherwise jeopardize the coach's relationship with the student-athlete. All these factors may ultimately lead to the recognition of punitive or exemplary damages in a student-athlete's action against an educational institution, coach or athletic association for bad faith or willful breach of contract.

In some instances the athlete may be satisfied in a remedial sense by obtaining a preliminary injunction. A preliminary injunction is an order from the court that maintains the parties' status quo until the court can decide the case. Examples of preliminary injunctions include ordering the school to preserve an athlete's scholarship during pendency of the trial or prohibiting the NCAA from declaring an athlete ineligible before the court has an opportunity to consider the matter. Thus, a student-athlete may assert a contract action merely to prolong his or her playing time or to prevent the educational institution from exercising its rights under the contract. In such cases, the athlete is more concerned with the court's granting of a preliminary injunction based on the contract action than with prevailing on the contract itself. While bringing a contract action on behalf of a student-athlete for the sole purpose of obtaining a momentary reprieve is ethically questionable for the athlete and the lawyer, the practice is sometimes successfully used. See chapter 4 *infra* for a discussion of preliminary injunctions and their use to enable an otherwise ineligible athlete to participate.

3.2 ANTITRUST LIMITATIONS ON REGULATORY AUTHORITY

Federal antitrust laws are principally contained in two statutes, the Sherman Antitrust Act, 15 U.S.C. §§ 1–7 (1982), and the Clayton Antitrust Act, 15 U.S.C. §§ 12–27 (1982). State antitrust laws, which generally mirror the federal statutes, also exist.

Federal antitrust laws are directed towards anticompetitive conduct involving interstate commerce, whereas state laws regulate business practices within that particular state. In reality, however, this distinction between state and federal laws is insignificant because a violation of one will most likely be a violation of the other. Thus, both federal and state antitrust statutes can restrict the regulatory authority of amateur and professional athletic organizations. Only the federal laws are considered here because they are the most frequent source of antitrust suits.

The Sherman Antitrust Act (Sherman) was passed in 1890 and was designed to promote a business environment with unrestricted competition. This law contains two main provisions, commonly known as Sherman I and Sherman II. These sections read, in part, as follows:

SHERMAN I

Every contract, combination in the form of trust or otherwise, or conspiracy, in restraint of trade or commerce among the several States, or with foreign nations, is declared to be illegal [and is a felony punishable by fine and/or imprisonment] . . . .

SHERMAN II

Every person who shall monopolize, or attempt to monopolize, or combine or conspire with any other person or persons, to monopolize any part of the trade or commerce among the several States, or with foreign nations, shall be deemed guilty of a felony [and is similarly punishable] . . . .

15 U.S.C. §§ 1, 2 (1982).

The Sherman Antitrust Act covers transactions in goods, land, or services. A transaction can be either a sale or a lease. Section I targets agreements, combinations, or contracts that restrain trade in interstate commerce, but not all restraints of trade are illegal. To be prohibited under Sherman I, the restraint of trade must be the product of two or more persons agreeing, combining, contracting, or conspiring to restrain trade and the restraint itself must be unreasonable.

In determining whether or not a particular business practice constitutes an impermissible restraint on interstate commerce, courts employ a rule of reason test. That is, courts balance the procompetitive effects of a challenged business practice against its anticompetitive results, and if the latter outweighs the former, the practice is held to be an unreasonable restraint of trade. In utilizing a rule of reason analysis, the existence of a less restrictive alternative is of vital concern to the courts. Although a particular business practice may have a legitimate (*i.e.*, procompetitive) objective, it may nevertheless be found to be unreasonable if the goal could have been achieved by another means less harmful to competition. The rule of reason test is a cumbersome procedure, which undoubtedly has led courts to develop what are termed "per se" violations of Sherman I.

Agreements to fix prices, tying contracts, group boycotts, and horizontal divisions of markets are all considered to be per se violations of Sherman I. Agreements to fix prices include not only agreeing to set a maximum price, but also setting a minimum price or otherwise entering into some agreement to control production. Tying contracts exist when the customer gets a particular good or service that he or she desperately needs, but only if the customer agrees to purchase another which he or she does not need. Group boycotts are concerted refusals to deal. An individual can lawfully refuse to trade with another, but it is generally a per se violation of Sherman I to combine with others in a joint refusal to deal with a third party. Finally, horizontal divisions of markets are per se violations. A horizontal division of markets occurs when competitors get together and agree to divide a geographic market.

Such conduct is considered by courts to be an automatic or per se violation of Sherman I. These particular business practices are considered per se violations because regardless of some present procompetitive benefit, they can eventually lead to the ultimate anticompetitive environment: a monopoly. If there is a per se violation, there is no balancing of the pro- and anticompetitive aspects of the business practice. It does not matter that the immediate effect promotes competition. If the conduct falls into the category of per se violations, it violates Sherman I regardless of any beneficial effect upon competition.

Unlike Sherman I, a Sherman II violation can occur without concerted action. One person acting alone can violate Sherman II. Sherman II focuses upon the creation and maintenance of monopoly power. Monopoly power is the power to set prices and exclude competition, and it is typically measured by the market share an individual or business organization enjoys in a particular product or service area.

Sherman II makes it illegal for a monopolist to engage in predatory conduct in order to maintain market position. One common predatory practice is below-cost pricing, or selling below cost, which drives a competitor out of business. If a corporation or association has a monopoly share of the market (which can be much less than 100 percent) and sells below cost, a violation of Sherman II has occurred. Of course, it is perfectly permissible for a monopolist to attain and maintain a monopolist's position through historical accident, business acumen, or superior products. However, any actions a monopolist takes to maintain or expand market share against challenges from a new entrant will be suspect. This has made Sherman II a prime source of litigation involving newly created sport teams and leagues, or athletic associations attempting to expand into an area long dominated by another sports entity. *See, e.g., Association for Intercollegiate Athletics for Women v. NCAA*, 735 F.2d at 577 (opposing NCAA's expansion into area of women's athletics as an unlawful use of monopoly power); *American Football League v. National Football League*, 323 F.2d 124 (4th Cir. 1963) (Sherman II action by then newly created American Football League).

Finally, Sherman II makes attempts at achieving monopoly power in interstate commerce illegal. To constitute an attempt under Sherman II, the person allegedly acting in violation of the law must have the intent to obtain a monopolist share of the market, engage in some anticompetitive (predatory) conduct, and have a dangerous probability of achieving his or her goal.

The Clayton Antitrust Act (Clayton) was passed in 1914 and was intended to strike at anticompetitive practices in their infancy. In other words, Clayton reaches conduct and persons before they commit a full-blown Sherman violation. Clayton was designed to complement the Sherman Act by attacking practices that were likely to substantially lessen competition (Sherman I) or tend to create a monopoly (Sherman II). Yet Clayton is much narrower than Sherman in that it principally applies to sales of goods in interstate commerce. The major provisions of Clayton are contained in §§ 1, 3, 7 and 8 which, respectively, prohibit: (1) price discrimination—sales of a product at different prices to similarly situated buyers; (2) tying and exclusive dealing arrangements—sales conditioned on an agreement that the buyer stop dealing with the seller's competitors; (3) corporate mergers—acquisitions of competing companies; and (4) interlocking directorates—common board members among competing companies. *See* 15 U.S.C. §§ 13, 14, 18, 19 (1982).

Although the Sherman Act imposes criminal sanctions upon violators, this law and Clayton also have a civil side to them. Anyone who has been injured in their business or profession as a result of another's violation of federal antitrust laws can sue for a variety of remedies. If a Sherman or Clayton violation is established, the aggrieved party may obtain an order from the court precluding the wrongdoer from engaging in similar acts in the future or may request the court to fashion other equitable remedies. *See* 15 U.S.C. § 26 (1982). In addition to relief of an equitable nature, an injured party is entitled to compensation for any damages sustained, and the party's actual damages are tripled. Stated otherwise, when the verdict is returned, the court automatically increases the damages to three times their actual amount and also awards the successful party other sums for attorney's fees and court costs. *See* 15 U.S.C. § 15 (1982). Having such a liberal damage provision not only makes antitrust violations an attractive theory to sue upon; but given the economic attractiveness of antitrust actions from a plaintiff's vantage point, and the basic complexity of antitrust law, such suits are dangerous as well as difficult for defendants.

A. Application to Sports

Federal antitrust laws were first applied to sports activities in 1922. The case was *Federal Base Ball Club of Baltimore, Inc. v. National League of Professional Base Ball Clubs*, 259 U.S. 200 (1922), a landmark decision in which the Supreme Court ruled that professional baseball was local in nature and that personal effort, unrelated to production, was not a subject of commerce. Ironically, this case has not been overturned and has thereby caused the creation of unique antitrust exception for the sport of professional baseball. *See, e.g., Flood v. Kuhn*, 407 U.S. 258 (1972) (the Court refused to consider whether or not baseball's reserve contract clause violated federal antitrust laws because major league baseball was immuned from those laws).

The *Federal Base Ball Club* decision has been challenged unsuccessfully numerous times since it was handed down in 1922. Interestingly, courts at various levels and jurisdictions have simply refused to consider alleged antitrust violations regardless of their nature, merely because the violations were associated with baseball. Some of the more recent decisions upholding the *Federal Base Ball Club* exemption principle include *Charles O. Finley & Co. v. Kuhn*, 569 F.2d 527 (7th Cir.1978) and *Professional Baseball Schools and Clubs, Inc. v. Kuhn*, 693 F.2d 1085 (11th Cir.1982).

The exemption from antitrust laws enjoyed by professional baseball is not absolute. It applies only to those activities central to the sport. *See, e.g., Henderson Broadcasting Corp. v. Houston Sports Association*, 541 F.Supp. 263 (S.D.Tex.1982) (baseball antitrust exemption does not cover broadcasting because it is not "central enough" to the sport). This exemption is also an anomaly, a tribute to the immutability of a Supreme Court decision, for once made it is rarely retracted.

The holding in *Federal Base Ball Club* case and its progeny are unique to professional baseball. Indeed, other sports with substantially similar commercial characteristics have never been granted this exemption. This exemption, like the case which spawned it, is rooted in the distant past. It is the product of a time when professional sports were not such a big business as they are today.

Whether one is talking about amateur athletics at the college level or a professional team, sports today resemble any other highly successful business enterprise capable of generating many millions of dollars in revenues. Sport is packaged and marketed nationwide. It has become an industry. This national marketing and industrial approach has, with the exception of professional baseball, exposed modern sports to the full affect of federal antitrust laws.

It has long since been established that professional football, unlike its baseball counterpart, is subject to the federal antitrust laws. The United States Supreme Court in *Radovich v. National Football League*, 352 U.S. 445 (1957), refused to accept the argument that *Federal Base Ball Club* compelled a finding that Congress did not intend professional football to be subjected to the antitrust laws.

Professional basketball has been held to be subject to the application of federal antitrust laws by various court rulings. The earliest of these is *Washington Professional Basketball Corp. v. National Basketball Association*, 147 F.Supp. 154, 155 (S.D.N.Y.1956), in which the court stated:

The business of professional basketball, as conducted by The National Basketball League and its constituent teams on a multistate basis, *coupled with* the sale of rights to televise and broadcast the games for interstate transmission, is trade or commerce among the several States within the meaning of the Sherman Act.

The clearest authority that professional hockey is subject to the federal antitrust laws is *Philadelphia World Hockey Club, Inc. v. Philadelphia Hockey Club, Inc.*, 351 F.Supp. 462 (E.D.Pa.1972). The reasons the court used in making its determination in *Philadelphia World Hockey*, are substantially similar to the reasons used by other courts in declaring football and basketball to be subject to antitrust law. These common factors include the transfer of players, equipment and communications across state lines. In other words, if a sport is found to conduct business or parts of its business in various parts of the country, it will be exposed to the application of federal antitrust law.

One of the first professional sports to be regulated by the antitrust laws was boxing. The Supreme Court decided in *United States v. International Boxing Club of New York, Inc.*, 348 U.S. 236 (1955), that the Sherman Act definitely applied to the business of professional boxing. Once again, the interstate nature of boxing appears to have been the rationale used by the Supreme Court in making that determination to apply the Sherman Act.

At least one decision has affirmatively established that professional golf is subject to the antitrust laws. The court in *Blalock v. Ladies Professional Golf Association*, 359 F.Supp. 1260 (N.D.Ga.1973), specifically stated that golf is included in the category of professional sports that are not exempt from antitrust application.

The most recent professional sport to be governed by federal antitrust law is tennis. In *Gunter Harz Sports, Inc. v. United States Tennis Association*, 665 F.2d 222 (11th Cir.1981), the court refused to give the United States Tennis Association a "blanket" exemption from the Sherman Act similar to that enjoyed by professional baseball.

The very factors that make professional sports vulnerable to federal antitrust laws (*i.e.,* interstate commerce and significant revenue generation), are also present in amateur athletics. Federal antitrust principles appear to have been applied to amateur athletics in *Amateur Softball Association of America v. United*

States, 467 F.2d 312 (10th Cir.1972). In *Amateur Athletics* a softball association was under investigation for possible violations of the Sherman Act. The association refused to produce its documents during the course of an investigation, and defended this refusal on the ground that as an amateur organization, it was exempt from federal antitrust laws. The court, however, rejected this argument and in doing so, made it clear that amateur athletics do not enjoy a specific exemption from the antitrust laws like that held by baseball.

Since the decision in *Amateur Softball,* amateur associations have been defendants in numerous antitrust cases. At the forefront has been the NCAA, which has been in the courtroom defending its practices and rules. *See, e.g., Association for Intercollegiate Athletics for Women v. NCAA,* 735 F.2d 577 (D.C.Cir.1984) (a case in which the NCAA successfully defended itself against allegations that it was attempting to monopolize women's intercollegiate athletics in violation of federal antitrust law); *Hennessey v. National Collegiate Athletic Association,* 564 F.2d 1136 (5th Cir.1977) (although a bylaw that limited the number of assistant coaches an NCAA member school could employ did not violate federal antitrust laws, the NCAA's rules had sufficient impact upon interstate commerce to be within the scope of the Sherman Act).

B. Labor Law Exemption

One further preliminary matter warrants discussion prior to an analysis of specific applications of federal antitrust law to various aspects of sports. Players in several professional sports have organized player associations to engage in collective bargaining with team owners and with the respective leagues in which they render their services. Sections 6 and 20 of the Clayton Act sought to exempt organized unions from antitrust review. *See* 15 U.S.C. § 17 (1982) (labor organizations shall not be construed to be illegal restraints of trade); 29 U.S.C. § 52 (1982) (restricting right of federal courts to issue an injunction in employment disputes between employer and employees). This position was further enhanced by the Norris-LaGuardia Act of 1932. *See* 29 U.S.C. § 101 (1982) (setting narrow jurisdictional parameters for federal courts to enter injunctions in labor disputes). The issue, therefore, is whether the labor exemptions in the Clayton and Norris-LaGuardia Acts will insulate certain owner-player activities from federal antitrust laws. Unfortunately, there is no definitive answer.

Caselaw indicates that the granting of an antitrust exemption depends on the nature of the player-owner activity. There are some general principles that do stand out, however. First of all, it appears that immunity is available only for those arrangements created between labor and management. The involvement of outsiders—those not directly involved in the immediate employment relationship—extends the reach of the agreement and will be condemned if it affects competition. *See, e.g., Allen Bradley Co. v. Local Union No. 3, International Brotherhood of Electrical Workers,* 325 U.S. 797 (1945).

A second general principle that has emerged from caselaw is that the scope of antitrust immunity is limited to matters that affect the *immediate employment relationship.* More specifically, the immunity is limited to matters concerning the terms and conditions under which the bargaining employees work. *See, e.g., United Mine Workers of America v. Pennington,* 381 U.S. 657 (1965) (bargaining employees may lose their protection from the antitrust laws if they attempt to influence the conditions that prevail in other employment settings).

One final general principle related to the existence of an antitrust labor exception in professional sports may exist. Although it has never been expressly articulated, the Supreme Court appears disinclined to interfere in the collective bargaining process between players and management. *See* Weistart and Lowell, *The Law of Sports,* 540 (1979) (containing a succinct analysis and statement of this principle).

C. Effect of Federal Antitrust Laws on Particular Practices in the Sports Industry

A review of the caselaw indicates that an antitrust suit involving a college, an athlete, or an athletic organization is likely to focus upon certain types of regulatory efforts. The activities that commonly generate a challenge on antitrust grounds will be discussed in the following sections, but it is important to note that the list is not all inclusive. There may be other practices equally violative of Sherman or Clayton that have yet to be attacked.

1. Control of Playing Facilities

The Supreme Court apparently first considered the question of facility control as a possible violation of federal antitrust law in *International Boxing Club of New York, Inc. v. United States,* 358 U.S. 242 (1959). Defendants in that case acquired control over many of the key boxing arenas in the United States, making it almost impossible for anyone else to stage a professional championship boxing event without first obtaining their consent. The Supreme Court held that the defendants had conspired in restraint of trade and to monopolize the business of professional boxing in violation of Sections 1 and 2 of the Sherman Act. *See also Hecht v. Pro-Football, Inc.,* 444 F.2d 931 (D.C.Cir.1971) (the plaintiff, owner of a professional football team in a rival league, successfully alleged that a lease which granted another team the exclusive use of a municipal stadium was a contract in restraint of trade because it was the only stadium in Washington, D.C. suitable for profootball).

Not all attacks on facility control have been successful. *See, e.g., American Football League v. National Football League,* 323 F. 2d 124 (4th Cir.1963) (unsuccessful action by American Football League challenging National Football League's operation of teams in most desirable cities); *Scallen v. Minnesota Vikings Football Club, Inc.,* 574 F.Supp. 278 (D.Minn.1983) (plaintiff seeking a United States Football League franchise unsuccessfully alleged that Minnesota Viking's exclusive lease of Metrodome violated federal antitrust laws).

2. Control of Franchise Movement

Perhaps one of the best examples of an actual league rule that seeks to prevent unauthorized relocation of a member team is provided by § 4.3 of the *Constitution and By-Laws For The National Football League* (1972). Section 4.3 reads:

Any transfer of an existing franchise to a location within the home territory of any other club shall only be effective if approved by a unanimous vote; any other transfer shall only be effective if approved by the affirmative vote of not less than three-fourths or 20, whichever is greater of the member clubs of the League.

Rules that restrict the movement of an existing franchise are particularly vulnerable to an antitrust challenge, and § 4.3 itself has been at the center of recent litigation concerning franchise movement. *See, e.g., Los Angeles Memorial Coliseum v. National Football League*, 726 F.2d 1381 (9th Cir.1984) (Oakland Raiders football team was permitted to move to Los Angeles because the court held that § 4.3 violated federal antitrust law).

3. Control of Participants

Control of a substantial percentage of the athletes engaged in a particular sport may also violate Sections 1 and 2 of the Sherman Act. In *International Boxing Club*, 358 U.S. at 242, the Supreme Court held that acquiring the exclusive promotion rights to the fights of four leading contenders violated both Sherman I and II.

A more recent attack on a league practice that effectively "controlled" a player came in *Kapp v. National Football League*, 390 F.Supp. 73 (N.D.Cal.1974), *aff'd*, 586 F.2d 644 (9th Cir.1978). The plaintiff in *Kapp* successfully challenged the NFL's "Rozelle Rule" under which a football club acquiring a free agent can be required to compensate the free agent's former club. The court determined that the "Rozelle Rule" imposed restraints that were virtually unlimited in time and extent, and went beyond any possible need for fair protection of the interests of the clubs, employees or the National Football League (NFL). Furthermore, it subjected player-employees to such undue hardship that the court declared it to be in clear violation of §§ 1 and 2 of the Sherman Act.

The reserve clause is another example of a regulatory practice that has consistently failed to withstand scrutiny under federal antitrust laws. Reserve clauses, once common in professional sports, are provisions in professional players' contracts that bind the players to one team indefinitely. A typical reserve clause provides that except for salary, the player agrees to accept the same contract for the next season.

During the early 1970s, the National Hockey League's standard player contract included the following reserve clause:

Clause 6. The Player represents and agrees that he has exceptional and unique knowledge, skill and ability as a hockey player, the loss of which cannot be estimated with certainty and cannot be fairly or adequately compensated by damages. The Player therefore agrees that the Club shall have the right, in addition to any other rights which the Club may possess, to enjoin him by appropriate injunction proceedings from playing hockey for any other team and/or for any breach of any of the other provisions of this contract.

· · ·

Clause 17. The Club agrees that it will on or before September 1st next following the season covered by this contract tender to the Player personally or by mail directed to the Player at his address set out below his signature hereto a contract upon the same terms as this contract save as to salary.

The Player hereby undertakes that he will at the request of the Club enter into a contract for the following playing season upon the same terms and conditions as this contract save as to salary which shall be determined by mutual agreement.

See Annot., 18 A.L.R.Fed. 515 (1974). This reserve clause, like those used in other professional sports, not only restrained the ability of athletes to sell their services in an open market, but it was also self-enforcing. Athletes were aware that if they refused to accept a new contract from their old team, other teams in the league would not hire them. They would, in fact, be boycotted. *See id.* at 516.

Antitrust challenges to reserve clauses usually take the form of defenses to a breach of contract action by a team. In a typical case, the team sues on the basis of a reserve clause to prevent the athlete from contracting with a new team for the next playing season. The athlete then asserts that because the reserve clause violates federal antitrust laws, it is unenforceable for public policy reasons. That is, enforcing any contract that violates the law is contrary to public policy. Courts appear willing to accept this argument, frequently striking down reserve clauses because they are per se violations under Sherman I (group boycotts or price fixing agreements) and because they improperly create or maintain monopoly power contrary to the prohibitions of Sherman II. *See, e.g., Mackey v. National Football League,* 543 F.2d 606 (8th Cir.1976) (NFL reserve clause was held by the court to be an unreasonable restraint of trade in violation of Sherman I); and *Robertson v. National Basketball Association,* 389 F.Supp. 867 (1975) (perpetual reserve system of the NBA was analogous to price fixing and violated §§ 1 and 2 of the Sherman Act).

Not all courts have viewed the reserve clause as being in clear violation of federal antitrust laws. *See, e.g. Nassau Sports v.*

Peters, 352 F.Supp. 870 (E.D.N.Y.1972) (the court refused to find an antitrust violation because some form of reserve system was necessary in professional sports; Peters had accepted employment under the allegedly illegal contract voluntarily, and only raised the antitrust question when it became economically beneficial to do so). The decision in *Nassau Sports*, however, does appear to be the exception rather than the rule. But given the rise of collective bargaining in professional sports and the availability of recourse to antitrust law, the use of reserve or related clauses has declined. For a discussion of the decline of the option or reserve clause and the use of player free agency, see § 5.1A *infra*.

4. *Control of Media*

When it enacted 15 U.S.C. § 1291 (1982), Congress granted a limited antitrust exemption to arrangements whereby members of a league pool the broadcast and telecast rights of their games to coordinate marketing. This exemption applies only to the professional team sports of baseball, basketball, football, and hockey, and it by no means constitutes an absolute exemption from antitrust laws.

College athletics enjoy no immunity like that granted professional teams. The NCAA's television broadcast provisions were successfully challenged under antitrust theories in *NCAA v. Board of Regents of University of Oklahoma*, 104 S.Ct. 2948 (1984). In *Board of Regents*, the Supreme Court affirmed a lower court's decision that the NCAA television plan for broadcasting college football constituted an unreasonable restraint of trade in violation of Sherman I. The NCAA's plan limited the total number of televised intercollegiate football games that an NCAA member might televise, and further forbade member institutions from selling television rights except in accordance with the basic plan. The Court found that by curtailing output and blunting the ability of member institutions to respond to customer preference, the NCAA restricted rather than enhanced the place of intercollegiate athletics in national life.

Immediately after the *Board of Regents* decision, most major universities with football programs began to renegotiate television contracts. Similarly, the television networks, particularly ABC and CBS, eagerly sought to acquire the broadcast rights previously disbursed by the NCAA. Less than a month after the Supreme Court's decision in *Board of Regents*, a large number of college conferences and independent football powers entered into an exclusive broadcasting contract with ABC under the new banner of the College Football Association (CFA). A much smaller, but nonetheless formidable group of schools (the twenty members of the PAC–10 and Big 10 conferences) signed a similar agreement with CBS for the 1984 season.

Shortly after the formation of these two new groups, a member of the latter association filed an antitrust suit against the CFA because two of the CFA's members had refused to allow the broadcast of games against PAC–10 teams. The CFA teams were enjoined from refusing to broadcast those games in *Regents of the University of California v. American Broadcasting Companies, Inc.,* 747 F.2d 511 (9th Cir.1984). The sums generated by televised college athletic events and the importance of those moneys to colleges and other athletic associations will undoubtedly make efforts to control the media a prime source of future antitrust litigation.

5. Merger With Competitors

The merger of professional football leagues is authorized in part by 15 U.S.C. § 1291 (1982), which essentially provides that:

> The antitrust laws . . . shall not apply to any joint agreement by or among persons engaging in or conducting the organized professional team sports of football, baseball, basketball, or hockey, by which any league of clubs participating in professional football, baseball, basketball, or hockey contests sells or otherwise transfers all or any part of the rights of such league's member clubs in the sponsored telecasting of the games of football, baseball, basketball, or hockey, as the case may be, engaged in or conducted by such clubs. In addition, such laws shall not apply to a joint agreement by which the member clubs of two or more professional football leagues, which are exempt from income tax under section 501(c)(6) of Title 26, combine their operations in expanded single league so exempt from income tax, if such agreement increases rather than decreases the number of professional football clubs so operating, and the provisions of which are directly relevant thereto.

Id. at § 1291. It is likely that this statute contributed enormously to the rather smooth merger of the American Football League (AFL) and the National Football League. Without this congressional blessing, antitrust litigation might have flourished as it has in mergers of other professional team sports.

6. Tying Contracts

Requiring those who purchase regular season tickets to also purchase other related items is probably the most commonly attacked "tying arrangement" in professional sports. Such attacks have, however, rarely met with success. In *Driskill v. Dallas Cowboys Football Club, Inc.*, 498 F.2d 321 (5th Cir.1974), the plaintiff argued unsuccessfully that the Dallas Cowboys had violated § 1 of the Sherman Act by requiring purchasers of regular season tickets to also purchase preseason tickets and low cost stadium bonds. The court identified the characteristics of an illegal tying arrangement as: (1) two separate products, the tying product and the tied product; (2) sufficient economic power in the tying market to coerce the purchase of the tied product; (3) involvement of a not insubstantial amount of interstate commerce in the tied market; and (4) anticompetitive effects in the tied market. The lower court reasoned that no Sherman Act violation was present in *Driskill* because the plaintiff had not been coerced to buy preseason tickets or stadium bonds, the purchasers of season tickets were granted certain privileges not given to single game ticket holders, and the arrangement was a reasonable business practice without any anticompetitive effect. The court of appeals affirmed the lower court's decision. Similar tying arrangements have been upheld as being a reasonable and not anticompetitive business practice by other courts. *See, e.g., Coniglio v. Highwood Services, Inc.*, 495 F.2d 1286 (2d Cir.1974) (alleged tying between season tickets and exhibition game tickets not illegal because seller was not using economic power to restrain competition); and *Laing v. Minnesota Vikings Football Club, Inc.*, 372 F.Supp. 59 (D.Minn.1973), *aff'd*, 492 F.2d 1381 (8th Cir.1974) (because of availability of single game tickets, no "coercion" existed when season ticket buyers were required to also purchase exhibition game tickets).

7. Eligibility Rules

Eligibility rules, whether imposed by a league or a players association, generally deprive a professional athlete of the opportunity to pursue his or her livelihood. Because different rules affect players in different ways, the courts have been unable to establish clear standards for determining whether or not such rules violate the federal antitrust laws. Depending on the circumstances, some rules have been held to violate the antitrust laws while others have not.

One decision holding that a league eligibility rule violated antitrust laws is found in *Denver Rockets v. All-Pro Management, Inc.*, 325 F.Supp. 1049 (C.D.Ca.1971). The rule in question was a National Basketball Association (NBA) bylaw which provided that no player was eligible to play basketball in the NBA until four years after he graduated from high school or four years after his original high school class graduated if he did not graduate. The court found that the so-called "Four Year Rule" was in fact a group boycott, the effect of which was an arbitrary and unreasonable restraint on the right of the plaintiff to bargain freely in a competitive market. The court therefore enjoined the use of the rule and declared it illegal under § 1 of the Sherman Act. *See also Linseman v. World Hockey Association*, 439 F.Supp. 1315 (D.Conn.1977) (a 19 year old plaintiff successfully challenged a league rule that prohibited persons under the age of 20 from playing for any team within the league).

Other courts, as was previously suggested, have not been similarly inclined to recognize antitrust problems with league or association rules. Those cases in which antitrust violations were not found appear to share a common rationale: the challenged rule was not so unreasonable as to clearly constitute an illegal refusal to deal. *See, e.g., Heldman v. U.S. Lawn Tennis Association*, 354 F.Supp. 1241 (S.D.N.Y.1973) (refusing player's request for injunction against USLTA rule that banned from its tournaments any player who had competed in non-USTLA tournaments). *See also Deesen v. Professional Golfer's Association*, 358 F.2d 165 (9th Cir.1966) (rule denying entrance to PGA sponsored tournaments because of a prolonged lack of adequate performance was not found to be a boycott in violation of the Sherman Act); and *Neeld v. National Hockey League*, 594 F.2d 1297 (9th Cir.1979) (because its primary effect promoted safety, an NHL bylaw making a player with only one eye ineligible to play for member clubs was held not violative of federal antitrust laws).

8. Disciplinary Rules

As was the case with eligibility rules, courts have not yet established a single standard for determining the legality of various league or association disciplinary rules under federal antitrust laws. Some cases have found that such rules violate the antitrust laws, while other courts have not found violations. Courts appear inclined to find an antitrust violation when the party seeking to enforce the disciplinary rule might gain financially, regardless of whether the gain is intended or not. *Compare Brenner v. World Boxing Council*, 675 F.2d 445 (2d Cir.1982) (court rejected boxing promoter's argument that his suspension by the WBC for disciplinary reasons was per se unlawful since he failed to prove that the executive committee which suspended him was composed of anyone who stood to gain financially from his suspension) *with Blalock v. Ladies Professional Golf Association*, 359 F.Supp. at 1260 (striking down disciplinary suspension of a female golfer as a "naked restraint of trade" in part because members of the PGA executive board ordering the suspension were competitors who stood to gain financially from their actions).

9. Player Draft

Numerous cases have determined that the principle behind the player drafts is a patent violation of federal antitrust law. These decisions are not peculiar to any one sport. Indeed, a player drafts system in any professional sport will probably be objectional on antitrust grounds. *See, e.g., Kapp v. National Football League*, 390 F.Supp. 73 (N.D.Cal.1974), *aff'd*, 586 F.2d 644 (9th Cir.1978) (NFL draft was patently unreasonable because it permitted a perpetual boycott of prospective draftees); *Smith v. Pro Football*, 420 F.Supp. 738 (D.D.C.1976), *aff'd in relevant part*, 593 F.2d 1173 (1978) (even under the rule of reason test, the draft violated antitrust laws because it was significantly more restrictive than necessary to maintain a "competitive balance" among teams in the league); *Drysdale v. Florida Team Tennis, Inc.*, 410 F.Supp. 843 (W.D.Pa.1976) (Pro Tennis Association's draft system was held to be anticompetitive in that it stifled competition between franchises that sought to obtain players' services); and *Robertson v. National Basketball Association*, 389 F.Supp. at 867 (NBA player draft was analogous to price fixing devices condemned as per se violations of Sherman I). Yet the draft system flourishes in the major professional sports despite its susceptibility to federal antitrust laws and the court decisions that have condemned this practice. Many courts have granted individual relief from the draft, but its use by various leagues has never been substantially thwarted. In fact, the draft stands as one of the most important recruitment devices used by professional sports leagues today.

10. Cross-Ownership Bans

One of the more recent league practices to which the federal antitrust laws may be applied is a cross-ownership ban. The NFL proposed an amendment to its bylaws that would prevent any owner of an NFL club or a member of his family from acquiring any interest in another major team sport. Those members holding interests in another major professional team would be required to divest themselves of this interest within a specified time period or face fines as well as other sanctions.

The NFL provided the following justifications for this proposed amendment:

a. Protection of commercial confidentiality;

b. Preservation of good relations with the public including:

(i) Avoiding dilution of the goodwill that a prominent local NFL "salesman" wins for the entire NFL;

(ii) Remaining untarnished by adverse fan reactions to publicly verbal owners whose activities in other sports may arouse local hostility;

(iii) Taking the procompetitive side of the public debate concerning the proper role of sports ownership "magnates" or "human conglomerates"; and

(iv) Encouraging of maximum cooperation and minimizing animosity and suspicion among the NFL member joint-venturers.

The North American Soccer League sued the NFL, claiming that this proposed rule would exclude it from a substantial share of the market for "professional sports capital and entrepreneurial skill" that it needed to be successful. *North American Soccer League v. National Football League*, 670 F.2d 1249 (2d Cir.1982). Using a rule of reason analysis, the Court of Appeals concluded that although the NFL's justifications for the ban were legitimate, there were less restrictive means of attaining these goals. In other words, the NFL could have accomplished its objectives in some manner other than by depriving the North American Soccer League of vital capital and expertise. The NFL's proposed cross-ownership ban was, therefore, illegal.

In reaching this decision, the court in *North American Soccer* rejected the NFL's argument that cross-ownership was barred by § 8 of the Clayton Act, which prohibits interlocking directorates. The court did, however, leave open the question of whether cross-ownership itself would be contrary to the law if it restrained or otherwise threatened competition.

3.3 CONSTITUTIONAL LIMITATIONS ON REGULATORY AUTHORITY

The Constitution, including the Bill of Rights and the Fourteenth Amendment, is the primary source of legal limitations on the regulatory power of institutions, associations, and other entities that govern student-athletes, coaches, and other athletic personnel. From the First Amendment's protection of religious exercise and free speech or expression to the Fourteenth Amendment's equal protection and due process clauses, the Constitution is the major repository of rights that limit regulatory authority in the athletic context. This section examines the nature of and extent to which constitutional rights serve as limitations on regulatory authority in the sports context.

A. Procedural Due Process

Procedural due process limitations on federal and state activity are found respectively in the Fifth and the Fourteenth Amendments to the Constitution. The Fifth Amendment applies to the federal government and provides that, "No person shall . . . be deprived of life, liberty, or property without due process of law . . . ." The Fourteenth Amendment serves as a limitation on state action by providing that no state shall "deprive any person of life, liberty, or property, without due process of law." Many state constitutions also prohibit the denial of due process, and occasionally a state constitution will be construed more liberally than the federal constitution. Hence, state as well as federal law should be considered when examining due process claims or other constitutional issues.

Procedural safeguards contained in the Constitution are possible legal limitations on regulatory activity. To determine the nature and extent of those limitations, however, one must examine: (1) when a procedural right of due process is implicated; and (2) the nature and extent of process available to the aggrieved party once a due process right is found to be implicated.

1. When a Procedural Right of Due Process Is Implicated

There are a number of elements that must be present before a right of procedural due process can be established: (a) state or federal action must be involved; (b) the aggrieved party must be a "person"; *and* (c) an interest in life, liberty, or property must be threatened or infringed upon.

(a) Government Action

As previously noted, the Fifth Amendment is a limitation on federal action and the Fourteenth Amendment is a limitation on state action. The standard for finding federal action under the Fifth Amendment is the same as that for finding state action under the Fourteenth Amendment. Both amendments apply to governmental rather than private action. (Indeed, even the "under color of law" standard of 42 U.S.C. § 1983 (1982) has consistently been treated as government action.) Taken literally, these limitations might render an action by a student-athlete or a coach against an athletic association or other seemingly private entity ineffectual on the ground that the act was private and not governmental. However, conduct that appears to be private may be so connected with governmental policy or may become so impregnated with governmental character as to constitute government action.

Courts have generally held that the action of collegiate and high school athletic associations constitute federal or state action for due process and other constitutional purposes. By taking upon themselves the role of coordinator and overseer of high school or collegiate athletics in the interest of its associated institutions, many of which are public, athletic associations have generally been declared to be performing traditional government functions. However, in three recent cases the Supreme Court examined state or federal action requirements in a manner that may yet influence decisions in the amateur athletic context. *See, Blum v. Yaretsky*, 457 U.S. 991 (1982) (actions of nursing home not "government action" despite state regulation of the home; plaintiff must show greater nexus than mere acquiescence by the state); *Lugar v. Edmondson Oil Co.*, 457 U.S. 922 (1982) (conduct of private party, acting jointly with the state constitutes "state action"); and *Rendell-Baker v. Kohn*, 457 U.S. 830 (1982).

In *Rendell-Baker,* the Court held that a private school whose income was derived primarily from public services and whose operation was heavily regulated by public authorities, did not act under color of state law when it discharged certain employees. Since the private school was not a governmental actor, constitutional limitations—*e.g.,* due process—did not apply. The court in *Rendell-Baker* examined a number of factors before declining to find government action despite the existence of a significant relationship between the private entity and the state. The Supreme Court emphasized that public funding does not make a program's administrative decisions the actions of the state. Thus, although the state provided nearly all funding for the school in *Rendell-Baker,* the state was not responsible for decisions concerning employee discharges. The Court likened the school to a private contractor who performs government construction contracts. Even when all revenue for a general contractor comes from government contracts, the contractor's acts cannot be attributed to the government for purposes of finding government involvement.

Neither does extensive government regulation related to a private entity's operations compel a finding of governmental action. The complaining party must first show a sufficiently close nexus between the government and the challenged action so that the activity of the latter may be fairly treated as that of the government itself. Applying that analysis, the Supreme Court concluded that the decision to discharge private school personnel was not state action even though the Justice Department had the power to approve persons hired for the positions. This nexus standard is obviously quite stringent, and may warrant re-examination of the regulatory nexus between private athletic associations and their membership.

The court in *Rendell-Baker* also examined the issue of whether the private school performed a public function, which would require a finding of government action. Although the school performed a function that served the public (*i.e.,* educating maladjusted students), that did not necessarily constitute a public function for government action purposes. The main inquiry was whether the function performed had traditionally been the exclusive prerogative of the state. The Court in *Rendell-Baker* concluded that the education of maladjusted students was not the exclusive prerogative of the state government.

Finally, the Court examined the issue of whether a symbiotic relationship existed between the school and the government. In holding that a symbiotic relationship was not present, the *Rendell-Baker* Court again likened the school to a private contractor. If a symbiotic relationship exists, so does a state involvement. However, the Supreme Court has clearly limited the symbiotic relationship to the definition originally enunciated in *Burton v. Wilmington Parking Authority*, 365 U.S. 715 (1961) (actions of restaurant operated by private owner under lease in building financed by public funds constituted "government action"). Anticipation that the *Burton* holding would continue to be read broadly by the Supreme Court was certainly dashed with the *Rendell-Baker* decision.

With its decision in *Rendell-Baker* and two other state or federal government action cases decided in 1982, the Supreme Court made clear its intention to closely examine assertions of government involvement in a challenged activity. It would not, therefore, be surprising to see courts re-examine the athletic association cases in light of the principles elucidated in the 1982 trilogy of government action cases. Furthermore, it is certainly conceivable that a court may find that government action is not present on public function or any other grounds, particularly given the courts' propensity to defer to the decisions of amateur athletic and other institutions in a sports context.

(b) Person

Both the Fifth and the Fourteenth Amendments are expressly intended to protect "persons." It is, therefore, conceivable that an entity would not have to be afforded due process. For example, if an academic institution were endeavoring to claim that it had been denied due process by an athletic association, of which it was a member, it might be asserted that the institution should not be afforded the protection of due process because it was not a "person," as required by the Fifth and Fourteenth Amendments. It is unlikely, however, that such an argument would be successful. For example, even corporations have been held to be "persons" for the purpose of the Fourteenth Amendment in some instances.

(c) Life, Liberty, or Property

The due process clause prohibits a governmental actor from denying a person life, liberty, or property without the due process of law. Since athletic associations and academic institutions rare-

ly deprive a person of life, the major interests that trigger application of the due process clause in the sports context are depriva-
tions of liberty or property. Unless an athlete or other party can
establish that he or she has been deprived of liberty or property,
he or she will not be able to establish a deprivation of due process.

(1) Liberty Interest. The liberty interest has been liberally
construed by courts. Courts have gone so far as to hold that a
party's liberty interest includes the right not to be "stigmatized."
See, e.g., Goss v. Lopez, 419 U.S. 565 (1975) (a liberty interest was
implicated when students were suspended from public school,
because future employers and academic institutions might find out
about the suspension and question the student's "good name,
reputation, honor, or integrity"). But the stigmatization must be,
as a general rule, accompanied by the threat or actual loss of some
property interest before a claim will be successful.

When presented with the issue of whether or not the right to
participate in athletics constitutes a liberty interest, the vast
majority of courts have held that it does not. However, it would
not be surprising to see courts begin to recognize the right to
participate in athletics as a liberty interest for due process purposes. This is especially likely given the rise in popularity and
importance of sporting activity as a form of expression, the desire
or interest of many athletes in participating in sports as a means
of obtaining a scholarship for educational purposes or, as in the
case of some college athletes, the desire of athletes to use participation at the collegiate level as a stepping stone to a professional
contract or coaching position. Courts are clearly more inclined to
find that a liberty interest is implicated when loss of the right to
participate involves an intangible interest, such as the avoidance
of psychological stigmatization coupled with some tangible interest, such as the opportunity for an education or a better livelihood.
Moreover, if there is a blending of the intangible and the tangible
in terms of the liberty interest, courts may be willing to depart
from their customary position that the liberty interest in the right
to participate in athletics is too speculative and should not be
recognized.

In *Goss v. Lopez,* the Court noted that students should have
been afforded due process before being suspended from school
because the act of suspension "could seriously damage the students' standing with their fellow pupils and their teachers as well
as interfere with later opportunities for higher education and

employment." Courts have also intimated that intangible interests like stigmatization might suffice to create a liberty interest
even when there are no tangible losses, such as a loss of educational opportunity or employment possibility. *See, e.g., Cleveland
Board of Education v. Loudermill,* 105 S.Ct. 1487, 1496 n. 13 (1985)
(a liberty interest may be implicated by accusations of dishonesty).
Thus, while courts have been reluctant to recognize a liberty
interest in the right to participate in athletics, it is certainly
conceivable that they may do so in the future, even in cases in
which only an intangible interest (such as freedom from personal
stigmatization) is implicated, as long as that interest can in fact be
established.

(2) Property Interest. A property interest, on the other hand,
will clearly trigger due process protection. Property interests are
not created by the Constitution. They are created, and their
dimensions are defined by existing rules or understandings stem-
ming from an independent source such as state law. Such interests are typically based on a state statute or regulation that
expressly creates a property right or entitlement. If a state or a
party acting in a governmental capacity extends a property right,
the state or the party acting in that capacity may not deprive
recipients of that right or interest without first affording them due
process.

In addition to finding a property interest in a state statute or
regulation, courts have found property interests in regulations and
similar documentation generated by athletic associations. Lower
courts have noted that NCAA regulations and documentation
regarding student athletic scholarships give rise to a property
interest on the part of the athlete. Given the broad power of the
NCAA and other athletic associations with regard to the regulation of scholarships and athletic participation in general, including their power to limit (through strict transfer rules) athletic
participation by an athlete who has lost his or her scholarship, it
is possible that courts may recognize a property interest on the
part of the student-athlete. But even if courts extend such a
right, they will no doubt limit the amount of process that will be
due. This approach will enable courts to recognize that a property
interest is involved, while simultaneously enabling them to give
ample deference to the athletic association as they (courts) are
inclined to do.

Lower courts have dealt with the issue of whether or not participation in extracurricular athletic activities constitutes a property interest for due process purposes. Most courts have held that participation in athletics does not constitute a property right for due process purposes, but it is conceivable that they will do so in the future if athletes can tie their participation to a concrete interest in employment or some similar benefit.

Courts seem to view the issues of whether a property right or a liberty interest exists in a seriatim fashion, deciding independently whether property or liberty interests are present. Nevertheless, there is an argument that might be raised in favor of cumulation of the property right and the liberty interest. In other words, one could argue that while a court might find that neither the property right nor the liberty interest standing alone in a particular case is sufficient to trigger due process, when cumulated or combined, the otherwise insufficient liberty interest and property right mandates application of due process principles. Although tenable, this argument has yet to be accepted.

The preceding analysis has dealt almost exclusively with the student-athlete's right to participate as a triggering mechanism for due process protection. There are, however, other possible applications of due process principles in sports. Before coaches or other athletic officials may be terminated by an institution or association, the institution may have to afford them due process. The coach or other athletic employee may have a property right in the continuation of his or her employment based on a state statute, or may have a liberty interest in remaining free from public stigmatization. In fact, the rights of these employees are not only well established, but they are also much more clearly protected than the student-athlete's right to participate in athletics.

2. *What Amount of Process is Due*

When a person is deprived of life, liberty, or property by state or federal action, some process must be extended. The extent of process due in a given case varies substantially. Normally, due process requires notice of the proceedings and a fair hearing. The nature, extent, and timing of the notice and hearing, are dependent on the court's determination of how much process is due in a given case.

(a) Balancing Test

Courts determine the requisite process due by applying a balancing test. Application of this test necessitates that the court weigh three factors in determining the amount of process due:

First, the private interest that will be affected by the official action; second, the risk of an erroneous deprivation of such interest through the procedures used, and the probable value, if any, of additional or substitute procedural safeguards; and finally, the Government's interest, including the function involved and the fiscal and administrative burdens that the additional or substitute procedural requisites would entail.

Mathews v. Eldridge, 424 U.S 319, 335 (1976).

To determine the process due, courts must unavoidably engage in some ad hoc decision making, at least until precedents develop concerning the particular type of case presented. When faced with the problem of determining what process is due in depriving a student-athlete of his or her liberty or property interest in athletic participation, for example, a court might analogize to decisions in similar areas. The court, however, would ultimately have to balance the three factors set forth above to determine how the factors applied in that particular case. Only after a line of precedent is established in that area will a student-athlete or an administrator know with any certainty what process is due.

When balancing these three factors (the magnitude or importance of the liberty and/or property interest involved; the extent to which the requested procedure would reduce possible errors in decision-making; and, the burden on the administrative body that would attend the providing of such safeguards), courts will probably continue to defer to the expertise of school administrators and rule-making bodies of athletic associations, both of which are likely to restrict the nature and extent of the due process safeguard accorded a student-athlete. This means that the notice and hearing due an athlete will also undoubtedly be limited. A coach or other athletic employee may be afforded more due process, however, simply because they are employees. Employees may likewise take advantage of a body of law protecting employees in general, and not just in the sports or recreational context.

(b) Notice

Once a court decides that some process is due under the Fifth or Fourteenth Amendments, it will require that notice be given.

A mere oral recitation informing an athlete or perhaps even a coach of the action being taken and a basic enumeration of the reasons for or charges supporting the action may suffice as proper notice. Determining the type of notice that must be given in each instance requires a balancing test. The court must balance the student-athlete's or coach's interests *and* the extent to which additional notice would reduce the possibility of an error by the decision-maker *against* the added administrative and fiscal burden on the school or athletic association of giving such notice.

(c) Hearing

The same factors considered in determining the notice requirement of procedural due process must also be balanced to ascertain the kind or form of hearing that must be afforded. When a party is being subjected to extreme privation or hardship similar to a criminal penalty, formal hearing procedures much like those used in a criminal trial may be required. In other less severe cases where the administrative burden is significant and the interest involved is limited, the required hearing procedure may be quite informal and still meet due process standards. Most cases, of course, fall between these two extremes and, therefore, require some formality in the hearing procedure.

In *Goss*, which involved the brief suspension of a student from school, the Supreme Court noted that a hearing in which the student could present his side of the story constituted the minimum hearing requirement. Courts have also required that students be given the name of witnesses against them and an oral or written report on the facts as to which each witness testified. Occasionally, courts will permit a party the right to cross-examine those witnesses. It should be clear, however, that the nature of the hearing varies greatly. For example, if a coach were being terminated for "immoral behavior," he or she would normally be entitled to a more formal hearing than a student-athlete whose scholarship was being terminated by a coach who was generally dissatisfied with the athlete's performance or attitude.

Questions may arise about the timing of a hearing; must it be held before taking action adverse to the athlete or employee's interest, or is due process met simply by providing an opportunity to be heard after termination? Sometimes due process will require a hearing before termination. As the Supreme Court recently noted in *Cleveland Board of Education v. Loudermill*:

The need for some form of pretermination hearing, recognized in these cases, is evident from a balancing of the competing interests at stake. These are the private interest in retaining employment, the governmental interest in the expeditious removal of unsatisfactory employees and the avoidance of administrative burdens, and the risk of erroneous termination.

105 S.Ct. 1487, 1494 (1985). The Court in *Loudermill* held that a pretermination hearing would have to be granted, but it also noted that the hearing need not be elaborate. A pretermination hearing does not have to resolve definitively the propriety of the discharge or termination—it need only provide an initial check against a mistaken decision. In other words, if the pretermination hearing enables the decision-maker to determine whether there were reasonable grounds to believe that the charges supported the accusation, the hearing is sufficient. Of course employees or athletes are also entitled to oral or written notice, an explanation of the evidence against them, and an opportunity to respond orally or in writing prior to the termination of some right or entitlement.

A tenured coach, like the employee in *Loudermill*, might be entitled to a pretermination hearing if his or her job were being terminated. A nontenured coach or employee, on the other hand, will usually be entitled to less due process in terms of the nature, extent, and timing of the notice and hearing. Less due process is required in those cases because nontenure employees seldom have a property interest in their jobs, mainly because statutes apply only to tenured or other specified employees and thus do not confer a property right on the untenured employee.

Athletes may not be entitled to as much due process as even nontenured employees. Even if student-athletes could successfully assert a property right in participation in athletics, they would doubtless be entitled to a lesser degree of protection since their interest in participation is not as weighty as that of employees in their jobs. Nevertheless, if the student-athletes could assert such a right and the timing of the hearing was significant, a pretermination hearing might be warranted.

(d) Limitations on the Notice and Hearing

Frequently, an institution or association will provide a set of termination procedures. A college might, for instance, establish procedures to follow when a tenured or nontenured coach's job or a student-athlete's scholarship is terminated. It has been argued that the school or other governmental entity should be permitted to limit the nature and extent of the due process hearing and notice requirements because it created the right in the first place. The Supreme Court in *Loudermill*, however, rejected this notion when it stated that "[w]hile the [state actor] may elect not to confer a property interest . . ., it may not constitutionally authorize the deprivation of such an interest, once conferred, without appropriate procedural safeguards." *Id.* at 1493.

An institution, therefore, will probably refrain from actions which might create property interests in its employees or athletes. Absent such a right, the employee or athlete is without recourse on due process grounds. With such a right, the institution must fashion a set of notice and hearing procedures which will withstand constitutional scrutiny. Nonetheless, there are a number of reasons why athletic associations and institutions might want to confer the right and simultaneously seek to establish a set of procedures: (1) it may be fairer to their employees and to athletes, thereby building good will; (2) courts, which are already inclined to defer to educational and athletic decision-makers, will in most cases find the procedures adequate, particularly if the procedures are originally fashioned in light of the balancing formula established by *Mathews*; (3) provided that the procedures are basically fair and balance the factors outlined in *Mathews*, they are less likely to be challenged by the student-athletes themselves, because some due process will already have been afforded the aggrieved party; and (4) it would contribute some certainty to an area otherwise fraught with ambiguity. Such certainty would benefit the institution as well as the athlete or employee, thereby reducing the role of the courts in fashioning and implementing required procedures.

3. Summary

Athletes and athletic personnel have been afforded due process rights when a liberty or property interest is implicated in a termination or related decision by a coach, department, institution, or association. To establish the right to due process, however, the athlete or employee must establish each of the elements of due process: (1) government action; (2) personhood; and (3) the presence of a life, liberty or property interest. Yet even when each of these elements is present, courts are inclined to defer to the educational and athletic decision-makers and limit the type of notice and hearing that must be afforded.

After the institutional decision-maker has met applicable procedural due process constraints, it may render its decision without fear of legal consequences unless some other right is implicated. In other words, procedural due process is designed only to secure fair procedures, it is not substantive in content and cannot be used by itself to challenge the merit or prudence of a given decision. Once proper procedures have been followed and a decision has been rendered, procedural due process is of no further service. If a substantive right exists, it must be found elsewhere.

B. Substantive Due Process—Privacy and Related Rights

In addition to providing a right of procedural due process, the Fifth and Fourteenth Amendments also guarantee what have been labelled substantive due process rights, the most notable of which is the right of privacy. Other fundamental rights, such as the right of interstate travel, have been found to exist implicitly within the contours of the Constitution's due process and equal protection clauses. Regardless of where these rights exist within the Constitution, they are rights which courts recognize as having a value so essential to individual liberty that governmental action regarding them is strictly limited. If the court finds a fundamental right, a government or state actor can typically limit it only when necessary to further a *compelling state interest.* In addition, the compelling state interest itself must be advanced in the least restrictive manner possible.

The right of privacy, which the Supreme Court has repeatedly reaffirmed, includes the right of freedom of choice regarding marital decisions, child bearing, and child rearing. It has even been invoked to protect the personal autonomy of one's body, thereby invalidating improper searches of one's person. Privacy can be used to prohibit state action that interferes with matters of private choice, and as such, might prohibit an institution or athletic association, as a state actor, from interfering with an athlete's or employee's private life. Consequently, contemporary efforts to subject athletes to blood or related testing for alcohol or drug abuse might be challenged as an invasion of privacy. Similarly, efforts to regulate marital or social activities may unduly abridge one's right of privacy. In such cases, of course, the institution may still regulate the privacy if it has a compelling state interest in the regulation as applied.

A number of cases have dealt with the dismissal of teachers and other personnel for immoral behavior such as, heterosexual improprieties, homosexuality, or the use of drugs or alcohol. The right of privacy limits the government's ability to regulate such matters, but courts continue to defer substantially to educational decision-makers, particularly when a nexus exists between the activity and the fitness of the individual to fulfill his or her employment or athletic responsibilities. This is even more true with athletic participation, which is considered to be more of a privilege than a right. Although there is a sense in which the government ought to have more power to regulate such behavior on the part of a teacher or coach (who is an agent assigned responsibility for teaching impressionable students) than a student-athlete (who acts as an individual for the most part), that is not the approach which courts have typically taken.

C. First Amendment Rights

Prior to the Civil War the Supreme Court held that the Bill of Rights did not apply to the states. However, during the twentieth century, courts selectively incorporated the Bill of Rights in state actions, making most of those amendments applicable to the states through the Fourteenth Amendment. The First Amendment has, by this process of incorporation, been made applicable to state action. Therefore, when an institution or association engages in state or governmental action violative of one's First Amendment rights, the courts will often declare the action unconstitutional.

1. First Amendment: Freedom of Religion

The religion clauses of the First Amendment provide that, "Congress shall make no law respecting an establishment of religion, or prohibiting the free exercise thereof." Two rights are stated: (1) the right of free exercise, and (2) the right to be free from a governmental establishment of religion. Free exercise and establishment clause issues can arise in the area of sports law. Both of these issues will be examined separately, looking first at issues typically raised by student-athletes and then examining freedom of religion challenges typically raised by coaches, athletic personnel, and other parties.

(a) Free Exercise

Once it has been established that a challenged governmental regulation imposes a burden on the free exercise of one's religion, the government has the burden of demonstrating that the regulation is necessary to further a compelling state interest. The state or governmental actor must also typically show that as applied to the religious exercise the regulation is the least restrictive means of achieving that compelling state interest. Courts usually distinguish between religious beliefs and religious action when examining regulations, asserting that actions may be more readily regulated than beliefs. However, if a free exercise right regarding action is involved, most courts apply the compelling state interest and least restrictive means tests in scrutinizing the offending regulation.

(1) Athletes. Student-athletes or sports participants have asserted claims in a number of different types of free exercise cases. In those cases an athlete generally argues that a rule or regulation promulgated by an institution or athletic association, as a governmental actor, interferes with the athlete's right to freely exercise his or her religion. Courts have been fairly reluctant to find for the athlete in these cases, despite the apparent stringency of the burden on the government to show that the regulation is the least restrictive means of achieving some compelling state interest. In fact, many lower courts balance the athlete's right of free exercise against the state's interest in regulation, and the athlete's right rarely outweighs the government's interest in such cases.

In a significant recent case, *Menora v. Illinois High School Association*, 683 F.2d 1030 (7th Cir. 1982), the Seventh Circuit Court of Appeals upheld a high school association rule forbidding basketball players to wear hats or other headwear, except headbands, while playing. The court upheld this rule despite a First Amendment challenge by Jewish student-athletes, who asserted that the rule was unconstitutional as applied to them because they could not exercise their religious beliefs by wearing yarmulkes during basketball games. Writing for the majority in *Menora*, Judge Posner noted that:

> The more valuable the benefit to the claimant and hence the greater the burden on him of forgoing it in order to continue to observe his religion, the greater must be the burden on the government of relaxing the condition it places on the benefit

for a refusal to make an exception for the claimant to survive a challenge based on the First Amendment.

Id. at 1033. With regard to the least restrictive means test, Judge Posner added that, "[w]e put the burden of proposing an alternative, more secure method of covering the head on the [student-athletes] rather than on the [athletic association] because the plaintiffs know so much more about [their religious law and doctrine]." *Id.* at 1035. The dissent criticized the majority's opinion on the ground that it overlooked established principles of free exercise jurisprudence, substituting an efficient solution for a constitutional determination.

Other lower courts are also inclined to balance constitutional rights and the efficiency of solutions in free exercise cases in the area of sports law. This may be due in part to the prevailing, albeit rarely articulated, view that participation in sporting or athletic events is a privilege and not a right, even when the regulation of participation directly implicates an athlete's right of free exercise.

In another recent case, a federal district court applied a similar balancing test in denying a student-athlete's claim of free exercise. *Keller v. Garden Community Consolidated Grade School District 72C*, 552 F.Supp. 512 (N.D. Ill.1982). *Keller* involved a coach's rule that punished student-athletes who had unexcused absences from practice by not allowing them to play in the next game. The court in *Keller* held that the basketball coach's rule requiring players to attend practice except in the event of illness or death in one's family did not infringe upon a student's free exercise right to attend catechism classes during the time scheduled for basketball practice. Relying heavily on the fact that the student could have attended catechism at another church, the *Keller* court held that the athlete's interest was de minimis and clearly outweighed by the school's interest in prohibiting participation by students who missed practice.

Similarly, a student-athlete's objection to a preparticipation physical examination on religious grounds was outweighed by the interest of the school in protecting the health and welfare of its student-athletes. Again, while the court conceded that the physical examination infringed upon the student's right of free exercise, it nevertheless held that the student may be forced to choose between religion and athletics.

A number of free exercise cases have dealt with transfer rules. In those cases, athletes transfer from one school to another for religious reasons and then are denied participation in athletics for a period of time due to the transfer. Courts typically have held that the transfer limitations are only minor infringements on the student's free exercise rights, which are outweighed by the school or association's interest in the transfer rule.

Students sometimes challenge such transfer rules on the ground that they violate the equal protection or privileges or immunities clauses, as well. See *infra* § 3.3D–1–(g). While the privileges or immunities clause insures that citizens of one state who venture into another state are afforded the same privileges which citizens of the second state enjoy, courts have been reluctant to enforce transfer rules under the privileges or immunities clause. In the case of privileges or immunities and equal protection challenges to transfer rules, judges generally find a sufficient basis for justifying the transfer limitations.

Another free exercise issue raised by athletes and coaches alike is the right to engage in religious exercises prior to or as a part of their participation in sporting activities. A coach or student-athlete might seek to have "voluntary" group prayer as a team, prior to a game. Such group activity, although arguably supported by the athlete's right of free exercise, violates the establishment clause limitation on government sponsored activity. A period for meditation prior to the event might, however, be supported on free exercise grounds if it does not involve the same coercive pressure on nonparticipants as entailed in "voluntary" group prayer. *See, e.g., Wallace v. Jaffree,* 105 S.Ct. 2479 (1985) (invalidating a "meditation or voluntary prayer" statute, but arguably recognizing the right of silent meditation, and possibly even silent prayer, in certain instances).

(2) Coaches. Coaches and other athletic personnel have free exercise rights too, but courts are more inclined to limit their free exercise rights. The rationale for limiting the rights of coaches and related personnel is that, while serving as coaches or in another related position, the free exercise of their religious convictions might influence the athletes they are assigned to coach. Since the coach is acting as an agent of the school or school district, public exercise of his or her religious beliefs might very well be viewed as a violation of the establishment clause, which generally prohibits governmental sponsorship of religious activity.

Indeed, the younger and presumably more impressionable the student-athletes are, the more restrictive the courts will be in permitting the coaches to lead or otherwise influence them in a religious manner. At the collegiate level, a coach has broader latitude, although even at that level, the coach should refrain from acting in a manner that might be deemed coercive of one of his or her student-athlete's rights.

A coach in a public elementary or secondary school, like a teacher, might therefore, for example, be precluded under the establishment clause from wearing religious apparel as a symbol of his or her religious devotion or from leading players in a prayer or other religious activity. The prohibition could be maintained despite the argument that religious activity furthers the free exercise right of the coach. This example illustrates the apparent conflict between the purposes of the free exercise and establishment clauses; free exercise of religious beliefs by a state agent may tend to establish state sponsorship of a religion. This conflict has troubled the courts and has led to some seemingly contradictory results.

(3) Other Entities. There are a number of cases in which religious schools have brought actions against athletic associations on free exercise grounds. In a number of these cases, private religious schools sued athletic associations alleging that the association's exclusion of church schools from participation in interscholastic activities violated their free exercise and equal protection rights. Generally, though, courts have held that the exclusion of a sectarian school from a league or association does not impermissibly burden free exercise rights nor does it create an invidious or discriminatory classification for equal protection purposes. These decisions are normally supported on the premise that the athletic association's interest in preventing athletic recruiting and in avoiding difficulties in the enforcement of its rules is advanced by the exclusion.

(b) Establishment Clause Limitations

The establishment clause prohibits government from making any law "respecting an establishment of religion." This clause likewise limits the regulatory authority of institutions and associations connected with state government. Whether it is providing for group prayers or recognizing particular religious groups and traditions, schools and associations (or their employees acting in an official, governmental capacity) are often precluded from engaging in public activities of a religious nature. Schools may, for example, violate the establishment clause by extending official school recognition to a religious and social group such as the Fellowship of Christian Athletes, particularly if the school refuses to grant other groups similar status. In instances in which the institution permits other nonreligious groups to meet, it may be required to permit student initiated religious groups to meet on an equal basis. To fail to do so might discriminate against religious speech or expression and might, therefore, possibly violate the Equal Access Act recently passed by Congress. *See, e.g.,* 20 U.S.C. §§ 4071 to 4074 (Supp. III 1984) (if a public secondary school has a limited open forum and is receiving federal assistance, this law makes it illegal to deny students access to that forum on the basis of the religious or other content of their speech).

The basic lesson of the establishment clause for school or related personnel is that, since they are acting in an official capacity, they will be precluded from exercising or promoting their own religious beliefs or those of others while serving in that official capacity. This is particularly true in the case of elementary and secondary school personnel, because their students and players are considered to be much more impressionable than college or university students. It must be noted, however, that schools and other institutions may and occasionally must permit some form of student-initiated as opposed to school-initiated, efforts to exercise one's religion in public.

2. First Amendment: Freedom of Expression

In addition to protecting religious liberty, the First Amendment provides that, "Congress shall make no law . . . abridging the freedom of speech, or of the press . . . ". This provision is made applicable to state action through the Fourteenth Amendment and has been rather broadly construed to protect the freedom of expression. Freedom of expression issues often arise in sports law and range from the rights of athletes and coaches to speak, to the interplay between the media, athletes, and the sports industry.

(a) Athletes, Coaches, and Athletic Personnel

Numerous cases have arisen in which student-athletes, coaches or others allege that they have lost their job or scholarship for engaging in expressive activity or speech that was offensive to their superiors. If the entity limiting the expressive rights is connected with the government, the one claiming the right may be able to bring a successful action to vindicate those rights.

Many coaches and athletic personnel have successfully challenged their termination or suspension from employment on First Amendment freedom of expression grounds. For example, in *Pickering v. Board of Education of Township High School District 205, Will County, Illinois,* 391 U.S. 563 (1968), the Supreme Court held that the dismissal of a high school teacher for openly criticizing the school board's allocation of funds between athletics and education was unconstitutional and therefore impermissible on First Amendment grounds. The Court noted that since Pickering's criticism was a "matter of legitimate public concern" upon which "free and open debate [was] vital to informed decision making by the electorate," it was protected by the First Amendment. *Id.* at 571–72.

Courts have continued to follow the principles outlined in the *Pickering* case when examining whether or not the employee's communication was directed to a matter of public or merely private concern. If the matter is public, the courts extend constitutional protection to the individual's right to express his or her views, but the protection is not absolute. Rather, as was true of decisions in free exercise cases, courts tend to balance the interests of the speaker against the employer's interest. Nevertheless, courts are more inclined to find that the employee's interest outweighs the school's interest in expression cases rather than in free exercise cases.

Both student-athletes and athletic personnel have enjoyed some success in asserting their right of expression, although courts appear more likely to permit regulation of student speech regarding sports issues. The courts are often able to get around potential First Amendment problems in this area by deciding that players' as opposed to students' and coaches' comments are not matters of public concern. Student-athletes do, however, retain First Amendment rights that have been upheld on occasion.

In *Tinker v. Des Moines Independent School District,* 393 U.S. 503 (1969), the Court held that the wearing of politically-motivated black armbands by students in a public high school was constitutionally protected expression. The Court in *Tinker* not only recognized that students' First Amendment rights do not stop at the schoolhouse (or gym) door, but also extended First Amendment protection of expression to forms of expression other than speech or written communication.

This right of expression, together with the right of privacy, has been expanded to cover matters related to personal appearance, such as dress or hairstyle. Dress and hairstyle codes have been promulgated by school districts for their employees, and by coaches for their players. In *Kelley v. Johnson*, 425 U.S. 238 (1976), the Supreme Court ruled that the hair-grooming of police officers could be regulated. In doing so, the Court noted that, "[t]he constitutional issue to be decided . . . is whether [the employer's] determination that such regulations should be enacted is so irrational that it might be branded 'arbitrary' . . . ." *Id.* at 248. Courts typically balance the state's interest in a hairstyle or dress rule against an individual's right, and in doing so, they often uphold the rule. Nevertheless, beginning in the early 1970s, over 100 cases dealing with students' hair styles were reported, and the students, some of whom were athletes, won many of them. The number of hairstyle cases has decreased in the past decade, but the issue of hair or dress style recurs. After the Supreme Court's decision in *Kelley*, it is possible that many hair and dress style cases will be decided in favor of the school district, especially if the rules have a rational basis and are not arbitrary. See *supra* at § 2.1G for association rules related to grooming.

(b) Professional Athletes

First Amendment issues do arise in professional sports. A major issue in any case in which a professional athlete claims that the league or club has abridged his or her freedom of expression is the existence of government action. Since professional teams are mostly privately owned and leagues are associations of those private entities, clubs or leagues frequently assert that they cannot be charged with infringing First Amendment rights because their action cannot be attributed to the government. Nevertheless, clubs often have leases and other close relationships with public entities. Those relationships might render the clubs sufficiently public for governmental action purposes. Given the nexus between professional clubs, leagues, and the government, it is possible that a court might find sufficient government involvement for First Amendment purposes, although this is less likely after the 1982 trilogy of government action cases discussed *supra* at § 3.3A–1–(a).

Once the government action hurdle is crossed, however, other obstacles confront the athlete. These are collective bargaining and contract problems, as well as difficult proof problems. Professional athletes and athletics may be covered by collective bargaining and other contractual agreements that expressly limit the athlete's right of speech or expression (e.g., gag rules prohibiting players from criticizing officials). Although there are arguments that can be raised by an aggrieved athlete, there may be reluctance to challenge the limitations for fear of jeopardizing all athletes covered by the agreement. Legally, the professional athlete faces the same public versus private distinction that arises in the employer-employee context. If the expression of the athlete is not public in nature, which it often is not, it may be regulated more readily. Nevertheless, a player may successfully challenge a club or league rule, related to expression, particularly if the rule's application is egregious.

3. Athletic Participation as Protected Expression

Sports participants have asserted that their athletic participation is a protected form of expression in a number of cases. These cases have met with little success. While expressive activity (conduct conveying a message) is often protected under the First Amendment, participation in athletics is not an expressive activity warranting First Amendment protection. Similarly, dancing, surfing and other recreational or sporting activities have usually not been considered to be expressive activities for First Amendment purposes.

Despite these holdings, some authority supports the proposition that sporting and related activities should be afforded some First Amendment protection. Analogous events such as plays, concerts, and even nude dancing have been declared to fall within First Amendment protection. See, e.g., Schad v. Borough of Mount Ephraim, 452 U.S. 61 (1981) (nude dancing is protected expression under the First Amendment). Furthermore, some support exists in legal opinions and commentary favoring the notion that sporting activity should be protected under the First Amendment. See, e.g., Note, Selfridge v. Carey: The First Amendment's Applicability to Sporting Events, 46 Albany L.Rev. 937 (1982). But even if a court ultimately treated participation in sporting events as expressive activity, it is likely that it would be reluctant to expand the right because of the ramifications such expansion would have for the management and operation of sporting activities.

4. First Amendment: Media and Sports

Many issues have arisen regarding the role of the media in the sports industry. With developments in broadcast and communications technology and a continuing public interest in sporting events, sports broadcasting has become a multi-billion dollar per year business. These ever-increasing revenues have probably contributed to the increase in the number of law suits filed, many of which involve First Amendment issues.

(a) Broadcast Issues

The First Amendment specifically provides for freedom of the press. It says nothing about the broadcast medium, which began to develop in the early part of this century with the advent of radio. From the beginning, the treatment of broadcast medium for regulatory purposes was an issue in First Amendment inquiries. In 1927, with the adoption of the Radio Act, broadcasting was subjected to more elaborate regulation than the press. By 1934 the Federal Communications Commission was formed and given regulatory authority over all broadcasting. Originally, the variations between the treatment of these two expressive mediums for First Amendment purposes was justified on the ground that the airways, unlike the press, constituted a limited access medium. Supposedly anyone could acquire a printing press or otherwise obtain virtually unlimited access to expression through the print medium; whereas, in broadcasting there were only a limited number of channels or frequencies available. Since access to the broadcast medium was initially more limited than access to the print medium, more extensive regulation of broadcasting was justified to assure access to broadcasting.

While the proliferation of cable and other broadcasting mediums has undercut the old limited access rationale, the tradition of permitting greater regulation of broadcasting has persisted. At the same time, however, courts have extended broad latitude to the press or print medium on First Amendment grounds. The courts have shown a willingness to recognize congressional and executive authority in regulating broadcasting, and this has had a significant influence on sports broadcasting.

A number of congressional and executive actions relating to broadcasting in the sports industry have arisen since the 1930s. See, *e.g.,* Garrett and Hockberg, *Sports Broadcasting and the Law,* 59 Ind.L.J. 155 (1984) (discussing many of the congressional and executive developments). The development of a property right in the accounts and description of games and sporting events has been particularly significant, and is amply illustrated by the case of *Zacchini v. Scripps-Howard Broadcasting Co.,* 433 U.S. 562 (1977).

Zacchini involved the televised broadcast of a fifteen-second tape of "Flying" Zacchini's human cannonball performance on a nightly news program. Zacchini never consented to the showing of the tape and ultimately sued the broadcasting company for unlawful appropriation of his professional property. The television station raised a defense based on its First Amendment rights as a news gatherer and disseminator. The Court declined to accept the television station's defense and held that "the First and Fourteenth Amendments do not immunize the media when they broadcast a performer's entire act without his consent." *Id.* at 575. Thus, the Court limited the scope of the First Amendment, and in the process, strengthened the individual's property right in his or her performance.

This property right of an athlete or a team to their performance in a game, match, or event has raised a number of vexing problems in sports law. Athletes (through their player associations), broadcasters, and clubs all claim that they have an interest in this property right and should be compensated for its use. While the club is generally deemed to be the primary beneficiary of this property right, broadcasters and athletes continue to assert, both in the courts and at the negotiation table, that they are also entitled to benefit from the right. Property rights have also been litigated on antitrust (see, *supra* at § 3.2A) and other grounds and will undoubtedly continue to be a source of substantial controversy in the future.

A player's right to the use of his or her name and likeness involves a somewhat similar interest. The use of the name and likeness of a player for advertisement or endorsement purposes is a common occurrence, and players often derive substantial income from such advertising. Sometimes, however, this right comes into conflict with the media's First Amendment rights or with the club's interests. For example, in *Namath v. Sports Illustrated,* 48

A.D.2d 487, 371 N.Y.S.2d 10 (1975), the court held that use of Joe Namath's name and likeness in advertisements for the sale of Sports Illustrated magazines was protected under the First Amendment because his original appearance in the magazine was newsworthy. As such, the Court treated the use of Namath's name and likeness by Sports Illustrated differently than their use for collateral endorsements of commercial products. Admittedly, there is a fine line between the athlete's property interest and the media's First Amendment rights, and that line cannot always be drawn with distinction, as illustrated by these two cases. See also *infra* at § 7.2B–5 for a discussion of the tort of misappropriation.

Another related issue that has arisen and that may constitute a substantial source of disagreement between players and management relates to the marketing rights of players. For example, under paragraph 18 in the current standard National Basketball Association agreement, players are prohibited from obtaining commercial endorsements without the written approval of the club, which approval cannot be unreasonably withheld. A number of players have been able to delete this paragraph from their individual contracts during the course of negotiations with their club, and other players are beginning to object to club efforts to restrict their (players') use of endorsements (a significant source of additional income to many players). While this issue will no doubt be discussed in the NBA collective bargaining negotiations in 1987, and possibly in arbitration to ascertain what club restrictions are reasonable, it is likely that the NBA clubs and the players will continue to have disputes over this issue, and that similar disagreements will occur in other sports regarding commercial endorsements. These disputes may even present First Amendment (commercial speech) issues, although at this juncture it is likely that these disagreements will be handled in collective bargaining or in the negotiations process, particularly in light of the state action problems (proving that the club is a governmental actor) attendant any such challenge on First Amendment or related grounds.

Courts have also held that a club's trademark and broadcast rights often outweigh countervailing First Amendment claims. *See, e.g., Dallas Cowboys Cheerleaders, Inc. v. Pussycat Cinema, Ltd.,* 604 F.2d 200 (2d Cir. 1979), for a case dealing with trademark protection; and *National Exhibition Co. v. Fass,* 133 N.Y.S.2d 379, *aff'd without opinion,* 136 N.Y.S.2d 358, 143 N.Y.S.2d 767 (1955) and *National Association of Broadcasters v. Copyright Royalty Tribunal*, 675 F.2d 367 (D.C. Cir. 1982) for cases recognizing the extent of the club's right to the accounts and descriptions of their games.

Another interesting issue that has arisen in the area of newsgathering is the right of reporters to have access to the players, in the locker room and otherwise. Since most athletic programs and professional clubs are very interested in maintaining favorable press coverage, liberal access to players and coaches is typically available. There have been cases, however, in which access has been successfully limited. An interesting case arose recently when a woman reporter was refused access to the players' dressing room pursuant to a policy determination by baseball's Commissioner. *Ludtke v. Kuhn*, 461 F.Supp. 86 (S.D. N.Y.1978). While Ms. Ludtke raised a First Amendment claim in support of her action seeking access, the court ultimately avoided the First Amendment question by holding for Ms. Ludtke on equal protection and due process grounds. The court held that Ms. Ludtke was entitled to injunctive relief under federal civil rights law (42 U.S.C. § 1983) and enjoined the club and the Commissioner from depriving her of access to the players, despite the argument that such access by a woman reporter violated the athletes' right of privacy. See *infra* at § 3.3D–1–(a)–(3) for a discussion of *Ludtke*.

(b) Defamation

Just as the property interests in athletic performances and the use of a player's likeness limit the scope of the First Amendment, so do libel and slander actions. The freedom of the press is not absolute. At times there are countervailing interests that limit that First Amendment right. One such limitation is the right of individuals to maintain their reputation free from libel, slander, or defamation.

Defamation is a communication that injures a person's good name or reputation and includes both libel, which is written or printed and seen, and slander, which is spoken and heard. While the First Amendment protects the media's freedom of the press, that protection does not extend to defamatory remarks. Because there are demands placed on the media to distribute information of concern or importance to the public, courts have been willing to permit the media broader latitude when public officials and public figures are involved. In those cases, courts look at the good faith of the media, and generally permit the public official or figure to recover damages only upon a showing of actual malice. See *infra* at § 7.2B–4 for a discussion of the tort of defamation as a theory for recovering damages for injury to one's reputation.

Sports figures whose public character is demonstrated by elaborate broadcast and print coverage are considered public figures for defamation purposes. However, the extent to which players' subject their private lives to scrutiny by the press and still remain protected by the First Amendment is limited. The balance between the public's right to know and the player's right of privacy is not always clear. Invasion of privacy is discussed *infra* at § 7.2B–5.

Another problem arises when the reporter's First Amendment privilege conflicts with an individual's discovery rights in a lawsuit. *See, e.g., People of the State of New York v. Bova*, 118 Misc.2d 14, 460 N.Y.S.2d 230 (1983) (involving a point-shaving scheme in which a criminal defendant sought production of virtually every document related to an article in possession of Sports Illustrated). Again, the courts are inclined to balance such fundamental rights.

5. Access to Public Sports Facilities

In *International Society for Krishna Consciousness, Inc. v. New Jersey Sports and Exposition Authority*, 691 F.2d 155 (3d Cir.1982), the Court of Appeals for the Third Circuit essentially held that a publicly-owned sports complex is not a public forum for First Amendment purposes. The court therefore concluded that the Exposition's policy banning religious and charitable solicitation at the complex did not violate First Amendment rights of solicitors. It is conceivable, however, that a court could find that a public sports facility is a limited public forum, thereby permitting some religious and charitable solicitation on the premises. *See, e.g., Heffron v. International Soc'y for Krishna Consciousness, Inc.*, 452 U.S. 640 (1981) (indicating that the First Amendment did afford limited protection for solicitation by adherents of the Krishna faith at the Minnesota State Fairgrounds, a public facility). Even if a court recognizes such a right, however, it will still permit the operator of the facility to enforce reasonable time, place, and manner restrictions on the First Amendment activities.

D. Unlawful Discrimination as a Limitation on Regulatory Authority

The Constitution, largely through the equal protection clause of the Fourteenth Amendment, provides a means by which certain regulatory actions of a discriminatory nature may be challenged. Additionally, with the passage of Titles VI, VII, and IX and other related congressional acts, statutory limitations have provided an increasingly fertile source of law with which to challenge discriminatory regulatory practices. Each of these sources of law prohibits discrimination of one form or another in various contexts, and thus limits the regulatory power of entities controlling sporting activities.

1. *Equal Protection*

The equal protection clause of the Fourteenth Amendment provides, in pertinent part, that, "no State shall make or enforce any law which shall . . . deny to any person . . . the equal protection of the laws." This amendment, which was passed shortly after the Civil War, was primarily intended to ensure "equal protection of the laws" for newly emancipated black citizens. However, its broader function has been to ensure equal treatment for other groups and individuals. In deciding an equal protection challenge, a court must first determine whether "state action" is involved, because the amendment applies only in cases of governmental as distinguished from private action. See *supra* at § 3.3A–1–(a) for a discussion of the state or government action issue.

Once state action is found the court must determine the applicable standard of equal protection review with which it will judge the constitutionality of the rule or regulation involved. The court determines the standard of review by looking both at the interest affected by the rule or regulation's classification and to the nature of the classification itself. If the court finds that the classification restricts a "fundamental right," strict scrutiny is applied. Under strict scrutiny, the party seeking to enforce the regulation must show that its classification is necessary to promote a compelling governmental purpose. Similarly, if the law involves a "suspect" classification, strict scrutiny is applied. To date, the only classifications considered suspect for federal equal protection purposes are those based on race, alienage, and national origin. Sex and other classifications may, however, be deemed "suspect" under an equal protection clause contained in state constitutions.

Federal courts and some state courts apply an intermediate standard of review in cases involving quasi-suspect classes. In these instances, the party seeking enforcement must show that the classification is substantially related to important government objectives. Classifications based on sex have been subjected to this intermediate level of review under the federal equal protection clause.

If neither a fundamental right nor a suspect class is involved, the court will apply minimum rationality review. The party seeking to enforce a regulation under this standard must merely show that the classification is rationally related to a legitimate government purpose. Almost any rational relationship will be sufficient to uphold the classification. Courts have consistently held that participation in interscholastic and nonprofessional athletics is an important interest, but not a fundamental right under the equal protection clause. This participation interest alone does not trigger application of strict scrutiny in evaluating a classification.

(a) Classifications Based on Gender

Most equal protection actions in amateur athletics have challenged a school or league rule prohibiting mixed-sex competition. With the growing importance of and attention given to women's rights in all areas, it is not surprising that women have begun to assert their right to participate in athletics free from gender-based discrimination. Women have been successful in asserting their right to participate on an equal footing with their male counterparts on a number of occasions, and one particular legal theory they have turned to in order to vindicate their rights has been the equal protection clause.

(1) Females on "Male" Teams. If no women's team exists for a particular sport, women generally may not be prohibited from participating on an all male team in a noncontact sport. When a women's team already exists, however, courts tend to uphold rules barring mixed-sex competition. Although most courts have held that a female has the right to try out for a "male" team in a noncontact sport when no women's team exists, some cases, such as *Bucha v. Illinois High School Association*, 351 F.Supp. 69 (N.D.

Ill.1972), hold the opposite. In *Bucha* a woman student sued to compete on the school's males-only swim team. The court upheld the association's rule requiring a male-only swim team, noting that physical differences between the sexes justified the separate programs. However, today it is unlikely that a court would reach a similar result because stricter review of classifications based on gender is required under federal and state equal protection or equal rights clauses and under Title IX.

When a separate women's team already exists in a sport in which an athlete wants to participate, courts usually uphold rules barring mixed competition. Generally, "separate but equal" teams for both sexes are constitutionally permissible. In *O'Connor v. Board of Education*, Justice Stevens, serving in his capacity as Circuit Justice, refused to require school officials to allow a female junior high student to try out for the male basketball team. The Court of Appeals had refused to accept the plaintiff's assertion that the higher level of competition on the male team would enable her to develop more fully her skills. Justice Stevens agreed, reasoning that:

> [T]here can be little question about the validity of the classification in most of its normal applications. Without a gender-based classification in competitive contact sports, there would be a substantial risk that boys would dominate the girls' programs and deny them an equal opportunity to compete in interscholastic events.

O'Connor v. Board of Education of School District 23, 449 U.S. 1301, 1307 (1980), *cert. denied*, 454 U.S. 1084 (1981). *O'Connor* supports the proposition that courts may permit separate but substantially equal men's and women's athletic teams in contact sports under the equal protection clause and Title IX. Nevertheless, state law may require mixed participation under a state equal protection clause or equal rights amendment, even if "separate but equal" programs are in place.

In *Commonwealth v. Pennsylvania Interscholastic Athletic Association*, 18 Pa.Commw. 34, 334 A.2d 839 (1975), the court held that a rule against mixed competition violated the state equal rights amendment. The court noted that

> [E]ven where separate teams are offered for boys and girls in the same sport, the most talented girls still may be denied the right to play at that level of competition which their ability might otherwise permit them. For a girl in that

position, who has been relegated to the "girls' team" solely because of her sex, "equality under the law" has been denied.

Id. at 842. *See also Darrin v. Gould,* 85 Wash.2d 859, 540 P.2d 882 (1975) (a rule denying a female the right to try out for male team violated the Washington Equal Rights Amendment).

In addition to the availability of a separate women's team, the nature of the sport involved has often been a factor in a court's determination of whether women must be allowed to participate on an all-male team. Rules prohibiting mixed competition in contact sports are often justified on the grounds that females are more prone to injuries than males. But several courts have rejected this reasoning, holding that women may not be prohibited from competing on men's teams, even in contact sports. Two such cases arose in Little League baseball. *See Fortin v. Darlington Little League, Inc.,* 514 F.2d 344 (1st Cir. 1975); and *National Organization for Women v. Little League Baseball, Inc.,* 127 N.J.Super. 522, 318 A.2d 33 (1974). The court in *Fortin* placed some emphasis on the fact that girls at the age of 8–12 have approximately the same physical capabilities as boys of that age. It is unclear whether the decision applies to contact sports involving older and more physically mature participants, where there may be more general deviation in terms of physical maturity between men and women. In 1974, the federal Little League Baseball charter was amended by Public Law 93–551 (Act of Dec. 26, 1974, 88 Stat. 1744). Where the word "boys" appeared, the phrase "young people" was substituted. Also, the goal of promoting "citizenship, sportsmanship, and manhood" was amended to read "citizenship and sportsmanship." The stated purpose of the amendment was to open Little League Baseball to girls.

While the age and physical maturation distinction may be of importance in some cases, other cases supporting a female's right to participate in contact sports have extended the right to football and baseball. It is conceivable, nevertheless, that the nature and extent of the contact in a given sport may make a difference to a court, and may along with age or physical maturation distinctions, restrict mixed participation in contact sports.

Whether an organization or association may require females to play a sport by different rules than those used by males is yet another issue. Many schools, for example, play by "split-court" rules in girls' basketball wherein each player is confined to one side of the court and shooting is restricted to forwards. Girls have challenged these rules with mixed success, claiming that the rules prevent them from developing the skills necessary for recruitment and competition at the college level, where the game is played by rules similar to those governing boy's basketball.

(2) Males on "Female" Teams.   A few cases have arisen in which males have sought to play on teams restricted to females. The desire to assure female participation in athletics and the belief that males usually dominate a mixed team make it unlikely that a court will allow males to play on female teams, especially when a male team is available in the same sport.   Nevertheless, courts have recently had to decide whether a school or association could restrict a team to women only when no men's team existed for the sport in question.

In *Clark v. Arizona Interscholastic Association,* 695 F.2d 1126 (9th Cir. 1982), a male athlete unsuccessfully asserted that he had the right, under the equal protection clause, to participate on his school's volleyball team, which had been reserved for females. Noting that boys are generally more physically adept in executing the fundamental skills necessary for volleyball, the court concluded that allowing boys to join the team would soon result in male domination of the team.   The court also observed that the policy of excluding males from the volleyball team was substantially related to the school's legitimate interest in redressing past discrimination against females and in promoting equal opportunity for women in sports.   *See also Petrie v. Illinois High School Association,* 75 Ill.App.3d 980, 394 N.E.2d 855 (1979) (state equal protection clause, requiring strict scrutiny review, was not violated by restricting the only available volleyball team to females).

Some courts have allowed boys a place on a girls' team.   In *Gomes v. Rhode Island Interscholastic League,* 469 F.Supp. 659 (D.R.I.), *vacated as moot,* 604 F.2d 733 (1st Cir. 1979), the court relied on Title IX in holding that a male student could be barred from a team reserved for women only if women's athletic opportunities had actually been limited in the past.   The court interpreted "limited" to mean limited within the sport in question, rather than limited overall.   Since women had not suffered an historical lack of opportunity in volleyball, the court allowed the boy to play on the team.   *See also Attorney General v. Massachusetts Interscholastic Athletic Association,* 378 Mass. 342, 393 N.E.2d 284 (1979) (barring males from female teams violates state equal rights amendment).

(3) Other Gender-Based Classifications. While many of the gender-based classifications that have been challenged on equal protection grounds relate to participation in athletics, there are a number of other areas in which classifications based on sex arise in sports law. In *Ludtke v. Kuhn,* 461 F.Supp. 86 (S.D.N.Y.1978), a woman reporter challenged a rule barring women from the locker room of a professional baseball team on equal protection grounds. In support of the rule, the Commissioner asserted that permitting a woman access to the men's dressing room would violate the players' right of privacy. Noting that there were clearly less restrictive alternatives available, such as hanging curtains or wearing a towel in the press area, the court rejected the Commissioner's argument and held that the reporter had indeed been denied equal protection because the rule barring women from the locker room was not substantially related to the purpose of protecting the players' privacy.

(4) Other Relief Available for Gender-Based Classifications. While many gender-based classifications have been attacked on federal equal protection grounds, there are other sources of law that may be used to challenge gender discrimination in sports. One example of other sources of law is state constitutions including equal rights and human rights amendments. In fact, when protection is not available under the federal equal protection clause of the Fourteenth Amendment, relief may still be available under a state equal protection clause. A state court may apply its equal protection clause to extend greater protection against gender-based classifications than that afforded under federal equal protection. For example, some state courts have held that their state equal protection clauses render any classification based on sex suspect. Those state courts then apply a stricter standard when scrutinizing classifications based on gender, and are more likely to find the classification unconstitutional than are federal courts which apply the less stringent standard of the federal equal protection clause. The federal equal protection clause prohibits only that state action which restricts rights afforded under the Fourteenth Amendment. The clause does not prevent state courts from affording broader rights under their state constitutions.

Other statutes must be examined when a gender-based classification is involved. These statutes include Title IX (*infra* at § 3.4A), Title VII and the Equal Pay Act (*infra* at § 3.4B), and various state statutes which perform similar and sometimes more extensive functions than their federal counterparts.

(b) Classifications Based on Race

Racial classifications are considered the most "suspect" of all for federal equal protection purposes, and are subject to very strict scrutiny. To survive such scrutiny, not only must the governmental entity establish that the classification is necessary to achieve a compelling purpose, but must likewise establish that there is no less restrictive alternative available to further that interest. This standard is rarely met, except when classifications are designed to effectuate equal opportunity or affirmative action.

After *Brown v. Board of Education of Topeka*, 347 U.S. 483 (1954), it became clear that with the elimination of the doctrine of separate but equal, racial segregation in athletics would be unconstitutional under the equal protection clause. It is not surprising, therefore, that a policy of segregating whole athletic associations based on the predominant race of member schools has been struck down. *See, e.g., Louisiana High School Athletic Association v. St. Augustine High School*, 396 F.2d 224 (5th Cir. 1968) (preventing an all-Black school from being admitted to a league violated the equal protection clause). Similarly, racially separate athletic systems were struck down in *Lee v. Macon County Board of Education*, 283 F.Supp. 194 (M.D.Ala.1968). The maintenance of a dual system was seen as an impediment to integration in general, and the leagues were ordered to merge.

Racial restrictions in professional athletics have also been struck down as being contrary to the equal protection clause since the 1950s. For example, as early as 1954, in *Harvey v. Morgan*, 272 S.W.2d 621 (Tex.1954), a court invalidated a state statute prohibiting Blacks and whites from boxing or wrestling with each other. *See also Dorsey v. State Athletic Commission*, 168 F.Supp. 149 (E.D.La.1958), *aff'd*, 359 U.S. 533 (1959) (invalidating a boxing commission rule against mixed-race matches).

Similarly, access to publicly-owned facilities, including recreational facilities, may not be restricted by race. In *Wesley v. City of Savannah, Georgia*, 294 F.Supp. 698 (S.D.Ga.1969), several Black plaintiffs successfully challenged their exclusion from a golf tournament, which was sponsored by a private club that played at a city-owned golf course, on equal protection grounds. Although the court held that Blacks could not be excluded from a prestigious tournament played on public land, it noted that the club itself was not required to admit Black members.

Recently, there have been indications that Black student-athletes may challenge the NCAA's new academic requirements (Proposal Number 48, *supra* at 1.2E–1) on equal protection grounds. The essence of the Black athletes' action is that those requirements based on standardized testing are racially motivated or have a much greater impact on Black student-athletes than on other athletes. Such a challenge may be successful. *See* Yasser, *The Black Athletes' Equal Protection Case Against the NCAA's New Academic Standards*, 19 Gonzaga L.Rev. 83 (1983/84).

(c) Classifications Based on Marital Status

High schools often have rules barring married students from participation in interscholastic athletics. Policy arguments frequently offered in support of these rules include:

1. Teenage marriage should be discouraged. Excluding married students from athletics will tend to discourage such marriages.

2. Students who marry in haste set a bad example for other students. The "hero worship" available to athletes should be avoided in these cases.

3. Supervision of emancipated married students and unmarried students requires the application of different standards. This may create morale problems within the athletic program.

4. If married students are present in locker rooms, the discussion could center around their sexual experiences. Exclusion of married students may reduce locker room discussion of sex.

In the past, rules barring married athletes have been upheld. *See, e.g., Kissick v. Garland Independent School District*, 330 S.W.2d 708 (Tx.1959), *o'ruled*, 507 S.W.2d 636 (Tx.1974) (the court noted that public policy disfavors underage marriages, and holding that the rule was sufficiently related to this policy objective). More recently, however, restrictions against married student-athletes have been struck down as violating the equal protection clause. For example, *Kissick* was itself overruled in *Bell v. Lone Oak Independent School District*, 507 S.W.2d 636 (Tx.1974). In *Bell* the court found no evidence that married students presented a danger to students, faculty, or the school and concluded that the school had failed to prove that the rule promoted a compelling interest.

In *Indiana High School Athletic Association v. Raike,* 164 Ind.App. 169, 329 N.E.2d 66 (1975), the court noted that two "almost fundamental" activities were involved—school athletics and marriage. Therefore, intermediate-level scrutiny rather than minimum rationality review, was appropriate. The asserted purpose of the rule was to prevent "unwholesome" influences in athletics. The court found the rule both over-inclusive, because it barred married students of good moral character, and under-inclusive, because it did not bar unmarried students of questionable character. Therefore, the court concluded that the rule did not have a substantial relationship to its goal and therefore violated the equal protection clause. Courts now typically hold that marital classifications are unconstitutional on equal protection grounds.

(d) Classifications Based on Alienage

Classifications based on alienage are inherently suspect under the equal protection clause and, are, therefore, subject to strict judicial scrutiny. A court applied strict scrutiny in *Howard University v. NCAA,* 510 F.2d 213 (D.C.Cir.1975) and struck down the NCAA's "Foreign Student Rule." The rule provided that if an alien participated in organized athletics in a foreign country, the time spent doing so counted against the athlete's period of collegiate eligibility. The policy or purpose asserted in support of the rule was to prevent older, more skilled players from dominating the NCAA. Even though the court accepted this purpose, it held that the rule was not closely tailored to achieve its goal, since it penalized foreign students for activities that citizens participated in without penalty.

In *Spaeth v. NCAA,* 728 F.2d 25 (1st Cir.1984), another NCAA rule was challenged as being discriminatory against aliens. Under the rule, any time an athlete spent in organized competition after the age of 20 would count against his or her period of collegiate eligibility. A Canadian athlete claimed that because Canadians spend five years in high school and are, therefore, older than Americans upon graduation, the rule was discriminatory as applied to Canadians. But the court noted that because the rule was facially neutral, the Canadian athlete had to show intentional discrimination—a showing of disparate impact would not suffice. After the athlete failed to do so, the rule was held to be constitutionally permissible. *See also Colorado Seminary v. NCAA,* 417 F.Supp. 885 (D.Colo.1976) (upholding an NCAA rule providing that anyone who played in the Canadian Amateur Hockey Association's Junior A program was ineligible to play NCAA hockey, despite the plaintiff's allegation that the rule constituted an unconstitutional classification based on alienage).

(e) Age and Longevity Classifications

Age restrictions on participation in interscholastic athletics are commonly upheld. *See, e.g. Blue v. University Interscholastic League*, 503 F.Supp. 1030 (N.D.Tex.1980) (upheld a high school league rule requiring all athletes to be under 19 years old). Since the rules need meet only a rational basis test, they are generally affirmed. The courts often find that the rules are sufficiently related to a legitimate goal of assuring fair competition by preventing more skilled and physically mature players from competing against younger high school athletes.

Courts also generally uphold rules that limit an athlete's eligibility to a specified period of time, typically four consecutive years. Like age restrictions, these time limits are justified on the basis of maintaining a competitive balance by preventing older, more physically mature athletes from participating. Such rules are likewise designed to prevent schools from abusing athletes by holding them back a grade ("red-shirting") to allow them to mature and develop their athletic skills. The rules often include exceptions allowing a student to maintain eligibility after academically failing a grade, since the retention was not related to athletics.

These rules are often upheld when the student's delay in school was unrelated to athletics or academic failure. For example, in *Smith v. Crim*, 240 Ga. 390, 240 S.E.2d 884 (Ga.1977), a student dropped out of school for a year to care for his invalid mother. Upon learning that his absence counted against his four-year limit of eligibility, he challenged the application of the rule as applied in his case. The court, however, upheld the rule as being sufficiently related to the goals of assuring fair competition and preventing red-shirting. Some courts, on the other hand, have limited the use of such rules when the reasons for the student's ineligibility were clearly unrelated to athletics. *See, e.g., Lee v. Florida High School Activities Association, Inc.*, 291 So.2d 636 (Fla.1974) (athletic association's declaration of ineligibility violated student's due process rights when he had to leave school for a year in order to support his family).

(f) Public-Private School Classifications

Athletic leagues comprised solely of public schools may deny the admission of private schools when the denial is designed to prevent inequities regarding recruitment of athletes. Courts have noted that private schools are free to recruit athletes from a wide area because they have no attendance boundaries. Public schools, on the other hand, are confined to attendance districts and have no such ability.

(g) Transfer Classifications

Many schools and athletic associations have a rule which provides that if a student voluntarily transfers from one school to another, without a corresponding move by the parent(s), the student will be barred from interscholastic athletics for a certain period of time (usually one year). Many cases have challenged these rules on equal protection, freedom of religion, right to travel, and due process grounds. However, the transfer rules are usually upheld. In transfer cases, the courts typically follow a policy of noninterference in the absence of fraud or arbitrariness. *See, e.g., Herbert v. Ventetuolo,* 480 A.2d 403, 407 (R.I.1984) (student declared ineligible to play interscholastic hockey; court will not intervene if eligibility rules are reasonable).

Courts usually note that transfer rules serve the legitimate purpose of controlling illegal recruitment of student-athletes, and also prevent students from "school shopping" for athletic purposes. Courts acknowledge that application of these rules sometimes work a hardship on a student who transfers for nonathletic reasons. Nevertheless, courts generally conclude that the rule need not be mathematically precise to be valid—it need only be rationally related to a legitimate state interest or purpose. If the student can prove that his or her transfer was not related to athletics, a few courts have held that application of the rule in those instances violated the equal protection clause. *See, e.g., Sturrup v. Mahan,* 261 Ind. 463, 305 N.E.2d 877 (1974) (because the student had moved to escape detrimental conditions at home and heavy drug use at his former school, the court concluded that the rule swept too broadly in restricting students who had transferred for nonathletic reasons).

3.4 STATUTORY LIMITATIONS ON REGULATORY AUTHORITY

In seeking to vindicate their right to participate in activities that have typically been male-dominated, women have found legal encouragement in state and federal constitutional provisions providing for equal rights or the equal protection of the laws. However, during the past decade and a half the various federal statutes aimed at curbing gender-based discrimination in education and employment in education have certainly proven to be a fruitful means of promoting equality for women in sports.

A. Title IX

In 1972 Congress passed Title IX, a law designed to prohibit discrimination on the basis of sex in educational programs and activities receiving financial assistance from the federal government. Competitive athletics for women have made extensive gains in recent years due in part to Title IX. Title IX has had a significant impact on athletic participation for women. Nevertheless, disparities between athletic programs for men and women continue to be the subject of considerable political debate and legal action, much of which will no doubt center on Title IX.

1. General Prohibitions

Title IX prohibits discrimination on the basis of sex in any educational program or activity receiving federal financial assistance. Title IX provides in part that "[n]o person in the United States shall, on the basis of sex, be excluded from participation in, be denied the benefits of, or be subjected to discrimination under any education program or activity receiving Federal financial assistance . . . ." 20 U.S.C. § 1681(a) (1982).

2. Regulations

In 1974 the Department of Health, Education and Welfare (HEW) proposed athletic regulations for the implementation of Title IX. The NCAA responded, in part, by attempting to exempt revenue-producing sports from Title IX coverage. This attempt resulted in adoption of a provision which extended Title IX regulations to all athletic programs.

Under Title IX, HEW issued athletic regulations, which were approved by President Ford in 1975. The regulations generally provide that no person shall be "discriminated against in any interscholastic, intercollegiate, club or intramural athletics offered by a recipient, and no recipient shall provide any such athletics separately on such basis." At present, the regulations expressly cover: permissibility of separate teams; factors used to determine whether equal opportunities are available to both sexes; and athletic scholarships.

(a) Separate Teams

Title IX regulations do not require separate teams. Instead, the regulations permit separate teams for members of each sex in two circumstances: (1) when the sport is a contact sport; or (2) when selection for a team in either a contact or noncontact sport is based on competitive skill. The rule forbidding separate teams when selection is based on competitive skill has one exception. It provides that when a school sponsors a team in a particular sport for one sex but not for the other, and the athletic opportunities for the excluded sex have been limited in the past, members of the excluded sex must be allowed to try-out for the sponsored team.

This exception does not apply if the sport is a contact sport such as boxing, wrestling, rugby, ice hockey, football, or basketball. HEW has, by its interpretation of this exception, required that past opportunities be assessed on the basis of the complete athletic program for the excluded sex, rather than on the basis of the excluded sex's past opportunities in the particular sport. Consequently, if a school sponsored a men's-only cross-country team and women sought membership on the team, Title IX would generally require that women be allowed to try-out and join the team *only* if the athletic opportunities for women at that school were historically more restricted than athletic opportunities for men. *But see Gomes v. Rhode Island Interscholastic League,* 469 F.Supp. 659 (D.R.I.), *vacated as moot,* 604 F.2d 733 (1st Cir.1979) (a case in which the court assessed past athletic opportunities in the specific sport under consideration).

(b) Equal Athletic Opportunity

Title IX regulations enumerate ten factors to be considered in determining whether an institution is providing "equal opportunity for members of both sexes" in its sports program:

(1) Whether the selection of sports and levels of competition effectively accommodate the interests and abilities of members of both sexes;

(2) Provision of equipment and supplies;

(3) Scheduling of games and practice time;

(4) Travel and per diem allowance;

(5) Opportunity to receive coaching and academic tutoring;

(6) Assignment and compensation of coaches and tutors;

(7) Provision of locker rooms, practice and competitive facilities;

(8) Provision of medical and training facilities and services;

(9) Provision of housing and dining facilities and services; and

(10) Publicity.

This list is not intended to be exhaustive. The Office for Civil Rights (OCR) of the Department of Education may use additional factors in assessing whether an institution has afforded equal opportunity. In contrast, some factors, such as publicity, academic tutoring, and housing and dining facilities and services, which are relevant in intercollegiate programs, are not generally relevant in evaluating a sports program in a secondary school.

The regulations do not require that the factors be exactly the same for men and women. In fact, the regulations expressly provide that unequal aggregate expenditures do not necessarily constitute noncompliance with Title IX. Nevertheless, significant disparities in spending may make it necessary for an institution to justify the disparities in light of Title IX's mandate of equal opportunity in athletic participation.

(c) Athletic Scholarships

Under Title IX an educational institution must provide equal opportunity in athletic scholarships. Essentially, the regulations require that scholarships be substantially equal for members of both sexes based on the proportion of students of each sex participating in the school's athletic program.

3. Policy Interpretation of the Regulations

After the adoption of Title IX and the implementation of its regulations, schools were given three years in which to comply. This period expired on July 21, 1978. By that time, HEW had already received numerous complaints alleging sex discrimination in athletic programs. In order to facilitate resolution of these complaints and compliance with Title IX, HEW published a policy interpretation. The policy interpretation provided basic guidelines relative to the Title IX regulations and thereby created a framework within which complaints could be resolved.

The policy interpretation focuses on three areas, which the OCR assesses to determine whether an institution complies with Title IX and its regulations. First, the OCR evaluates the availability of an institution's athletic scholarships on a "substantially proportional" basis. To determine whether a school's athletic scholarships are awarded on a substantially proportional basis, the OCR divides the amount of scholarship money available for each sex by the number of male or female participants in the athletic program and compares results. If the comparison of the results shows "substantially equal amounts" of money spent per athlete, or if a disparity is explained by legitimate and nondiscriminatory factors, the OCR will find compliance.

The second area of evaluation is the degree to which the institution provides equivalent treatment, benefits, and opportunities in certain program areas. The factors the OCR considers in determining whether equal treatment exists are equipment, coaching and tutoring, locker rooms, recruitment, and support services.

The final area of concern of the OCR is the extent to which the school has met the interests and abilities of men and women students. The policy interpretation requires that an institution "equally and effectively" accommodate the athletic interests and abilities of both men and women students. A determination of the extent of compliance requires examination of the institution's assessment of the athletic interests and abilities of its students, its selection of offered sports, and its available competitive opportunities.

To determine the interests and abilities of its students, an educational institution may choose any nondiscriminatory method or methods. The methods, however, must take into account the nationally increasing levels of women's interests and abilities, and must refrain from disadvantaging members of the underrepresented sex. The methods must also consider team performance records and the expressed interests of underrepresented students who participate in intercollegiate athletic competition.

Effective accommodation is likewise mandated in the institution's selection of offered sports. The guidelines do not require an institution to provide exactly the same choice of sports to men and women or to provide integrated teams. But, if an institution sponsors a team in a particular sport for members of one sex, it may be required to permit members of the opposite sex to try out for that team. It may also be required to sponsor a separate team for members of the excluded sex, in contact as well as noncontact sports. In assessing effective accommodation, the OCR examines whether the excluded sex has been historically precluded from participation, whether the excluded sex has sufficient ability to maintain a viable team, whether the team has a reasonable expectation of intercollegiate competition, and in the case of noncontact sports, whether the excluded sex has sufficient skill to actively compete on the integrated team if selected.

Finally, the OCR evaluates the level of competition available to students when it assesses a school's accommodation of the interests and abilities of male and female students. An educational institution must provide both male and female athletes opportunities to participate in intercollegiate competition and must provide competitive team schedules that equally reflect the abilities of each sex. The OCR assesses compliance with this provision in one of three ways. First, the OCR determines whether an institution provides opportunities for men and women students in intercollegiate competition in numbers substantially proportionate to their respective enrollments. Second, it determines whether the institution's historical and current practice of program expansion is responsive to the athletic interests of the underrepresented sex. Third, the OCR determines whether an institution that cannot fully and effectively show a continuing practice of expansion accommodates the abilities and interests of the underrepresented sex in the institution's current program. If the OCR finds that an institution complies *with any one* of these three tests, the institution is deemed to have effectively accommodated the interests and abilities of its student-athletes.

4. *Title IX Enforcement Provisions*

Title IX provides that upon the discovery of an express violation and after an opportunity for notice, voluntary compliance, and hearing, federal funding may be terminated. Termination of funds, however, is subject to the following limitation contained in 20 U.S.C. § 1682 (1982):

> [S]uch termination . . . shall be limited to the particular political entity, or part thereof, or other recipient as to whom such a finding has been made, and shall be limited in its effect to the particular program, or part thereof, in which such noncompliance has been so found . . . .

This language and the requirements of notice, hearing, and an opportunity for voluntary compliance reflect the congressional intent that termination of federal funding is not to be lightly imposed.

Under the regulations, the OCR has two methods of enforcing Title IX. The enforcement process can be initiated by compliance reviews and complaints. In compliance reviews, the Department of Education (Department) periodically selects colleges and universities that operate intercollegiate athletic programs and investigates the institutions' compliance with Title IX.

In addition to filing complaints with the Department, aggrieved individuals may sue an institution directly, without being required to rely on the administrative enforcement mechanism. *See Cannon v. University of Chicago*, 441 U.S. 677 (1979). In either event, the Department conducts an investigation. If the investigation reveals that the institution is in compliance, the Department so informs the institution, and the matter is dropped. When violations are discovered, the Department outlines the violations and provides the institution with the results of its investigation.

The Department has ninety days in which to conduct an investigation and ninety additional days thereafter to negotiate a voluntary compliance agreement with the institution violating Title IX. When a voluntary settlement is reached, the Department and the institution agree on the steps the institution will take and the resources that it will use to achieve compliance. They also agree on a timetable for interim goals and full compliance. The Department then periodically reviews the institution's implementation of the plan.

When the Department finds that an institution is not in compliance with Title IX and a voluntary compliance agreement cannot be reached, the formal administrative process leading to termination of federal funds will commence. An institution targeted for termination of federal funding is entitled to a hearing before an administrative law judge. The administrative law judge will make an initial determination on the institution's compliance, and both the Department and the institution may appeal that determination to the Department's reviewing authority. If the reviewing authority affirms the administrative law judge's decision, the institution may request a review by the Secretary of Education. The secretary's review, however, is discretionary. If the Secretary of Education decides to withdraw funding, it must report that decision to the appropriate congressional committees thirty days prior to the termination of funds. Having exhausted its administrative remedies, the institution may now seek judicial review of the Department's actions.

The Department rarely invokes the formal administrative process to terminate funds to enforce Title IX or its regulations in the area of athletics. When an institution is not in compliance, the formal enforcement process is usually avoided because institutions have typically developed voluntary compliance plans acceptable to the OCR.

5. *Caselaw*

Although Title IX has existed for more than a decade, few cases have provided judicial interpretation regarding its effect on sports. Even the general caselaw on Title IX has been sparse, but a handful of cases have interpreted substantive aspects of Title IX. *See, e,g., Yellow Springs Exempted Village School District Board of Education v. Ohio High School Athletic Association*, 647 F.2d 651 (6th Cir.1981) (high school athletic association's rule prohibiting coed teams in contact sports violated Title IX); *O'Connor v. Board of Education*, 645 F.2d 578 (7th Cir.1981) (an athlete failed to show a reasonable likelihood of success on the merits of her claims that the school board's policy of providing for "separate but equal" boys' and girls' interscholastic athletic teams violated Title IX); and, *Gomes v. Rhode Island Interscholastic League*, 469 F.Supp. 659 (D.R.I.), *vacated as moot*, 604 F.2d 733 (1st Cir.1979) (defendant athletic league had to permit a male volleyball player to participate in interscholastic volleyball either by establishing a separate men's team or by permitting Gomes to participate on the women's team).

As previously noted, the issues of separate teams and the related opportunity to participate in individual sports have been the subject of litigation based on grounds other than Title IX. Typically, these other cases raise equal protection or equal rights objections, particularly if the state has an equal or human rights amendment.

While caselaw discussing substantive Title IX matters has been sparse, some cases have discussed the issue of enforceability under Title IX. Section 1682 prohibits discrimination on the basis of sex in "any educational *program or activity* receiving Federal financial assistance . . . ." (emphasis added). Schools have argued that their athletic programs are not programs or activities receiving direct funding from the federal government and that, therefore, the strictures of Title IX do not apply to these programs. Athletic departments rarely receive direct financial assistance from the federal government in the form of money earmarked for the athletic department. The issue thus arises as to whether Title IX coverage extends to an athletic program in an educational institution that receives federal funds in departments other than its athletic department.

Courts have disagreed over the proper interpretation of the term "program." Historically, some courts interpreted the term broadly, holding that aid to any part of an institution renders the entire institution subject to Title IX. Other courts interpreted the term narrowly, holding that Title IX applies only to the specific part of the institution receiving the assistance. The Supreme Court dealt with this conflict in *Grove City College v. Bell*, 104 S.Ct. 1211 (1984).

The Court of Appeals in the *Grove City* case read the statute broadly, holding that receipt of federal financial assistance by one program rendered the entire institution subject to the strictures of Title IX. The Supreme Court stressed, however, that no evidence had been presented establishing that the receipt of federal money by the students in that case resulted in the diversion of funds from the college's financial aid program to other areas in the college. The Supreme Court also noted that the Court of Appeals incorrectly assumed that Title IX applied when one program benefited from federal funding in another program. This interpretation was held to be inconsistent with the program-specificity requirement of Title IX. Accordingly, the Supreme Court concluded that the receipt of basic educational opportunity grant money by some of

Grove City College's students did not trigger institution-wide coverage of Title IX. The "purpose and effect" of the money received by the students at Grove City was to aid the college's financial aid program. The Court found that federal grants of financial aid to students subjected only the college's financial aid programs to Title IX coverage. Grove City College was, therefore, required to file an Assurance of Compliance for its financial aid program, but not for other programs.

The Supreme Court's decision in *Grove City* may limit Title IX claims in athletics. The decision seems to require that to invoke Title IX to prohibit discrimination in a particular program or activity the "purpose and effect" of the federal funding must aid that particular program or activity. In his opinion for the Supreme Court, Justice White distinguished between nonearmarked grants to an institution, which subjects the entire institution to Title IX requirements, and student aid of the type involved in *Grove City* which only subjects the earmarked program or area to Title IX coverage. Additionally, Justice White left open the possibility of proving a nexus between any federal aid and the discriminatory program by emphasizing that no proof had been offered in *Grove City* of such a nexus.

Justices Powell and O'Connor and Chief Justice Burger concurred, emphasizing that the Department of Education acted with overzealousness in pursuing Grove City College, despite the fact that no actual discrimination was alleged. The votes of Chief Justice Burger, Justice O'Connor, and Justice Powell were required to reach a majority consensus in *Grove City*. Thus, it is possible that the Supreme Court might rule differently in a subsequent case with more egregious facts. Since most institutions receive more forms of federal aid than did Grove City College, it would be an error to read the case as constituting a complete barrier to all discrimination actions brought against athletic programs under Title IX.

With its direct funding requirement, however, *Grove City* does constitute a difficult hurdle to overcome when asserting Title IX claims in athletics and other areas. Recognizing this, there has been some congressional effort to overrule *Grove City*. Several bills have been introduced that would limit the Supreme Court's ruling and reestablish broad applicability for Title IX. If such legislation is successful, it is likely that even private institutions like Grove City will be covered by Title IX if their students received federal financial assistance. Additionally, it should be noted that the *Grove City* funding requirement limitation may sometimes be avoided by bringing a cause of action under the equal protection clause of the fourteenth amendment or state law.

B. Employment Discrimination: Title VII and the Equal Pay Act

The Equal Pay Act, 29 U.S.C. § 206(d)(1) (1982), provides that:

No employer having employees subject to any provision of this section shall discriminate, within any establishment in which such employees are employed, between employees on the basis of sex by paying wages to employees in such establishment at a rate less than the rate at which he pays wages to employees of the opposite sex in such establishment for equal work on jobs the performance of which requires equal skill, effort, and responsibility, and which are performed under similar working conditions . . ..

Title VII of the Civil Rights Act of 1964 (42 U.S.C. § 2000e–2(a) (1976)) states that:

[i]t shall be an unlawful employment practice for an employer to fail or refuse to hire or to discharge any individual, or otherwise discriminate against any individual with respect to his compensation, terms, conditions, or privileges of employment, because of such individual's race, color, religion, sex, or national origin . . ..

Both of these statutes have been applied to athletics, primarily in suits brought by women coaches claiming sex discrimination. Under the Equal Pay Act, the party asserting discrimination must establish that his or her job is substantially equal to that of another employee of the opposite sex who is being paid more for performing similar services. Courts have held that Congress did not intend to put them or the Secretary of Labor in the position of evaluating jobs and determining what constitutes a proper differential for unequal work. One court added that "judicial determination of the relative economic value of unequal work may be particularly ill-advised in the context of faculty salaries in a private school." *Horner v. Mary Institute*, 613 F.2d 706 (8th Cir. 1980) (involving a claim by a female physical education instructor and coach).

The Equal Pay Act requires that differences in wages must not be based on the gender of the employee for work that is substantially equal in terms of skill, responsibility, and effort, and performed under similar working conditions. Title VII's impact is broader than that of the Equal Pay Act. Title VII covers wage discrimination in work that is not substantially equal, and prohibits discrimination in conditions and terms of employment. The latter prohibition covers many issues that are not strictly matters of pay.

Thus, even though Title VII and the Equal Pay Act are not coextensive, they both may be asserted to challenge gender discrimination in employment. Given apparent disparities in treatment of athletic personnel based on gender, it is likely that both Title VII and the Equal Pay Act will be asserted to eliminate those disparities. *See, e.g., Horner,* cited *supra,* and *Erickson v. Board of Education,* 120 Ill.App.3d 264, 75 Ill.Dec. 916, 458 N.E.2d 84 (1983), for two cases relating to sports or physical education law.

3.5 SPORTS AND THE DISABLED

Many schools have a policy of prohibiting physically disabled students from participating in interscholastic athletics. The decision to bar a student from participation is often based on guidelines provided by the American Medical Association (AMA), which recommends that students with particular disabilities be disqualified from participation in certain sports. When a party challenges a disqualification based on these guidelines, courts generally defer to the judgment of the school and uphold the disqualification unless the school's action was arbitrary or capricious. *See, e.g., Spitaleri v. Nyquist,* 74 Misc.2d 811, 345 N.Y.S.2d 878 (1973) (upholding disqualification based on AMA recommendation that students with the loss of one paired organ be barred from contact sports).

Recently, however, courts have been more willing to recognize the right of disabled students to participate in athletics. On at least two occasions, students who were blind in one eye successfully challenged their disqualification from playing college football on equal protection grounds. Students have prevailed in similar cases by relying on state law as well. *See, e.g., Kampmeier v. Harris,* 66 A.D.2d 1014, 411 N.Y.S.2d 744 (1978) (high school student with vision in only one eye successfully challenged her disqualification by asserting rights under New York Education

Law 4409, which provided that disabled students may participate in athletics if it is reasonably safe for them to do so, and if participation is in students' best interest); *Neeld v. American Hockey League*, 439 F.Supp. 459 (W.D.N.Y.1977) (professional hockey league rule barring athletes with vision in only one eye from participating in the league violated the plaintiff's rights under the New York Human Rights Law prohibiting employment discrimination based on disability).

The primary legal theory asserted by disabled students seeking to participate in athletics is based on Section 504 of the Rehabilitation Act of 1973, 29 U.S.C. § 794 (1982). The Act provides that:

> No otherwise qualified handicapped individual in the United States . . . shall, solely by reason of his handicap, be excluded from the participation in, be denied the benefits of, or be subjected to discrimination under any program or activity receiving Federal Financial assistance or under any program or activity conducted by any Executive agency
> . . . .

A § 504 regulation directly addresses the disabled student's right to participate in organized athletics:

> In providing physical education courses and athletics and similar programs and activities to any of its students, a recipient . . . may not discriminate on the basis of handicap. A recipient that offers physical education courses or that operates or sponsors interscholastic, club, or intramural athletics, shall provide to qualified handicapped students an equal opportunity for participation in these activities.

45 C.F.R. § 84.37(c)(1) (1984).

The identification of an "otherwise qualified" individual under § 504 has presented some difficulties for the courts. In an early § 504 case, a court permitted enforcement of a rule barring the plaintiff, who was blind in one eye, from participation in contact sports because medical testimony indicated a high risk to his good eye. *See Kampmeier v. Nyquist*, 553 F.2d 296 (2d Cir. 1977) (the court concluded that the plaintiff was not "qualified" to participate).

In 1979, however, the Supreme Court clarified the term "otherwise qualified" when it decided *Southeastern Community College v. Davis*, 442 U.S. 397 (1979). The Court stated in *Southeastern* that "[§ 504] requires only that an 'otherwise qualified handicapped individual' not be excluded from participation in a federally funded program 'solely by reason of his handicap,' indicating only that mere possession of a handicap is not a permissible ground for assuming an inability to function in a particular context." The Court also noted that "[a]n otherwise qualified person is one who is able to meet all of a program's requirements in spite of his handicap." *Id.* at 406.

Following *Southeastern*, students have been more successful in bringing § 504 claims against school or athletic league rules or regulations that discriminate against the disabled. For example, in *Poole v. South Plainfield Board of Education*, 490 F.Supp. 948 (D.N.J.1980), the court held that a youth who had been born with only one kidney should be permitted to participate in interscholastic wrestling. Poole and his parents were well aware of the risks involved in his participation and were willing to sign a waiver releasing the school from liability. The court stated that the school board's only duty was to advise the family of the risks, not to impose its own view of the proper course of action on the family.

In *Grube v. Bethlehem Area School District*, 550 F.Supp. 418 (E.D.Pa.1982), the court held that § 504 required that a high school student with one kidney be allowed to play football if his parents signed a waiver. In *Wright v. Columbia University*, 520 F. Supp. 789 (E.D.Pa.1981), a college student with vision in only one eye brought suit to play football. The university claimed that § 504 was not applicable to the football program because the program did not receive federal funds. The court noted that under the applicable regulations, a "recipient" of funds was defined as ". . . any public or private agency, institution, organization, or other entity, or any person to which Federal financial assistance is extended directly *or through another recipient* . . . ." 45 C.F.R. § 84.3(f) (1984) (emphasis added). The court concluded that federal funds need not go specifically to the football program to bring it within § 504's reach. The court noted further that even if the football program were not a recipient, the decision to prohibit the plaintiff from participation was ultimately made by the University itself, a direct recipient of funds.

The court in *Wright* distinguished the Second Circuit's decision in *Kampmeier* in two ways. In *Kampmeier*, the high school was acting *in loco parentis* when it disqualified the plaintiff from participating. In *Wright*, however, the plaintiff was an adult college student, deciding for himself whether to assume the risks of participation. The facts of the cases also differed with respect to the likelihood of injury.

Emotionally disabled students have also used § 504 to enforce their right to participate in interscholastic athletics with some success. The cases in this area reveal several developments that are worthy of note: (1) an increased willingness on the part of courts and lawmakers to recognize the right of disabled individuals to participate in athletics, even though their participation carries certain risks; and (2) significant weight is placed on a maturation distinction, evidencing a greater willingness to permit older, more mature disabled individuals to decide whether to assume the risk attendant with participation in athletics or other endeavors.

Section 504 and related acts (*e.g.,* Education for All Handicapped Children Act, Pub.L.No. 94–142) are designed to ensure that disabled individuals have an opportunity to participate in physical education classes. As a general rule, therefore, disabled students should be permitted to participate, if possible, with other students, or in programs specifically designed to meet their needs.

3.6 OTHER LIMITATIONS ON REGULATORY AUTHORITY

Before concluding with this chapter devoted to limitations on regulatory authority, brief mention should be made of other areas of law which may impinge upon an athletic association, league, professional team, or other sports entity's ability to control its affairs. These other potential sources of regulatory limitation are consumer protection laws and eminent domain rights.

A. Consumer Protection Laws

Many states now have what are commonly known as "consumer protection statutes." These laws are typically patterned after § 5(a)(1) of the Federal Trade Commission Act, 15 U.S.C. § 45(a)(1) (1982), and they usually outlaw both unfair methods of competition and unfair or deceptive acts and practices in the conduct of any trade or commerce.

Although these consumer protection laws may provide for a criminal penalty, their real significance lies in the fact that they create a private cause of action (*i.e.,* statutory tort) for those persons and businesses harmed by the illegal act. In addition to any actual damages sustained, those injured by conduct in violation of a state consumer protection act are often entitled to recover punitive damages, costs, and attorney's fees from the wrongdoer.

It is important to note from the outset that suits under state consumer protection statutes are governed by a specialized body of trade law, and not the more traditional legal principles of contract and tort law. Under trade law, an act or practice is deceptive if it has a tendency or capacity to mislead. To recover under consumer protection laws, it is not necessary that the person suing show either actual deception or reliance upon some false representation of fact. *See, e.g., Fisher v. World-Wide Trophy Outfitters, Ltd.,* 15 Wash.App. 742, 551 P.2d 1398 (1976) (big game outfitter's magazine advertisement representing "100% chance for each hunter to obtain a shot at a trophy" animal, was found sufficiently deceptive to entitle unsuccessful hunters to damages).

In determining whether a deceptive representation has been made, the statement is judged in its entirety and upon the overall impression it conveys to consumers. Words mean what they are intended and understood to mean. Therefore, deception may result from the use of statements not technically false or those which may be literally true. If a statement can be construed as either truthful or misleading, most jurisdictions require that it be interpreted as misleading.

This law that has developed around deceptive advertising has certainly made state consumer protection statutes a troublesome source of liability for manufacturers and sellers of athletic equipment, as well as others who advertise their services in a sport or recreational activity. The Federal Trade Commission has recently tried to retreat from this liberal tendency to mislead standard to a more stringent test for deceptive advertising: material misrepresentation likely to mislead consumers. *See Cliffdale Associates,* 103 F.T.C. 110, 165 (1984). How, if at all, this new federal standard will influence state consumer protection laws remains to be seen. *See generally* J. Karns, *Redefining "Deceptive" Advertising Under Illinois Consumer Fraud And Deceptive Business Practices Act After Cliffdale Associates,* 1985 S.Ill.U.L.J. 1 (for an excellent discussion of this recent change in the federal deceptive advertising test and its potential impact upon the Illinois Consumer Fraud and Deceptive Business Practices Act).

Consumer protection statutes also make unfair acts and practices illegal, and provide for a civil cause of action for these activities as well. In deciding whether a particular act or practice is unfair, courts seem to consider a number of factors: (1) does it offend public policy; (2) is it immoral, unethical, oppressive or unscrupulous; and (3) does it cause substantial injury to consumers or competitors? Among those practices which have been determined to be unfair are failure to promptly fill orders, giving secret rebates, refusing to make refunds and shipping unordered goods. Violations of other laws (*e.g.,* antitrust laws) are against public policy and per se unfair practices subject to sanction under a state's consumer protection act as well.

B. Eminent Domain Rights

Professional sports franchises are normally matters of pride to the citizens of the cities where they are located. Sports fans seem to take a proprietary interest in their local team. It is also economically rewarding for the city and local merchants to have a professional team. It may not, however, be rewarding for the team, and this brings up the possibility of moving the franchise to another, hopefully more lucrative location. Fans frequently object to the move, and the city government may resist it through exercise of the right of eminent domain.

Eminent domain is a government's power to condemn private property. It is an inherent attribute of state and federal governments, and a sovereign power which most municipalities are expressly authorized by law. No constitutional restraints limit the nature of the property that may be taken by eminent domain. All that is constitutionally required for condemning private property located within the territorial limits of a city are: (1) that the taking be for a "public purpose," and (2) that the owner receive "just compensation."

Assuming it can show a valid public use for the property, a city can condemn and operate a professional sports franchise. *See, e.g., City of Oakland v. Oakland Raiders,* 646 P.2d 835, 183 Cal. Rptr. 673 (1982) (recognizing City of Oakland's right to condemn a professional football team if it could establish the requisite public use). "Public use" has been defined as a use which concerns the whole community or promotes the general public's interest in relation to any legitimate objective of government. Courts have recognized a valid public use in condemnation of recreational facilities, and they may likewise someday approve the taking of a professional sports franchise as a proper subject for eminent domain. *See, e.g., City of Los Angeles v. Superior Court,* 51 Cal.2d 423, 333 P.2d 745 (1959) (city's acquisition of a baseball field was obviously for proper public purposes). Thus, this governmental power of eminent domain may severely restrict the movement of some professional sports franchises.

Chapter Four

AVOIDING A DECLARATION OF INELIGIBILITY

A simple and effective method for athletes to avoid being declared ineligible is to obey the regulations of the associations or conferences to which they belong. This, however, may not always be possible. Some athletes knowingly violate association or conference eligibility rules while others do so unknowingly or because they were deceived into doing so by a third party. *See, e.g., Shelton v. National Collegiate Athletic Association*, 539 F.2d 1197 (9th Cir.1976) (college basketball player remained ineligible even though he had been induced to sign a professional contract through fraud and undue influence on the part of his agent). Still other athletes have done nothing wrong, but are declared ineligible as a part of a general sanction placed upon their college or university. *See, e.g., Justice v. National Collegiate Athletic Association*, 577 F.Supp. 356 (D.Ariz.1983) (University of Arizona football players were ineligible for post season competition and prohibited from appearing in televised college football games as a part of the NCAA sanctions levied against the school).

If an athlete is declared ineligible, the individual's first response should be to exhaust all remedies he or she has with the governing body. Exhaustion of remedies means that the athlete appeals the decision, asks for a reconsideration, or employs any other established procedures for having the association or conference re-evaluate its initial determination of ineligibility. *See, e.g.,* NCAA Enforcement Procedure § 9–(b) (appeals permitted on behalf of student-athletes determined to be ineligible under Association rules).

Only after these procedures have concluded and proven unsuccessful should the athlete consider a law suit. If the athlete does sue, he or she should realize that there is little possibility of prevailing on the merits of the case. The vast majority of suits challenging NCAA or other athletic association rules have resulted in losses for the athletes involved. See *supra* §§ 1.2E, 2.1 and 3.3D for a representative sample of athletic association rules which have withstood court challenges by ineligible athletes. These cases have been lost in the sense that a particular rule was upheld by the court, but it is still possible for athletes to achieve what they most desire (*i.e.,* another season of competition) notwithstanding the eventual outcome of trial. With a little bit of luck and with the help of a skillful attorney, an otherwise ineligible athlete may be able to participate even though he or she ultimately loses the law suit.

This ability to win the objective, another season of competition while losing the challenge to the particular rule, is possible through a legal procedure known as a "preliminary injunction." Properly employed, a preliminary injunction may be used to gain the athlete an additional season of competition he or she is not otherwise entitled to. This result is possible because a preliminary injunction is used to maintain the status quo until a court of law can render a decision on the merits of the controversy.

To obtain a preliminary injunction, the athlete sues the NCAA, conference, or interscholastic association that declared the student ineligible, asking that the particular rule an individual violated be declared unenforcible. Grounds typically alleged for declaring eligibility rules unenforcible are violations of the due process and equal protection clauses of the state and federal constitutions, violations of federal antitrust laws, violation of other federal laws, or breach of contract. In conjunction with this attack upon the rule making him or her ineligible, the athlete asks for a court order enjoining enforcement of the rule until the court hears the case and renders its decision. This order is a preliminary injunction.

A preliminary injunction is considered an extraordinary remedy. To qualify, the athlete must demonstrate (1) a strong likelihood of success on the merits of the case, (2) the possibility of irreparable injury, (3) a balance of hardships in favor of the athlete, and (4) furtherance of some public interest in granting the injunction. In practice these criteria mean that the athlete need convince the court only that the legality of the challenged rule is in doubt, the athlete will forever lose a year of eligibility if forced to sit out competition until the case is decided, the athlete will suffer more harm than the defendant association if he or she is not allowed to compete during the legal proceedings and that the public interest is well served by allowing an athlete to participate while the case is being heard.

Once the trial court is convinced that the preceding criteria for a preliminary injunction have been met, it may prohibit the NCAA, conference, athletic association, or institution from declaring the athlete ineligible. If not declared ineligible, the athlete can compete. When the preliminary injunction is issued, the athlete's attorney immediately puts the brakes on the legal proceedings. It does not serve the athlete's interest to rush to trial and possibly lose on the merits of the case. But it does serve the athlete's interest to have the injunction in place and have the law suit drag out until after the season has expired. An excellent example of this use of a preliminary injunction may be found in the case of *Kite v. Marshall,* 454 F.Supp. 1347 (S.D.Tex.1978).

Greg Kite was a 6'11" high school senior, and considered to be one of the finest high school basketball players in the United States. During the summer before his senior year, Kite attended a basketball camp, which was against the state interscholastic association rules. Kite was declared ineligible for the 1978–79 season and he sued, alleging that this rule was unconstitutional. In conjunction with the suit, Kite asked for a preliminary injunction restraining the state high school athletic association from enforcing its training camp rule against him. The trial court granted the preliminary injunction. The court believed that Greg Kite had a strong likelihood of success on the merits, that he would suffer irreparable harm if he lost his senior year of competition, that it served the public interest to have Kite eligible, and that when the hardships were balanced, Greg Kite would suffer material harm if the injunction were denied, whereas the interscholastic association would suffer little if any harm in having the young man compete until the matter came to trial.

Compete Kite did, for the trial court never reached a decision on the merits until 1980, and it was not until 1981 that the court proceeding finally terminated in favor of the association. It was more than two years after Greg Kite graduated from high school that the law suit concluded and the interscholastic association won. The association won because its training camp rule was found constitutional; but Greg Kite also won because he competed in his last year of high school.

Kite is illustrative of the effective use of a preliminary injunction to obtain an additional season of competition. But it would be erroneous to conclude from this case that every ineligible athlete can qualify for injunctive relief; many do not. A key factor in *Kite* was that the athlete challenged the legality of a rule that had never been previously subjected to judicial scrutiny. Had Kite been ineligible because of a minimum grade-point average rule, he would probably not have obtained the preliminary injunction because such rules have been uniformly upheld by the courts. If the rule had already been declared constitutional, Kite would have had little likelihood of prevailing on the merits, and the injunction would not have issued. Therefore, the conference, athletic association, or institution may defeat the request for a preliminary injunction by directing the court's attention to other cases that have upheld similar rules. If this tactic fails, the association or institutional defendant should make two additional requests of the court.

The first request is for a bond to cover payment of any costs and damages the association, conference, or enjoined party sustains because of a wrongfully issued injunction. Wrongfully issued means that after a trial on the merits, the court decides that the preliminary injunction should not have been entered because the challenged rule is in fact constitutional or otherwise lawful.

Requesting the athlete to post a bond before getting an injunction is significant for a number of reasons. When a bond is requested, the court may not ignore the request and grant the preliminary injunction. If the court issued the injunction without either the posting of a bond or a specific finding that the enjoined party would not incur any damages as a result of the injunction, most jurisdictions consider the order void. If the injunction is void, it cannot be enforced through the court's contempt powers.

Another important reason for requesting that the athlete post a bond is that many courts view the bond as a limit on the amount of damages a wrongfully enjoined party may recover. Stated otherwise, the defendant's only source of recovery is the bond. If no bond is posted and the preliminary injunction is later found to have been wrongfully issued, the defendant athletic association or school has no recourse against the athlete for any damages sustained as a result of the injunction. Conversely, if a bond is posted, the defendant may recover up to the value of the bond, but no more.

Since the amount of the security is crucial to the defendant's subsequent remedies, a large bond should always be requested. In convincing the court to require a substantial bond before issuing the injunction, a college might, for instance, calculate its potential economic loss if the injunction is later dissolved and the institution is sanctioned by its athletic conference or association for permitting the athlete to play in violation of the rules. *See, e.g.,* NCAA Enforcement Procedure § 10 (permitting the NCAA to sanction institutions which play an ineligible student-athlete under a wrongfully issued preliminary injunction). The loss of television revenues and other potential injury to the college because of NCAA sanctions can be quite significant, and the court should be asked to require a bond sufficiently large to cover this eventuality. Of course, the ultimate decision on the amount of any bond rests with the court, but the court is not likely to set a low bond when the enjoined party might suffer a substantial economic loss because of the court's restraining order. *See, e.g., Kite v. Marshall,* 454 F.Supp. at 1347 (plaintiff athlete was only required to post a $50 bond because court specifically found that only nominal harm would be inflicted upon the defendants by enforcement of the preliminary injunction). Moreover, if the court does require a substantial bond to be posted and the athlete cannot afford the cost of that bond, then he or she is not entitled to a preliminary injunction!

The second request a party subject to a preliminary injunction should make relates to the form of the court's order. An enjoined party has the right to request that the court not order the athlete played. Whether or not an athlete participates is a decision more properly left up to the coach. The court cannot and should not substitute its judgment for that of the coach. Since the court cannot order that the athlete actually compete in a game, it will be difficult for the court to find the association or school in contempt for not allowing the athlete to participate.

In a law suit, the ineligible athlete's energies and resources are directed at obtaining a court order which allows the student to compete until the trial is completed. After the case is tried, the court will either dissolve the injunction if the association rule is lawful, or make the injunction permanent if the rule is unlawful. In most instances, however, the athlete has little interest in the eventual outcome of the trial, for the student-athlete will have long since used his or her four years of eligibility.

For similar reasons, it is incumbent upon an athletic association, college, or other person to commit its resources early in opposing issuance of the injunction. The fight to deny the athlete that final season of eligibility has to be made early, because once the preliminary injunction is issued, it may take years for the matter to wind its way through the court system. It is much less expensive for the athletic association or school to prevent the injunction. If the athlete does not obtain an injunction, the same lengthy court process will work against that individual and the final season will have passed long before the trial. When the association commits sufficient legal resources early in the case and prevents the injunction, the athlete will most often drop the suit. This brief but intense battle over the issuance of a preliminary injunction will be much less costly than a protracted trial on the merits.

Chapter Five

REPRESENTATION OF THE PROFESSIONAL ATHLETE

While boxing and other related sports have been professional for centuries, most organized professional sports are of more modern origin. Professional baseball came into being with the Cincinnati Red Stockings in 1869, professional football with the Latrobe, Pennsylvania YMCA football club in 1895, and professional basketball with the Trenton, New Jersey club in 1896. During the past 100 years, substantial changes in professional sports have occurred, but the most significant changes have undoubtedly occurred in professional team sports. Creation of the business-oriented franchise and the arrival of the player's representative are the two events that have most profoundly changed professional sports.

5.1 HISTORICAL DEVELOPMENTS

Just twenty years ago, most professional athletes negotiated their own contracts. The thought of having an agent was foreign to clubs and athletes alike. But over the past few years agents have had an ever-increasing role in professional athletics. The primary reason for the rising influence and role of agents is that professional team franchises have turned sports into a profitable industry, and athletes can now demand increased compensation for their participation. In less than two decades, athletes have seen their salaries rise from the thousands into the millions of dollars. There are a number of factors that have contributed to increased compensation for professional athletes.

A. Rise of Free Agency and Arbitration

Option and reserve clauses, which were present in most professional contracts, left athletes with very little bargaining leverage because the clauses precluded athletes from negotiating with other clubs. Since they could not negotiate with other clubs, athletes had to choose between two unpalatable alternatives: either accept the contract and play or refuse to play and receive no compensation. The players' bargaining position with a club was, therefore, severely limited. The only threat to the club was that players might elect not to play, or more commonly, that they might in their dissatisfaction, play with a negative attitude. Regardless of which choice an athlete might make, the overall effect kept the salaries of professional athletes artificially low. Section 6.1 *infra* contains an in depth discussion of option and reserve clauses in the player-management context, and a typical reserve clause is shown in § 3.2C–3 *supra*.

Beginning in the 1960s, however, some countervailing influences ultimately weakened management's bargaining position relative to option clauses and the reserve system. While such provisions effectively prohibited clubs within the league from negotiating with players under contract with a different club, the option clause or reserve system could not prevent clubs in new leagues from negotiating with players. Thus, competition for players' services developed between the National Football League and the American, World, and United States Football leagues; between the National Basketball Association and the American Basketball Association and the World Basketball League; and, between the National Hockey League and the World Hockey Association. This competition for players' services shifted bargaining power to the athletes. With the rise of rival leagues, athletes had a new and more viable alternative: they could enter into negotiation with a rival league and thereby undermine the reserve system or option clause in their contract. If their club refused to match or at least substantially raise their salaries to the level offered by the rival league, players could go elsewhere and play for increased compensation.

As competition increased for the services of professional athletes, athletes enjoyed the fruits of increased bargaining power in areas other than compensation. They were able to bargain as a group for the actual elimination or weakening of the reserve system and option clauses. Players were also able to bargain for a right of free agency, whereby an experienced athlete whose contract with a club had expired could declare himself a free agent and thereby allow other clubs within the league to negotiate for the athlete's services. Free agency is ominous for many clubs. Because they risk the loss of their better, experienced players to other teams, clubs have extended the duration of players' contracts to avoid the threat of losing an athlete whose contract has expired and who, therefore, qualifies for free agency status.

Since free agency is often only available to more experienced players, younger athletes remain at the mercy of the club that drafted and signed them to multiple-year, fixed-term contracts. To help equalize their bargaining power with the club during these initial years, players have increased minimum salaries through collective bargaining. Players have also, in the case of baseball, established mandatory arbitration between the younger player and the club. After three years (it used to be two) in the league, baseball players can seek arbitration of their compensation. Arbitration and free agency, together with competition among clubs, contributed to the escalation of player salaries. Another factor that has helped promote free agency in professional sports has been the federal antitrust laws and their effect upon reserve clauses. For a discussion of antitrust challenges to reserve and option clauses see *supra* § 3.2C–3.

B. Collective Bargaining

Collective bargaining is discussed in much greater detail in the next chapter and in subsequent portions of this chapter, but here it is important to note the influence collective bargaining has had on the escalation of salaries. As players gained bargaining power on an individual basis, they likewise recognized that they could gain power by joining collectively in players associations. By presenting a unified front, these associations were able to increase the bargaining power of players regarding salaries, pensions, and other matters. They were particularly successful in increasing minimum salaries for players, in strengthening the position of middle-level (nonsuperstar) and younger athletes, and in assisting even the superstars by stimulating development of free agency.

C. Media Exposure, Increasing Popularity of Sports, and the Advent of the Agent

First with radio and later with television in its many forms (*e.g.*, cable, pay television, network coverage), the popularity of sporting activities and the athletes who participate in them has increased dramatically. Literally millions of people watch sporting activities on a daily basis. Given the popularity of sporting events, particularly at the professional level, advertising and related commercial activities have converted the sports business into a multi-billion dollar a year industry. A number of companies each spend over $100,000,000 yearly to obtain advertising time during televised sporting events. Public and media attention has clearly contributed to escalating salaries in professional sports. Players, like actors in the entertainment industry, have become the focus of much of this media attention, and like their acting counterparts, they have come to expect compensation for their personality status as well as for their athletic performance.

The large amounts of money involved in the sports industry have contributed to escalating player salaries and have lured agents into the professional sports industry. With many athletes commanding annual salaries in excess of $1,000,000, and with average salaries often in the hundreds of thousands of dollars, players recognize that they need professional assistance, not only in negotiating their contracts but also in managing their financial affairs. Agents perform some or all of these services, and are often compensated well for their services.

By the mid-1970s, however, excesses on the part of some agents in representing athletes became a matter of common knowledge and some commentators began to assert that competent and honest agents were the exception rather than the rule. This sobering assessment led to regulatory efforts to control agents and their excesses. Many entities, including the NCAA and the players associations, have sought to regulate or at least screen agents, limiting the likelihood of an unscrupulous agent preying on a talented young and financially naive athlete. The relationship between agents and players must, therefore, be examined, not only to point out excesses but also to establish how athletes can best protect themselves.

5.2 PLAYER–AGENT RELATIONSHIP IN PROFESSIONAL SPORTS

An agent is someone who is given authority to transact business for another. A contract between a sports agent and an athlete forms the basis of agreement regarding both compensation for the agent and the nature and extent of the agent's authority to act on behalf of the athlete. The nature of compensation and scope of authority varies, depending on the particular contract.

While there is a statute of frauds which requires that some agreements be in writing (for example, if they are over one year in duration), the agreement between an agent and a player can be oral unless either state law or the players association requires a written contract. Nevertheless, a written contract is customary and preferable because it requires the parties to put their agreed terms down on paper, allowing them to be scrutinized by both themselves and by an arbitrator or a court, if necessary.

Even if an agent is an attorney, it is still advisable for the athlete to obtain separate legal advice on the proposed agreement. Reputable attorney-agents will, as an ethical matter, encourage the player to obtain such advice from another attorney or players association. Indeed, it is not unusual for a players association to either require the signing of a standardized player-agent contract or to require submission of a newly drafted contract to the association for review. *See, e.g.,* the National Football League Players Association's standard player-agent agreement, which is included in § 10.5 *infra.* *See generally* R. Ruxin, *An Athlete's Guide to Agents* (1983) (presenting a fairly comprehensive introduction to the problems which often arise in a player-agent relationship).

A. Selecting An Agent

Prior to entering into a contract with an agent, the athlete must select one. Some of the factors that should be considered in the selection process are discussed in this section. The athlete and the agent should be comfortable with one another—not every agent and every athlete will be compatible. They need not be best friends, but their aims *and* their views as to how those aims or goals can best be achieved should be compatible. Both the player and the agent should understand and be comfortable with their respective roles. Their relationship should engender faith and trust on the part of both parties.

The agent should also be competent to perform the agreed tasks. Competence, along with basic honesty, is a major concern in selecting an agent. Similarly, the agent should be able to expect that the athlete will merit trust. Competence on the part of an agent includes more than a general educational background—it requires an understanding of the sport, its management, and its business aspects. An agent is under a legal duty to conduct the representation with the same degree of competence displayed by others who engage in the representation of athletes. Failure to act with that degree of competence might subject the agent to a negligence or related claim by an athlete. However, since such a claim might be difficult to prove, particularly in marginal cases where the agent's incompetence is not extreme, and since some agents may not have the financial resources necessary to pay a judgment, an agent's potential liability for malpractice is hardly a cure-all for damage caused by incompetence.

Similarly, efforts by state legislatures to require agents to post a bond to protect their clients have often proven inadequate due to the limited amount of the required bonding. It is not likely that many states will pass legislation requiring professional agents to post bonds in an amount sufficient to satisfy the potential claims of the athletes they represent. In addition, the language of the bond itself often limits the availability of the security in marginal cases. An athlete should, therefore, examine both the professional and character qualifications of a prospective agent. An agent does not have to be an attorney to represent an athlete. However, there are some advantages to having an attorney as an agent: (1) an attorney must comply with a set of ethical standards; (2) he or she presumably has a legal background which is often helpful in analyzing problems that arise during negotiations; and (3) an attorney has experience in negotiating, drafting legal documents, and in modeling provisions for inclusion in the player's contract. Of course, many competent agents are not lawyers. Nevertheless, any competent agent will seek legal assistance when needed. Additionally, it should be noted that attorney-agents are often at a practical disadvantage in obtaining clients because they are ethically limited in their ability to approach or solicit athletes as clients. There have been efforts to regulate the ethical conduct of non-attorneys and even unscrupulous attorney agents, although these efforts have been only minimally effective. See *infra* § 5.6 for an examination of the ethical constraints imposed upon attorney-agents, and the appendix, *infra* at § 10.1, for a copy of the Association of Representatives of Professional Athletes' Code of Ethics.

If the agent handles the athlete's money or any financial matters, the athlete should require that the agent be bonded. Furthermore, just as an agent must be competent to negotiate contracts, if the agent manages financial matters, competence sufficient to warrant acting on the player's behalf as a financial planner is necessary. Some states require financial managers to be licensed.

State regulations applicable to the services being rendered by the agent must be complied with. For example, California regulates sports agents through a licensing statute and many other states regulate financial and other professional planners. (A copy of the California athlete agent law, Cal.Labor Code §§ 1500 to 1547 (West Supp.1985), is reproduced *infra* at § 10.2 of the appendix.) The NCAA and other organizations and institutions are developing a screening system to help athletes select agents. If such a screening mechanism is available, the athlete should take advantage of it. The athlete should not treat it as a panacea, however, since screening mechanisms are fairly new and offer variable results in terms of the quality of the agents selected.

Players, particularly those with college eligibility remaining, should be careful in discussing contract matters with a would-be agent. The athlete may lose eligibility and may also cause NCAA sanctions to be invoked against his or her school if such negotiations take place prior to the athlete's final game. One agent sought to get around the rule forbidding an athlete from entering into an agreement with an agent prior to the last game by creating an "offer sheet," whereby the player signed an offer to have the agent serve as a representative. The agent argued that the offer could not constitute an agreement until accepted, and since the agent did not accept it until after the season, it did not violate the NCAA's rule. The NCAA rejected this reasoning, recognizing that the agent's action was little more than a sham to circumvent the NCAA's rule regarding the timing of player-agent contracts. Players should not only be careful to avoid discussing substantive contract matters during their playing days, but they should likewise avoid any agent or player representative who encourages such activity. The NCAA rules on agent contracts are set out *supra* at § 1.2A.

Once a player has selected an agent and the agent has agreed to be employed, the parties generally enter into an agreement. Some agents or players representatives maintain that such agreements are unnecessary, but entering into a formal written contract is always a good precaution for the sake of both parties. The athlete should have the agreement examined by an independently selected attorney. Additionally, when a player has an investment agreement, financial management contract, or an endorsement agreement, those should likewise be in writing and reviewed by independent legal counsel. Those agreements should also be separate from the basic agent-player contract because they cover different material, and are often between the athlete and a party other than the agent. An agent may even want added protection by including a provision in the contract recommending that the athlete have the agreement reviewed by independent counsel. This is particularly desirable if the agent or the agent's attorney drafted the agreement.

B. Compensation

Obviously, the terms of an agent's compensation are critical to the contract. Typically, an agent receives payment in one of four ways: (1) by the hour (compensation at an hourly rate, *e.g.*, $100 per hour); (2) by a flat rate (*e.g.*, $2,000 for the services rendered); (3) by a percentage of the salary or income received by the athlete (*e.g.*, five percent of the total package negotiated by the agent); or (4) a combination of any of the preceding modes of payment (*e.g.*, a flat fee plus a percentage). It is critical that the compensation provision be clear and precise. In some instances, (*e.g.*, the National Football League (NFL)) compensation provisions are expressly limited by the players association. It is also important to specify how much the agent will receive for what services *and* when that payment will be received. For example, there may be a serious problem if an athlete signs for $450,000 over three years ($150,000 per year) with only the first year guaranteed, and for an additional signing bonus of $75,000. A problem arises when the player's agreement with the agent fails to specify when the agent is to receive payment. If the agreement fails to specify that the agent will be paid at the time the athlete actually receives money from the club or team, the agent might claim an entitlement to the entire payment upfront. The agent might assert upfront entitlement to five percent of the $75,000 and the $450,000 requiring the player to immediately pay $26,250 of the $75,000 bonus over to the agent. Furthermore, in the example used, if payment is made up front on the $450,000, only $150,000 of which is guaranteed, the player may end up paying the agent for negotiating a salary never received.

A second problem exists in determining what part of the athlete's compensation is included in the computation of the agent's fee. The agent will often contend that such items as the player's expense allowance, bonuses, incentives, investments, and personal appearances are to be included in the base from which the agent's fee is computed. These matters should be clearly spelled out in the player-agent agreement. Furthermore, the players association may preclude an agent from negotiating or receiving compensation for an incentive provision in a player's contract.

Another problem with the sample agreement is that it does not provide for a method of resolving disputes regarding compensation. Player-agent contracts should include an arbitration clause or some other mechanism for handling differences expeditiously and at minimal cost to the parties. Such clauses may be required by the players association. See paragraph four of the National Football League Players Association's standard player-agent contract, *infra* at § 10.5, for an example of an arbitration clause.

C. Duration, Renewal, and Termination

The actual duration of the contract between the athlete and the agent should be stated in the agreement. A term providing for automatic renewal of the contract may be included in some instances, but it should be specific in nature. Again, the players association, as with the NFL Players Association, may limit the initial term and any renewals. The actual terms of automatic renewal must be included, or a player might be bound indefinitely to an agency arrangement that becomes very unsuitable.

A provision in the agreement should also cover the right of the player or the agent to terminate the agreement. The agreement should specify the period covered by the contract, as well as what constitutes cause, permitting a party to terminate the agency relationship during the life of the agreement.

D. Services to Be Performed

For a contract to be enforceable, it must provide for consideration, or some substitute therefor. Each party must, in other words, offer the other party some service or compensation—there must be a bargained for exchange. The player agrees to compensate the agent, and the agent agrees to perform certain services in exchange for that compensation. The services rendered by the agent should be specified in the contract.

Some agents limit their services to negotiating the contract with the club, while others offer a large range of services. A few agents even offer a complete management service, whereby the athlete turns his or her entire income over to the agent or the agent's management firm. The athlete receives an allowance back in return, with the firm managing the remainder on behalf of the athlete. Whatever the services rendered may be, from mere negotiation of the player's contract with the club to complete management, those services should be clearly enumerated in the agreement.

Again, when the agent performs multiple services such as negotiation, investment, or management, it is often advisable, and sometimes even required by law, that separate agreements for differing services be executed. With separate agreements, it is a good practice to refer to these additional agreements in the player-agent contract, and to specify whether the player-agent agreement (or any other agreement) is severable from the remaining agreements. In other words, the player-agent agreement should specify whether breach of any one term results in the breach and termination of the agreement itself.

A provision indicating whether the agent has the sole or exclusive right to represent the athlete, and for what purposes the agent retains such an exclusive right, is desirable too. Such a provision should, however, be consistent with the services provision of the agreement.

A player should be reluctant to provide an agent with a general power of attorney, giving the agent full power to make all of the player's business and related decisions without the player's signature. Even a limited power of attorney, designed merely to allow the agent to act on the player's behalf without written consent in isolated and specific transactions, should be carefully drafted to ensure that the agent is not given too much authority.

An athlete should seek independent legal counsel before signing any power of attorney.

E. Standards and Practices

Another common provision in player-agent contracts is a clause specifying uniform standards or practices, ethical and otherwise, under which the agreement is to be performed. For example, the contract might specify that the agent will conform to the standards and practices published by the Association of Representatives of Professional Athletes (ARPA). A copy of the ARPA Code of Ethics is contained in the appendix, *infra* at § 10.1. Membership in ARPA is voluntary and the Code, therefore, is only enforceable against those agents who agree to abide by its terms. An athlete would be wise to incorporate the ARPA or related standards by reference into the player-agent agreement and attach a copy of the standards to that agreement. Incorporation of such standards would assure to a limited extent that an express set of ethical standards apply to the particular agent-athlete relationship.

F. Boilerplate

Virtually every contract contains boilerplate provisions. Boilerplate provisions are the general terms normally included to protect the contracting process. Some of the provisions that ought to be included, or at least considered, in the player-agent contract are: (1) a dispute resolution provision requiring arbitration of disputes and prescribing the method of selecting arbitrators; (2) a notice provision indicating the manner and method required for parties to provide one another with notice of matters arising under the contract; (3) an integration term providing that the final agreement constitutes the full and final agreement of the parties, limiting the legal effect of prior or contemporaneous written and oral statements or documentation; (4) a choice of law provision indicating which state's law governs the transaction; (5) indemnification clauses, indemnifying the athlete or the agent against acts of others; (6) a force majeure clause dealing with the treatment of unforeseen occurrences or acts of God; and (7) other clauses necessary to deal with general problems arising in the contract context.

G. Recitals

Recitals are provisions typically included at or near the beginning of the contract which specify the facts or underlying intent of the parties in entering into the contract. If included, recitals should be drafted carefully. They are often useful to courts in resolving ambiguities or differences arising out of the contractual relationship. Unless there is actual evidence of the intent of the parties, when contract disputes arise courts or other entities are left to their own devices to ascertain the intent of the parties when they made the contract. A well crafted recital will often disclose the intent of the contracting parties, and help to resolve disputes regarding the intent of the parties relative to a contract provision.

H. Other Essential Provisions

Basic provisions that ought to be included in an agreement are fairly standard, yet many transactions involve unique parties with unique needs. The contract should fit the needs of the parties, not vice versa. Standardized or form contracts are convenient to use, but are generally just the beginning point. The essence of a particular contract is seldom fully embodied in any general or standardized contract. Provisions must be added or deleted to meet the needs of a particular arrangement. However, a standardized player-agent contract may be required by the players association, and may limit the right of the parties to deviate from the terms of that agreement. (*See, e.g.,* the NFLPA's standard player-agent contract, which is included in the appendix, *infra* at § 10.5).

If a contract fails to embody all of the essential details of the parties' agreement, it may be unenforceable or may have to be modified by a third party's addition of implied provisions. Courts have usually been the third party called upon to add implied contractual provisions, and they have been willing to imply or add terms to save a contract, provided the parties sincerely intended a contract. Drafting a general contract and trusting in the future is not without risk, however. A court may add terms that are harmful to one or both of the parties, or may simply declare the contract unenforceable.

The authors do not pretend to include a comprehensive catalog of all the provisions necessary in a player-agent contract. However, they do intend to make two things clear: (1) a written contract is desirable; and (2) its drafting is no simple matter—care must be taken to draft an agreement that fully expresses all of the particulars of the player-agent relationship.

There are additional problems in the player-agent relationship that transcend the substance of the parties' agreement. Unscrupulous agents who take advantage of naive or inexperienced athletes present a major problem. Problems arise when the agent develops a trust relationship with the athlete and then takes advantage of that relationship. The NCAA, various players associations, and even state and federal governments have intervened on occasion to protect athletes. These efforts to aid the player range from informing the athlete about unscrupulous agents through screening groups and registration efforts to actual regulation of agents, as in the case of the California legislation. Collectively, these efforts are new and remain largely untried. Nevertheless, they have served to heighten player sensitivity to potential excesses. Professional athletes are increasingly aware of excesses on the part of some agents, and this awareness has helped remedy problems among veteran players.

Many agents have tried to improve their tainted group reputation. They formed the Association of Representatives of Professional Athletes in an effort to create and ultimately enforce a code of ethics applicable to the industry. Regulation of this sort is in its infancy and remains largely voluntary. Even where applicable, the provisions of such codes are most effective against major excesses and remain largely ineffective against less egregious but more common problems, like general incompetence and conflicts of interest.

Conflicts of interest are common in sports representation, even among some of the most reputable agents. Some agents represent both individual athletes and players associations, creating a potential conflict of interest between the desires of their individual clients and the association as a whole. Another common and potentially harmful conflict arises when an agent represents multiple players, particularly when the players are on the same club. This conflict is exacerbated when an agent represents two players who are in competition with each other for the same position on a team or when the players must seek remuneration from a limited fund, such as is the case in the National Basketball Association (NBA) where each team has a cap on total salaries payable. Anytime an agent might benefit from playing the interests of one client against another, the agent has a serious conflict of interest.

Another serious conflict arises when the agent's interests in being paid conflict with the client's interest in deferring income or in obtaining a benefit, such as education, that does not translate into financial compensation for the agent. In those cases, an agent may be more interested in seeking a large bonus upon execution of the agreement rather than protecting the client's interest in deferring taxes or in obtaining future benefits.

A potential conflict of interest also arises when the agent receives anything of value from a club or management. Whenever the club offers anything of value to the agent, the agent runs the risk of compromising his or her client's interest in order to obtain the perk or benefit offered by the club.

Many conflicts of interest present only the potential for wrongdoing. When an agent appears to fully and adequately represent clients despite an apparent conflict, there has been a general reluctance to question the representation on conflict of interest grounds. However, an athlete should be sensitive to the potential for conflicts of interest, and the agent should disclose any potential conflicts of interest to the athlete.

Some competent agents abide by ethical limitations that preclude them from approaching athletes, and thus find it difficult to compete with agents who do not feel similarly constrained. Therefore, a potential pool of competent and ethical agents often remains largely untapped. Screening groups who act on behalf of athletes are often able to circumvent this problem by inviting attorneys and other agents to submit their credentials for review by the screening committee and for possible employment by athletes. These screening committees, however, are not without their potential problems, including the following: (1) the committee recommending competent representation for athletes must know what such competence entails; (2) the committees are subject to being "bought" or persuaded by matters unrelated to the selection of competent player representatives; (3) the committees may be viewed as cure-alls by an impressionable athlete more interested in playing than in selecting an agent, and the athlete may place too much reliance on them; (4) by screening potential agents and limiting the accessibility of those found to be unqualified to athletes, the committees may incur their own legal liability either to an athlete who was victimized by an agent the committee approved (*e.g.*, negligence or warranty theories) or to an aspiring agent who was rejected from the pool (*e.g.*, antitrust violation). *See, e.g.*, Note, *The NFL Players Association's Agent Certification Plan: Is It Exempt From Antitrust Review?*, 26 Ariz.L.Rev. 699 (1984). At best, such screening committees are a buffer between the student-athlete and a horde of agents. The committees can help the athlete acquire helpful information about possible representatives without taking up too much studying and playing time. As screening and registration efforts develop, these committees may be very productive in eliminating excesses that have been all too common in the player-agent relationship.

With the recent massive increases in compensation paid to athletes and skyrocketing sports revenues due to media attention and related factors, problems in the player-agent relationship have arisen and are bound to continue to arise. Nonetheless, the potential for such problems can be limited by careful selection of an agent, careful drafting of an agreement, and if necessary, by increased regulation of agents by entities interested in maintaining the integrity of the sport.

5.3 CONTRACT WITH THE CLUB

Once the player and the agent have entered into an agreement, the agent must negotiate with the club. Negotiations with the club, however, should not commence until the agent is prepared. Adequate preparation includes knowing the needs of the client and that of the interested professional teams, as well as a basic understanding of the negotiations process itself.

A. Evaluating the Value of Player's Services

In evaluating the value of a client's services, the agent should be aware of what similar players have received and are receiving for their services. For instance, if the player is a linebacker drafted in the first part of the second round of the draft, the agent needs to know what other players who play similar positions and are drafted at a similar point have received. Players associations are often a very fruitful source of such information.

An agent should accumulate any other information that might enhance the value of the player such as the athlete's skills and personality and the needs of the club. The agent must be gathering as well as packaging information about his or her client in preparation for the negotiations. The value of a professional athlete's services and presence on a team are necessarily subjective, but the agent must endeavor to cast these somewhat subjective factors in an objective form—a form that translates into specific contractual terms.

B. Evaluating the Needs of One's Client

To be effective, an agent must determine the needs of the client. To do so, the agent must look at issues other than how much money the club is willing to pay for the client's services. An agent must be concerned not only with the client's economic future, but must also be concerned with the player's other needs. Thus, although the agent might determine that holding out during the preseason could help the client obtain a larger contract, the agent may recommend against holding out if it might ultimately hurt the player by foreclosing the opportunity to get in shape or to prepare for the season. Similarly, the agent must often be willing to balance a client's economic interest with other noneconomic interests, such as the athlete's need for privacy. The club should be encouraged to respect a player's rights in this regard. Unfortunately, as was pointed out in the previous section, sometimes the economic interest of the agent conflicts with the interests, economic and otherwise, of the client. When this happens, the agent must be aware of the client's interests and must respect them.

Another somewhat intangible need of a player eligible for the draft may be the desire for an education. Several ways of dealing with this need have developed. The agent may bargain for an education incentive bonus, or may encourage the athlete to stay in school. When the latter course is taken, insurance is often necessary to protect the athlete from the economic effect of a debilitating injury that could end a professional career before it even begins. A substantial insurance policy will protect the athlete from the economic effect of such an injury by requiring payment in the event of injury much like payments made under a disability insurance policy. Care must be taken, however, to ensure that receipt of sums used to make the premium payments on such a policy do not violate NCAA rules regarding compensation.

C. Evaluating the Needs of the Club

After ascertaining the value of the client's services and the client's needs, the agent must next determine the needs of the club. Knowledge regarding this triad—the value of the player's services, the needs of the player, and the needs of the club that can be met by signing the player—is crucial in preparing for negotiation. The agent should, however, avoid trying to make management decisions such as the position at which a client should play and how much the client should play or shoot. Nevertheless, suggestions and even firm requests may occasionally be in order when the client's needs could be substantially enhanced, particularly if it can be done without harming the club.

Increasingly, a club's economic position (whether it is profitable or not) has become a factor in the negotiations process. When the club asserts that it is in a precarious financial situation, it may be necessary for the player's agent to request access to the club's financial records. The agent should likewise consider some method of securing contract payments to his or her client when the club or a league is or has experienced financial difficulties. Absent some form of security, there would be nothing preventing the professional team from declaring bankruptcy and thereby discharging its contractual obligations to the players.

D. Know the Opposition

To adequately convince the club of the client's value, the agent must know as much as possible about the negotiations process. The negotiation style and position of the club's representatives and owner are particularly helpful aspects to know. The club should likewise familiarize itself with the style and position of the player's representative. Being prepared in this sense enables the agent and management to increase the likelihood that an agreement will be reached.

E. Be Aware of the Context

Just as the agent and management must know the player's and club's interests they must also be aware of the context in which redress or compensation is being sought. For example, preparation for an arbitration hearing requires much of the same information as negotiating head-on-head for a first year contract with the club. However, the information in an arbitration hearing will probably be presented in a more formal manner, much like that of a courtroom.

F. Provide the Athlete With Other Necessary Services

During the course of contract negotiations, the player may need access to many other services. The player may, for instance, need tax counseling to evaluate the tax ramifications of given proposals and to help with initial planning of tax and investment matters. Occasionally, an agent will be competent in these other areas, but the agent must be careful to secure competent advice for the player on matters the agent cannot handle. As an ethical consideration, the athlete's consent should be obtained whenever possible before the expense of such services are incurred.

G. Assist Player in Dealing With Media, Fans, and Others Affected by the Negotiations Process

An effective agent cannot disregard matters that might be affected by the negotiations process, such as coping with the stress caused by prolonged negotiations. If the agent is insensitive to these matters, the client's performance and attitude may suffer. The effective agent may serve as a buffer, protecting both the club and the player from the acrimony that sometimes accompanies negotiations, thus ensuring a productive working relationship between the club and the player after the contract is signed.

5.4 NEGOTIATING AND DRAFTING THE AGREEMENT BETWEEN PLAYER AND CLUB

Nearly all professional team sports are governed by a collective bargaining agreement between players and management. In collective bargaining, the players' union and management can agree to a standardized contract covering all terms of the player-club relationship, leaving nothing to future negotiation. However, while the parties begin with a standardized agreement (a copy of the National Football League Players Association's agreement is included *infra* at § 10.4), substantial latitude for supplementing this standard contract exists in a number of areas.

The term or length of the contract is an open issue. Players often threaten arbitration, free agency, or in some cases, jumping to another league, giving clubs good reasons for extending the length of the contract. Many other factors such as health, age, marketability, and the nature of the player's skills make the duration of the contract a significant issue from the athlete's perspective. For example, the Kansas City Royals and three of their top players agreed to long-term contracts in 1985. The creative contracts were designed to keep the players in Kansas City, to facilitate economic planning, thereby enabling the club to avoid free agency in the future, and to prevent disruption of the nucleus of a very successful team.

A uniform players contract commonly includes a renewal provision that may provide for an automatic extension of the contract for an additional year, unless otherwise provided for in an additional agreement between the parties. The compensation for the additional year may be limited by the applicable collective bargaining agreement.

A signing bonus is also subject to negotiation. The amount of the signing bonus is typically based on the player's position in the draft, though other factors may be taken into account. Of course, the signing bonus does not stand alone—it is related to other forms of compensaton. The form of the bonus is always open to negotiation. Some signing bonuses may take the form of money payable on signing, or may come in the form of an automobile, property, or investment opportunities. Timing the receipt of the bonus is a proper subject of negotiation. The player may want to defer the bonus payment for tax or economic reasons. The variety of bonuses available is limited only by the imagination of the negotiators and the needs of the parties.

The base salary is similarly negotiable, subject to a minimum that players must be paid pursuant to the collective bargaining agreement between management and the players' association. Additionally, some clubs or leagues (*e.g.*, NBA) have caps on the total amount of compensation they can pay to their players. The agent generally negotiates: (1) the base amount payable to the player on a yearly basis over the term of the contract, (2) whether any part of the base will be deferred, and (3) other matters related to payment of base compensation.

Incentives or bonus provisions are open to negotiation too. Incentives bonuses frequently depend on performance, such as touchdowns, tackles, points scored, shooting percentages, goals, and games or minutes played. Incentive bonuses may be structured in a manner to reflect the statistics the club would like to see the player amass. In basketball, the league has been reluctant to permit performance bonuses, and in the NFL's standard player-agent contract, incentives are not treated as compensation for the purposes of calculating the agent's fee.

Not all incentive bonuses are tied to statistical performance. Clubs are sometimes willing to give educational bonuses to encourage a player to complete or continue his or her formal education. This clause is particularly effective when a player turns professional before completing college, despite pressure from family to finish school. Bonuses can also be given for increases in attendance above a certain level to compensate a player whose personality or background draws crowds. Weight bonuses are given for keeping one's weight below or above a certain level. Bonuses are also given for attendance at practice. Incentive bonuses serve as a good example of why an agent must be aware of the club's needs or expectations and the client's personality and skills. Such bonuses may benefit both the club and the player if they are effectively presented and well thought out (e.g., Pete Rose's attendance incentive during the 1985 season). Incentive bonuses may likewise be helpful in resolving impasses when the club and the agent differ as to their respective appraisals of a player's anticipated performance.

Many items of compensation are included in the standardized player contract. Workmen's compensation, insurance, publicity, and expense reimbursement are a few of the subjects normally included in the standard contract. These may, of course, be supplemented by agreement between the club and the player. The collective bargaining agreement serves a sort of ratchet function: the agent may increase but may not decrease a player's benefits under the agreement. However, even some individual benefits may be unacceptable if they jeopardize the rights of other players under the bargaining agreement.

A matter of significant concern in many negotiations is the issue of tax benefits attributable to various compensation proposals or packages. The tax ramifications should be carefully weighed, and this will usually require expert tax advice. Given the volatility of tax law, tax considerations related to long-term or other intricate compensation packages must be carefully thought out. The parties might even want to specify who bears the risk of a change in tax law that affects a given provision in a player's contract.

In the case of professional sports played in Canada or other countries, the tax laws of other nations along with fluctuations in the value of the currency must be considered. It is common for these athletes playing in other countries to contract for payment of their salaries in United States dollars, rather than the local currency.

Negotiating a player's contract is much more than just agreeing on a base price for the player's services. Both the player's agent and the club must be aware of each other's needs. As is true in most contract negotiations, there is no substitute for careful preparation. The players associations recognize this and try to provide agents with helpful information, but this does not replace the need for additional work by an agent to learn the unique needs of the client and the club.

5.5 PROBLEMS ARISING AFTER NEGOTIATION OF THE CONTRACT

A number of post-negotiation problems often arise and must be dealt with during the term of the contract. These include protecting the player's interest under the contract, counseling the player about post career security and negotiating a contract during its term or preparing for subsequent free agency, arbitration, or negotiation with another club.

Renegotiating a contract during its term often engenders an emotional response on the part of team management. Some clubs stubbornly resist efforts by players to renegotiate a contract during its term. Under the pressure of the possibility of free agency and the intense competition between leagues, however, most teams are willing to consider renegotiating a contract in exchange for an extension in its duration. Generally, as a matter of law and prudence, a player should abide by the terms of the contract during the course of good faith negotiations, even though some agents argue that the right to breach is a part of every contract.

Whenever a player contemplates renegotiation of a contract, the agent should be prepared to give advice on any legal or practical issues that may arise. Legally, the agent should apprise the player of the impact of the player's actions if they ultimately are held to constitute a breach of the contract. If a player is encouraged to breach a contract in the course of renegotiation, the club might be able to enjoin the breach or possibly even bring an action for tortious interference with the contractual relationship. An agent should inform the player of these and other likely reactions of management and the possible impact of such matters on the player's professional reputation.

The parties should be prepared to deal with arbitration or free agency during the latter stages of the player's contract. Seeking arbitration or free agency often carries less severe consequences than seeking to renegotiate one's existing contract, but either course requires substantial preparation on economic and noneconomic issues.

Other matters that the agent should cover in the post-contract stage include: (1) protecting and asserting the player's rights under the contract with the club and the collective bargaining agreement; (2) assisting the client in efforts to obtain wider media exposure if desired; (3) assisting the player in efforts to obtain endorsements and to earn extra income by virtue of the client's status as a professional athlete; and (4) advising the player about the effect of personal actions on the professional career. If the agent is an attorney, the agent may have to provide legal advice to the client in matters totally unrelated to athletics. An agent should realize, however, that when undertaking to give advice to an athlete, the agent owes the player a duty to perform each task with the same expertise or competence as is generally possessed by those who are in *that* trade or business. In addition to concern about malpractice, an agent must be concerned with ethical constraints and conflicts of interest that arise out of representing a player in many differing areas.

If an agent undertakes to represent an athlete in areas other than contract negotiations (such as helping the athlete obtain commercial endorsements) the agent has a duty to use his or her best efforts in promoting the athlete. The agent may, therefore, have to establish by documentation that such efforts were made. As a practical matter, an agent can often avoid these problems by consistently communicating with the client about the nature and extent of the agent's efforts.

5.6 ETHICAL LIMITATIONS ON LAWYER–AGENTS

The attorney who seeks to represent athletes may face special problems not applicable to nonlawyer-agents. A lawyer is bound by a code of ethics or rules of professional responsibility adopted by the jurisdiction in which he or she is licensed. These codes or rules are based, in most states, on the American Bar Association's (ABA) 1970 Model Code of Professional Responsibility or its 1983

Model Rules of Professional Conduct. A few states have developed rules that are not derived from the ABA model provisions.

Lawyer-agents may see these professional conduct standards as obstacles in the fiercely competitive world of sports agents. Some lawyer-agents attempt to avoid the application of these standards to their activities by refraining from traditional aspects of legal practice or formally obtaining inactive status from the state attorney licensing authority. These devices should not be effective, however, since ABA Formal Opinion 336 has interpreted the ABA ethical provisions as binding on attorneys, "whether acting in [their] professional capacity or otherwise."

The well-informed athlete will often view the legal profession's ethical standards as an incentive to choose an agent who is bound by these standards. Absent statutes like the comprehensive California law on athlete agencies, or some voluntary (ARPA Code of Ethics), or league-imposed ethical codes applicable to all agents, athletes have no protection against unscrupulous conduct by nonlawyer-agents. The lawyer's professional strictures, on the other hand, protect the athlete-client by limiting the lawyer's conduct. The most relevant specific limitations contained in these standards are described below. It should be emphasized, however, that even when the attorney clearly violates these canons of professional conduct, the athlete-client must look elsewhere for a remedy.

These ethical requirements govern the attorney's actions and he or she may be sanctioned for violating them, whereas the client's remedy, if any, will be in the form of a law suit against the lawyer-agent for breach of contract or tort. Breach of contract and tort are the theories under which agents are sued regardless of whether or not they are attorneys, but the professional standards imposed upon attorney-agents are a ready marker by which to judge their conduct. The lawyer-agent whose conduct falls short of that required by the rules of professional responsibility will generally incur some liability towards his or her athlete-client.

A. Advertising and Solicitation

A lawyer cannot be an agent unless he or she has some athletes as clients. Traditionally, lawyers have been bound by advertising and solicitation rules that have succeeded more in protecting established lawyers from competition from other lawyers than they have in helping potential clients locate qualified counsel. Starting with *Bates v. State Bar of Arizona*, 433 U.S. 350 (1977), the United States Supreme Court has decided a series of cases that emphasize the public's interest in receiving truthful and meaningful information about legal services.

As a result of these Supreme Court decisions, lawyers should be able to use advertisements so long as they are not false or misleading. The *Bates* decision upheld the lawyer's constitutional right to advertise truthful information about fees for routine legal services. After *Bates*, the ABA revised the advertising rules in the Model Code of Professional Responsibility, but the amended provisions restricted ads to items included in a "laundry list." *See* Model Code of Professional Responsibility DR 2–101(B) (1980). The "laundry list" approach is contained in the codes of many states but it is inconsistent with two recent Supreme Court cases. *See, e.g., In re R.M.J.*, 455 U.S 191 (1982) (Missouri Supreme Court's rule limiting attorney advertising to ten categories of information was held to be an invalid restriction upon speech), and *Zauderer v. Office of Disciplinary Counsel*, 105 S.Ct, 2265 (1985) (Ohio Code of Professional Responsibility rule which prohibited attorneys from including pictures in their business advertisements was found to be an invalid restriction upon commercial speech). The ABA Model Rules reject the "laundry list" approach in favor of the "false or misleading" standard. *See* Model Rules of Professional Conduct Rule 7.1 (1983). The California athletic agent statute also establishes a "false, fraudulent or misleading" standard for agents' advertisements and other information. *See* Cal. Labor Code § 1537 (West Supp. 1985) reproduced *infra* at § 10.2.

While truthful advertising is permitted, the Model Rules retain traditional restrictions on in-person solicitation of clients. Model Rules of Professional Conduct Rule 7.3 (1983); *see also* Model Code of Professional Responsibility DR 2–103 (1980). In *Ohralik v. Ohio State Bar Association*, 436 U.S. 447 (1978), the Supreme Court upheld disciplinary action against a lawyer engaged in egregious "ambulance chasing." An early draft of the Model Rules would have lifted the blanket prohibition on in-person solicitation in favor of a rule permitting solicitation absent physical, emotional, or mental conditions diminishing the client's judgment about selection of a lawyer, a client's express desire to avoid solicitation, and coercion, duress, or harassment by the lawyer. Model Rules of Professional Conduct Rule 9.3 (Discussion

Draft 1980). Given the disparity in sophistication between lawyer-agents and many athletes, some limitation on in-person solicitation of athletes seems desirable. Until the Supreme Court rules otherwise, though, most states are likely to retain the blanket prohibition found in both the Model Code and the Model Rules.

Lawyer-agents may be tempted to try to circumvent the anti-solicitation rules by cultivating the favor of other persons close to an athlete. To the extent this cultivation includes the transfer of money or other items of value to third parties, both the Model Code and Model Rules explicitly prohibit such conduct. Model Code of Professional Responsibility DR 2–103(B), 2–101(J) (1980); Model Rules of Professional Conduct Rule 7.2(c) (1983).

Despite language in the *R.M.J.* case suggesting that direct mail advertising is constitutionally protected commercial speech, the ABA Model Rules treat direct mail contact as prohibited solicitation. *See* Model Rules of Professional Conduct Rule 7.3 (1983). Until the Supreme Court decides a case directly on point, lawyer-agents will find such letter writing (a popular method of contacting clients) to be prohibited by most states.

B. Conflict of Interest

Attorneys are expected to give their undivided interest to their clients. They are not to permit their own financial or other interests or the interests of other clients or third persons to diminish their representation of any particular client. *See generally* Model Code of Professional Responsibility DR 5–101–5–107 (1980); Model Rules of Professional Conduct Rules 1.7–1.10 (1983). The conflict of interest rules also reinforce another important ethical standard, the duty to preserve a client's confidential information. *See generally* Model Code of Professional Responsibility DR 4–101 (1980); Model Rules of Professional Conduct Rule 1.6 (1983).

Numerous situations common to the practice of sports agency may violate conflict of interest rules applicable to a lawyer's representation of an athlete. An agent who encourages an athlete to seek cash payments instead of educational benefits may be subordinating the athlete's best interests to those of the agent. Representation of several players on one team, and especially athletes who play the same position, may force the agent to rank the relative worth of the clients. Direct payment of an agent's fee by the player's team violates a specific conflict of interest rule.

See Model Code of Professional Responsibility DR 5–107(A) (1980); Model Rules of Professional Conduct Rule 1.8(f) (1983). So does a contract giving the lawyer-agent the literary or media rights to the subject matter of the representation. *See* Model Code of Professional Responsibility DR 5–104(B) (1980); Model Rules of Professional Conduct Rule 1.8(d) (1983).

Under both the ABA Model Code and the Model Rules, the client may consent to most conflict of interest situations. *See* Model Code of Professional Responsibility DR 5–101(A), 5–104, 5–105(C), 5–106, 5–107 (1980); Model Rules of Professional Conduct Rules 1.7, 1.8(a). The prohibition against contracts giving the athlete-client's book or movie rights to the lawyer-agent is an exception. Model Code of Professional Responsibility DR 5–104(B) (1980); Model Rules of Professional Conduct Rule 1.8(d) (1983). Consent provisions would permit two catchers on the same baseball team, for example, to retain the same agent because of that agent's track record with that particular team. Even when consent is permitted, the client has some protection, since the attorney must ensure that the client has sufficient information to make a sound decision when consenting to a conflict of interest. *See, e.g.*, Model Code of Professional Responsibility DR 5–101(A) (1980) ("consent . . . after full disclosure"); Model Rules of Professional Conduct Rule 1.7(b) (1983) ("consents after consultation . . . includ[ing] explanation of the implications of the common representation and the advantages and risks involved").

C. Fees

The ABA Model Code prohibits illegal or clearly excessive fees, while the Model Rules require that a lawyer's fee be reasonable. They contain identical factors to be considered in evaluating the reasonableness of the fee. *Compare* Model Code of Professional Responsibility DR 2–106(B) (1980) *with* Model Rules of Professional Conduct Rule 1.5(a) (1983). These factors include the time, labor, and skill required by the legal service, the reputation, experience, and ability of the attorney, the amount involved, the results obtained, customary fees, and the nature and length of the lawyer's professional relationship with the client.

While the typical sports agent's fee of three to ten percent may seem high in light of the absolute dollars involved, many of the reasonableness factors could be used to justify such fees. More important than the provisions for measuring the excessiveness or reasonableness of fees is a provision now included in the Model Rules that requires contingency fee arrangements to be in writing. *See* Model Rules of Professional Conduct Rule 1.5(c) (1983). The writing must include specific information, including the method by which the contingent fee is computed. If applied thoughtfully to sports agency contracts, this provision could provide substantial protection to athletes. With a carefully drafted fee arrangement in writing, the athlete who is cut from a team should be less likely to owe a substantial fee to an agent who negotiated the un-guaranteed contract.

D. Preserving Client's Funds and Property

The tragedy of an agent's misappropriating the funds of an unsuspecting athlete is a major, even if infrequent, problem. Lawyers are ethically bound to notify clients of the receipt of the client's property, to segregate the property, to account for it, and to deliver the property to the client upon request. *See* Model Code of Professional Responsibility DR 9–102 (1980); Model Rules of Professional Conduct Rule 1.15 (1983). While the fear of disbarment seems unlikely to deter an attorney-agent who is willing to violate criminal laws or incur civil liability in order to defraud a client, the ethical principles discourage carelessness if not dishonesty.

E. Unauthorized Practice of Law

Perhaps the least defensible provisions of the Model Code and the Model Rules are those that deal with unauthorized practice of the law. *See* Model Code of Professional Responsibility DR 3–101–3–103 (1980); Model Rules of Professional Conduct Rules 5.4, 5.5 (1983). These rules discourage lawyers from practicing with other professionals, such as accountants and advertising experts. The complex business dealings of professional athletes demand multi-disciplinary advice. As more attention is given to the full range of services needed by professional athletes, perhaps sports law will force a re-examination of the unauthorized practice of the law provisions.

Chapter Six

LABOR LAW: DEVELOPMENTS IN PROFESSIONAL SPORTS

The development of organized professional sports in America is of fairly recent origin. Baseball itself was created in 1839 by Abner Doubleday, and became the first organized professional sport in 1869 with the formation of the Cincinnati Red Stockings baseball club. As athletes began to receive compensation for playing and as clubs began to make money by marketing the wares of their players, professional athletics became a business enterprise, with rudimentary management and labor components. This chapter will hopefully provide the reader with a basic understanding of the development of collective bargaining in professional sports, as well as introducing the legal principles that typically give rise to labor law issues in a sports context. For a fuller treatment of this subject, the reader should see L. Sobel, *Professional Sports and The Law* (1977) (containing an excellent chapter on the history and development of the reserve clause); Weistart and Lowell, *The Law of Sports* (1979) (providing in depth coverage of labor law in professional sports); Barry, Gould and Staudohar, *Labor Relations in Professional Sports* (1985) (presenting the most current discussion of labor law and sports); and Gorman, *Basic Text on Labor Law* (1976) (an excellent treatise on labor law).

6.1 HISTORICAL DEVELOPMENTS

By 1875, professional baseball clubs became painfully aware of the need to secure their labor force. That year four players from Boston's championship team signed with another club for the succeeding season, leaving Boston without the services of a number of its finest players. These and related actions contributed to soaring salaries. In turn, salary demands were a contributing factor in causing clubs to fold or to experience significant economic dislocation. Responding to this threat, club owners met secretly in 1879 and created what became known as the "reserve clause." The reserve clause gave individual clubs exclusive rights to their players' services for succeeding seasons and put an end to the players' jumping from one club to another. If a player was unwilling to sign with his club for salary or other reasons, he could find himself blacklisted and his career terminated. The reserve clause largely put an end to the spiraling salary demands that management believed threatened the existence of professional baseball in the 1870s. (See § 3.2C–3 *supra* for an example of a reserve clause.)

The players countered by forming the Brotherhood of Professional Baseball Players in 1887, the predecessor of today's players associations. The Brotherhood, however, lasted only four years, disbanding after its abortive effort to form a Players League to challenge the existing National League and American Association. John Montgomery Ward, the President of the Brotherhood, who was both a player and an attorney, summarized the plight of players under the reserve system by noting that:

> Like a fugitive slave law, the reserve rule denies [the player] a harbor or livelihood, and carries him back, bound and shackled, to the club from which he attempted to escape . . . . He goes where he is sent, takes what is given him, and thanks the Lord for life.

While the Brotherhood was unsuccessful in eliminating the reserve clause, it did engage in a significant court battle during its brief existence. In *Metropolitan Exhibition Co. v. Ewing*, 42 F. 198 (1890), the court upheld the reserve clause between teams in the National League and American Association, but it also held that the clause did not preclude a player from signing with a new league.

After disbanding in 1891 for financial reasons, the Brotherhood reappeared in 1900, for two years, but it was again unable to establish an effective and lasting players association. In 1912 another association, the Baseball Players' Fraternity, was created to organize the players. The Fraternity proved powerful enough to gain eleven concessions from the National Commission in 1914, and almost succeeded in calling a general strike. When the strike effort failed to materialize in 1917, the Fraternity faded.

With the Brotherhood's limited success in *Metropolitan Exhibition Co.* and the minor concessions gained by the Fraternity in 1914, the stage was set for the formation of a new baseball league that could take advantage of existing player dissatisfaction. Responding to these and other factors, the Federal League was formed. Although the Federal League merged into today's existing leagues after a brief independent existence, it did leave a significant legacy. The Baltimore club refused to agree to the merger and claimed that the merger violated existing antitrust law. This case ultimately reached the Supreme Court, which, in an opinion written by Justice Holmes, held that the Sherman Act did not apply to the restrictive practices of the National League and the American Association. *Federal Base Ball Club of Baltimore Inc. v. National League of Professional Base Ball Club's*, 259 U.S. 200 (1922). Baseball, in the eyes of Justice Holmes and the Court, was not subject to antitrust law.

The *Federal Base Ball Club* case constituted a significant setback for the players, because it deprived them of the legal means to challenge the reserve clause other than through negotiation and player unionization or organization. After *Federal Base Ball Club*, resentment against management excesses continued among the players. But, given the *laissez faire* mood in the country at that time, little could be done to vindicate the players' interests. Nevertheless, the players eventually tried again. In 1946, several players from the Pittsburgh Pirates, under the leadership of Robert Murphy, a former examiner for the National Labor Relations Board, formed the American Baseball Guild.

The Guild attempted to bargain collectively with the management of the Pittsburgh club. The Guild sought to obtain a minimum wage of $7,500 per year, security, insurance, bonus and other welfare payments, as well as the submission of general disputes between players and management to existing labor dispute resolution mechanisms. When the club refused to bargain and to permit a representation election, Murphy was left with no recourse other than to threaten a strike. The club remained steadfast, and the National Labor Relations Board (NLRB) refused to review the Guild's claim that baseball was in "commerce" and should, therefore, be subject to an election for union representation purposes. With defeat in the form of the refusals of both the club and the NLRB, even Guild members sensed the futility of proceeding further and voted not to strike.

Even though the Guild was largely unsuccessful in achieving its goals, it is generally credited with providing the impetus for certain concessions on the part of management. Those concessions included the adoption of minimum salary (at a much lower level than the $7,500 sought by the Guild), the establishment of a limited pension fund, the shortening of spring training, and the payment to players of a spring training allowance that is to this day referred to as "Murphy Money." A player-representative system was also established shortly after the demise of the Guild. This system is considered to be the forerunner of present day players associations, although as originally constituted, it was little more than a medium through which players could raise and submit objections to their respective clubs.

During this period and into the early 1950s, there were other efforts to declare baseball to be "commerce" for the purpose of antitrust law, but the reserve system remained in tact. One of these efforts was undertaken in response to the failure of Ernie "Tiny" Bonham, a veteran pitcher of 10 years, to receive his pension. Two league representatives, Allie Reynolds of the Yankees and Ralph Kiner of the Cubs, questioned league owners relative to the status of Bonham's pension and requested that the amount of the minimum salary be raised. They also requested that players making under $10,000 per year be permitted to play for compensation in the winter leagues.

When their requests remained unanswered, Reynolds and Kiner hired J. Norman Lewis, a lawyer, on a part-time basis to represent the players' interests. Lewis was excluded from meetings with the owners, however. In response to their relative lack of success the players representatives met in December of 1953 and created the Major League Baseball Players Association (MLBPA), which continues to represent professional baseball players to this day.

By 1955, the players had made substantial gains on the pension issue and had received an increase in the minimum salary to $6,000 per year. Even though the MLBPA was in its infancy, it managed to get many other concessions. At this point in the Association's history, players were not required to pay dues and Lewis continued to work on a part-time basis. Nevertheless, the notion of a players association was well on its way to becoming an integral part of the world of professional athletics. The National Basketball Players Association was formed in the 1950s and was formally recognized as a collective bargaining unit by the NLRB in 1962; the National Football League Players Association was organized in 1956 and formally recognized in 1967; and the National Hockey League Players Association was formally organized and recognized in 1967. Associations in other sports (*e.g.*, soccer and rodeo) have also been formed and recognized as collective bargaining units by the NLRB.

Ironically, while professional athletes were gaining leverage in the collective bargaining area, due in part to the failure of the baseball players to gain redress through the antitrust laws, the antitrust exemption for professional sports itself began to erode as applied in contexts other than baseball. Baseball has continued to retain its exemption, largely due to the Supreme Court's application of the doctrine of stare decisis and congressional inactivity in removing the exemption from the antitrust laws. Other sports, however, beginning with boxing in *United States v. International Boxing Club of New York Inc.*, 348 U.S. 236 (1955), have been held to be subject to antitrust laws. Thus, in most professional sports, players are armed with two often complementary weapons (antitrust law and collective bargaining) in their efforts to win concessions from management.

With the development of the Major League Baseball Players Association, the contemporary era of collective bargaining and labor dispute resolution was under way. A look at more recent developments will aid in understanding the contemporary role of collective bargaining and the labor movement in the professional sports context.

6.2 CONTEMPORARY DEVELOPMENTS IN COLLECTIVE BARGAINING

Upset with the owners' position regarding contributions to their pension fund, National Basketball Association (NBA) players threatened a boycott of the League All Star game in 1964. The start of the game was delayed until the players received assurances that the owners would take action relative to the players' demands. Finally, in 1967 the NBA Players Association and management, on behalf of the club owners, entered into the first collective bargaining agreement in professional sports history. Agreements in baseball and football followed shortly thereafter. And, in 1969, the National Labor Relations Board indicated that it would accept jurisdiction over labor issues in professional sports.

With the advent of the collective bargaining agreement and recognition by the NLRB, the resolution of labor or employment issues in professional sports has taken on a new form, a form similar to that in other industries governed by labor law.

In 1968, when the National Football League Players Association and the club owners were commencing negotiations over a collective bargaining agreement, a significant controversy developed. Most issues were disposed of quickly, but the question of contributions to the pension fund remained unsettled. As negotiations deteriorated, the players considered and ultimately authorized the Players Association to call a strike. After the Association had advised the players to boycott training camps until an agreement could be reached on the pension issue, management responded with a lockout, barring the players from attending training camp. With pressure applied on each side, an agreement was soon reached. This dispute, which arose after the parties had reached an impasse, foreshadowed subsequent disputes, with threats of strikes by the players and corresponding threats of lockouts or other economic pressure by management.

It was baseball's turn to experience strife in 1969. In that year, a dispute arose over the percentage of television receipts that baseball owners were to contribute to the players' pension fund. After a short-lived training camp boycott, which culminated in intervention by the Commissioner of Baseball, the matter was tentatively settled. In 1972, however, the pension issue erupted anew and led to a walkout that delayed the baseball season for 13 days. The public was dismayed by the strike, and even President Nixon publicly called for a prompt resolution of the dispute. The owners ultimately responded to this pressure by increasing their contribution to the pension fund by approximately $500,000, and the issue was temporarily laid to rest.

At about the same time that the differences were being tentatively settled in baseball, a controversy was brewing in the National Football League. An actual dispute arose in 1970 over the Football Commissioner's role in collective bargaining, player compensation for participation in exhibition games, and contributions to the pension plan. When negotiations regarding the pension contribution reached an impasse, the players voted to strike and refused to attend training camp. After a seventeen day lockout and a three day strike, the matter was settled. Thus, a pattern had developed, whereby disputes in one sport were influenced by similar disputes or developments in other sports. In a related sense, as players in one professional sport made various gains, players in other sports raised their expectations.

While developments in the collective bargaining were occurring in the early 1970s, the players were also seeking relief in the courts on antitrust grounds. *See, e.g., Haywood v. National Basketball Association,* 401 U.S. 1204 (1971) (affirming Justice Douglas' decision that basketball does not enjoy an exemption from antitrust laws and noting the significance of the group boycott issue in professional sports); *Flood v. Kuhn,* 407 U.S. 258 (1972) (baseball's exemption from antitrust laws was anomalous but nevertheless was "fully entitled to the benefits of stare decisis"); *Philadelphia World Hockey Club, Inc. v. Philadelphia Hockey Club, Inc.,* 351 F.Supp. 462 (E.D.Pa.1972) and *Boston Professional Hockey Association, Inc. v. Cheevers,* 348 F.Supp. 261, *rem. on other grounds,* 472 F.2d 127 (1st Cir.1972) (both held that hockey was subject to antitrust laws and that the labor exemption from antitrust laws could not be used as a sword to protect monopolistic or anticompetitive activity). See *supra* at § 3.2C for a general discussion of antitrust principles as developed in these and other cases. As pension contributions were challenged in the early 1970s, the reserve clause was being challenged in the courts on antitrust grounds. Players and their representatives were beginning to sense a relationship between the collective bargaining process and antitrust law.

With the expiration of the NFL's collective bargaining agreement in 1974, the players submitted a list of sixty-three separate demands. These demands turned the attention of collective bargaining from the pension contribution issues of the early 1970s to the so-called "freedom issues" that were to dominate the remainder of the 1970s. The freedom issues challenged the reserve, option, and related clauses that restricted the freedom of players to make the best deal possible on an individual basis. When negotiations over these issues bogged down, the players initiated a strike that lasted forty-four days and ended in a whimper after all the players returned to camp under a fourteen day no strike moratorium. The moratorium itself became moot when the players decided not to resume the strike at the end of the fourteen day period, even though management's offer was unacceptable to the players. While the players apparently suffered a significant defeat in their inability to reach an acceptable collective bargaining agreement in 1974, the owners were also under pressure, both from irate fans and from the courts and Congress. Congressional leaders threatened to re-evaluate their legislative position regarding antitrust and related issues unless the owners reached a fair compromise with the players. The dispute continued into 1974 despite congressional pressure and the filing of unfair labor practices charges with the NLRB by the players. As the battle continued in professional football throughout 1975 and 1976, developments in the National Basketball Association, together with pressure from other sources, helped bring the parties in the football dispute closer together on the "freedom issues."

The NBA competed with the American Basketball Association during the early 1970s. As a result of that competition, salaries of many of the players increased dramatically. As a result, the owners sought to merge the stronger American Basketball Association teams into the National Basketball Association. After the merger appeared complete, the NBA Players Association tried to have it enjoined. The Players Association also attempted to bar the college draft system, the reserve clause, and the standard players' contract as unreasonable restraints on trade under the antitrust laws. The owners argued that the NLRB had primary jurisdiction to determine whether these three issues were conditions of employment, and thus exempt from antitrust law. The lower court, which was subsequently affirmed by the Court of Appeals in *Robertson v. National Basketball Association,* 389 F.Supp. 867 (S.D. N.Y. 1977) *aff'd,* 556 F.2d 682 (2d Cir. 1977), rejected the NBA's claim and held that the labor exemption was not available and that the mobility restrictions on players were suspect under applicable antitrust law.

After the court rendered its opinion in *Robertson,* the parties settled the case. The owners agreed to compensate the players for their damages, and ultimately eliminated the option clause, allowing certain players to become free agents at the expiration of their contracts. Under this agreement the reserve or option clause was severely weakened, leaving the clubs without a unilateral right to renew a player's contract. By 1980, the NBA clubs discontinued their demand to receive compensation when one of the club's players was signed as a free agent by another club. Instead, the clubs accepted a much less stringent (from the players' perspective) right of first refusal, permitting them to match an offer received by a free agent. Management likewise negotiated a salary cap on the amount payable by clubs to all of the players on their roster.

These developments in the National Basketball Association did not bode well for the reserve, option, and related clauses in other professional sports contracts. In baseball, for example, the MLBPA was successful in challenging the reserve clause in arbitration. In that case, a player desired to play out his option and become a free agent. The arbitrator concluded that the grievance could be heard by the grievance board and that the player was free to negotiate with other clubs. After this decision and the related developments in basketball, baseball's management was induced for the first time to negotiate with the MLBPA over the reserve system. The parties were able to reach an agreement in 1976. Under that agreement, the player was bound to a club for six years before becoming a free agent. During each of the final years of that six year period, if the parties could not reach an agreement on player's compensation, the compensation could be submitted to arbitration. While these developments in baseball hardly eliminated the reserve clause, they constituted an important step in that direction.

After the reserve clauses in baseball and basketball contracts were attacked, mobility restraints in other professional sports were soon challenged. In *Mackey v. National Football League*, 543 F.2d 606 (8th Cir. 1976), *cert. dism'd*, 434 U.S. 801 (1977), the court held that the Rozelle Rule, football's version of the reserve clause, constituted an unreasonable restraint of trade under applicable antitrust law. This ruling forced league management to negotiate an agreement with the NFL Players Association that included the reserve clause, something they had adamantly refused to do from 1974 to 1976.

In the 1977 NFL collective bargaining agreement, management agreed to limit the Rozelle Rule, but retained a right of first refusal. Had it been unilaterally imposed, the right of first refusal itself might have been challenged under antitrust law, but the fact that it was bargained for collectively strengthened the right of first refusal. Given the past unwillingness of management to bargain over "freedom issues," one of which is the reserve clause, the agreement was a victory of sorts for the players.

In *McCourt v. California Sports, Inc.*, 600 F.2d 1193 (6th Cir. 1979), the court held that the reserve clause contained in the collective bargaining agreement between the National Hockey

League (NHL) and the Players Association had been bargained for in good faith, and that the league was exempt from an antitrust action challenging that provision of the contract. The NHL was exempt because the labor exemption to antitrust law applied. In exempting the NHL, the court sought to accomodate the antimonopoly and procompetitive aspects of the antitrust law with the preference for bargaining under federal labor law. Thus, as the players gained bargaining power in the collective bargaining process, they lost some of their capacity to successfully challenge rights of refusal or other limitations on player mobility under antitrust theories. *See also Reynolds v. National Football League,* 584 F.2d 280 (8th Cir. 1978) (rejecting the plaintiff's argument that the labor exemption did not apply because not all individual members or players were properly represented in the collective bargaining process).

With the onset of the 1980s, the nature and complexity of the disputes in collective bargaining changed, and developments in one sport often mirrored developments in others. Early in 1980, negotiations were underway in baseball to update that collective bargaining agreement. On April 1, 1980, negotiations came to a halt in the midst of the preseason. The players struck for eight days during the exhibition season, resulting in the early closing of training camps and the cancellation of ninety-two exhibition games. At issue was the recurrent dispute over free agency. The players wanted to reduce the six year period during which a player could not become a free agent to five years, and management countered with a proposal that clubs be compensated for the loss of a free agent. The compensation requested by management was a selection from a list of possible candidates from the free agent's new team.

A strike during the regular season was barely avoided when the owners agreed to grant several additional benefits to the players. The free agency issue was postponed for later determination. In 1981 the parties tacit postponement of the free agency issue deteriorated when the owners implemented their free agency compensation plan. The players responded by calling a strike. After a record-setting strike of fifty days that substantially disrupted the baseball season, players and owners reached an agreement.

In the National Football League the following year, 1982, labor unrest centered on revenue-sharing issues. The players initially sought a fixed salary structure, under which players' salaries would account for fifty-five percent of each team's revenues. Later, however, the players withdrew their demand, substituting a plan whereby they would receive a share of television revenues. The owners initially rejected this approach. When an agreement could not be reached, the players called a strike that lasted for fifty-seven days, surpassing the fifty day record set by the baseball players in 1981. This strike eliminated seven of the sixteen regular season games scheduled for 1982. However, the eventual settlement resulted in a five-year collective bargaining agreement.

The 1982 NFL agreement left the mobility (option, free agency, and right of first refusal) aspects of the contract largely intact. (*See* Weistart and Lowell, *The Law of Sports* 86 (Supp. 1985) for a more thorough examination of this and other collective bargaining issues, and § 10.3 *infra* for a copy of the NFL agreement.) Thus, rather than focusing on the reserve or option clauses concerning player mobility and compensation, as the parties did in the 1970s, the dispute largely centered on the players' desire to share in the gross revenues received by the owners. Revenue sharing dominated collective bargaining in professional sports during the 1980s in much the same way that pensions dominated early collective bargaining negotiations and free agency dominated the second half of the 1970s.

In order to settle the 1982 NFL strike, management guaranteed that it would incur total player costs of $1.28 billion over a four year period, prior to the lapse of the agreement. Management also agreed to increase the minimum pay scale and to provide for "money now" payments to the players. These money now payments were based on a player's time in the league, and compensated players for a portion of their personal financial losses incurred as a result of the strike.

The National Basketball Association's collective bargaining agreement expired in 1982, and the parties narrowly averted an April 2d strike date by reaching an agreement on March 31, 1982. Under the new agreement, management and the players accepted a gross revenue sharing plan, which was designed to place both a floor and a ceiling on players' salaries. During the negotiations, the owners claimed that less than a third of the clubs were profitable (a postition that has been taken by management in subsequent negotiations, *e.g.*, baseball in 1985), and that they should be able to negotiate a ceiling on salary payments for all clubs. Not only was this ceiling intended to help financially ailing clubs, it was also intended to equalize access to talent in the league.

Baseball's collective bargaining agreement expired again in 1985. Five primary areas of dispute developed. First, the owners had initially claimed extensive losses in 1984 and projected losses of $155 million by 1988 in an effort to counter economic demands made by the players. The players challenged these figures after examining some of the financial records upon which they were based. The clubs ultimately withdrew the amounts projected, but remained steadfast in their assertion that losses would be substantial. Second, the players had traditionally received about one-third of baseball's television revenues as a contribution to their pension plan, but after the $1.1 billion television contract was negotiated by management in 1984, the owners contended that the traditional one-third was excessive. Third, management voiced its objection to the arbitration system, contending that it unfairly benefited the players. Management likewise argued that the amount of time a player should have to spend in the majors before he could file for arbitration should be extended. Fourth, the players challenged the free agent compensation system, whereby clubs losing a free agent were compensated with players and draft picks from the clubs signing free agents, arguing that this compensation program inhibited the free agency process. Finally, the clubs argued for a salary cap much like that in the NBA.

With average player salaries exceeding $350,000 per year, and with management's $1.1 billion television deal, the public grew restless when the players' August 6th strike date approached without much promise for a resolution of the issues. Management, the players and Commissioner Ueberroth recognized the volatility of fan support and how that support affected the fragile economic status of baseball. As a result, a flurry of "last minute" bargaining resulted in an agreement after a strike of a single day.

The parties resolved the dispute over television revenues for pension funds by splitting the difference. The players' pension fund had been receiving $15 million per year, but the players sought $60 million. The players ultimately settled for $32.5 million per year. The owners likewise agreed to divide an additional $20 million among clubs in financial difficulty, although it is not clear how such an assessment of "difficulty" will be made.

The parties settled their dispute over the arbitration issue when management gave up its effort to limit pay hikes to 100% and when the MLBPA agreed that players must have three, rather than two, years of major league experience before qualifying for salary arbitration. The free agency issue was resolved when the parties agreed to eliminate the free agency draft and replace it with a player compensation system, whereby teams signing a highly rated free agent would surrender one or two amateur draft choices to the club losing the free agent. Finally, management abandoned its efforts to obtain a salary cap, although such an effort will no doubt be renewed if management's projected losses materialize in the future.

Developments in the National Hockey League have mirrored developments in other major professional sports. However, the league has maintained a compensation formula or "Rozelle Rule" whereby clubs are compensated when they lose a player who exercises his right of free agency. This rule may be challenged in the future if the hockey players gain further bargaining power. (Article XV of the 1982 NFL collective bargaining agreement, a copy of which is reproduced *infra* at § 10.3, contains the free agency/compensation terms.)

Professional soccer players have also won a number of concessions from management, but the soccer owners were initially very reluctant to give any ground. The owners even resisted the efforts of the Players Association to gain certification as the exclusive bargaining unit for players in the league. Given the relative infancy of professional soccer in the United States and its weaker financial position in terms of media coverage and other sources of revenue, it is not surprising that the soccer owners have been more successful than owners in other sports in resisting economic overtures by players. However, with antitrust and labor law precedents, competition for the services of players between leagues, and the growing popularity of soccer as a youth sport, it is likely that, as soccer expands its financial base, players will win further concessions. Other professional sports, such as rodeo, will probably experience similar developments as they grow in popularity.

In summary, during the 1980s players have largely turned from their effort to gain concessions relative to the reserve, option, and compensation clauses contained in prior agreements, to winning economic concessions, particularly in the form of revenue sharing from gross or other receipts. If management's projections of financial losses materialize, however, some of the economic and related concessions made to the players may be retracted in the future.

6.3 LEGAL ISSUES

Understanding the historical development of collective bargaining and labor law in professional sports is helpful not only in anticipating developments in subsequent negotiations, but also in understanding the legal issues that have arisen and will in all likelihood arise in the professional sports. Therefore, the following section discusses general legal principles and developments in the labor area of sports law.

A. Coverage of the National Labor Relations Act and Role of the NLRB in Professional Sports

Before the National Labor Relations Act (NLRA) is applied to an industry, the activities of that industry must be in interstate commerce. This is as true of the sports industry as any other industry. Originally, in *Federal Base Ball Club,* 259 U.S. at 200, the Supreme Court held that baseball was not subject to antitrust law. In writing about the interstate commerce issue as it arises in the antitrust context, Justice Holmes noted that baseball games "are purely state affairs," and that the travel involved in staging games is "merely incidental." He, therefore, concluded in *Federal Base Ball Club* that since the interstate contacts "were not substantial enough to change the local nature of the business," professional baseball was not in interstate commerce. However, with changing attitudes toward the commerce clause and changes in the nature of professional sports (including the rise of media coverage spanning many states) Justice Holmes' reasoning has largely been rejected. *See, e.g., Flood v. Kuhn,* 407 U.S. 258, 282 (1972) ("Professional baseball is a business and it is engaged in interstate commerce"). While to this day the Supreme Court has clung tenaciously to the ultimate holding in *Federal Base Ball Club* by refusing to apply antitrust law to baseball, it has nevertheless expressly held that baseball is "in commerce." Similar decisions have been reached in basketball, football, hockey, soccer, golf, and even rodeo.

Nevertheless, even when an industry is in interstate commerce and the NLRA is applied, the National Labor Relations

Board may, in its discretion, decline jurisdiction over a particular industry. The Board does so when it determines that the impact of the industry is insufficient to justify the exercise of its jurisdiction, even though the industry may be "in commerce." The NLRB has not yet declined jurisdiction over any major team sport. However, even after the National Labor Relations Board has decided to exercise its jurisdiction under the NLRA, it still must determine whether the issues raised are proper subject matter for collective bargaining. The National Labor Relations Board must also ascertain the nature and extent of the rights and obligations of the parties before exercising jurisdiction.

B. Subject Matter of Collective Bargaining

In defining the obligations of parties to bargain collectively, the NLRB has divided the relevant subject matter into two categories: "mandatory" and "permissive." These categories are treated differently by the NLRB. As to "mandatory" matters, which include all subjects related to "wages, hours, and other terms and conditions of employment," parties have an obligation to bargain in good faith. Bargaining in good faith does not require that the parties reach an agreement. Rather, it only requires that they bargain in good faith until an impasse is reached. On "permissive" matters, those arising outside the scope of "wages, hours, and other terms and conditions of employment," the parties are not required to bargain, although they are permitted to do so.

The distinction between mandatory and permissive subjects determines whether or not a party has a duty to bargain in good faith, and can therefore be a critical issue. For example, if the players seek to have management bargain in good faith over compensation for players signed as free agents, the players must establish that this compensation relates to "wages, hours, and other terms and conditions of employment" of the players. The definition or meaning of these terms often cause problems in determining whether a subject deserves mandatory bargaining. *See, e.g.,* Weistart and Lowell, *The Law of Sports,* at 814–818; *Mackey v. National Football League,* 543 F.2d at 606 (the Rozelle Rule in football, which provided for compensation to a player's former team from the team signing him as a free agent, was a mandatory subject for bargaining purposes); *Smith v. Pro-Football,* 420 F.Supp. 738 (D. D.C. 1976), *aff'd in pt.,* 593 F.2d 1173 (1978) (the college draft in football was a mandatory subject for collective bargaining purposes). *But see Robertson v. National Basketball Association,* 389 F.Supp. at 867 (the draft, option clause, and the compensation rules were not necessarily mandatory subjects for collective bargaining purposes).

Owners in most professional sports have shown increasing willingness to bargain over these issues, hence it is not surprising that few recent cases have challenged the good faith of management. Most significant issues negotiated today are economic and are often directly related to salary or wages. In most instances these economic issues are mandatory subjects requiring good faith bargaining. However, future disputes over safety and related noneconomic issues may blur the mandatory/permissive distinction.

C. Challenging Substantive Provisions

Another problem that occasionally arises is whether a party may challenge a substantive provision that was the subject matter of collective bargaining and has been included in a collective bargaining agreement. Given the strong freedom of contract notions inherent in the collective bargaining process, courts and the National Labor Relations Board alike are normally reluctant to hold bargained for provisions to be unenforceable. Courts and the Board may intervene on occasion to see that the collective bargaining procedure is operating as it should, but they are generally reluctant to deal with substantive issues.

However, there are two grounds upon which courts have held substantive terms of collective bargaining agreements unenforceable: when the terms are illegal or when the terms violate antitrust laws. Collective bargaining terms have been held illegal and, therefore, unenforceable when the terms themselves are unlawful or contravene the policies of the National Labor Relations Act, such as creating closed shops, or discriminating against nonunion members. A particular term in a collective bargaining agreement that is illegal or contravenes the policies of the NLRA will be unenforceable, but an exception may exist when the illegality involves a violation of antitrust laws.

Courts have consistently held that terms included in a negotiated collective bargaining agreement are exempt from antitrust laws. Thus, the only way a party may attack a term included in a collective bargaining agreement on antitrust grounds is by establishing that it was not really subject to negotiation. Because parties to collective bargaining agreements in professional sports have increasing parity, it is unlikely that a party challenging a term on antitrust grounds could prove that it was not subject to negotiation. See *infra* at § 6.3I, for discussion of the relationship between antitrust law and collective bargaining.

D. Rights of the Parties

Section 7 of the National Labor Relations Act provides employees entering into collective bargaining agreements with certain rights. Section 8 of the Act deals with unfair labor practices by an employer or union. Section 7 expressly provides the employee with the right to engage in or refrain from: (1) self-organization (forming, joining, or assisting labor organizations); (2) bargaining collectively through representatives of his or her own choosing; and (3) involvement in other concerted activities for the purpose of collective bargaining or other mutual aid and protection. In early collective bargaining in the sports industry, owners often pressured players to withdraw support from their union. In such instances, if the players proved that the employer acted with an antiunion motive, the employer's activity would be considered violative of § 7 and could be thus declared an unfair labor practice under § 8(a)(1).

Players have also challenged the owners for interference with union activity based on players' allegations that the clubs terminated or otherwise punished them for participating in union activities. This conduct by owners or league management could be challenged under § 8(a)(1) or § 8(a)(3) of the NLRA and, if proven, would violate § 7.

As noted previously, the clubs and the players have a duty to negotiate in good faith on mandatory issues related to collective bargaining. The violation of this duty to bargain in good faith may constitute an unfair labor practice. Given the bitterness that developed during the past decade and a half of collective bargaining in the professional sports, it is likely that the number of actions initiated by the parties for alleged unfair labor practices will increase in the future. *See, e.g.*, E. Lock, *Employer Unfair Labor Practices During the 1982 National Football League Strike: Help on the Way*, 6 U.Bridge.L.Rev. 189 (1985).

E. Duties of the Parties

Just as the parties to collective bargaining have rights, they also have duties. They have the duty to bargain in good faith on mandatory issues. The duty to bargain in good faith includes the obligation to furnish information related to the bargaining process. The latest series of collective bargaining negotiations in baseball illustrate the relevance of the need for information. In those negotiations, management argued that an economic crisis had developed, and the union sought access to management's books. While the parties were unable to agree on the magnitude of the economic crisis besetting the owners, access to relevant economic information clearly was relevant to good faith bargaining. *But see Silverman v. Major League Baseball Player Relations Committee, Inc.*, 516 F.Supp. 588 (S.D.N.Y.1981) (comments about economic difficulties by the Commissioner instead of by the owners' bargaining committee were not sufficient to place a duty to provide economic information on the owners).

The union-employee (player association-player) relationship likewise generates certain rights and responsibilities. Once the players select a bargaining unit to represent them, they must permit that unit to serve as their exclusive bargaining agent. After the selection, neither individual players nor the players on a given club (if the unit is league-wide) may assert that they are represented by a rival union. To terminate this exclusive right, a majority of the players have to vote the union out in a formal election. Absent such an election, the union retains its right of exclusive representation with only minor limitations.

As a corollary to the union's right of exclusive representation, the union has the duty to represent fairly the players. Typically, before a court will hold that the union has breached the duty of fair representation owed to its individual members, the player(s) must establish that the union has acted arbitrarily or in bad faith.

Pursuant to the right of exclusive representation, an individual player does not have a right to enter into a contract wholly separate from that reached in the course of collective bargaining. Effectively, the extent or ambit of individual contracting depends on the consent of the union since the union negotiates all terms, including the right to individual negotiation of the collective bargaining agreement. The bargaining unit theoretically holds very extensive control over the terms and conditions of a player's agreement with his club. However, in the professional sports context, significant disparity exists among union members in terms of their respective marketable skills. Consequently, the players associations have permitted individual players broad latitude to negotiate more favorable terms or additional benefits with their clubs. If, in the future, the unions begin to limit the rights of individual players to bargain for better terms by exerting expansive authority under their right to serve as exclusive bargaining agent for the players, some higher paid athletes may challenge the union's authority on the ground that their individual interests have not been fairly represented.

Management too must recognize the exclusive authority of the players' union in the bargaining process and cannot circumvent that exclusive authority by dealing directly with the players. *See Morio v. North American Soccer League*, 501 F.Supp. 663 (S.D.N.Y. 1980), *aff'd*, 632 F.2d 217 (2d Cir. 1980) (a temporary injunction prevented the clubs from enforcing contracts entered into with the players prior to certification by the Players Association). The reasoning in the *Morio* case may also help to determine the enforceability of contracts entered into after a collective bargaining agreement has terminated and before a new collective bargaining agreement has been entered into between the parties.

F. Appropriate Bargaining Unit

As previously noted, the players union has exclusive authority to reach an agreement with management on behalf of the players. Nevertheless, the nature of the appropriate bargaining unit is occasionally questioned. Initially, the owners and the players agree on the size of the bargaining unit. Typically, the scope of the appropriate bargaining unit in professional sports is league-wide. *See, e.g., North American Soccer League v. NLRB*, 236 N.L. R.B. 1312 (1978), *enforced*, 613 F.2d 1379 (5th Cir. 1980), *reh. den.*, 616 F.2d 568 (5th Cir.), *cert. den.*, 449 U.S. 889 (1980) (in a dispute between the Players Association, which argued that the appropriate bargaining unit was league-wide, and the owners, who argued that the individual clubs were the appropriate unit, the court determined that the league was the appropriate unit).

The size of the unit may be changed, however, in the same manner that it is formed—by an agreement or consensus between management and the employees through their union. Similarly, a subgroup of players might argue that they have identifiable interests apart from the broader interests of the represented group. If the union and management agree, the subgroup may be allowed to create a new unit. In most instances, such an agreement would not be forthcoming because it is unlikely that the union would consent to a withdrawal. When the union refuses, the subgroup might seek recourse from either the NLRB or the courts.

G. Role of the Commissioner

Professional players have historically viewed the role of the league commissioner with some skepticism, typically believing that the commissioner is more a pawn of management than an unbiased intermediary. This skepticism has been central to a number of disputes that have arisen concerning actions taken by the commissioner's office.

The players argue that the commissioner should be included on management's side of the bargaining process. If the commissioner were included on the employer side of the collective bargaining process, the player could treat him as an agent of management. For example, statements made by the commissioner could be binding upon management, and more importantly, the disciplinary powers of the commissioner would be subject to collective bargaining. Not surprisingly, the owners have resisted the players' efforts to draw the commissioner to their side. To date, the owners' resistance has largely been successful. Nevertheless, the threat that the commissioner might be treated as a part of management for collective bargaining purposes serves as an incentive for the commissioner's office to remain as neutral as possible. *See, e.g., National Football League Players Association v. NLRB,* 503 F.2d 12 (8th Cir. 1974) (the NFL Commissioner was held to have acted on behalf of the owners). As the 1985 baseball strike illustrates, the Major League Baseball Commissioner's office appears to be gaining greater independence in that sport and may, therefore, develop into a more genuine and oft-needed neutral intermediary. If the Major League Baseball Commissioner gains independence, it is likely that the commissioners in other sports will seek additional independence, as well.

H. Disputes: Economic Pressure and Resolution Mechanisms

The sports industry has had its share of strikes and lockouts, as a means of exerting pressure on the parties to the collective bargaining process. The parties, particularly the players, when they were just beginning to establish their bargaining power, have also turned to the courts for the resolution of disputes. The court cases, like strikes and lockouts, have often been used as leverage to encourage a recalcitrant party to relent on disputed issues or positions. In addition to strikes, lockouts, and court fights, a grievance and arbitration system has increasingly been used to resolve many disputes.

1. Strikes

Strikes and threats of strikes commonly occur in virtually every professional sport, especially during the final year of the term of any collective bargaining agreement. This is not surprising, because the strike is the players' ultimate weapon. With it, they may attack an apparent impasse with management. As noted in the historical overview in § 6.1 *supra*, threats of a players' strike have materialized on a number of occasions, disrupting seasons and increasing the willingness of all parties to overcome their bargaining disputes.

A strike is a refusal by players to work as a means of coercing the owners into accepting all or a portion of the demands that were previously rejected. Strikes bring considerable economic pressure to bear on both the clubs and the players. Without the revenue generated by sporting activities, both parties feel the adverse economic implications of the strike. Therefore, as a practical matter, a strike or a genuine threat of a strike often encourages agreement and dislodges impasses.

The National Labor Relations Act guarantees players the right to strike, provided that the players association has bargained in good faith to an impasse and that the parties have not agreed to an enforceable "no strike" clause as a part of their bargaining agreement. Even when a strike is permitted, it must be carried out by acceptable means. Thus, the players, who retain their status as employees, may engage in strike-related activities as long as those activities would not otherwise allow the owner to justify discharging them as an employee. For their part, owners are generally permitted to replace the striking players without the obligation to rehire the striking players upon settlement of the strike. As a practical matter, however, professional clubs have not been able to successfully replace striking players for a couple of reasons. First, the players have maintained a fairly strong resolve to strike. Second, replacement of known, skilled athletes with lesser known, unskilled athletes has not been a viable alternative.

Even if clubs have not successfully replaced players on a wholesale basis during or after a strike, they have been able to replace individual striking players on occasion. Marginal, or even unduly costly striking players may find themselves without a position on the team when the strike concludes. Since individual players are much easier to replace than whole teams, clubs may use the strike as a convenient means of unloading some players. However, clubs may have some problems related to dropping a striking player from the team after the strike, particularly if that player was active in supporting the strike. In such cases, the player must usually be given a fair opportunity to make the team. This very general and amorphous standard is meant to avoid impermissible retaliation by the club against a player engaged in legitimate labor activity. The club may replace individual striking players, but it may not do so in a discriminatory fashion, or as a means of retaliation against individual players exercising their right to strike.

2. Lockouts

Just as players may strike to put economic pressure on the owners, the owners "lockout" the players to place economic pressure on the players. Like the strike, the lockout has its legal limitations. If the lockout is used to defend against actual or threatened action by the union, it is permissible. If, however, the owners' motive in using a lockout is to interfere with or manifest hostility toward the collective bargaining process, it is impermissible. As long as the owners intend to support their economic position at the bargaining table, they may engage in a lockout.

3. Grievance and Arbitration

In addition to more extreme bargaining or dispute resolution devices, professional sports leagues have developed a grievance and arbitration procedure for resolving disputes. This procedure may be divided into two basic categories: (a) the resolution of salary disputes; and (b) the resolution of general disputes.

(a) Salary Disputes

The rise of arbitration as a means of resolving salary disputes and differences over the option or reserve clauses in baseball contracts was discussed earlier in this chapter. *See supra* at 6.1. Salary arbitration has received mixed reviews, particularly from management. Although the players have been its strongest supporters, arbitration has generally proven to be a viable, if not always equitable, means of resolving certain salary disputes for both players and management. It has also provided younger baseball players who do not qualify as free agents with a leverage in salary negotiations. *Compare* R. Grebay, *Baseball Arbitration: Another Look at Baseball's Salary Arbitration,* 38 Arb. J. No. 4, 24 (1983) (salary arbitration has become a technical, highly formal process with a devastating impact upon professional sports) *with* M. Miller, *Arbitration of Baseball Salaries: Impartial Adjudication,* 38 Arb. J. No. 4, 36 (1983) (salary arbitration serves a vital, productive function in professional sports), for two differing views of the effectiveness of salary arbitration in baseball.

(b) Arbitration of General Disputes

While salary arbitration is primarily a baseball phenomenon, disputes in other professional sports have been subject to arbitration. When a player disputes an aspect of his contract with the club or an action by the league, resolution of that dispute can frequently be achieved by filing a grievance before an arbitrator. A whole body of law governs the grievance and arbitration process. An elaborate discussion of those principles is beyond the scope of this introductory book. *See* Weistart and Lowell, *The Law of Sports,* at 408–454, 829–836 and the supplement thereto for more in depth discussion of these issues.

Two general points concerning arbitration are worth noting. As their caseloads have increased, the courts, and particularly the Supreme Court, have shown an increasing willingness to defer to the decisions rendered by arbitrators. Second, while the courts remain free to interpret the scope and enforceability of the arbitration clause itself, they are generally reluctant to do so. *See, e.g., Dryer v. Los Angeles Rams Football Company, Inc.,* 151 Cal. App.3d 266, 198 Cal.Rptr. 497 (1984) (although the court declined to find the arbitration clause in an NFL collective bargaining agreement to be adhesionary, it did find that the Commissioner had too much discretion to remove a matter from arbitration).

The *Dryer* case serves as a reminder of the general unwillingness of courts to meddle in arbitration. *Dryer* points out that giving the commissioner or any other potentially biased person or entity too much authority to remove a matter from the designated arbitration procedure may render that procedure legally unacceptable. Thus, while an arbitration procedure should be carefully drawn to ensure "due process," arbitration will usually be accorded great deference by the courts, both as a matter of procedure and as a matter of substance. *See, e.g.. Cincinnati Bengals, Inc. v. Thompson,* 553 F.Supp. 1011 (S.D. Ohio 1983) (dispute over whether team obligated to pay player during strike must be settled by arbitration pursuant to arbitration clause); *Erving v. Virginia Squires Basketball Club,* 468 F.2d 1064 (2d Cir. 1972) (pursuant to terms of contract, arbitration was the proper procedure for resolving question of whether player had been fraudulently induced to sign the agreement); and *Southland Corporation v. Keating,* 465 U.S. 1 (1984) (Federal Arbitration Act pre-empts state law that forecloses arbitration).

The National Labor Relations Board typically defers to arbitration decisions and proceedings, but the arbitration process has not displaced or altered the NLRB's jurisdiction. Deference does not constitute a reduction in the NLRB's authority. The NLRB customarily defers to arbitrators because arbitrators have special skill and experience in deciding matters in a given industry. This would certainly appear to be true of arbitration in the professional sports. Yet it should be noted that the role of the commissioner's office in the arbitration process may undermine the assumption of expertise and the deference shown by the NLRB to the arbitration process, because the commissioner may be viewed as being biased.

Not all issues lend themselves to arbitration. The language of the arbitration provision in the collective bargaining agreement will generally determine which issues can be arbitrated. Courts may rule on the issue of arbitration, unless the collective bargaining agreement expressly provides that the determination is to be made by the arbitrator. When there is no such clause, the courts have tended to resolve doubts in favor of arbitration, holding that a given dispute should be arbitrated even though the agreement is not as clear as it ought to be. Once a substantive issue has been decided by an arbitrator, who has the authority to decide that issue, the decision will generally be honored by both the courts and the NLRB.

I. Antitrust Laws and Collective Bargaining

Professional baseball is not subject to antitrust law, but all remaining major professional sports are. However, even for those sports that are subject to antitrust law, an exemption from antitrust laws exists for the terms and conditions of bona fide collective bargaining agreements. See *supra* at § 3.2 for a more in depth discussion of federal antitrust laws.

The collective bargaining exemption from federal antitrust laws balances the labor law policy favoring collective bargaining with the antimonopoly policy of antitrust law. This exemption forecloses a major avenue of redress that was historically available in professional sports. As a result, aggrieved parties are frequently required to resolve their differences at the bargaining table instead of in the courts through antitrust law. As collective bargaining agreements have become more encompassing, the players, who originally were at a disadvantage at the bargaining table, gained more power and presumably had less need to vindicate their rights through antitrust law.

If the parity between the players and management shifts again in favor of one of the parties, the balance between the policies of collective bargaining and antitrust law may likewise shift. If so, the disadvantaged party may seek judicial or congressional redress to amend or otherwise alter the Sherman Antitrust Act or the National Labor Relations Act. Due to the popularity of professional sports, recourse to Congress for the purpose of resolving an intractable dispute or some other irregularity remains a distinct and potentially viable possibility.

The concurrent existence of collective bargaining and rigorous antitrust litigation concerning matters not covered by a collective bargaining agreement has significantly influenced professional sports. On this subject, Professors Weistart and Lowell have examined the nuances of the interrelationship between antitrust and labor law, and have concluded that as unanswered issues are resolved by the courts, the relative bargaining power of the parties may be significantly changed. Weistart and Lowell, *The Law of Sports,* at 839.

The dynamics of the interplay between collective bargaining and antitrust law will continue to have interesting implications for professional sports. The parties to collective bargaining will almost assuredly keep this interplay in mind as they negotiate and frame their respective positions.

Chapter Seven

TORT LIABILITY

With increasing frequency the media carry news stories about athletes who sue because of sports injuries and recover many hundreds of thousands or perhaps millions of dollars in damages. The defendants in these cases are generally the coach, a school or university, an athletic team, club, or association, or perhaps even the people who make and sell athletic equipment. These law suits are a genuine concern of school administrators, officials, and other persons associated with athletics at both the amateur and professional level.

Speak with any college athletic director or the manager of a local health club and they will inevitably complain about the cost of insuring against a sports injury law suit. Sellers and manufacturers of sports equipment are equally vocal in opining that sports injury litigation is destroying the athletic equipment industry. These and other people give numerous reasons why sports litigation is on the increase, the more common reasons being: attorneys; a litigious society; and people today have more leisure time to devote to sports and an increase in participation has resulted in a corresponding increase in sports related injuries. While all of these proffered reasons for the increase in sports injury litigation may sound plausible and have some validity, they are not the real reason for the increase in litigation. The real reason for the increase in sports injury law suits and large jury verdicts is a specialized body of law known as tort law.

Tort law refers to the law of injury and includes injury to property as well as people. The term "tort" has its origins in the latin word "*torquere*," meaning twisted, and this may explain why the word has become synonymous in Anglo-American law with wrongs done to others. Torts, however, are not crimes. Crimes are public wrongs; wrongs against society that are punishable by fines, imprisonment, or death. Torts include certain specific private wrongs that are committed against another person. Not all harm done to others constitutes a tort.

A tort is harm done to another for which the law holds the wrongdoer responsible. It is the manner in which the injury is done, rather than the injury itself that creates a tort. People can be severely injured or even killed by the actions of others, but a tort is not committed if the person causing the injury did not act in a wrongful manner. In other words, a tort occurs only if the harm was done in such a way that the one causing the harm is held legally responsible for the results.

This chapter will briefly review the development of sports and recreational torts. It will discuss general principles of tort law in a sports context. Liability of teachers, coaches, participants, spectators, administrators, officials, owners, and other athletic personnel will be considered with emphasis upon the most common torts. The chapter will conclude with a brief section on minimizing risk of tort liability for sports related injuries.

7.1 HISTORICAL DEVELOPMENTS

Law is a reflection of society's values. Sports are a microcosm of society. It is therefore not surprising that sports and the law have had a long and varied association. This association has largely been dictated by the societal function and role of the individual at a particular time and place in history.

The early Olympic Games, for instance, were designed to promote better relations among the varied and often hostile Greek city states. To accomplish this goal, a sense of fairness and harmony throughout the competition had to be maintained. Therefore, rules were passed and strictly enforced by judges who punished competitors for violations.

Even then, sports involved a risk of serious injury or death. Under the Ancient Greek system, an athlete who killed another during competition was not punished. Instead, he was expected to placate the victim's family with the payment of money. Greek law enforced this system of compensation and the survivor was not permitted to raise defenses. This compensation system helped to dispell the bitterness or animosity associated with an athlete's death. *See* J.A. Scanlan, Jr., and G.E. Cleveland, Sr., *The Past as*

Prelude; The Early Origins of Modern American Sports Law, 8 Ohio N.U.L. Rev. 433, 433–39 (1981).

Over the next several millenniums participation in sports was restricted by law and continued to serve the purposes of the state. The gentry in Tudor, England, for example, enjoyed tennis and similar activities, while the lower classes were confined to the more pragmatic sports, such as archery. It was not until the industrial revolution created leisure time that sports became the passion of all strata and segments of society. *See id.* at 439–444.

The industrial revolution, however, did more than begin the declassification of sports. It also commenced a redefinition of the worth of the individual in western society. From creating a shorter work day and better working conditions to passing child labor laws and expanding public education, society began to recognize the merit of individuals and started to place a value on an individual's life. More importantly, though, the respect for the individual was reflected in the evolution of tort law. Courts began to strike down many legal barriers that had prevented an injured person from bringing suit, thereby making it easier for those who had suffered harm to be compensated by the wrongdoer.

These legal barriers have endured longer in the area of sports injury litigation, but they are slowly crumbling. They are crumbling because courts today are increasingly willing to apply tort law principles to injuries sustained on neighborhood playgrounds, in school-sponsored athletics, and during professional sports events. The development of sports injury law has been identical to the general evolution of tort law in other circumstances, and there is no reason to expect that this trend will change. Indeed, one can expect an increase in the application of tort law principles to recreational and athletic activities, and that the outcome of sports injury suits will be increasingly determined by the application of common law tort concepts.

7.2 GENERAL PRINCIPLES OF TORT LAW

Torts are either of a statutory or common law origin. Statutory torts are created by legislative enactment. They are frequently intended to redress the violation of some statutory or constitutional right. Typical statutory torts are those that redress injuries caused by racial, sexual, religious, and age discrimination, or the infringement of some other civil right. Common law torts, on the other hand, are wrongs established, recognized, and preserved by courts of law.

Under the common law tort concept, courts define the wrong and prescribe a remedy, not the legislature. Most common law torts are historically rooted in English common law, and became part of American common law during this nation's tenure as an English colony. Since English common law was retained by most of her former colonies, the tort principle discussed herein have widespread application in countries such as Great Britain, Canada, Australia, and New Zealand.

The statutory torts related to sports law are discussed elsewhere in this book. *See supra* §§ 3.2 (antitrust) and 3.4 (Title IX discrimination). This section and the remainder of this chapter are devoted to an application of common law tort principles to sports. Discussion will focus upon the unintentional and intentional torts most likely to be committed by an athlete, spectator, coach, club owner, or others involved in athletic or recreational activities.

A. Unintentional Torts

The person who commits a tort is called a tort-feasor. A tort-feasor may or may not intend to injure another person. The intent to injure another person is not required to establish a cause of action under an unintentional tort theory. Liability for an unintentional tort exists because the tort-feasor either acted or failed to act in a manner required by law, or otherwise engaged in some harm-producing conduct for which the law will ultimately hold him or her responsible.

Sports injury litigation involving unintentional torts is based upon two theories: negligence or strict liability. Since the same wrongful conduct can give rise to liability under several different torts, it is possible for an injured party to sue under both negligence and strict liability and, given the right facts, prevail under each theory. While it is possible to sue under both theories, negligence is undoubtedly the most common source of liability.

1. Negligence

The law requires people and corporations to act in a way that avoids creating an unreasonable risk of injury to others. Negligent conduct is that which falls below this standard. Negligence consists of either doing something a reasonable person would not do because it poses an unreasonable risk of harm to others, or failing to do some act necessary to protect others which the law requires one to perform. *See* Restatement, Second, Torts §§ 281–284 (1965).

a. Duty of Care

The cornerstone of a negligence case is the duty of care required of the defendant. "Duty of care" refers to the standard or level of care the law has established for the protection of others. It is important to realize that the law does not require one to protect others from all injuries; it merely requires that every adult act or not act in such a manner as to create an unreasonable risk of harm to another. Tort law emphasizes not causing injury to others rather than preventing an injury which one in no way caused.

The general rule is that there is no duty to warn, protect or otherwise aid another person who is about to be harmed or has been harmed by situations, forces, or persons one neither contributed to nor controlled. For example, so long as he or she did not cause or add to the hazard, a spectator at an athletic event is not required to warn others of broken glass, slippery steps, or similar dangers. The spectator is also not required to aid another person injured by such conditions. *Id.* at § 314. If there is no duty to warn of a danger, prevent harm, or aid an injured person, then there is no liability for failing to do so. But there are several important exceptions to this general rule. These exceptions are discussed elsewhere in this chapter, and they apply to common carriers, who are under an obligation to protect and care for their passengers; owners of athletic clubs, stadiums, and other facilities open to the public who have a similar duty; and coaches, teachers, and administrators, who often have a very high responsibility to their charges. *See infra* at §§ 7.4A–8 and 7.7.

The level of care owed to others will vary. The more immediate, likely, or serious the foreseeable harm, the more careful one must be to avoid causing an injury to another, or to prevent injury to someone he or she is under a duty to protect. The standard against which one's actions or inactions are measured is always the same: that of a reasonable person under the same or similar circumstances. One is expected to know the law and obey the law because that is what the reasonable person would do. Therefore, the standard of care required of a reasonable person may be determined by statutes or administrative rules designed to protect people or to prevent a particular type of harm. *See* Restatement, Second, Torts §§ 286, 290 (1965).

If state law requires that all high school athletes be given a physical examination before participation in school sponsored sports, that is the standard of care which must be met by the coach, school administrator, and others in charge. If an examination is not given and the athlete is later injured as a result of an undetected physical condition, those responsible for seeing that an examination was done are automatically negligent. An unexcused violation of a law or governmental regulation defining conduct is considered negligence per se. *See, e.g., Ogando v. Carquinez Grammar School District of Contra Costa,* 24 Cal.App.2d 567, 75 P.2d 641 (1938) (liability for death of child during recess play was based on teacher's violation of board of education rules governing playground supervision). Violating a club or league rule may likewise constitute negligence if that rule is recognized by the court as establishing the standard of care required for the protection of others. *See, e.g., Nabozny v. Barnhill,* 31 Ill.App.3d 212, 334 N.E.2d 258 (1975) (violation of "F.I.F.A." rule against making contact with goalkeeper who has possession of the ball in penalty area was basis for injured soccer player's recovery against the player who injured him). Even when a court refuses to adopt a rule or regulation as the standard of care required of the reasonable person, violation of that rule may nevertheless be evidence of negligence. *See e.g., Toone v. Adams,* 262 N.C. 403, 137 S.E.2d 132 (1964) (violation of minor league rules was evidence of negligence in a case involving injury to an umpire).

The absence of a legislative or regulatory standard of care will not prevent a finding of negligence. Compliance with all existing statutes, rules, and regulations will also not preclude a finding of negligence. If no statutes or rules govern conduct, one is expected to act as a reasonable and prudent person would act under the same or similar circumstances. Likewise, if a statute or regulation governs conduct, compliance will not prevent a finding of negligence if a reasonable person would have been more careful. *See* Restatement, Second, Torts §§ 283, 288C (1965).

If one has superior knowledge, intelligence, or special training and skills, his or her actions are judged in light of a reasonable person possessing similar knowledge, intelligence, training, and skills. *See id.* at §§ 289–290. Moreover, one who acquires additional knowledge about professional, amateur, and recreational sports and sports related injuries is expected to act with greater care. Thus, the standard of care required of a reasonable person often increases from year to year. What once was good coaching technique may no longer be acceptable. The modern coach, trainer, or athletic doctor using out-dated techniques may be negligent.

(b) Breach of Duty

Once the court determines that the person charged with negligence owed a duty of care to the injured person, the next step is determining whether or not that level of required care was met. The fact that an injury occurred or that someone was harmed is not in and of itself evidence of negligence. Before liability can be established, the injured person must show that the person accused of negligent behavior failed to act as a reasonable person would under the same or similar circumstances. The law expects every adult to have the intelligence, perception, understanding and judgment of an ordinary prudent person. As such, one is expected to recognize that his or her conduct may involve an unreasonable risk of harm to others if a reasonable person would realize the risk. *See* Restatement, Second, Torts §§ 289–90 (1965).

When confronted with an emergency situation requiring immediate decisions, actions are judged in terms of what a reasonable person would have done under like circumstances. *Id.* at § 296. That the decision was wrong or that another reaction may have prevented or greatly reduced the injuries inflicted upon another does not matter. If one acted reasonably under the circumstances that person is not negligent.

A person is also not negligent in nonemergency situations when the acts are performed in the manner of a reasonable person. One is not an insurer of the safety and well being of others. The law requires only that conduct comport with that of a reasonable person under similar conditions. Consequently, if the injury-producing situation was not foreseeable by a reasonable person or could not have been prevented by the exercise of reasonable care, no liability results, regardless of how seriously another may have been hurt. *Curtis v. Portland Baseball Club,* 130 Or. 93, 279 P. 277 (1929), provides a good example of this principle of law. In *Curtis,* the Oregon Supreme Court concluded that a minor league baseball team was not responsible for the injuries sustained by a fan who was struck with a foul ball.

The Portland Baseball Club had constructed 150 feet of wire screen 40 feet high to protect patrons from foul tips. This screen was maintained in good condition and the spectator was seated behind it when he was injured by a foul ball which hit the screen and made an approximately 180 degree turn to land behind the barrier. The Oregon Supreme Court reasoned that the ball club owed a duty to use reasonable care and diligence to protect its patrons from harm, but concluded that the club had met this duty of care with the existing screen.

The baseball club was not required to protect spectators from all injuries, but only to use reasonable efforts to guard against foreseeable harm. This incident was of such an unusual nature that no one could have reasonably foreseen it. Since it could not have been anticipated by a reasonable person, it was an unavoidable accident for which no one was responsible.

Again, the emphasis under negligence law is avoiding the creation of an unreasonable risk of harm to others. It is not enough that conduct poses a mere risk of injury to others; an unreasonable risk must be both foreseeable by a reasonable person and preventable with exercise of ordinary care. If the potential harm is neither reasonably foreseeable nor avoidable through the exercise of ordinary care, no negligence liability exists.

Sometimes a person is required to foresee the creation of an unreasonable risk of harm to another from the negligence, reckless or intentional conduct of third parties, animals, or even nature. If a person realizes or should realize that their conduct exposes another to the unreasonable risk of injury from third parties, animals or forces of nature, then he or she will be negligent for acting in that manner. See Restatement, Second, Torts §§ 302–03 (1965). A coach could therefore be negligent for requiring an athlete to compete while injured, and ultimately responsible for subsequent injury the athlete sustains even though it was in fact caused by other participants.

In most situations the injured party must prove that a duty of care existed and that this duty was breached by the defendant. If the plaintiff cannot prove both the defendant's legal duty to conform to the standard of care required by law *and* the breach of that duty, the plaintiff loses the negligence action. See Restatement, Second, Torts § 328A (1965). However, in some instances the law places upon the defendant the burden of proving the absence of negligence. The burden of proof is placed upon the defendant in these situations because certain events give rise to an inference of negligence. Once it is raised, the defendant must dispel the inference of wrongdoing.

This policy of shifting the burden of proof is the legal doctrine of *res ipsa loquitur*. The doctrine applies when the injury-producing event was one which ordinarily would not occur in the absence of someone's negligence, and when the defendant was in exclusive control of the agent or instrumentality causing the harm. *Id.* at § 328D. In other words, the only reasonable explanation for the cause of the harm is someone's negligence, and the defendant was the person most likely negligent. *Res ipsa loquitur* is not common in negligence cases, but it is applied in sports injury law suits when appropriate. *Res ipsa loquitur* was, for instance, applied in the recent case of *Parker v. Warren,* 503 S.W.2d 938 (Ct.App.Tenn.1974), which involved the collapse of bleachers at a wrestling match.

The plaintiff in *Parker* was a 52 year old woman who fell and was injured when the bleachers upon which she was seated gave way. Mrs. Parker sued the match promoter and others under a negligence theory, contending that they were negligent in failing to inspect and repair the bleachers. The *Parker* court observed that the seats breaking under the weight of a patron was a most unusual occurrence and that, absent negligence, such things do not happen. Since the promoter had the duty to use reasonable care to render the premises safe for the public, including the duty to inspect bleachers and seats for cracks or other structural weaknesses, the case was a proper one for application of the doctrine of *res ipsa loquitur:*

> Where the thing causing the harm is shown to be under the management of the defendant, and the accident is such as in the ordinary course of things does not happen if those who have the management use proper care, it affords reasonable evidence, in the absence of explanation by the defendant, that the accident arose from want of care.

Id. at 942. Because of *res ipsa loquitur* the promoter was required to prove that he was not negligent, and this he could not do.

(c) Causation

Once the plaintiff establishes that the defendant acted in a negligent manner, the plaintiff must still show that the tortious conduct caused a legally compensable injury. The injury required for a negligence action may be death or physical harm, as well as damage to property or economic interests. A negligence suit can be brought when the harm suffered consists only of lost wages or property damage. *See* Restatement, Second, Torts §§ 328A (1965) and 906 (1979).

Obviously, though, the magnitude and type of harm suffered will have a direct bearing upon the compensation an injured party is entitled to receive. Compensable injuries are discussed elsewhere in this chapter. *See infra* at § 7.2E–1. To recover for injuries, the plaintiff must show that the defendant's conduct was a legal cause of the harm done. *See* Restatement, Second, Torts §§ 328A(c) and (d), 430 (1965). Legal or proximate cause indicates there is a causal connection between the defendant's negligence and the harm sustained by the plaintiff.

Proximate cause exists if the defendant's negligence either caused or was a substantial factor in bringing about the resultant injury. The defendant's negligence need not be the only cause nor the most important cause of the injury-producing event. Two or more persons may be responsible for the same injury. If each defendant's negligent conduct contributed in a substantial way to the resulting harm, those defendants can be liable even though they acted independently of each other. The case of *Welch v. Dunsmuir Joint Union High School District,* 326 P.2d 633 (Cal.App.1958) illustrates the principle of multiple causation.

Welch involved a high school football player injured during a scrimmage. Although he suspected that the young man had a neck injury, the coach instructed several other players to carry the injured athlete off the field so the team doctor could examine him. As a result of being moved in this manner, the athlete suffered additional spinal injuries which rendered him a permanent quadriplegic.

The plaintiff did not claim that the coach was negligent in supervising the scrimmage or in otherwise failing to prevent the initial injury. Rather, the injured athlete contended that the coach was negligent in moving him, and that this transportation caused his permanent paralysis (the athlete had feeling in his lower body prior to being moved). Had the force of the initial contact rendered the athlete a quadriplegic, the coach would not have been liable because he did not cause the harm. Proximate cause does not exist if the plaintiff would have sustained the same injury regardless of the defendant's negligence. *See* Restatement, Second, Torts §§ 430–432 (1965).

The court agreed that the coach's conduct was negligent and was a substantial cause of the permanent injury. Furthermore, the fact that the original injury had been caused without any negligence attributable to the coach was no defense. Neither was it a defense that the team doctor had allowed the athlete to be moved off the field instead of examining him where he lay. In fact, the *Welch* court recognized that the doctor was likewise negligent and possibly more so than the coach. However, since each man's conduct was a substantial cause of the injury, both could have proximately caused the harm, regardless of whether they acted independently or in concert.

The effect of the proximate cause requirement is to place a limit on the extent of a negligent person's liability. The tortfeasor is not automatically responsible for all of the harm directly caused by his or her negligence. Before liability is established, the plaintiff must show that the negligence and resulting harm was not considered "highly extraordinary." Restatement, Second, Torts § 435 (1965).

Parties are not responsible for the bizarre or otherwise unforeseeable events that their negligence causes. But proximate cause does not require that the particular injury or exact manner of its occurrence be readily foreseeable. It is sufficient if the negligent conduct posed a reasonably foreseeable risk of injury. Stated otherwise, if a reasonable person could have anticipated some injury to another as a result of the negligent conduct, the defendant will be responsible. Additionally, as a matter of policy courts have determined that proximate cause automatically exists in certain circumstances regardless of how extraordinary the harmful event may be. For example, it is often stated that negligent defendants "take their victims as they find them." This means that if a person is negligent and injures another, that individual cannot avoid responsibility by claiming that the injuries were greatly aggravated or enhanced by the victim's own physical susceptibility to harm.

If a defendant's negligence is a substantial factor in bringing about injury to another, that defendant is responsible for the full extent of those injuries, even when the injuries were enhanced by the victim's own peculiar physical condition. A negligent defendant will likewise be responsible for additional injuries caused by the victim's weakened condition, including those resulting from subsequent accidents, disease or negligent medical treatment. Furthermore, if a defendant's negligence places another in a perilous situation, the defendant is responsible for harm sustained in reasonable efforts to escape the peril, injuries incurred in rescue attempts by others, and for injuries to those who reasonably attempt to rescue the person negligently placed in danger. *Id.* at §§ 435–461.

(d) Defenses

Contributory negligence is the common law defense to a negligence suit. Contributory negligence is conduct by plaintiffs that falls below the standard of care the law requires them to exercise for their own protection. *See* Restatement, Second, Torts § 463 (1965). If a plaintiff does not use reasonable care for his or her own personal safety, and this lack of care contributes substantially to causing the injuries, the defendant may rely upon the plaintiff's contributing negligence as a defense. The rules used to determine a plaintiff's contributory negligence are the same as those used to determine a defendant's negligence. Like ordinary negligence, contributory negligence requires existence of a duty of care which the plaintiff owes to himself, breach of that duty, and a resulting injury.

In its original form, contributory negligence constituted a complete defense. If the plaintiff was the least bit responsible for the injuries, recovery was completely denied. This is a harsh rule, for many times the contributing fault of the plaintiff is insignificant in comparison to that of the defendant. The existence of any contributory negligence, regardless of how slight, is nevertheless sufficient to preclude the plaintiff from recovering for injuries. *See, e.g., Harrison v. Montgomery County Board of Education,* 295 Md. 442, 456 A.2d 894 (1983) (because he had not acted with the care a reasonably prudent person would exercise for his own safety, a fourteen year old boy paralyzed in a physical education class accident could not recover against the more negligent school district and teachers).

To alleviate some of the injustice of the contributory negligence defense, some courts have adopted the "last clear chance" doctrine. If the defendant could have, with the exercise of ordinary care, avoided the plaintiff's carelessness, the defendant had the last clear chance to prevent the accident and contributory negligence is no defense. Other states, however, have abandoned the harsh total bar defense of contributory negligence in favor of comparative negligence.

Either by legislative action or judicial decision a majority of states now adhere to a comparative form of the contributory negligence defense. Under this comparative form, the defendant's fault is compared to that of the plaintiff's. Some states employ "pure comparative negligence," under which the plaintiff can recover that portion of the damages caused by the defendant's negligence. Recovery is allowed even if the plaintiff's negligence exceeds that of the defendant. Other jurisdictions recognize a modified form of comparative negligence. Under this form, the plaintiff recovers proportionate damages only if the plaintiff's own negligence is less than that of the defendant. If the plaintiff's negligence exceeds the defendant's under this modified form the plaintiff is denied recovery. The plaintiff's contributory negligence is, in other words, a complete defense.

Regardless of which variation of comparative negligence a state uses, engaging in certain types of activities may be considered to be per se contributory negligence by the injured plaintiff. In these cases no comparison is made of the plaintiff's and defendant's relative fault. The plaintiff's conduct constitutes a complete defense as a matter of law, much as it would have under the older common law form of contributory negligence. Injuries to athletes and spectators at athletic events are two areas in which the common law complete contributory negligence defense still exists to some extent. Both of these are discussed *infra* in §§ 7.4A–9 and 7.7C–6, respectively.

2. *Strict Liability*

The tort doctrine of strict liability is one of the more recently recognized tort theories. For policy reasons, those persons who participate in certain activities are held responsible for the harm they cause to others despite the care or caution employed. Strict liability is, in essence, liability without fault. Strict liability applies to those who either engage in ultrahazardous activities, or are in the business of selling defective products which are unreasonably dangerous to consumers. This section will examine the strict liability associated with abnormally dangerous activities. The strict liability of sellers of defective products is discussed elsewhere. *See infra* at § 7.10B.

People who carry on abnormally dangerous activities are liable for harm caused to others notwithstanding the exercise of reasonable care. It is no defense that an injury was in fact caused by the negligent conduct of others, animals, or the forces of nature. By choosing to carry on an ultrahazardous activity, the tort-feasor has for his or her own purposes created a risk that is not common to the community. When this risk causes harm to others, the one who undertook to create the dangerous situation is responsible regardless of the fact that other persons or forces may have contributed to causing the injury.

To determine whether an activity is ultrahazardous or abnormally dangerous, courts consider a variety of factors: (1) does the activity pose a high risk of harm to others; (2) will the potential injury be great; (3) can the risk of harm be eliminated with reasonable care; (4) is the particular activity commonly carried on in the community; (5) is the activity carried on in an appropriate location; (6) to what extent does the value of the activity to the community outweigh its potential danger. These criteria are usually weighed by the jury or by the court in a nonjury trial. In some cases a particular activity may be found to be ultrahazardous, while in other cases the same conduct might not give rise to strict liability. Regardless of how the court or jury rules on a particular set of facts, the type of sports activities that might be considered abnormally dangerous are readily recognizable.

Automobile racing at an established race track is probably not an ultrahazardous activity, but a race through city streets might be. The combination of speeding vehicles and volatile fuel creates an ever-present risk of a serious accident. No amount of care will eliminate the risk of serious injury, and the promoters may be strictly liable for crash-related injuries to the person or property of nonparticipants. Cf. Saari v. State, 203 Misc. 859, 119 N.Y.S.2d 507, aff'd, 282 A.D. 526, 125 N.Y.S.2d 507 (1953) (automobile race on public streets was sufficiently dangerous to constitute a public nuisance). Additional examples of possibly abnormally dangerous sports activities might include airplane races, skydiving, and any other event involving a substantial risk of serious harm that cannot be eliminated by any degree of care.

(a) Causation

The tort-feasor, however, is not responsible for all conceivable harm that may result from an abnormally dangerous activity.

The tort-feasor is strictly liable for the harm that the conduct substantially caused, but only if the harm is of the type that makes the activity abnormally dangerous. Thus, the promoters of an inner city Grand Prix race would probably be responsible for personal injury and property damage caused by a crash, but strict liability would not apply to the spectator who suffers heat stroke while watching the race. The injury-producing crash is the very kind of harm that makes the race abnormally dangerous, whereas the spectator's heat stroke is totally unrelated to the ultrahazardous nature of the activity.

(b) Defenses

The main defense to strict liability in tort is assumption of risk. Assumption of risk is essentially a plaintiff's express or implied consent to encounter a known danger. A plaintiff's ordinary negligence is not sufficient to give rise to an assumption of risk defense. Although if the plaintiff's conduct is sufficiently reckless to constitute assuming a known risk, it will also be contributorily negligent.

Assumption of risk is a commonly encountered defense in suits by injured athletes and spectators. *See infra* §§ 7.4A–9 and 7.7C–6. The doctrine is normally considered a complete bar to a plaintiff's recovery, but those states that compare negligence also tend to compare fault under this defense. *See, e.g., Lamphear v. State*, 91 A.D.2d 791, 458 N.Y.S.2d 71 (1982) (if they could be proven, defenses of assumption of risk and contributory negligence would only serve to reduce recovery of injured collegiate softball player, not completely bar the recovery).

B. Intentional Torts

The state of mind required for an intentional tort is the intent to harm others. Lack of due care or engaging in an abnormally dangerous activity have nothing to do with intentional torts. Liability for an intentional tort is premised upon whether the tort-feasor acted with the express purpose of causing harm to another person, or whether the tort-feasor committed a nonaccidental act substantially certain to harm someone, even though the resulting injury was not actually intended. Restatement, Second, Torts § 8A (1965).

The law treats intentional tort-feasors differently than other tort-feasors. Unlike the situation for tort-feasors under negligence and strict liability, there is no limit on liability for those who intentionally harm others. In an intentional tort case, the wrongdoer is responsible for the actual or direct consequences of his or her actions, regardless of how remote, unforeseeable, or bizarre they may be. Once the court or jury determines that the tort-feasor acted to cause a particular harm or engaged in some activity that was substantially certain to cause another injury, the tort-feasor will be responsible for all the harm that is a direct result of the initial wrong doing. The difference in recoverable damages for intentional torts is discussed in § 7.2E–1 *infra.*

The intent to injure can be transferred to different persons, significantly increasing the potential exposure for the initial wrong doing. Under the doctrine of "transferred intent," if a tort-feasor intends to harm one person but injures another instead, the intent to harm is transferred to the person actually injured. Thus, an intentional tort is deemed to have been committed. By holding intentional tort-feasors responsible for the natural and probable consequences of their actions, and by transferring the intent to harm from person to person, it is possible for a single occurrence to give rise to any number of intentional torts among several injured plaintiffs. There are many intentional torts, but discussion will be limited to the ones most frequently encountered in sports litigation.

1. Assault

The tort of assault consists of intentionally placing another in fear or apprehension of immediate harmful or offensive bodily contact. Harmful contact is capable of producing pain, illness, or injury, and offensive contact is that which would offend a reasonable person's sense of personal dignity.

The threat must be of a present harmful or offensive touching, rather than a future touching. The person assaulted must have been aware of the threat at the time it occurred, and words alone are not sufficient to constitute an assault. However, threatening language coupled with some other act or circumstance that puts the other person in reasonable apprehension of an imminent harmful or offensive bodily contact may constitute an assault. *See* Restatement, Second, Torts §§ 31–34 (1965). A typical assault case involves one person threatening another with harmful or offensive bodily contact by means of feet, hands, fists, sticks, clubs, bats, guns, knives, or similar instruments.

2. Battery

A battery occurs when one person intentionally touches another person in a harmful or offensive manner. Because fear is not an element of the battery tort, the plaintiff need not be aware of the bodily contact at the time it occurs. It is sufficient if the victim subsequently learns of the harmful or offensive touching.

A battery can be committed by touching the clothing, equipment, or apparel on the person of another. Although it is not necessary to have an assault in conjunction with a battery, the two torts frequently occur together. *Hogenson v. Williams*, 542 S.W.2d 456 (Tx.App.1976) is illustrative of an assault and battery case.

Hogenson was a seventh grade football player. During a practice session the young man missed a blocking assignment, which apparently angered the coach, who started yelling and struck the athlete's helmet with sufficient force to knock him down. The coach then grabbed Hogenson's face mask. The athlete was hospitalized for neck and muscle injuries and brought an action against the coach. The Texas Court of Appeals recognized the player's right to sue under both assault and battery theories. It was not necessary for the coach to actually touch Hogenson to commit an assault; the threatened contact was sufficient if the athlete either saw the blow coming or saw the coach reaching for his face mask. A battery occurred when the athlete was actually struck.

3. False Imprisonment

Intentionally confining another within fixed boundaries forms the basis for the tort of false imprisonment. The confinement can be accomplished with physical barriers, such as walls and locked doors; with physical force, such as restraining another; or by threats of violence and other forms of duress used to deprive someone of his or her freedom of movement. If the person is left with a reasonable means of escape, no confinement is present and the tort has not been committed. The victim, however, must be aware of the avenue of escape. A means of escape is not reasonable if it involves a risk of injury or otherwise requires the person to do something that would be offensive to a reasonable person's sense of decency or personal dignity.

The confinement need not be in a small area, nor must it be of a specific duration. The tort is completed once the victim learns that he or she is confined without a reasonable means of escape, or is otherwise harmed by the confinement. Restatement, Second, of Torts §§ 35–45A (1965). False imprisonment cases most often occur as a result of an invalid arrest or other improper seizure of a spectator. The tort may also be committed by coaches and other persons who engage in misdirected efforts at maintaining discipline and control.

4. Defamation

Defamation is publishing a false *and* defamatory statement of fact about another. Publishing requires that the false statement be communicated to at least one other person. A statement is defamatory if it tends either to lower someone's reputation in the community or to otherwise deter third persons from associating or dealing with that person.

If the defamatory matter is communicated by radio, television, or by written or printed words it is termed libel. Those who have been libeled can sue without showing actual injury to their reputation. Publication of defamatory material by the spoken word and not through a print or electronic medium is slander. To sue for slander, the defamed person must show an actual injury to his or her reputation unless the false statement is considered by law to be slanderous per se. Slander per se is like libel in that injury to reputation is presumed. Restatement, Second, Torts §§ 568–576 (1977).

A statement is slanderous per se if it accuses another person of criminal conduct, being homosexual or unchaste, having a loathsome disease like gonorrhea, syphillis, or perhaps "AIDS," or otherwise affects that person's trade, business, or profession. Disparaging comments about a coach's lack of good sportsmanship or penchant for being rowdy certainly impact upon him or her professionally and may therefore be per se defamatory. *See, e.g., Grayson v. Curtis Publishing Company,* 72 Wash.2d 999, 436 P.2d 756 (1968) (recognizing coach's right to sue for such statements).

Defamation does not cover false statements injurious to the reputation of those already dead, but corporations, partnerships and associations can be defamed. Defamatory material about a group or class of people will not support a libel or slander suit by a member of the group unless the group is either so small that the disparaging remarks can be reasonably understood as defaming that member, or they otherwise make a personal reference to the individual. Restatement, Second, Torts §§ 560–564A (1977). Defamation of an entire team was the issue in *Fawcett Publications, Inc. v. Morris*, 377 P.2d 42 (Okla.1962).

In *Fawcett* a magazine publisher printed an article alleging that drug use was prevalent among members of the 1956 University of Oklahoma football team. Morris was a regular starter on that team. While he was not specifically mentioned in the article, Morris nevertheless brought a libel suit against the magazine publisher. A jury awarded Morris $75,000 in damages. The publisher appealed, but the jury verdict was affirmed by the Oklahoma Supreme Court. The Oklahoma Supreme Court held that the statement was not only false and defamatory per se, but that despite not being named in the article, Morris had been personally defamed because he was well known and commonly identified with that team.

Those who hear and repeat defamatory matter are equally as liable as the originator of the false and slanderous statement. It is usually no defense that one believed the statement to be true. Yet, notwithstanding the highly defamatory nature of what was said, written, or printed, a defamed person may not always be able to recover in a law suit. Truth is an absolute defense to a defamation suit. Even if not true, a defense exists if the statement amounted to no more than a "fair comment" about the other person's performance or ability. A defense also exists for otherwise defamatory comments made during the course of judicial, administrative, and similar proceedings. Yet, the most significant defense to a sports defamation suit will probably be the First Amendment barrier to suits by public figures. *See* Restatement, Second, Torts §§ 581A–612 (1977).

The First Amendment to the United States Constitution grants to citizens the privilege of freely commenting about public figures without fear of being sued for defamation. To prevail in a libel or slander suit, a public figure must not only show the usual false and defamatory statement of fact, but he or she must also prove that the statement was made with malice. "With malice" means that the false and defamatory material was published by someone who knew that it was false or who acted (published) with reckless disregard for the truth. *See id.* at §§ 577–581A.

A statement is published with reckless disregard for the truth when it is made without a reasonable basis for belief. Hence, in the case of statements about public figures, believing the material to be true may constitute a defense if that belief is based upon some reasonable ground, such as a source close to the athlete, team, or management. Since athletes, coaches, and owners often receive enough media coverage to qualify as public figures, the requirement that they prove actual malice has greatly restricted the likelihood of a defamation suit arising out of comments about their personal lives or performance. The impact of constitutionally protected speech upon defamation suits by public figures is considered in greater detail *supra* at § 3.3C–4–(b).

5. *Invasion of Privacy*

There is a constitutionally protected right to privacy (*see supra* at § 3.3B), and interference with another's right to privacy can also give rise to a tort. Like defamation, invasion of privacy involves harm caused by making public statements about or disclosing matters concerning another person. Unlike libel and slander, an intentional invasion of another person's privacy will sometimes permit that individual to sue and recover damages for harm caused by the disclosure of nondefamatory statements, or even true facts about his or her private life. Damages can be awarded in that instance because the focus of an invasion of privacy is upon repairing harm caused by an intentional, unwarranted, and unprivileged intrusion into the private life of another. Neither truth of the personal facts revealed, nor injury to an individual's reputation from the disclosure of private facts are elements of this tort. The crux of the tort of invasion of privacy is an intrusion into another person's right to be left alone.

An individual's right of privacy can be invaded in many ways. The first and perhaps most common source of sports oriented invasion of privacy suits relates to the public's curiosity about sports figures. From the littlest Little Leaguer to the highest paid professional athlete, newspapers, radio, and television are full of details about the lives of athletes. Most of what one hears and reads about sports figures cannot be the basis for an invasion of privacy suit. By their public athletic accomplishments or by choosing a profession in which there is a legitimate public interest, players, coaches, team owners and other sports personalities have relinquished a part, but not all, of their right to privacy.

Sports figures, like ordinary citizens, can have their right to privacy tortiously invaded, but the intrusion must affect purely private as opposed to public matters before a court will find that a wrong has been done. Public matters, for example, include any-thing related to an athlete's sports association, performance, or character. In most instances no cause of action for the public revelation of true facts about a sports notable will exist. Never-theless, some details of an athlete's life even superstars are enti-tled to keep secret, such as sexual relations. The unprivileged disclosure of these matters may entitle the athlete to compensa-tion for the mental distress and other harm suffered as a result of the invasion of privacy. Restatement, Second, Torts § 652H (1977).

There is admittedly no clear line between the public's right to know and the individual's right to privacy. The line between legitimate public interest and an improper prying into another's private life is often loosely determined on the grounds of common decency. A tortious invasion of privacy occurs if a reasonable person with decent standards would view the invasion as a prying into a matter which was of no concern to either the intruder or the public.

Once a person has attained the status of a widely recognized sports figure, that person cannot regain his or her former standing as a private citizen. Past events and the heroes of yesterday may still be the proper objects of legitimate public interest. The same is true of a public figure's family. Legitimate public interest may include those persons closely associated with a sports figure, such as a member of the family, a business partner or a girlfriend. *See id.* at § 652D comments h and k.

Although the facts disclosed may be privileged as matters of genuine public interest, a sports figure's privacy is wrongfully invaded if the information was acquired in an improper manner. For example, prying into another person's private affairs by searching his or her locker, tapping another's telephone, opening someone else's mail or any similar act that is highly offensive to a reasonable person is an invasion of privacy. *See id.* at § 652B.

An invasion of privacy might likewise occur if the newspaper, television sports commentator, or other person makes a false statement about a sports figure. If the statement injures the athlete or coach's reputation, it could give rise to a libel or slander suit as well. An injury to reputation is not necessary for a plaintiff to recover for false statements under an invasion of privacy theory. When the statements are directed at a public figure, however, he or she must prove that the false statements were publicized with malice.

This malice requirement is the same as that necessary to establish the tort of defamation of a public figure. Proving malice requires proof that the false facts were publicized by one knowing them to be false or with reckless disregard for the truth. *See* Restatement, Second, Torts § 652E (1977). Unauthorized biographies are a frequent source of invasion of privacy suits. *See, e.g., Spahn v. Julian Messner, Inc.,* 21 N.Y.2d 124, 286 N.Y.S.2d 832, 233 N.E.2d 840 (1967), *appeal dismissed,* 393 U.S. 1046 (1969) (although Warren Spahn's status as a public figure made him newsworthy and thus placed his biography in the public domain, the author was not entitled to publish an unauthorized biography containing many factual errors, distortions, and fanciful passages). It is also an invasion of privacy to appropriate another's name or likeness for commercial purposes.

Product endorsements by athletes are important to the promotion and sale of many products from beer to underwear. Commercials are also a significant source of revenue for the athletes. It should therefore come as no surprise to discover that the commercial exploitation of a sports figure's name or image is another type of conduct likely to generate an invasion of privacy suit.

Adults are vested with the exclusive use of their own identity, which includes both name and likeness. Using another person's identity may be the basis for liability under an invasion of privacy tort theory. One may authorize others to use his or her name or photograph, and to the extent such a license has been granted, there is no action for invasion of privacy. Likewise, no invasion of privacy claim exists if the use is of an incidental nature, such as a sports magazine's promotional advertisement that includes photographs from past issues. *See, e.g., Namath v. Sports Illustrated,* 48 A.D.2d 487, 371 N.Y.S.2d 10 (1975) (since it was used to show the magazine's quality and content, photograph of Joe Namath originally published by Sports Illustrated in conjunction with an article on the 1969 Super Bowl Game could properly be included in the magazine's subscription advertisements). In the absence of consent or a privileged incidental use, appropriating or exploiting another's identity for any purpose is a tort. *See, e.g., Palmer v. Schonhorn Enterprises, Inc.,* 96 N.J.Super. 72, 232 A.2d 458 (1967) (Arnold Palmer, Gary Player, Doug Sanders, and Jack Nicklaus successfully sued corporate manufacturer of a game which, without their permission, included these well-known golfers' names and career profiles).

6. Interference With Contract

A person who breaches a contract is legally responsible for damages the other party sustains as a consequence of the breach. The person harmed can sue the breaching party under contract law. A tort action may nevertheless exist if the breach was caused by the willful conduct of some third party. This tort is known as interference with contract. It consists of intentionally inducing another to breach his or her contractual obligations. The person who induces the breach of contract is liable in tort; the party who actually breaches the contractual obligations remains liable in contract rather than tort.

A valid contract must exist before this tort can be committed, and the tort-feasor must also be aware of the contract. Even though one may cause another's failure to perform a contractual obligation, the act cannot be done intentionally for the purpose of inducing a breach of contract unless the actor knows the contract exists and is aware of the interference with its performance. Interference is simply inducing a party to breach the contract. Inducement can take many forms; promises of a better deal with more money or benefits, a simple request not to perform, threats of physical or economic harm, or any other conduct conveying the actor's desire that the contract not be performed. *See* Restatement, Second, Torts § 766 (1979).

Because the existence of a valid enforceable contract is necessary, interference with contract will normally be restricted to the recruitment of coaches, professional athletes, and other paid persons. Yet, it is possible that the recruiting of scholarship athletes from colleges may be a tortious interference with contract. *See* § 3.1 *supra* for a discussion of the contractual nature of athletic scholarships.

Once a contract has been interfered with, the nonbreaching party has at his or her disposal any or all of the following remedies; sue the breaching party under contract law for damages incurred as a result of the breach, sue the interfering party under tort law for money damages, or ask the court for an order prohibiting the breaching party from working for another team during the remainder of the contract term. The one remedy not available to the injured party is a court order requiring the coach or player to perform his or her contract. *See infra* § 7.2E for a more complete discussion of tort remedies.

7. Trespass

The unauthorized, intentional intrusion upon the land or premises of another constitutes a trespass. Although the initial entry may have been consensual, trespass can occur when one remains upon another's property after being told to leave. A trespass can be accomplished by intentionally causing a third person to enter land in possession of another or by propelling some object onto or across the property. *See* Restatement, Second, Torts § 158 (1965).

It is no excuse that the trespasser acted under the mistaken belief of the right to enter and remain upon the property. Trespassers are liable for all the injury which they cause to the property and person of another. A trespass can occur even when there is no actual harm done as a result of the intrusion. *See* Restatement, Second, Torts §§ 158, 163, 164 (1965). These characteristics of trespass make that tort an ever present source of liability for hunters, fishermen, joggers, and outdoor recreationalists in general. This threat of liability is reduced somewhat in those western states where property owners must post their land with no trespassing signs to exclude sportsmen.

8. Breach of Fiduciary Duty

An agent is authorized to represent and act for a principal. Professional representatives who act for athletes in contract negotiations and other matters are agents, but they are not the only examples of agents in sports law. Employees may be agents if they are authorized to transact business for their employers. Thus, the term "agent" can include both employees and those who are not, but regardless of this distinction, all agents owe their principal the fiduciary duty of loyalty.

This duty requires that the agent act with complete honesty in all dealings with the principal. An agent must avoid conflicts between the agent's interests and those of the principal. Agents must serve the undivided interest of the principal, and cannot represent two principals on the same transactions. Finally, the agent must not receive secret compensation or profits from a third party for transacting the principal's business, nor may the agent take advantage of any business opportunity that rightfully belongs to the principal. For a full discussion of an agent's duty of loyalty to the professional athlete, *see* §§ 5.2H and 5.6B *supra*.

If the agent fully discloses a conflict of interest or other potentially improper conduct and receives the principal's prior consent to the action, the agent's subsequent acts will not constitute a breach of fiduciary duty. Without this full disclosure and prior approval, however, the agent acts at his or her own risk. When a breach of the duty of loyalty occurs, the agent will be liable for the resulting harm to the principal.

An agent's liability is predicated upon a tort known as "breach of fiduciary duty." Breach of fiduciary duty is closely akin to the intentional torts because it may result in an award of punitive damages. Moreover, in addition to damages, the principal may be able to set aside a contract which the agent negotiated in violation of the duty of loyalty. *See, e.g., Detroit Lions, Inc. v. Argovitz*, 580 F.Supp. 542 (E.D. Mich.1984) (Billy Sims was permitted to rescind his contract with Houston Gamblers of the USFL because the agent who negotiated that contract owned a substantial interest in that club, a fact that was not disclosed to Sims). The principal is also entitled to any secret profit or other compensation the disloyal agent received. The principal normally does not have to compensate the agent for work performed in violation of the duty of loyalty.

9. *Defenses*

Consent is the most commonly asserted defense to an intentional tort. One who effectively consents to participate in harm-producing activities cannot recover in tort for the injuries later sustained. To be effective, consent must be freely and knowingly given. When one's consent is obtained under duress or by misrepresentation, it is not a defense to an intentional tort. Consent given by mistake will likewise be invalid if the person to whom it is given realized that the person consenting was mistaken. *See* Restatement, Second, Torts §§ 892–892C (1979).

The essence of consent as a defense is the injured person's willingness to allow the otherwise tortious conduct to occur. This willingness can be shown by deeds as well as words. Mere participation in a harm-producing activity may be interpreted as consent to risk incurring the injuries which result therefrom. If consent is restricted to a particular time, place, or person, or is limited in any other respect, its effectiveness as a defense will be limited by the conditions set. The consenting party must likewise have the capacity to consent. Lack of capacity will sometimes invalidate consent obtained from children or mentally incompetent individuals. *See id.* at §§ 892–892C. The effectiveness of consent obtained from minors and the mentally handicapped is considered in § 7.2C *infra*. Consent as a defense to tort actions by participants and spectators is addressed in §§ 7.4A–9 and 7.7C–6 *infra*.

C. Children and the Mentally and Physically Infirm

Sporting events are no longer the exclusive province of mentally and physically healthy young adults. Today numerous athletic and recreational programs are run for the mentally or physically impaired of all ages. Youth sports have similarly attained a level of sophistication and intensity few would have foreseen a generation ago. With the increase in participation by children and the handicapped in sports activities, the likelihood of injuries has also increased. More importantly, though, the legal responsibility for those injuries will be largely determined by special principles of law applicable to children and the handicapped.

Society has an important interest in the welfare and protection of its children. It is likewise generally understood and accepted by society that children do not always act in a mature and responsible manner. These factors undoubtedly contributed to the development of a special legal standard of behavior for children.

Children approaching the age of majority or those engaging in activities such as driving, which are normally only undertaken by adults, are typically held to the same standard of care as adults. They are required to exercise the skill, judgment, and competence of a reasonable person under the same or similar circumstances. No allowance is made for their immaturity. On the other hand, children below a certain age, usually four, are thought to be so immature that they cannot intelligently perceive those situations and activities that pose risks either to themselves or others. These very young children are incapable of committing a negligent act. This means that very young children cannot be liable for injuries they inflict upon others, and they are incapable of being contributorily negligent. Since young children cannot be contributorily negligent, persons legally responsible for injuring small children are deprived of the defense of contributory negligence. *See* Restatement, Second, Torts § 283A comment b (1965). For a discussion of the contributory negligence defense *see supra* at § 7.2A–1–(d).

If a child is beyond the age of innocence but not yet treated as an adult, to avoid being negligent the child must conform his or her conduct to that of a reasonable person of like age, intelligence, and experience under similar conditions. A majority of the children involved in athletics come under this standard of required conduct. Whether children are very bright or mentally impaired is taken into account in judging their actions. A child's education and experience must be considered too. Hence, those children who are very intelligent, well educated, and have enjoyed many experiences in life are required to exercise the judgment of a child with like intelligence, education, and experience. Conversely, handicapped or inexperienced children are held to a lower level of care for their own safety and the safety of others around them; their conduct is evaluated by comparing it to the expected actions of a reasonable child of like age, intelligence, and experience under the same or similar conditions. *See* Restatement, Second, Torts §§ 283A, 464(2) (1965). Thus, if two youngsters of differing age, experience, or intelligence, engage in the same activity and either injure themselves or a third person, the brighter, more experienced child may be judged negligent while the other is not. Younger, less experienced, and less intelligent children are least likely to be judged negligent either towards themselves or towards others.

Physically handicapped or impaired adults are expected to conform their conduct to that of a reasonable person with the same disability. Under certain circumstances, a disabled person may be required to exercise greater care for his or her safety and that of others than would a nonhandicapped individual. For example, the handicapped athlete must carefully avoid engaging in activities in which his or her physical limitations may expose others to an unreasonable risk of harm. While a motocross racer who has a sudden and unexpected seizure is generally not negligent in losing control of the motorcycle and crashing into spectators, if the racer knows about a propensity for seizures, the racer may very well be found negligent for having entered the race in the first place. *See* Restatement, Second, Torts §§ 283C comment c (1965); 895J comment a (1979).

The mentally handicapped, retarded or insane adult does not enjoy the same treatment as children and the physically handicapped receive under the law. Regardless of their mental retardation or mental illness adults are held to the same standard of care as a reasonable person who is not mentally deficient. *See* Restatement, Second, Torts § 283B comment b (1965). It is indeed ironic that many times adults who participate in recreational programs for the mentally impaired are expected to exercise a degree of care that is admittedly beyond their capacity. Although it may seem unfair to hold mentally handicapped adults to the same standard of conduct as a person of normal intelligence, any injustice is more than offset by the higher care required of those persons sponsoring, supervising, or controlling recreational activities for the mentally impaired.

Organizations and individuals who sponsor, control, or supervise activities for the mentally or physically handicapped must be extremely careful to protect the participants, fans, and other persons who could be injured. This increased level of care also applies to those individuals who run recreational programs for children. A reasonable person working with children or handicapped adults should recognize the need for increased supervision and additional safety measures, and act accordingly. Consequently, whether they are aware of it or not, people involved with youth programs or with recreational activities for the impaired are expected to meet this higher level of care in the performance of their duties. They may be found negligent for failing to do so. This duty to exercise greater care for the handicapped is further complicated by federal and state laws that guarantee handicapped people the right to participate. Rights of the handicapped in sports are considered *supra* at § 3.5.

D. Vicarious Liability

The person who commits a tort remains personally liable for injuries inflicted on others. Yet there are occasions when an innocent third party may be legally responsible for the tortious conduct of another. This is called vicarious or imputed liability. Vicarious liability usually arises under the doctrine of *respondeat superior.*

Respondeat superior literally means "let the master answer." It is a legal theory whereby a principal is made jointly and severally liable for the torts an agent commits. Employees are considered to be agents. An employee may have any number of principals; everyone who has control over the details of an employee's job performance is a principal. A high school coach would, for example, be an agent of the school athletic director, school principal, district superintendent, school board, school district, and city that operates the school system, and all of these principals might be sued for the coach's negligent acts. *See, e.g., Larson v. Independent School District No. 314*, 289 N.W.2d 112 (Minn. 1980) (gymnast paralyzed as a result of coach's negligence sued coach, high school administrator, and school district).

The principal's liability is joint and several with that of the agent. "Joint and several liability" means that one harmed by an agent's negligent conduct may, at his or her option, sue the agent, one or more of the principals seperately, or any combination of agent and principals. However, a principal's liability for the agent's actions is not automatic.

Since the principal's liability is based upon the conduct of the agent, if the employee has not committed a tort, no wrong can be imputed to the employer or supervisors. Moreover, even when an agent has committed some tortious act, liability will not be charged to the principal unless the agent was acting within the scope of the agency or employment when the wrong was committed. An agent is acting within the scope of the agency or employment when he or she is carrying out the tasks assigned by the principal.

Disputes about whether the employee was acting to further his or her own personal interest rather than the employer's when the injury-producing event occurred are common. As a general rule, though, the harmful act is deemed within the scope of employment if the employee performed it during regular working hours and as a part of assigned duties. As long as the agent is acting within the scope of his or her agency, liability can be imposed upon the principal even though the agent is not compensated for the services and the activity takes place either after hours or away from the usual place of employment. *See, e.g., Chappel v. Franklin Pierce School District*, 71 Wash.2d 17, 426 P.2d 471 (1967) (because its faculty had participated in supervising and planning a campus social club's activities, the school district could be vicariously liable for injuries a student suffered at an off-campus initiation ceremony).

Vicarious liability is usually encountered in a negligence rather than intentional tort case. It is not often found in an intentional tort action because the harm producing conduct must be within the scope of the agency before liability is imputed to the principal. Not many employees are acting within the scope of their employment when they intentionally harm another human being. However, if they are, it is proper to hold the employer or supervisor liable for the employee's intentional torts. Contact sports may create situations in which a participant's intentional tort will be imputed to the team or owner. *See, e.g., Hackbart v. Cincinnati Bengals, Inc.,* 601 F.2d 516 (10th Cir. 1979) (recognizing right of Denver Bronco defensive back Dale Hackbart to sue the Cincinnati Bengals for disabling injuries recklessly inflicted upon him by a Bengals player).

E. Remedies

Remedies are employed by a court of law to enforce a right or redress a wrong. Remedies are the relief to which a successful litigant is entitled. Tort victims traditionally seek remedies in the form of an award of damages or injunctive relief. These remedies can be awarded individually or collectively, but they are not always jointly applicable and the same remedies are not automatically granted for the same injury. Instead, the court or jury fashions the appropriate relief for each individual case from these two basic remedies, and there are infinite possibilities.

1. Damages

The term "damages" refers to a sum of money awarded to the person harmed by another's tortious conduct. Damages intended to compensate a tort victim are "compensatory damages." Sometimes the actual injury is so slight that a tort victim is only entitled to nominal damages. "Nominal damages" are a trivial sum of money, such as one dollar, awarded against a wrongdoer whose tortious conduct has caused no harm or insignificant injury. *See* Restatement, Second, Torts §§ 901–07 (1979). However, when a significant injury has been sustained, compensatory damages may be awarded, and these can be substantial.

Compensatory damages include the value of any property injured or destroyed by the tortious act. The more valuable the property and extensive the injury, the greater the damages. Compensatory damages also include an award of money for personal injury or death. Damages in injury or death cases vary according to the extent of harm. The more permanent and disabling the injury, the greater the compensation due the victim or his family. It would, however, be incorrect to assume that death is the most costly injury of all.

Various elements of compensatory damages are applied to personal injury or wrongful death cases, and these elements largely dictate the size of the damage award. When the tort victim dies, some states permit his or her heirs to recover only for their pecuniary loss. "Pecuniary loss" is the financial support lost as a result of the victim's death. A widow's pecuniary loss would be the husband's earnings for the remainder of his life. The children would be entitled to the financial support their father would have provided them had he lived. If the victim died without children or a spouse, his or her parents or other relatives may be able to sue, but again, only for their pecuniary loss. In other words, relatives are entitled only to the financial support the decedent would have given them throughout the course of his or her life. Unless a wrongful death or survivor statute allows recovery for grief, sorrow or other emotional harm suffered as consequence of a loved one's death, no recovery can be had for those particular elements, nor can suit be brought on the victim's behalf for the death itself.

If the deceased person is a professional athlete with great earning potential and leaves a widow with young children, the compensatory damages for his wrongful death could be great. Many times, however, the person killed in a sports accident will be a young, unmarried, nonprofessional athlete. These factors will greatly reduce the legal liability of those responsible. Although it may appear callous and bordering on the macabre, from a tortfeasor's perspective, the younger the victim the better; the law usually permits less compensatory damages for the death of a child.

While the law may not appear to place much value on a young person's life, the same is not true for nonfatal injuries to young people. The most costly compensatory damage cases will typically involve a severely injured child. This difference in valuation between children's death and injury cases is caused by the additional elements of damages permitted in personal injury actions.

A person injured by another's tortious conduct is entitled to recover his or her pecuniary losses. These damages include not only income already lost due to disabling injuries, but wages which will be lost throughout the remainder of the victim's working life if the disability is permanent. Furthermore, the injured person is entitled to compensation for all medical expenses which he or she has or will incur as a result of the injuries. The injured person is also compensated for any pain, suffering, mental anguish and loss of the ability to enjoy life that results from the injuries.

Since the elements of damages in personal injury actions are measured over the remainder of the victim's life, the younger the person and more serious the injury, the greater will be the lost wages, medical expenses, pain, suffering, mental anguish and loss of the ability to enjoy life. Because of the numbers of young participants and the great potential for serious bodily harm, sports and recreational activities will always be a source of substantial compensatory damage awards. *See, e.g., Pell v. Victor J. Andrew High School*, 123 Ill.App.2d 423, 78 Ill.Dec. 738, 462 N.E.2d 858 (1984) (award of $3.4 million in compensatory damages to a high school gymnast who suffered a severed spine and paralysis as a result of a mini-trampoline accident).

In addition to nominal and compensatory damages, a tort victim may be entitled to an award of punitive damages. "Punitive damages" do not compensate the injured party, but are added to compensatory or nominal damages. The purpose of awarding this extra money is to punish the tort-feasor and to deter that tort-feasor and others from engaging in similar conduct. *See* Restatement, Second, Torts § 908 (1979). Punitive damages are also known as exemplary damages. They are never authorized for mere mistakes, carelessness, or similar errors in judgment constituting ordinary negligence. Instead, punitive damages are reserved for tort-feasors who act with intent to injure or with a reckless indifference to the rights of others.

If the tort-feasor has committed an intentional tort, or otherwise acted with a reckless or wanton disregard for the safety of others, exemplary damages may be awarded in addition to substantial compensatory damages. Punitive damages are even awarded when the tort victim has suffered no significant harm, as long as the tort-feasor acted in a deliberate, reckless, or wanton manner. *See* Restatement, Second, Torts § 908 comment c (1979). Punitive damages may be awarded against the employer for the actions of an employee if: (1) the employer either authorized or approved the injury producing act; (2) the employee was acting in a managerial capacity and within the scope of the employment when he or she committed the tort; or (3) the employer was reckless in hiring or retaining an unfit employee. *See id.* § 909.

In determining the amount of exemplary damages, if any, to award in a particular case, the court or jury considers not only the nature of defendant's conduct and the degree of harm caused, but an award of punitive damages can be based on the defendant's wealth. If the purposes of exemplary damages is to punish and deter the wrongdoer, then it is necessary to know the wealth of the tort-feasor. For example, an award of $10,000 in punitive damages could be crushing to one defendant, while ten times that amount might be insignificant to another defendant. Serious injuries and a wealthy defendant frequently combine to expose manufacturers of athletic equipment to large exemplary damage awards when they act with a callous or reckless indifference for the safety of others. *See, e.g., Rawlings Sporting Goods Co. v. Daniels,* 619 S.W.2d 435 (Tex.Civ.App.1981) (awarding brain injured high school football player $750,000 in compensatory damages and $750,000 in exemplary damages against football helmet manufacturer for its failure to warn about helmet's inability to prevent head and brain injuries).

2. *Injunctions*

An injunction is a court order for one of the parties to a law suit to behave in a certain manner. Failure to comply with that order can be punished as contempt of court. Injunctive relief is designed to prevent future wrongs, not to punish past acts. Past wrongs are compensated by an award of damages, while future harm may be prevented by a court order enjoining the other party from engaging in the harmful conduct.

The order can require the defendant to perform a particular act or to refrain from performing a harmful act. Injunctions are either temporary or indefinite in duration. Temporary orders are traditionally issued during the course of a trial to preserve the status quo until the rights of all the litigants can be determined. After the court has made a final decision, it may then enter a permanent injunction. Permanent injunctions usually continue in effect until removed by order of the issuing court or some higher authority.

Injunctive relief is an extraordinary remedy. It is only used to prevent an irreparable injury. Irreparable injury is suffered when monetary damages cannot be calculated with a reasonable degree of certainty or when money will not adequately compensate the injured party. An injury is most likely to be considered irreparable when it involves the risk of physical harm and death, the loss of some special opportunity, or the deprivation of unique, irreplaceable property.

Their limited application notwithstanding, injunctions can order athletic associations, colleges, school athletic directors, coaches, and other institutions or individuals to declare an otherwise ineligible athlete eligible. This technique was discussed in considerable detail in chapter 4 *supra*, and is a common means of circumventing eligibility rules. The court cannot order that an athlete participate. This discretionary decision is vested in the coach. But if a coach abuses his or her discretion by not playing a superior athlete, the coach may be guilty of contempt of court and punished accordingly.

An injunction may be used to reinstate a fired or suspended coach, teacher or other employee. A professional athlete may be enjoined from playing for another team if doing so would violate a contractual or other duty owed to another organization. *See, e.g., Philadelphia Ball Club v. Lajoie*, 202 Pa. 210, 51 A. 973 (1902) (order prohibiting outstanding second baseman and rival of Ty Cobb from playing for another team during pendency of his contract with Philadelphia). An injunction cannot, however, be used to compel one person to work for another. Courts have even enjoined an activity or use of a recreational facility. *See, e.g., Easterly v. Carr*, 361 So.2d 279 (La.App.1978) (neighbor's complaints of excessive noise and dust resulted in enjoining motorcycle racing on adjoining property); *Sans v. Ramsey Golf and Country Club, Inc.*, 29 N.J. 438, 149 A.2d 599 (1959) (order prohibiting country club from using certain golf tees because balls struck from these tees endangered nearby residents).

7.3 LIMITATIONS ON TORT LIABILITY

When a tort has been committed and a grievous injury incurred, the injured party may have no recourse under the law because of the various immunities or limitations upon liability that certain defendants enjoy. Immunities are different from defenses. A defense justifies or excuses what would otherwise be a tortious wrong. Immunities and limitations on liability do not justify the wrongful conduct; they simply deprive the injured party of the right to sue.

Historically, immunities and limitations upon liability were broader in scope and favored by both the courts and state legislatures, but this is no longer the case. In recent years limitations on liability have come under frequent attack and are no longer approved of nor readily accepted. Legislatures and courts in many states have abrogated some of the more traditional limitations on liability, and severely restricted the application of others. Yet this abandonment or retrenchment of exemptions from tort liability is nowhere near complete, nor is it unanimous. While some states may reject a particular immunity or limit it in scope, other jurisdictions approve of the doctrine. Depending upon the jurisdiction, many of the limitations on tort liability discussed in this section may not only exist, but they may completely bar a tort victim's right to recover for his or her injuries.

A. Charitable Immunity

For many years American courts held that charitable organizations were immune from tort liability. Charitable institutions were immune for a variety of reasons: (1) donations to charities might decrease if they were held liable; (2) those receiving the benefit of charities should not be allowed to sue the charity for injuries caused by them; (3) *respondeat superior* did not apply to charitable institutions; and (4) holding a charity liable in tort would divert donated trust funds to a purpose for which they were not given. The policy reasons for charitable immunity are less persuasive to modern courts. Today most states have rejected *total* immunity for charities by either abrogating the doctrine or by recognizing exceptions which permit certain tort victims, but not others, to sue. *See* W. Keeton & W. Prosser, *The Law of Torts* § 133 (5th ed. 1984).

Although it is currently in disfavor with many courts, charitable immunity is not an extinct legal concept, nor is it likely to become extinct in the very near future. *See e.g., Pomeroy v. Little League Baseball of Collingswood,* 142 N.J.Super. 471, 362 A.2d 39 (1976) (spectator injured when bleachers collapsed during baseball game could not maintain suit against local Little League Association because of that organization's charitable work). To the extent charitable immunity remains a viable doctrine in a particular state, it will apply to the Little League, Y.M.C.A., Y.W.C.A., Boy Scouts, and any other nonprofit corporation, society, or association organized exclusively for religious, charitable, educational, or hospital purposes. However, even if charitable immunity exists, it is not automatically applied to every case involving a charitable organization. The doctrine will not bar suit when the injured person is not a beneficiary of the charity's work, such as a stranger or passerby. Employees of a charitable institution are sometimes permitted to sue for injuries not otherwise covered by workmen's compensation. (*See infra* chapter 8 for a general discussion of employer liability under state workmen's compensation statutes.) A charity may also be held accountable for its own negligence because the doctrine of charitable immunity affords protection only from vicarious liability for torts of organizations, agents, and employees. *See, e.g., Young Men's Christian Association of Metropolitan Atlanta v. Bailey,* 107 Ga.App. 417, 130 S.E.2d 242 (1963) (being negligent in providing an insufficient number of life guards at its swimming pool in which a child drowned, or giving the lifeguards inadequate instructions on the performance of their duties, constituted original negligence of the Y.M.C.A. which was beyond the scope of charitable immunity). Finally, charitable immunity is often denied to those organizations operating public swimming pools, race tracks, or engaged in other activities open to the general public and to which an admission fee is charged. *See, e.g., Langheim v. Denison Fire Department Swimming Pool Association,* 237 Iowa 386, 21 N.W.2d 295 (1946) (because it charged an admission fee, nonprofit organization which operated a public swimming pool was not entitled to the exemption from liability provided by charitable immunity).

B. Governmental Immunity

Also known as sovereign immunity, governmental immunity from tort liability shields federal, state, and local governmental entities in certain instances. Simply put, governmental immunity means that unless the federal, state, or local government has consented to be sued for tort liability, it is immune. This immunity may extend to governmental agencies as well as political subdivisions. It protects public school boards, school districts, state colleges and universities, and other instrumentalities of the government. Sovereign immunity even extends to Indian tribes.

Sovereign immunity will not always protect athletic associations, leagues, or their officers even though they regulate the sports activities of public schools. *See, e.g., Coughlon v. Iowa High School Athletic Association,* 260 Iowa 702, 150 N.W.2d 660 (1967) (immunity not granted to state high school athletic association and its officers in suit by a spectator injured when bleachers collapsed at a basketball tournament). Nor will governmental immunity serve as an absolute shield for a coach, school administrator, or other employee responsible for the tort. If the public officer or employee is carrying out a discretionary rather than a purely ministerial function, governmental immunity may be accorded for the discretionary acts. *See* Restatement, Second, Torts § 895D (1979). Discretionary acts often involve policy decisions at an upper management level. In contrast, decisions that create direct personal risks to others and involve ordinary safety considerations are usually ministerial. These ministerial acts are not immune. *See* W. Keeton & W. Prosser, *The Law of Torts* § 1060 (5th ed. 1984). Because they do not function at a policy-making level, public school coaches, teachers and other athletic personnel do not often qualify for the sovereign immunity enjoyed by their employers.

Governmental immunity has been the subject of much criticism by lawyers, courts and other commentators, but remains a viable doctrine in most jurisdictions. Hence, the first step for anyone injured in a sporting activity sponsored, supervised, or controlled by a governmental entity is to determine the status of sovereign immunity in that jurisdiction. If the doctrine exists, it may shield not only the entity, but negligent employees as well, thereby foreclosing any possibility of compensation for the injured party.

Some state courts have abrogated or restricted sovereign immunity. A common method of doing away with governmental immunity is limiting the doctrine to governmental functions. Governmental functions are those acts and services that only the government can provide. Fire and police protection, education of children, and other programs for the protection of property, public health, and safety are typical governmental functions. These are activities done for the common good. The government is immune from tort liability for any harm done in carrying out its governmental functions, but it is not immune from tort liability for injuries caused while performing a proprietary function.

Proprietary functions are the services a state or local government provides which are commonly performed by profit making businesses. Proprietary activities include the operation of government-owned utilities such as power and water, community swimming pools, stadiums and arenas for which admission and other fees are charged. In providing these services and collecting a fee the government is behaving very much like a private enterprise. Since private businesses are not immune from tort liability for injuries they cause, the government should not be immune when performing proprietary services.

This proprietary-governmental distinction has been a popular tactic for curtailing the immunity from tort liability claimed by city and local governments. Yet the common means of abolishing governmental immunity for state and federal governments is by consent, which is achieved by the passage of legislation known as tort claims acts. Tort claims statutes specify the conditions under which the United States or a state government gives up its sovereign immunity. These laws frequently contain procedural and substantive provisions to which the injured party must strict- ly adhere before immunity is waived, and anything less than total compliance may result in a denial of the claim.

C. Federal Tort Claims Act

With the enactment of the Federal Tort Claims Act, 28 U.S.C. § 1346(b) (1982), Congress gave its permission for the United States to be sued in federal district courts for loss of property, personal injury or death caused by the negligent or wrongful acts of government employees. Some express exceptions to the waiver of sovereign immunity still exist, however, and when these excep- tions apply the original absolute immunity remains intact. The United States is not, for example, liable for punitive damages, nor has it waived sovereign immunity for intentional torts. *See* 28 U.S.C. §§ 2674, 2680(h) (1982). The federal government is likewise immune from suit based upon the acts or omissions of an employee who carries out a duty imposed by statute or regulation, or performs a discretionary duty. *See id.* at § 2680(a) (1982). Yet perhaps the most significant hurdle to recovery posed by the federal tort claims law is a requirement that the injured person's claim be submitted to the appropriate federal agency before a suit can commence.

The claim must be in writing, state the facts upon which the federal government's tort liability is based, and contain a demand for a specified amount of damages for the property loss, personal injury, or other harm incurred. *See id.* at § 2675 (1982). Failure to include the demand for money damages deprives the claimant of the right to bring suit if the claim is denied. If a suit is brought, the injured party cannot recover more than the sum demanded in the administrative claim.

The administrative claim must be filed within two years of the time it accrued. A tort claim normally accrues when the injury is incurred. Failure to submit a claim within two years from date of injury bars a tort action against the federal government. If a claim is filed, the agency has six months within which to accept or deny it. If accepted, the damages are paid and the matter is amicably resolved. A denial of the claim entitles the injured party to commence suit against the federal government. The tort action must be brought within six months of the agency's denial of the claim or the case will be dismissed. *See* 28 U.S.C. §§ 2401, 2675 (1982).

A person with a claim against the United States government must strictly comply with notice and related requirements of the Federal Tort Claims Act. These requirements also apply to children. It is therefore necessary that the parents or guardians of any child with a potential claim against the United States preserve that child's right to sue by timely compliance with the federal tort claims statute. *See Smith v. United States*, 588 F.2d 1209 (8th Cir.1978) (child's claim against United States not tolled by his minority).

D. State Tort Claims Acts

Many states have consented to be sued in tort through passage of their own tort claims statute. These state laws are often patterned after the federal act and contain exceptions for intentional torts and the exercise of discretion on behalf of state or local governmental agencies and their employees. State tort claims laws typically limit governmental exposure by placing a ceiling on liability. The government's liability is limited to a certain dollar maximum above which the injured person cannot recover. Some state acts do, however, permit the injured party to recover more than the statutory limits when the excess is covered by insurance.

State tort claims laws often have strict notice and time requirements. Failure to comply with these will bar the action, and again exceptions are normally not made for children. State tort claims statutes generally have a much shorter filing time than that for the federal law, often six months or less. Those persons with tort claims against public schools, state colleges and universities, or other state agencies, must be especially diligent in preserving their right to sue by filing a proper and timely claim. Moreover, even if a tort claim is timely filed and rejected, the law suit must be commenced before the appropriate statute of limitation has expired.

E. Statute of Limitation

State legislatures often prescribe the time period within which a law suit can be brought. These time periods are referred to as a "statute of limitation." Statutes of limitation vary from state to state, and even within states, depending upon the nature of the claim. Breach of contract claims will have to be brought within a prescribed time, and other time limits are set for tort actions. Regardless of the actual time limit, all statutes of limitation have one thing in common: a law suit must be commenced before the time limit has expired. Failure to bring a law suit before the statute of limitation has expired will completely bar a tort action if the defendant promptly raises the statute as a defense, but this defense is waived if not asserted in a timely manner.

A statute of limitation usually begins to run for an adult when the injury is incurred, even though with some injuries the time does not commence until it is discovered. Insane or mentally incompetent individuals may be given additional time within which to commence an action, and a majority of states suspend or toll statutes of limitation for minors. The time limit for suing may not begin to run on a child's cause of action until he or she reaches the age of majority, but the same is not true for the child's parents. Any claim parents may have for their child's injury is immediately subject to the statute of limitation; it is not tolled until the child attains the age of majority. The parents' right to sue may therefore expire years before the child's.

F. Statute of Repose

Products liability laws have been enacted by a number of states. These laws reduce or limit the right of one injured by a defective product to sue the people who made or marketed it. This infringement upon the injured party's right to sue purportedly advances the public interest by encouraging manufacturers, wholesalers, and retailers of certain necessary products to remain in business. *See, e.g.,* N.D.Cent.Code § 28–01.1–01 (Supp.1985) (articulating similar legislative intent for North Dakota's Product Liability Act).

These laws are particularly significant to the manufacturers of athletic equipment. Athletic equipment can be extremely durable while at the same time, defective and dangerous. Dangerously defective equipment is capable of producing injury or death as long as it is in use. This longevity exposes those manufacturing or selling such equipment to liability for injuries incurred in the very distant future. Statutes of repose lay this potential liability to rest by providing that no recovery can be obtained for injuries incurred more than a certain number of years after the product was manufactured or initially sold.

Statutes of repose are similar to statutes of limitation, but rather than fixing a time period in which a tort action must be brought, these laws fix a time period within which the injury must occur. If the harm is not incurred within the designated time period, no action may be brought nor is recovery possible. These laws apply to tort as well as implied warranty theories, and some even go so far as to allow the injured party to sue only the manufacturer.

G. Interspousal Immunity

The common law doctrine of interspousal tort immunity precludes tort actions between husband and wife. Numerous public policies have been suggested to support interspousal tort immunity. Some courts stress the need to preserve marital harmony and assert that without interspousal immunity, tort actions between husband and wife will further divide and eventually destroy many marriages. Still other jurisdictions suggest prevention of fraud as the main rationale for immunity. These courts theorize that without interspousal tort immunity, couples will fabricate claims and suppress evidence to collect from their insurance company; although the husband or wife is being sued, the real target is the family liability insurance carrier.

Interspousal tort immunity has been rejected in a number of states, but still remains the law in others. Where it does exist, spousal immunity tends to be restricted to negligence cases. The doctrine is not favored in intentional tort actions, nor are the parties likely to proceed under an intentional tort theory when insurance is involved. Most home owner's insurance policies do not cover intentional torts, and by proceeding under an intentional tort theory the couple loses coverage.

There are other exceptions to the doctrine which may or may not be followed by a jurisdiction recognizing general spousal immunity. These exceptions exist because of the absence of public policy support in a particular case. Since the main purpose of spousal immunity is to preserve marital bliss, there is no reason to apply the doctrine when one of the parties has died, or if the husband and wife are separated or divorced by the time the tort suit is commenced. Interspousal immunity has likewise not been applied to torts committed prior to marriage, nor to law suits involving injuries incurred in motor vehicle accidents. Suits are ironically permitted in motor vehicle cases because insurance exists; marital harmony is not threatened since an insurance company is the real defendant.

H. Parental Immunity

A majority of states prohibit tort actions between a parent and an unemancipated child. Known as "parental immunity," this doctrine is justified by public policy arguments similar to those advanced in support of interspousal tort immunity; fostering familial harmony and preventing fraudulent or collusive law suits when the parents are covered by liability insurance. A few courts even base their support for parental immunity upon the parents' right to care for, control and discipline their children.

Immunity is most often applied when the child's injury occurred as a result of ordinary negligence involving either an exercise of parental authority, or an exercise of ordinary parental discretion with respect to the provision of food, clothing, housing, medical and dental services, and other care. Parental immunity can have widespread application in sports injury cases because of the degree of parental discretion and control involved. Permitting a child to participate in a sports activity and providing the necessary athletic equipment and supervision are proper parental concerns. In exercising discretion on these matters, a parent will normally enjoy immunity. *See, e.g., McCallister v. Sun Valley Pools, Inc.*, 100 Mich.App. 131, 298 N.W.2d 687 (1980) (failure to maintain swimming pool in a safe condition and to properly supervise child involved an exercise of reasonable parental control and discretion which barred their paralyzed son's tort action).

As with interspousal immunity, courts are reluctant to apply parental immunity when it no longer furthers a legitimate public policy. The doctrine has no application to willful, malicious or intentional wrongs or when the parents have abandoned their parental responsibilities. Neither will the doctrine shield parents when the child reaches the age of majority or is otherwise emancipated. Courts have likewise refused to recognize parental immunity when the parent-child relationship has been terminated by death, or when there has been a loss of custody and control over the minor.

I. Disclaimers, Exculpatory Agreements, and Releases

"Disclaimers" are a disavowance of responsibility, usually for some future injury to another. Disclaimers can be oral, a simple statement that one will not be responsible for someone else's safety, or written, as in the case of the carefully drafted documents supplied by the manufacturers of athletic equipment. A properly worded disclaimer may effectively eliminate a manufacturer's liability for breach of warranty (*see infra* § 7.10C–3), but disclaimers will not always eliminate or limit tort liability.

One who expressly agrees to accept a risk of harm arising from another's conduct enters into an "exculpatory agreement," which may be enforceable against that individual. These agreements ordinarily take the form of a contract, but they can also be noncontractual. Signs warning ball park patrons that if they sit in a certain section they do so at their own risk, or that stadium parking is at automobile owner's risk are frequently encountered examples of noncontractual exculpatory agreements; the agreement is reached when the patron parks or sits in the section referred to in the signs or warnings. An exculpatory agreement may be broad in scope, relieving one of all responsibility for the safety of another, or it may be narrowly drafted covering only specific risk such as theft.

Exculpatory agreements are not favored by courts. If an agreement is ambiguous or covers a definite time, place, or risk, it will not be interpreted to absolve a tort-feasor of liability for harm caused at another time and place, or in a different manner. Exculpatory agreements are usually not enforced against persons not a party to them. For example, the wife of spectator injured by a foul ball would not be precluded from suing because of warning on her husband's ticket. Nor are the agreements likely to be effective against children. Minors may always rescind or disaffirm any exculpatory agreement they execute, and courts are not inclined to permit parents to assume risks for their child. *See, e.g., Santangelo v. City of New York,* 66 A.D.2d 880, 411 N.Y.S.2d 66 (1978) (waiver of liability signed by parent did not deprive son of right to sue for injuries sustained during ice hockey clinic).

Disparity in bargaining power is the reason commonly given for invalidating liability waivers contained in parental consent forms. When schools, athletic clubs, or organizations require that parents sign a waiver of liability as a precondition for their child's participation, the parent is saddled with an unfair burden. A parent may refuse to sign a waiver and deprive the child of participation, or the parent may execute the liability waiver. No other options are available to either the parent or the child under these circumstances, and courts are inclined to view these agreements as contrary to public policy. *See, e.g., Fedor v. Mauwehu Council, Boy Scouts of America, Inc.,* 21 Conn.Supp. 38, 143 A.2d 466 (1958) (waiver declared contrary to public policy insofar as it purported to free defendant from liability for its own negligence).

Exculpatory agreements that contravene public policy are not enforceable. It is against public policy to allow a waiver of liability for intentional or reckless misconduct, because to do so would foster such behavior. It is likewise against public policy to enforce liability waivers between an employee and employer, because these are likely to be coerced. For similar reasons, bus companies, airlines, motels, and others providing services to the public may not relieve themselves of their responsibility to patrons by contract or agreement. *See* Restatement, Second, Torts § 496B (1965).

Exculpatory agreements are usually enforced when signed by adult participants in athletic events. The more dangerous the activity and higher level of skill required, the less reluctant courts are in permitting a participant to waive his or her right to recover for injuries. *See, e.g., Garretson v. United States,* 456 F.2d 1017 (9th Cir.1972) (waiver signed by ski-jumping contestant barred his suit for injuries allegedly caused by negligence of event promoters and owners of contest site). Courts, however, seem hesitant to enforce similar waivers against spectators and members of athletic clubs when they are not signed, when the waiver is so inconspicuous that the party was not aware of it, or when the language did not clearly indicate what rights were being relinquished.

A "release" is the surrender of the right to sue, usually given in return for the payment of money or other consideration. It is a means whereby an existing tort claim can be resolved without resorting to a court of law. Releases are similar to exculpatory agreements in that they are both consensual attempts to absolve a party of tort liability, but they differ in one material sense. Releases are negotiated and entered into *after* the tort has been committed, while exculpatory agreements are entered into *before* commission of the tort.

Releases are often negotiated between a tort-feasor's insurance carrier and the injured person. The usual release will explicitly extend to "all known and unknown, foreseen and unforeseen injuries and the consequences thereof," and once signed and delivered it will effectively bar any additional recovery. Releases are final even if the injuries later turn out to be more serious and extensive than the tort victim originally thought. Of course, if the release was the product of a mutual mistake or was obtained by fraud on the part of the insurance company, a court can set it aside and allow the injured party to sue. Some states have even passed laws giving an injured party the absolute right to rescind a release if rescission takes place within a designated time period. Absent such statutory authorization, however, it is difficult to vacate a release. Since sports and recreational injuries may initially seem insignificant but later prove quite disabling, quick settlement with the tort-feasor's insurance carrier is not always wise. *See e.g., Hendricks v. Simper,* 24 Ariz.App. 415, 539 P.2d 529 (1975) (upholding $2,500 settlement for personal injuries sustained in fall from a horse, and refusing to set aside release despite plaintiff's contentions that injuries and treatment costs turned out to be much greater than initially anticipated).

Persons who obtain releases for a child's tort claim or the claim of a mentally impaired adult should exercise caution. Not only must the settlement and release be effected by a lawful guardian or conservator, but it is wise to have the entire agreement approved by the court. Tort victims must also be aware of the danger of releasing one of a number of co-tort-feasors. The general release of one tort-feasor may release all other tort-feasors who are jointly responsible for the wrong.

J. Workmen's Compensation

Among the more significant limitations on tort liability is the protection accorded an employer under workmen's compensation law. If the injured person is an employee and the employer belongs to a state workmen's compensation insurance plan, under most circumstances the employer is immune from tort liability for the employee's job related injuries. Athletes as well as coaches may be subject to workmen's compensation immunity. A more thorough discussion of this subject and workmen's compensation in general is found in chapter 8 *infra*.

§ 7.4 LIABILITY OF COACHES AND ATHLETIC PERSONNEL

Coaches, teachers and sports instructors are not insurers of the safety of those under their control, nor are they strictly liable for injuries caused to others by the athletes they supervise. A basis for liability must exist before a coach or teacher is charged with responsibility for injuries to a participant or spectator. Some accidents are unavoidable and although they may have tragic consequences, no one is to blame. Yet because coaches and teachers have the most control over the injury producing activity, any fault that exists is likely to be theirs.

A. Injury to a Participant

The term "participant" includes not only those individuals directly involved in an athletic contest or event, but also includes referees, umpires, and other officials involved in the game. The team physician in attendance is a participant as is a life guard at a municipal pool. A participant is thus anyone who is either directly or indirectly involved in an athletic or recreational sports activity. Spectators, however, are not participants but merely observers. A coach or sports instructor's liability for injuries to spectators is addressed *infra* at § 7.4B.

The level of care that a coach or sports instructor owes to athletes and other participants will vary from activity to activity, but the standard by which that care is measured will always be the same: a coach must use reasonable care to avoid the creating a foreseeable risk of harm to others. Whether care is reasonable depends upon the circumstances surrounding that particular activity.

Greater care must be exercised if the participant is required to come in contact with an inherently dangerous object, or to engage in an activity likely to produce injury. Personnel supervising children or the handicapped must employ a higher degree of care than the coach of a professional team. The level of care required will vary according to the skill and experience of the participant. A world class athlete may need less supervision than a beginner.

A coach or instructor who fails to exercise the requisite degree of care is negligent. Negligence by a teacher or coach may sometimes be referred to as malpractice. Negligence can consist of either doing an act that should not have been done, or in failing to do an act that should have been done.

In determining whether a coach has been negligent, some states apply the "locality rule." The locality rule requires that a coach be held to the standard of reasonable skill and care exercised by other coaches in that same locality. In other words, the coach's actions are judged by a local rather than a state or national standard. The locality rule originated at a time when it was not reasonable to expect a rural professional to have access to centers of learning and the latest information. Today's professional organizations, clinics, and sports magazines make the exchange of coaching ideas and techniques so widespread that there may no longer be a legitimate reason for applying the locality rule.

Some states have rejected the locality rule. Other jurisdictions have simply modified it to permit a coach's conduct to be judged by the standard of care observed in similar localities. Existence of the locality rule, however, will not generally affect the outcome of a sports injury negligence case because the standard of care for a professional or college coach is set at a national level. The same is true for instructors at health clubs and resorts that are either located in urban areas or draw their clientele from beyond the nearby community. Even the high school coach will have difficulty limiting the locale to anything less than the league to which the coach's school belongs, including schools from other communities. In some cases a coach's actions are so deficient that he or she would be considered negligent by any community's standards.

1. Failure to Provide Competent Personnel

Supervision is the primary responsibility of a coach or athletic instructor. A coach has the duty to instruct and warn athletes of any hidden dangers which the coach either knows or in the exercise of reasonable care should know are present in a sports activity. A coach must instruct pupils in methods which will safeguard them from these dangers. A coach will often delegate these duties to an assistant, but delegation does not relieve the coach of the ultimate responsibility for proper supervision. If the coach hires incompetent assistants, the coach will be considered negligent, as will the school administration for hiring an incompetent coach.

A coach may be negligent in failing to supervise and instruct assistants in carrying out their duties. Even if the coach or supervising instructor was not personally negligent in the hiring and training of assistants, vicariously liable may still exist for an assistant coach's negligence under the doctrine of *respondeat superior*. *See supra* § 7.2D. Both the coach and the negligent assistant are responsible for any harm caused. Of course, if the assistant is not negligent, neither the assistant nor the coach is liable.

Coaches and teachers are not insurers of their students' safety even when supervising the very young. While more care will undoubtedly be required for the younger more inexperienced pupil, if that level of care is provided, the coach or instructor is not negligent.

2. *Failure to Provide Instruction*

The duty to instruct is undoubtedly one of the broadest responsibilities placed upon coaches and teachers. Injuries are inherent in contact sports, and no one expects a football or hockey coach to prevent them. Neither is it the responsibility of an instructor or coach in a noncontact sport to prevent all injuries. It is, however, the coach's function to minimize the possibility that participation will result in serious injury. A coach does this through the instruction given the athletes and students.

The duty to instruct includes the duty to teach the fundamentals of the game. This means not only that the athletes must be taught the skills necessary to make the team, but also that they be instructed about how to reduce the possibility of injury to themselves and other participants. This duty to instruct requires the coach to properly advise athletes on the selection and use of proper equipment to minimize injury.

Since participant safety is one of the purposes for rules, athletes should be taught the rules of the game. Conditioning is another aspect of the duty to instruct. It is the coach's responsibility to see that students are in sufficient physical condition to receive the lumps, bruises, and other rough treatment they encounter in actual competition.

The coach or teacher who fails in the duty to instruct is negligent. But when the coach or teacher has used reasonable care to instruct students, neither the coach nor the employer is legally responsible for the injuries sustained by a student during the course of an athletic event. *See, e.g., Vendrell v. School District No. 26C, Malheur County*, 233 Ore. 1, 376 P.2d 406 (1962) (although high school football player became a permanent paraplegic as a result of being injured during a game, the coach and school district were absolved of liability because the athlete had been properly instructed and conditioned for playing the game).

3. *Failure to Provide Proper Equipment*

The school, team, owner, or sponsoring organization ordinarily has a duty to provide proper equipment. The coach shares some responsibility for the equipment. If the coach is given the responsibility of selecting the equipment to be purchased either by the team or parent, more than ordinary care must be used to choose equipment that is not dangerous for its intended use. *See, e.g., Everett v. Bucky Warren, Inc.*, 376 Mass. 280, 380 N.E.2d 653 (1978) (because of superior knowledge and experience, hockey coach was negligent in ordering dangerously defective helmets). This does not mean that the coach must personally purchase the necessary equipment when the school or parent refuses to do so. But the coach's responsibility goes much further than merely requesting particular equipment. If the proper equipment is not provided, it may be necessary for the coach to forbid a particular student's participation, or perhaps cancel a game.

A coach must similarly use reasonable care to instruct athletes on the use of athletic equipment, and to see that they follow instructions. It may be necessary to establish a procedure for inspecting equipment for damage or replacement. Even when good equipment is purchased, the coach should exercise reasonable care to see that it is maintained in a safe and suitable condition.

4. *Failure to Warn*

Closely akin to a coach's duty to instruct, is the obligation to warn. Coaches and sports instructors have a duty to warn students of any dangers that are known to them or should have been discovered in the exercise of reasonable care. This duty to warn extends only to those dangers that are not obvious. A coach has no duty to warn pupils of dangers which the pupils are aware of, or those a reasonable person would have known existed. This duty to warn applies not only to dangers associated with the use of equipment and athletic facilities, but also includes dangers involved in a particular sports activity or technique.

The obligation to warn is especially important when the instructor is working with children or the mentally handicapped. Dangers that might be obvious to a normal adult may not be discovered by a child or handicapped person. Even if discovered, it is not reasonable to expect the young or mentally impaired athlete to appreciate a dangerous condition. Coaches and instructors working with children and handicapped people are thus required to exercise a higher degree of care in the matter of warnings. It may not only be necessary to advise these students of the most obvious dangers, but coaches supervising children and the handicapped should also make reasonable efforts to see that their warnings are obeyed.

5. *Failure to Supervise*

Another fundamental obligation placed upon a sports instructor is the duty to supervise. Coaches and instructors must exercise reasonable supervision over their pupils commensurate with the age and experience of the students and the nature of the activity. A greater degree of care, therefore, must be exercised in supervising young children or the unskilled as opposed to mature, experienced athletes. The law requires additional supervision if the student will come in contact with an inherently dangerous object or engage in an activity that is likely to produce an accident or injury.

The duty to supervise may include observing and controlling both participants and spectators. Examples of negligent supervision range from leaving children unattended in a swimming pool to allowing spectators to encroach upon the playing field where they pose a danger to both themselves and the athletes. A coach has to use reasonable care in supervising athletic activities to avoid the unreasonable risk of harm to students and others associated with the event. When a coach exercises this level of care, no negligence exists.

A failure to properly supervise will not automatically result in liability for the coach. If the injury could not have been reasonably anticipated or prevented by reasonable care in supervising the event, the coach is not liable. However, when children are involved, the coach may be required to anticipate or guard against a greater range of dangers, including the misconduct of others. *See, e.g., Dailey v. Los Angeles Unified School District*, 2 Cal.3d 741, 470 P.2d 360, 87 Cal.Rptr. 376 (1970) (lack of supervision may have been a proximate cause for death of a 16 year old injured in an unauthorized "slap fight" with fellow gym student).

6. *Moving or Improperly Treating Injured Athlete*

Part of a coach or instructor's duties is providing medical care to an injured participant. The duty to provide medical care raises several questions. When is medical treatment required? What medical care is required? Who should provide it?

It is not necessary that the coach understand what is wrong with an athlete for the coach to be negligent in not providing proper medical care. If a reasonable person would have recognized the need for immediate medical attention, then the coach who does not do so is negligent. In *Mogabgab v. Orleans Parish School Board*, 239 So.2d 456 (La.App.1970), a high school football coach was found negligent for failing to provide prompt medical assistance to an athlete who collapsed and subsequently died of heat stroke. The coach was negligent because he waited over two hours following the first appearance of heat stroke symptoms before summoning medical aid. A coach may likewise be held liable for injuries caused when he or she moves an injured athlete, when the coach provides medical treatment in a negligent manner, or when he or she permits a seriously injured player to participate.

Coaches and sports instructors are not required to act as physicians. The law requires only that they act with reasonable care under the circumstances. Of course, a coach may or possibly should have sufficient first aid training or experience with injuries to be held to a higher standard of care than that of the average person. But even under this higher standard, the care required is that of a reasonable person with similar skills and training, a level of care far lower than that required of medical personnel.

A coach can often meet this duty by removing the injured athlete from competition, and directing the athlete to seek medical treatment. If the athlete is a child, the coach should also advise the parents of the injury and the need to see a physician. Sometimes the coach may be required to render temporary first aid until a doctor arrives. If so, the first aid must be given in a nonnegligent manner. A coach may also be liable for rendering unnecessary medical aid. *See Guerrieri v. Tyson,* 147 Pa.Super. 239, 24 A.2d 468 (1942) (teacher who immersed 10 year old pupil's hand with infected finger in scalding water when no medical emergency existed was found liable for damages).

A more difficult question concerns the coach's duty to arrange for medical treatment. In an emergency situation, it may be necessary for the coach to not only contact a physician and ambulance, but to pay for these emergency services. Most states, however, have laws entitling the coach to reimbursement from the athlete or the parents of a minor athlete.

A coach will not be required to pay for a doctor in attendance at an athletic event. This duty is usually imposed upon the school district or sponsoring organization. But the coach may be negligent in allowing the event to take place in the absence of a physician.

7. Selecting Participants

The ultimate decision as to who participates lies with the coach, but the coach must exercise discretion in a nonnegligent manner. If a coach knows or should have known that an athlete is physically unable to compete the coach is negligent and may be liable for any injuries which result from that athlete's participation. A coach can be negligent for playing an injured athlete as well as an athlete who is overweight or out of condition. *See, e.g., Morris v. Union High School District A., King County,* 160 Wash. 121, 294 P. 998 (1931) (liability for requiring injured football player to play). It is possible that a coach could be negligent for mismatching opponents. If a reasonable person would have anticipated injury to a particular athlete because of a mismatch in physical condition with an opponent, the coach who permits the participation is negligent. *See, e.g., Brooks v. Board of Education of the City of New York,* 29 Misc.2d 19, 205 N.Y.S.2d 777 (1960), *aff'd,* 15 A.D.2d 495, 222 N.Y.S.2d 184 (1961) (physical education instructor was negligent for not matching the participants in a dangerous game by height and weight).

8. Other Breaches of Duty

Listing all of the areas of potential negligence for coaches and sports instructors would be impossible. They are too numerous to mention. However, coaches and teachers have five additional duties that often serve as a source of liability. These are the duties related to transportation, facilities protection, the duty not to intentionally injure and the duty to obey association rules.

(a) Transportation.

Coaches are usually involved with transporting their athletes or students to and from athletic events and practices. Whether a coach is personally driving or merely travelling with the team, reasonable care for the safety of others must be exercised. If the coach is driving, the coach has to operate the vehicle in a reasonable manner and must obey all traffic laws. If a passenger, the coach should insist that assigned drivers do likewise. The coach is responsible for maintaining order and discipline in the vehicle, and must act in a prudent manner to secure transportation for the students under his control. *See, e.g., Hanson v. Reedley Joint Union High School District*, 43 Cal.App.2d 643, 111 P.2d 415 (1941) (teacher was negligent in directing students to ride home from tennis practice with driver he knew to be reckless and in a vehicle known to be unsafe.)

(b) Facilities.

Many sports facilities are old or in a poor state of repair. While others were never designed to house athlete contests. Yet sports and athletic events routinely take place under these unsafe or inadequate conditions, posing a serious problem for coaches and instructors. Although it may not be the coach's responsibility to furnish a safe athletic facility, a coach may not be absolved of liability for injuries caused by unsafe playing conditions. If the coach is aware or should have been aware of the danger, the coach can be negligent in failing to warn others of the danger. A coach must take reasonable care to inspect the facilities for hidden dangers, such as water on the court, and may have an obligation to refuse to proceed with the event if the facilities are so inadequate that they pose an unreasonable risk of serious injury to the participants.

(c) Protection.

Parents are forced to rely upon school employees to protect their children during school activities. School teachers and coaches stand partially in place of the student's parents, and in doing so they assume a duty to protect the student or athlete in their charge. This duty to protect includes using reasonable care to prevent foreseeable assaults and other intentional harm caused by third persons. *See* Restatement, Second, Torts § 320 (1965). Coaches may be negligent if they fail to promptly break up a fight, or if they do not take reasonable precautions to prevent an attack which they know is imminent. The law does not require that the coach risk incurring serious injury to save the student. However, the coach must act in a reasonable and prudent manner to prevent the harm.

(d) Duty Not to Intentionally Injure.

International torts are discussed in detail elsewhere in this chapter. *See supra* § 7.2B. Assault, battery, invasion of privacy, and defamation are intentional torts that may be brought against coaches or instructors by participants. Assault and battery actions normally occur during the disciplining of an athlete or perhaps as a result the coach's frustration at the athlete's performance. School teachers, including coaches, can use reasonable force to discipline and control their students. This same right to discipline may extend to Little League coaches and others charged with a parent's duties. An instructor enjoys no privilege to threaten or strike an adult. Nor does the instructor's privilege to discipline permit the use of physical violence against a child merely because the child is unable or fails to perform at a desired level of athletic ability.

Coaches are often asked to publicly comment about an athlete or team's performance. Thus, when an athlete is suspended or disciplined a coach's comments may appear in the media. The increase of drug use by athletes may prompt coaches to initiate locker searches and mandatory drug testing. These are but a few of the activities that could subject a coach to a defamation or invasion of privacy suit. If the coach's statements are truthful or constitute fair comment, the coach has an absolute defense to any defamation suit. If they are considered public figures, college and professional athletes have to prove that the defamatory comments were made with malice. Some courts have extended the malice requirement to defamation suits by high school athletes. *See, e.g., Iacco v. Bohannon*, 70 Mich.App. 463, 245 N.W.2d 791 (1976) (in defamation suit by high school athlete against his basketball coach, the athlete had to show that allegedly defamatory remarks were made with actual malice). Showing actual malice is difficult, and this requirement affords some measure of protection to a coach's comments. *See* § 7.2B–4 *supra* for a more detailed examination of the proof necessary to establish malice in a defamation case against a public figure.

As far as invasion of privacy is concerned, disclosure of embarrassing details about an athlete's life can be privileged as newsworthy if the athlete is a public figure. High school athletes may not qualify for public figure treatment as frequently as the college or professional athlete. Furthermore, if the information is part of a student-athlete's school records, its disclosure may constitute a violation of both federal and state educational privacy laws. *See, e.g.,* 20 U.S.C. § 1232(g)(b) (1982) (Family Educational Rights and Privacy Act of 1974); Ill.Ann.Stat. ch. 122, §§ 50–1 to 50–10 (Smith-Hurd Supp.1985) (Illinois School Student Records Act).

When the coach has reasonable grounds for believing that an athlete has violated or is violating the law or school rules, a search may be conducted. The United States Supreme Court, however, has not extended this privilege beyond the high school level, nor should searches of the person and possessions of even younger children be undertaken in a cavalier manner. Searching a person or another's personal possessions is a substantial invasion of privacy. This is true for children as well as adults. The Supreme Court recognized public school officials' right to search in *New Jersey v. T.L.O.,* 105 S.Ct. 733 (1985), but required reasonable grounds for the search. The Supreme Court further required that the search not be excessively intrusive in light of the student's age and sex, and the nature of the infraction. Courts are reluctant to accept a child's consent to be searched as a valid consent; it is often viewed as coerced. The decision to search lockers, personal items, or the participant is fraught with danger, and should not be undertaken without the advice of legal counsel. Mandatory testing of athletes for drug use is even more likely to generate invasion of privacy suits.

(e) Violation of Association or Conference Rules.

Coaches are agents of the college or university that employs them. As an agent, the coach has a duty to act with ordinary care and skill in coaching. A coach's duty to obey rules and regulations promulgated by the athletic associations to which the employer belongs is part of the duty to use ordinary care and skill. Since a violation of association rules breaches the duty to exercise skill and care, the coach could be liable for any harm caused by violating athletic association rules. Stated otherwise, when the college is sanctioned for a coach's violation of association rules, the school has a cause of action against the coach for any harm it sustained.

9.   *Defenses and Limitations on Liability*

The limitations on tort liability discussed in § 7.3 *supra* generally apply to coaches.   Some jurisdictions do not extend sovereign immunity to protect coaches and other governmental employees from liability for their own negligence, but others do.   A few states even expand parental immunity to include teachers and coaches.   *See, e.g., Kain v. Rockridge Community Unit School District No. 300*, 72 Ill.Dec. 813, 117 Ill.App.3d 681, 453 N.E.2d 118 (1983) (football coach standing *in loco parentis* should not be subjected to greater liability than parents).

Consent and assumption of risk are normally a defense to an intentional tort.   Both of these defenses are firmly rooted in sports law, but are frequently merged into a hybrid defense which applies to intentional and unintentional torts.   Courts may consider players, coaches, referees, and any one else who voluntarily participates in an athletic activity to have consented to and assumed the risk of the kind of injuries normally associated with that sport.

The risks assumed and consented to are only those ordinarily encountered in that particular sports activity.   Participants do not consent to or assume the risk of injury from another's intentional or willful acts, or the risk of injury from fellow players behaving in an unexpected, unsportsmanlike, and reckless manner.   *See* Weistart and Lowell, *The Law of Sports* at 942.   Neither do the participants consent to or assume the risk of being injured by the negligence of others not actually involved in the competition.   *Id.* at 942–44.

The football player who is properly coached, trained and equipped will, as a matter of law, consent to the blows and bodily contact that are so much a part of the game.   By choosing to participate the athlete also assumes the risk of being injured during play.   This same player, however, does not consent to being intentionally struck by the other team's coach nor does he assume the risk of being injured by defects in the equipment.

If consent or assumption of risk is not available as a defense, the coach or instructor may be able to raise the defense of contributory negligence.   Consent and assumption of risk depend on the plaintiff's state of mind; the recognition, understanding, and full appreciation of the potential risk involved in a particular activity and the voluntary assumption of that risk. Contributory negligence, on the other hand, depends on the plaintiff's failure to use due care for his or her own personal safety and well-being. Although a football player may not have assumed the risk of injury from playing with defective equipment, the player may be contributorily negligent in doing so.

Consent, assumption of risk, and contributory negligence may be viable defenses to the tort claim of an injured child. But in many cases, a child lacks the understanding and maturity to appreciate the dangers. If a child cannot fully comprehend the risks involved, the child cannot consent to or assume them. Contributory negligence may likewise be inapplicable because children are subject to a reduced standard of care. Section 7.2C *supra* contains a general discussion of the tort principle governing the conduct of children.

B. Injury to Spectators

In this era of escalating sports violence, confrontations with and between spectators is a source of liability for coaches. Emotions run high at athletic events, both on and off the field of play, and the coach who is assaulted by irate fans may have a right to self-defense and to defend others for whom there is a duty to protect. But the coach who uses more force than is reasonably necessary will have committed an assault and battery. Assaults and batteries can occur when coaches hit, shove, or throw objects such as chairs at cameramen or other persons along the side lines. The privilege of self-defense does not exist under these circumstances.

A coach can commit an intentional tort by directing the players to threaten or harm spectators. A coach may also be liable even when he or she neither directs nor encourages the attack upon a spectator. In these cases, however, a coach's liability must be premised upon negligence. If the coach knows or should have known that an athlete might attack a spectator, the coach may be found negligent for failure to use reasonable care to prevent the attack. Even if the coach was not aware beforehand, once the assault begins, he or she cannot allow the attack to continue unchecked. The coach has a duty to use reasonable efforts to bring the athlete under control.

Another frequent cause of spectator injuries is their presence too near the playing field. Crowd control can be the coach's responsibility, especially at amateur and high school events. The coach may have a duty to police the sidelines and take reasonable precautions to see that spectators do not encroach upon the field and pose a danger to themselves and the participants. Reasonable care can be as simple as asking the spectator to step back and stopping play until he or she does, or summoning a police officer to have an unobliging fan removed.

Spectators, like participants, may consent to and accept the risk of being injured when they attend a sports activity. Spectators may also be contributorily negligent in not using reasonable care for their own safety. These and other defenses are available to a negligent coach, and are discussed in § 7.2B–9 *supra.*

7.5 LIABILITY OF OFFICIALS

Umpires, referees, and other officials must supervise athletic events. Supervision includes enforcing the rules governing competition. Sports officials have a duty to see that the rules for participant and spectator safety are obeyed. To the extent that the duty is not performed, both they and their employers may be negligent. *See, e.g., Carabba v. Anacortes School District No. 103,* 72 Wash.2d 939, 435 P.2d 936 (1967) (liability may be imposed upon school district for referee's negligence in failing to detect an illegal wrestling hold that left a high school athlete permanently paralyzed).

A referee obviously cannot prevent all violations of the rules, nor does the law require this. Referees and game officials need only use reasonable care to see that the rules of competition are complied with. Reasonable care might consist of advising the contestants about illegal holds, punches, and similar tactics. Reasonable care will require referees to be diligent in detecting infractions of the rules and in sanctioning violators. First offenses might properly be dealt with by a warning to the guilty party; continued offenses may require ejecting the athlete from the game. Every situation is different, and in evaluating a referee's conduct the law will judge it against that of a reasonable and prudent person with similar training and experience. While a reasonable person in the position of a game official may not be able to prevent the first violation, that person will certainly take precautions to see that it does not happen again.

An official's responsibility goes much further than enforcement of rules. Officials control the competition, and in this capacity are saddled with a general duty of care. They are expected to anticipate reasonably foreseeable dangers, and to take reasonable precautions to protect both participants and spectators from those dangers. If a reasonable person would conclude that weather conditions posed a danger to contestants, the referee who does not cancel or delay the event will be negligent. If the official is aware of some potentially dangerous condition on the field, that official may be required to warn the participants or even terminate the competition. A referee can not ignore a participant's lack of proper equipment, and may bear some responsibility in the decision to permit a seriously injured athlete to continue. There are, however, no hard and fast rules governing a referee's decisions. Instead, the referee will be judged by the reasonable person standard, and when the referee fails to exercise the judgment of a reasonable and prudent person, negligence will be found.

7.6 LIABILITY OF SPECTATORS

Courts have no difficulty imposing general principles of tort law upon spectators at sporting events. Purchasing a ticket to an athletic event does not entitle one to assault other spectators or to attack the participants. The fan who throws a bottle or strikes another person will be liable for the intentional torts.

A sports fan must use reasonable care to avoid creating situations which present an unreasonable risk of injury to others. The fans must conduct themselves in the same manner as would reasonable and prudent persons under similar conditions. A reasonable person does not shove or jostle others on steep and narrow stadium steps. Reasonable people in the upper deck of a ballpark do not place bottles or heavy objects on the rail where they may be knocked off and strike someone below. A spectator who does these and other things which a reasonable person would not do is negligent.

7.7 LIABILITY OF OWNERS, OPERATORS, AND ADMINISTRATORS

Coaches, athletes, umpires, and anybody else directly involved in a sports or recreational activity are considered to be participants. People who attend an athletic contest for the purpose of viewing it are spectators. Participants and spectators are not the only persons with potential tort liability for a sports injury. There are also the people and organizations who sponsor, promote, or control the athletic event or facilities where it is held. This section will address the tort liability of these latter individuals and organizations.

Within this group is a broad range of people and business entities who are simply referred to as owners, operators, and administrators. "Owners" include not only the corporation or individuals who own a professional team but anyone else who owns the facilities where a sports or recreational activity is taking place. School districts, colleges, universities, park boards, and even cities may be owners.

"Operators" are those people and associations who do not own a team or athletic facility, but control it. The promoter who leases a municipal arena for a sporting event is an operator, as are the many league associations and athletic conferences that schedule or control athletic contests.

The term "administrators" covers those who are in actual charge of the facilities or event. The head of a local park board is an administrator. So are the league president, school principal, athletic director, and arena manager. Administrators have the basic obligations to supervise both the premises and activity. If the administrator is liable for the injury to a spectator or participant, the administrator's negligence or other tortious conduct will frequently be imputed to the employer. Owners and operators are vicariously liable for the torts of their employees under the doctrine of *respondeat superior,* which was discussed in § 7.2D *supra.*

Owners, operators, and administrators are liable for their own intentional torts. They can be liable for their negligence in maintaining or providing facilities and equipment, as well as for failure to properly supervise. This liability is commonly referred to as "premises liability." When a person is injured during a sports activity, liability of the owner or those in control of the premises will often depend upon the status of the injured person as either an invitee, licensee, trespasser or passerby.

People who are present at the athletic event at the invitation of the owner or operator are "invitees." The invitation can be expressed or implied. Invitees are owed the highest duty of care. Owners and those persons in control of an athletic event are not insurers of an invitee's personal safety, but they must use reasonable care to protect the invitee and to provide a reasonably safe premise.

"Licensees" are also upon the premises with the owner or occupant's permission but they are there solely for their own benefit or entertainment. An owner or occupant's duty to the licensee is to exercise reasonable care to advise him or her of any dangerous conditions that are known to the owner *and* are not likely to be discovered by the licensee. There is no duty to inspect for hidden dangers, as there is in the case of an invitee. *See* Restatement, Second, Torts § 343 comment b (1965).

"Trespassers" are people who enter the building or grounds of another without permission. Liability for injuries to trespassers depends in large part upon the owner or occupant's actual or constructive knowlege of their presence on the property. An invitee or licensee may become a trespasser if they enter an area where they are not authorized to go, or when they refuse to leave after being told to do so. When the proprietor knows or has reason to know of a trespasser's presence upon the premises, the proprietor must use reasonable care to warn the trespasser of any artificial condition which poses an unreasonable risk of harm. *See id.* at § 335.

A "passerby" is someone who lives adjacent to or happens by a sporting event but is not present upon the premises where the activity is taking place. Proprietors of sports facilities must use due care not to expose passersby to an unreasonable risk of injury. *See id.* § 371.

Everyone injured on the premises of a sports or recreational facility will fall into one of the above categories. The tort liability of owners and operators in each of these categories will be discussed, but before doing so it should be noted that when the facilities are leased there may be a dispute over whether the owner or tenant-operator will be ultimately responsible.

A. Leased Premises

The owner and the operator of leased athletic facilities will both be responsible for tortious acts when they have joint control over the premises or activity. *See, e.g., Atlantic Rural Exposition, Inc. v. Fagan,* 195 Va. 13, 77 S.E.2d 368 (1953) (both automobile race track owner and track lessee held liable for injuries resulting when wheel from race car detached and struck spectator). The owner-lessor alone will be liable when the lease requires him to keep the premises or equipment in a good state of repair, the failure to keep the property in repair creates an unreasonable risk of injury to others, and someone is in fact harmed because the owner-lessor did not use reasonable care to perform the contract. *See* Restatement, Second, Torts § 357 (1965). When the lease is for a short period of time, the owner usually remains liable for any nonapparent defects. *See, e.g., Novak v. City of Delavan,* 31 Wis.2d 200, 143 N.W.2d 6 (1966) (because school district leased city football stadium on a game by game basis, its use of the facilities was so temporary that the city had the duty to inspect and repair bleachers upon which spectators were injured).

The owner will likewise be liable if he or she fails to disclose an unreasonably dangerous condition on the premises which the owner knows or should know will not be discovered or realized by the tenant. *See* Restatement, Second, Torts § 358 (1965). Finally, if the owner of a sports facility has actual or constructive knowledge of an unreasonably dangerous defect on the premises but nevertheless leases that property for a purpose involving the admission of the public, the owner will be liable for any harm which results if there is reason to suspect that the tenant will admit members of the public without putting the facilities in a safe condition. *See id.* at § 359. However, the owner will not be liable to the tenant or anyone else for physical harm caused after the owner surrenders custody, control, and possession of the premises, unless one of the foregoing exceptions applies. *See, e.g., City of Fort Worth v. Barlow,* 313 S.W.2d 906 (Tex.Civ.App.1958) (lease of its lake property for construction of public swimming facility did not make city liable for injuries sustained by patron in absence of an agreement to repair, or concealment of dangerous conditions).

B. Injured Participant

In analyzing the care required of owners, operators, and administrators, the physical and mental condition of the participants is extremely important. Those involved with recreational activities and sports for the handicapped will be required to exercise a greater degree of care for participant safety. A higher degree of care is similarly imposed upon individuals, institutions, and organizations that conduct youth activities. Greater care is required for children and the handicapped because they are less able to protect themselves, and because they may not have the capacity to observe and appreciate the dangers confronting them. See § 7.2C *supra* for a discussion of tort law principles generally applicable to children and the handicapped.

A review of existing caselaw involving personal injury suits by participants against owners or operators of sports facilities and their administrators, reveals that such suits are likely to have arisen out of some incident involving transportation, condition of the premises, the furnishing or failure to furnish proper equipment, and a lack of supervision. This section will briefly consider these activities as potential sources of liability, and review the defenses an owner, operator or administrator might assert against a personal injury suit by an injured participant.

1. *Common Carrier*

If the activity involves the transportation of a participant for a fee, the owner or operator becomes a common carrier. Common carriers are required to take every precaution for their patron's safety. *See, e.g., Fisher v. Mt. Mansfield Company,* 283 F.2d 533 (2d Cir.1960) (ski lift operator considered a common carrier). In all other cases the owner or operator owes participants the same duty of care as an invitee: the owner or operator is required to use ordinary care to keep the premises in a safe and suitable condition, and to protect participants from an unreasonable risk of harm.

2. *Facilities*

Owners and those in control of sports and recreational facilities have a duty to provide a reasonably safe place for participants. This duty extends to the physical condition of the premises as well as equipment that may be in use there. Proprietors are required to exercise ordinary care and diligence in keeping both the premises and sports apparatus in a reasonably safe condition. This may require establishing a cleaning, inspection, or maintenance schedule. How frequently the facilities and equipment should be inspected will depend upon the potential harm anticipated.

If a particular condition poses a risk of serious injury or death, then a reasonable and prudent person will be extremely diligent in establishing a stringent inspection policy. When a recognizable risk of serious injury or death is present, reasonable care might require that the equipment or premises be inspected and serviced following each use. On the other hand, a less rigorous inspection and maintenance schedule will be sufficient when the potential harm is slight or not likely to occur. Thus, the operator of a scuba diving school might be derelict by inspecting and servicing equipment on a daily basis, whereas a daily inspection of the grounds might be reasonable care for a golf course manager.

Regardless of the care they exhibit, owners and operators are not insurers of participant safety. This means that they are not liable if the injury could not have been prevented by the exercise of reasonable care. The law emphasizes the prevention of probable injury by requiring those in control of sports facilities to undertake reasonable precautions for maintaining their premises in a reasonably safe condition. Premises liability is based upon the duty of those in charge to use ordinary care and diligence in discovering and remedying potentially dangerous conditions.

It is not necessary for the owner or operator to have actual knowledge of the dangerous condition; only that they knew or should have known. Part of the duty that proprietors owe to participants and other invitees is to use reasonable care to inspect the premises for hidden damages. Those in charge of sports facilities will be liable for any harm caused by the dangers they should have discovered. Moreover, if their employees are aware of the danger, this awareness is imputed to the owner or operator, who become liable if they fail to take reasonable steps to remedy the problem or to warn participants. *See, e.g., Dawson v. Rhode Island Auditorium, Inc.,* 104 R.I. 116, 242 A.2d 407 (1968) (basketball player injured when he slipped and fell on puddle of water caused by a leaking arena roof). Owners and operators are not, however, liable for dangers which are not concealed and are known or should have been known to the participant. *See, e.g., Rock v. Concrete Materials, Inc.,* 46 App.Div.2d 300, 362 N.Y.S.2d 258 (1974), *appeal dismissed,* 36 N.Y.2d 772, 368 N.Y.S.2d 841, 329 N.E.2d 672 (1975) (recovery denied for snowmobiler killed when he drove into a metal gate).

3. Equipment

The duty which owners, operators, and administrators owe to participants extends to the furnishing of equipment. If it is required for participant safety, owners or operators are negligent if they fail to provide or allow the participant to compete without proper equipment. *See, e.g., Kopera v. Moschella,* 400 F.Supp. 131 (S.D.Miss.1975) (owner of swimming pool negligent in not keeping rescue and resuscitation equipment on premises).

4. Supervision

The exercise of reasonable care for participant safety includes the duty to supervise. Supervision entails requiring the presence of adequate lifeguards, referees, or similar personnel when necessary to prevent an unreasonable risk of injury. Supervision may require those in charge to establish and enforce rules for the protection of participants. Supervision requires the proprietor of a sports facility to protect participants from injury caused by the misconduct of employees, customers, and third persons if the occurrence was reasonably foreseeable and could have been prevented through the exercise of ordinary care and diligence. Conversely, if the resulting injury to a participant happened suddenly and without warning and the proprietor could not, by the exercise of reasonable care, have discovered or prevented it, the proprietor is not negligent. *See, e.g., Lincoln v. Wilcox,* 111 Ga.App. 365, 141 S.E.2d 765 (1965) (owner or operator of swimming pool was not negligent, as a matter of law, because injury to child swimmer was not preventable through the exercise of reasonable care). Sports violence and misconduct have become so common that it is not only anticipated, but expected. Those in control of athletic events must be aware of expected misconduct and must implement reasonable security measures for the safety of participants, such as restricting the sale of alcoholic beverages and maintaining an adequate police presence.

5. Defenses

Assumption of risk and contributory negligence are the defenses normally available to owners, operators, and administrators against an injured participant's suit. Sovereign immunity may be a viable defense when the defendant is a school district or other governmental entity, but it will not always protect administrators and athletic associations.

If the injured participant is an employee, workmen's compensation may bar recovery in negligence cases against an owner or operator. In many jurisdictions, the existence of workmen's compensation coverage will even prevent the participant from recovering for intentional torts.

The proprietor of a sports or recreational facility should also explore the possibility of a statutory defense. To make more property available for public recreation, some state legislatures have enacted laws limiting a landowner's liability for injuries to participants. A landowner cannot, however, use the liability limitation unless the public is allowed access to the premises. *See, e.g., Georgia Power Co. v. McGruder,* 229 Ga. 811, 194 S.E.2d 440 (1972) (statute limiting liability of recreational landowners did not apply where property was posted with "keep out" signs).

C. Injured Spectator

Proprietors of sports and recreational facilities are liable not only for any unintentional injury of a spectator, but they may also be liable for the intentional torts of their employees. The owner and operator's most likely source of liability for the intentional wrongs of an employee will be associated with security. If stadium police or security personnel use excessive force in controlling unruly spectators, there is a very real possibility that they will commit the intentional torts of assault, battery, and false imprisonment. Since they are acting in furtherance of their employer's interests, any injury done to a spectator by over-zealous security personnel will be charged to the proprietor who employed them. *See, e.g., Alamo Downs, Inc. v. Briggs,* 106 S.W.2d 733 (Tex.Civ. App.1937) (affirming award of damages to a patron for assault, battery, and false imprisonment committed by race track security personnel). Owners and operators are vicariously liable for the torts of their security force under the legal doctrine of *respondeat superior.* See § 7.2D *supra.*

1. Intentional Torts

Professional athletes can be employees. Professional athletes have been known to assault and batter fans. If the attack was committed within the scope of the athlete's employment, then the team owner will also be responsible for the tort under *respondeat superior.*

2. Unintentional Torts

Although intentional tort actions are certainly not uncommon, the most frequent basis for an injured spectator's suit will be negligence. Spectators are invitees. Proprietors of sports and recreational facilities owe spectators the same duty of care that they owe to participants. Owners, operators, and administrators have to maintain the premises in a reasonably safe condition, and to use reasonable care to protect the spectator from an unreasonable risk of harm.

In maintenance of the facility and equipment, the spectator is entitled to expect that the proprietor will exercise ordinary care and skill to make the premises safe. The owner or operator is thus required to exercise care in the original construction of the premises and in regulating the activities of employees that may affect the conditions of the premises. The owner must likewise inspect for any latent dangers. Once a dangerous condition is discovered, the owner or administrator in control of the athletic facility must take reasonable precautions to protect spectators from injury by implementing such repairs, safeguards, or warnings as may be reasonably necessary. *See* Restatement, Second, Torts § 343 comment b (1965).

The duty of care that proprietors owe spectators includes taking reasonable precautions to protect them from being injured by the misconduct of others. If it is foreseeable that a spectator may behave in a manner that creates a serious risk of injury to others, the proprietor must take reasonable precautions to prevent the harm. This duty to protect has even been extended to the parking lot of a sports facility.

In *Bearman v. University of Notre Dame,* 453 N.E.2d 1196 (Ind.App.1983), two drunk men who were fighting injured a spectator as she approached her vehicle in the stadium parking lot. There were no ushers or security police in the area, and the injured fan alleged that this was negligence on the part of Notre Dame University, owner of the stadium. The trial court dismissed the case, and the plaintiff appealed.

The Indiana Court of Appeals reversed and remanded the case for trial because Notre Dame had a duty to exercise ordinary and reasonable care to protect patrons from injury caused by third persons. Notre Dame was aware of drinking and tailgate parties in the stadium parking lot, and whether Notre Dame had taken reasonable precautions for the protection of those attending its football games was a matter for the jury to decide.

3. Spectator Searches

Responding to the increase of spectator violence at sporting events, many proprietors have instituted search policies. A spectator must consent to a limited search of person and property for weapons, alcohol, drugs, and missile-like containers prior to admission to the sports facility.

Spectators attending professional football games in the Pontiac, Michigan Silverdome see the following four-foot by four-foot sign prominently displayed over each entrance:

NOTICE: FOR YOUR PROTECTION BOTTLES, CANS, LIQUOR CONTAINERS, HORNS OR OTHER MISSILE–LIKE OBJECTS ARE NOT PERMITTED IN STADIUM. PLEASE RETURN SUCH ITEMS TO YOUR VEHICLE. PATRONS SUBJECT TO VISUAL INSPECTION OF PERSON, PARCELS, BAGS AND CONTAINERS OR CLOTHING CAPABLE OF CARRYING SUCH ITEMS. PATRONS MAY REFUSE INSPECTION. IF SO, MANAGEMENT MAY REFUSE ENTRY.

Uniformed unarmed guards are stationed at the stadium's entrances and are authorized to stop any person carrying a container large enough to conceal bottles, cans, or other missile-like objects of similar size. Patrons are first asked permission by the guards to visually inspect the package. The guards advise the patron that the patron may refuse to allow the inspection. If the patron does refuse, the container may be discarded in a nearby waste can or returned to the vehicle, after which the patron will be allowed to enter the stadium. The spectators who refuse the search and refuse to dispose of the container are denied admittance. Those patrons denied admittance may receive a refund of their ticket price.

If the patron consents to the search, the stadium guards do not at any time touch their person or property. If a patron has a large container or package, the guards ask the patron to move things around within the container so they (guards) can visually inspect the contents.

The Silverdome search policy was challenged in the case of *Jensen v. City of Pontiac,* 113 Mich.App. 341, 317 N.W.2d 619 (1982). A patron who objected to the warrantless stadium search brought suit claiming that the policy violated both state and federal constitutional prohibitions against unreasonable search and seizures. The *Jensen* court reasoned that the constitutionality of the preadmission stadium search procedures should be determined on the basis of three factors: (1) public necessity for the search, (2) effectiveness of the search in achieving the purpose for which it was implemented, and (3) the degree and nature of the intrusion upon the patron's right to privacy.

The court recognized a public necessity for the search. This public necessity was evaluated by examining the nature of the threat to public safety and likelihood that this threat would materialize. Public necessity for the search policy existed because football games tend to encourage violence in the stands, and injuries to patrons from thrown objects were widespread.

The second factor, efficacy of the search, focused upon the likelihood that the search procedure would avert the potential harm. The court concluded that injuries caused by thrown objects were in fact reduced by the search policy. Silverdome stadium searches were thus effective in promoting public safety.

Next, the court balanced the public necessity and efficacy of stadium searches against the degree and nature of the intrusion upon patrons. Emphasizing that stadium guards touched neither patrons nor their property, and that the guards were unarmed, the *Jensen* court upheld the stadium search procedure. The court, however, ordered stadium management to maintain the signs warning of the search policy over every gate, and to instruct guards to request permission for a visual search while simultaneously advising patrons of their right to return the package to their car if they did not want to be inspected. The stadium management was likewise ordered to instruct guards to inspect the bag or purse of *every* patron that was large enough to conceal a bottle or can. By inspecting everyone, no selective enforcement of the rule would occur and all patrons would be treated equally.

In implementing a policy such as that of the Silverdome's, proprietors of sports facilities should bear several things in mind. First, the search in *Jensen* was implemented to prevent serious threat of injury to the public attending professional football games, not to enforce alcohol or drug laws. Searches solely to enforce alcohol and drug laws might not supply the requisite public necessity to justify a stadium's search policy. By implementing the search to protect spectators from injury from thrown objects, however, the stadium's management indirectly curtailed alcohol and drug violations.

Second, the importance of a visual, rather than physical search cannot be over emphasized. It is extremely difficult to justify a bodily search of a patron's person or possessions by a stadium guard. An unlawful search subjects the owner or operator of a sports facility to liability for violating the patron's civil rights.

Lastly, in addition to the procedures in *Jensen,* other safeguards can be effectuated to reduce the likelihood that stadium searches will be declared unconstitutional. Notice of the search policy should be printed on the tickets. Perhaps a separate screening area should be set aside for carrying out visual searches. Patrons who agreed to have their packages or containers searched should voluntarily enter a designated search area. The spectator's knowledge of and voluntary participation in the search somewhat mitigates the offensiveness of the screening process.

4. Excluding Spectators

Excluding or expelling spectators from a sporting event is closely related to stadium searches. Unlike persons engaged in a public calling, such as innkeepers and common carriers, the proprietor of an athletic facility has a common law right to eject or deny admission to any spectator not desired upon the premises. *See, e.g., Flores v. Los Angeles Turf Club, Inc.,* 55 Cal.2d 736, 13 Cal.Rptr. 201 (1961) (denying damages to convicted bookmaker who was forcibly ejected and excluded from Santa Anita Race Track). Even though the right to exclude or expell a fan exists, a security guard's use of excessive force in ejecting a spectator may expose the proprietor to liability for an intentional tort.

The common law right to exclude patrons has been further modified by constitutional due process requirements and civil rights laws. Excluding fans on the basis of race, sex, religion, or national origin is illegal, and if the facility is operated by a governmental entity, the expelled patron may be entitled to notice and an opportunity to be heard. *Cf. Saumell v. New York Racing Association, Inc.,* 58 N.Y.2d 231, 460 N.Y.S.2d 763, 447 N.E.2d 706 (1983) (due process required notice of alleged misconduct and presuspension hearing for jockey excluded from race tracks). There is, however, the possibility that a sports facility may qualify as a limited public forum, which raises other constitutional speech and religious issues involving a denial of access. See § 3.3C–5 *supra,* for the constitutional implications of a denial of access.

5. Waivers and Exculpatory Agreements

Owners and operators of sports facilities often try to avoid liability for spectator injuries with waivers or exculpatory agreements. Waivers and exculpatory agreements are strictly construed against the proprietor, and courts are generally reluctant to enforce them. *See, e.g., Celli v. Sports Car Club of America, Inc.,* 29 Cal.App.3d 551, 105 Cal.Rptr. 904 (1972) (waiver of liability on pit pass at automobile races did not bar recovery by injured spectators).

6. *Defenses*

Assumption of risk is the traditional defense that proprietors of recreational facilities assert against suit by an injured spectator. Spectators attending an athletic contest are generally considered to have assumed the risk of injury caused by the commonly recognized hazards of the game. Known as the "common knowledge rule," this principle of law has effectively banned spectators from recovering for personal injuries resulting from the risks a reasonable person would recognize as inherent in attending the sports activity. Thus, the owner of a baseball park has a duty to use reasonable care to provide protective screening for the most dangerous portion of the park, but the spectator who opts to sit elsewhere voluntarily assumes the risk of being struck and injured by batted or thrown balls. *See, e.g., Williams v. Houston Baseball Association,* 154 S.W.2d 874 (Tex.Civ.App.1941) (denying plaintiff recovery for injury resulting from being struck by a foul ball).

The basis of the common knowledge rule is that the potential danger involved in attending a particular sports activity is known and appreciated by a reasonable person. If the danger is clearly incident to that particular sport, courts conclude that the spectator consented to or assumed the risk of injury as a matter of law. When the court finds that a spectator assumed the risk of injury as a matter of law, it will dismiss the law suit. *See, e.g., Stradtner v. Cincinnati Reds, Inc.,* 39 Ohio App.2d 199, 68 Ohio Ops.2d 384, 316 N.E.2d 924 (1972) (affirming dismissal of personal injury suit by fan struck by batted ball). In other cases, the jury decides whether a particular risk would have been recognized and assumed by the reasonable person. *See, e.g., Perry v. Seattle School District No. 1,* 66 Wash.2d 800, 405 P.2d 589 (1965) (whether plaintiff had assumed risk of being struck by ball carrier when she stood on sidelines of high school football game was a question for the trier of fact).

Existence of a comparative negligence statute may modify the common law defense of assumption of risk. *See, e.g., Lamphear v.*

State, 91 A.D.2d 791, 458 N.Y.S.2d 71 (1982) (New York's comparative negligence statute abolished assumption of risk and contributory negligence as absolute bars to recovery by an injured athlete). The defense of assumption of risk likewise has limited application to children and the handicapped because of their inability to recognize and appreciate many dangers. Assumption of risk is not a defense to intentional torts, nor does it relieve proprietors of liability for their own negligence and that of their employees.

A spectator's contributory negligence or general lack of care for his or her own personal safety is also a defense to a proprietor's negligence. This defense may completely bar recovery by an injured spectator or reduce the amount of damages awarded.

D. Injured Licensee

Unlike invitees, licensees are those persons who are on the premises of a sports or recreational facility with the proprietor's permission rather than by invitation. Licensees include social guests, members of the possessor's household, and anyone else present upon the property solely for their own benefit. *See* Restatement, Second, Torts § 330 comment h (1965). A licensee supposedly enters the premises with the understanding that the proprietor owes him no duty to prepare a safe place, or to inspect the property in order to discover possible or even probable dangers. *Id.* at § 342 comment d (1965).

Sports injury law suits by licensees typically arise from the use of private property for recreational purposes. When land, such as parks and public school grounds is held open to members of the general public, people using these facilities are considered public invitees. As public invitees, they are entitled to expect that the proprietor will exercise due care in making the premises safe for their use. *See id.* at § 332 comment d (1965). When the land is privately owned, people using the land are considered to be licensees. For example, a homeowner who invites guests to use the backyard swimming pool, or the farmer who allows cross country skiers on his or her property are only required to exercise reasonable care in disclosing any dangerous conditions known to the owner and not likely to be discovered by the licensees. There is no duty to inspect the premises for unknown dangers. *See, e.g., Telak v. Maszczenski,* 248 Md. 476, 237 A.2d 434 (1968) (social guest injured at swimming pool party was only a licensee who took premises as he found it and could not expect the host to take special precautions for his protection).

Landowners are of course liable for any intentional or willful injury they cause a licensee. Additionally, a landowner may be negligent for not taking reasonable precautions to protect guests once their peril is discovered. The law also requires more precautions by a landowner if the property constitutes an attractive nuisance to childen.

In a majority of states, liability depends upon the status of the injured party as either an invitee or licensee. Some states, however, have abandoned these common law classifications of a landowner's duty of care. These states have adopted a uniform standard. This uniform standard is: the duty to maintain the property in a reasonably safe condition in view of all the circumstances. More states are likely to adopt this new standard for several reasons. First, the old common law invitee-licensee-trespasser classification system is confusing; second, the new system is more equitable because a licensee is entitled to the same level of care as an invitee. *See, e.g., Mounsey v. Ellard,* 363 Mass. 693, 297 N.E.2d 43 (1973) (duty of reasonable care owed to all lawful visitors). "Reasonable care in all circumstances" is determined on the basis of the foreseeability of the visitor's presence on the premises, the likelihood of serious injury or death, and the burden of removing the danger.

Persons sued for the death or injury of a licensee will often be able to assert the same defenses that are asserted against suits by injured participants and spectators. These defenses include assumption of risk and contributory negligence. Exculpatory agreements and waivers are other potential limitations on the proprietor's liability. State laws exist which reduce liability for recreational property owners who make their land available to the general public. These defenses are discussed in detail *supra* in §§ 7.7C–5 and 7.7C–6.

E. Injured Trespasser

A trespasser is anyone, regardless of age, who is present upon the property of another without permission. Invitees and licensees may become trespassers when they are asked to leave and refuse to do so, or when they enter upon an unauthorized portion of the premises. A few states have abandoned the common law status classification for the duty owed trespassers and have substituted a reasonable care under the circumstances standard. This new standard requires one in possession of land to act as a reasonable person in maintaining the property in a safe condition for all foreseeable visitors. *See Webb v. City and Borough of Sitka*, 561 P.2d 731 (Alaska 1977) (liability of city for failure to use reasonable care in maintaining sidewalk does not depend upon the status of the plaintiff). Most states, however, still adhere to the common law status classification, which relieves the owner or occupier of any duty to trespassers unless the owner knows or should have known of their presence, or otherwise intentionally harms them. *See, e.g., Carlson v. Tucson Racquet and Swim Club, Inc.*, 127 Ariz. 247, 619 P.2d 756 (1980) (swim club had no duty to warn trespasser of obvious dangers inherent in diving head first into shallow pool).

Once the proprietor knows or has reason to suspect the trespasser's presence on the premises, several duties arise. The owner or occupier must use reasonable care in carrying on activities so the unauthorized visitor is not endangered. *See* Restatement, Second, Torts §§ 333–34 (1965). The proprietor or one in possession must likewise warn the trespasser of any highly dangerous artificial condition of which the occupier is aware and the trespasser is not likely to discover. An "artificial condition" is one which has been created or maintained by the proprietor, and a "highly dangerous" condition is one reasonably capable of causing serious bodily injury. *See id.* at § 335.

If the property owner fulfills the foregoing limited duties, the owner is not liable for the unintentional injury or death of a trespassing adult. The property owner may, however, have a higher standard of care towards children who trespass. A property owner *or* occupant must exercise reasonable care to protect children from any attractive nuisance on the property.

The attractive nuisance doctrine is accepted by most jurisdictions. It provides in essence that one in possession of land is liable for physical harm to children caused by an artificial condition upon the premises if the possessor knows or has reason to know that: (1) children are likely to be present; (2) the condition poses an unreasonable risk of serious injury or death; (3) children are not likely to realize the danger because of their youth; and (4) the utility of maintaining the dangerous condition and the burden of remedying the danger are slight in comparison to the risk involved. If these four factors are present, the owner or occupier of the property must use reasonable care to eliminate the danger or otherwise safeguard children from harm. *See* Restatement, Second, Torts §§ 339 and 343B (1965). Attractive nuisance suits have commonly proven successful against the swimming pool owner who fails to adequately fence his or her property to keep out neighborhood children. *See, e.g., McWilliams v. Guzinski,* 71 Wis.2d 57, 237 N.W.2d 437 (1976) (complaint alleging that pool was inadequately fenced was sufficient to state cause of action against owner for drowning of four-year-old child).

The defense that owners and occupiers of property have against personal injury suits by licensees are also available against suits by trespassers. Additionally, a person subject to a personal injury suit by a trespasser might wish to consider a countersuit. Trespass is an intentional tort. The landowner may recover his or her actual damages as well as punitive damages from the trespasser. These damages might serve as a set-off to any recovery by the injured trespasser.

F. Injured Passerby

"Passerby" includes anyone not on the premises of a sports or recreational facility. Proprietors and those in possession owe passersby many of the same duties that they owe visitors on their property. Owners and occupiers of land have a duty not to willfully and intentionally injure a passerby. Those in possession or control of a sports facility have a duty to use reasonable care in the maintenance and repair of the premises so passersby are not exposed to an unreasonable risk of harm or the rights of adjoining property owners are not unreasonably interfered with.

Operators of golf courses, driving ranges, outdoor tennis clubs, or similar sports facilities need to be especially careful because of errant balls. Golf courses, for example, are frequently sued over stray balls and liability has been established under trespass, negligence and nuisance theories. But regardless of the theory, liability seems to depend upon how frequently balls are driven onto adjoining property.

Those who deliberately choose to live next to a golf course have necessarily accepted the risk of an occasional errant ball falling onto their property, and neither the country club nor the golfer who hit the ball will be liable for injuries to a passerby. *See, e.g., Nussbaum v. Lacopo,* 27 N.Y.2d 311, 317 N.Y.2d 347, 265 N.E.2d 762 (1970) (denying recovery to owner of property adjacent to golf course). However, when the course is designed in such a manner that balls are continually being hit onto adjoining property, then the operators of the golf course may be liable under either trespass or negligence theories. *See, e.g., Fenton v. Quaboag Country Club, Inc.,* 353 Mass. 534, 233 N.E.2d 216 (1968) (320 golf balls hit onto adjacent homeowners property within a period of one year constituted a continuing trespass); *Kirchoffner v. Quam,* 264 N.W.2d 203 (N.D.1978) (golf course which used a public waterway as a hazard was liable for injuries to boater struck in the eye by an errant ball).

The operation of a sports facility will often interfere with an adjoining property owner's right to use and enjoy land, or with the rights of the public in general. If the interference is unreasonable it may constitute a nuisance. A private nuisance exists when the sports activities unreasonably interfere with the rights of the private property owner. There is a public nuisance if it interferes with the rights of the general public.

When a private nuisance is involved the private landowner has the right to sue. Law suits based on a public nuisance theory must normally be brought by the city or other responsible governmental entity, but a private person may sue for a public nuisance if a special injury is shown. *See* W. Prosser & W. Keeton, *Prosser and Keeton on Torts,* § 86 (5th ed. 1984).

Nuisance suits related to sports activities are usually brought by people who own or occupy property adjoining golf courses, stadiums, and race tracks. Their complaints center around the noise, dust, rowdy crowds, lights, and balls hit out of the playing area, as well as other annoyances and dangers. The infrequent ball hit out of play or a similar infrequent disturbance will not support a successful nuisance suit. A nuisance exists only when the intrusions are so regular that they constitute a material and unreasonable interference with the rights of persons occupying adjacent lands, or the rights of the public in general.

Whether one sues under a trespass, negligence, or nuisance theory, he or she can recover for property damage as well as personal injury or death. Property damage includes broken windows and other actual physical injury to property as well as any reduction in market value due to the nuisance. In addition to money damages, the injured may be entitled to an injunction. Injunctive relief is only appropriate when the wrong is of a continuing nature—that is, when it will continue to occur in the future, as with errant golf balls—or when money damages are an inadequate remedy. See § 7.2E *supra* for a general discussion of remedies, including injunctive relief.

7.8 LIABILITY OF ATHLETES FOR INJURY TO SPECTATORS AND PARTICIPANTS

Athletes may be liable for tortious injury to spectators and participants. "Participants" include other athletes, coaches, umpires, and those directly involved in the sport or recreational activity. The respective liabilities of coaches, officials, and spectators are discussed elsewhere in this chapter. See §§ 7.4–7.6 *supra*.

If the athlete is an employee or sufficiently controlled by others, the athlete's tortious conduct may be imputed to the employer or principal. Vicarious liability of team owners and controlling persons for the actions of their athletes is analyzed in § 7.2D *supra*.

A. Injured Participant

An athlete's liability for tortious injury to another participant is based upon willful, wanton, deliberate, or recklessly inflicted harm, not simple negligence. Whether they are athlete, coach, or official, those who participate in an athletic event have willingly submitted to the bodily contact or restrictions of liberty permitted by the rules of the game. See Restatement, Second, Torts § 50 comment b (1965). Participants have no legal recourse for injuries which are a normal and inherent risk of the game. See generally R. Yasser, *Sports Law: Cases and Materials* 609–38 (1985) (discussing tort liability of one participant to another).

Ordinary negligence does not usually establish liability for injury to another participant even when a safety rule is violated. *See, e.g., Oswald v. Township High School District No. 214,* 84 Ill.App.3d 723, 40 Ill.Dec. 456, 406 N.E.2d 157 (1980) (affirming trial court's dismissal of law suit by high school gym student for injuries allegedly sustained as a result of fellow student's violation of rules governing the protection and safety of participants in basketball games). To recover for injuries, a participant must typically allege and prove that the other athlete's conduct was either deliberate, willful, and wanton, or a reckless disregard for the safety of other players.

Coaches, players, referees, managers, and others who voluntarily participate in a sport must accept the risks to which their roles expose them. The participants in a softball or baseball game assume and consent to the risk of being hit by a bat or ball occurring as a result of competition. Players do not consent to the risk of injury caused by another athlete intentionally striking them with a ball or bat. The distinction between injuries natural to and ordinarily encountered in a sports activity, and deliberate, or willful injuries is aptly illustrated by two cases involving second basemen. These cases are *Tavernier v. Maes*, 242 Cal.App.2d 532, 51 Cal.Rptr. 575 (1966) and *Bourque v. Duplechin*, 331 So.2d 40 (La.1976), *cert. den.* 334 So.2d 210 (1976).

The second baseman in *Tavernier* suffered a fractured ankle when he was struck by the sliding base runner. This was a family softball game in which the runner was sliding to avoid a throw from an outfielder. The base runner did not intentionally slide into the second baseman—the runner was merely trying to safely reach the base.

In *Bourque*, the second baseman was standing four or five feet from the base when he was struck under the chin by the base runner's left arm. This incident occurred in a summer league softball game between teams sponsored by local businesses. To make contact with the second baseman, the runner purposely left the base path in order to break up a possible double play. The second baseman suffered a broken jaw and loss of teeth as a result of the blow. An umpire ejected the base runner from the game because of this incident.

Both injured second basemen sued, but only in *Bourque* was the base runner found liable. There was no liability for injuries caused by the sliding base runner in *Tavernier* because this contact was a reasonable risk inherent in and incident to the game, while the blow struck in *Bourque* was not. In one case the second baseman consented to and assumed the risk of injury; in the other he did not.

Players who stand in the base path assume the risk of injury from being spiked by someone sliding into the base because this is a common incident in both softball and baseball. The participant assumes all of the risks incidental to that particular activity which are obvious and foreseeable. A player does not assume the risk of injury from fellow players acting in an unexpected or unsportsmanlike way with a willful, wanton, or reckless lack of concern for the safety of other participants. Thus, the injured second baseman in *Bourque* did not assume the risk of injury from or consent to contact with the base runner who went out of the base path to run into him at full speed.

Assumption of risk is an affirmative defense which the defendant must prove by a preponderance of the evidence. In deciding whether a particular injury is within the risks a participant assumes, courts consider such things as the skill of the athletes, the rules and nature of the game, the foreseeable contact, and any potential dangers which normally attend the activity. It is not enough that the injury was caused by a deliberate or even flagrant breach of rules for participant safety. Courts are not unmindful of the heat of competition, and athletes are accorded a certain margin of error. In order to maintain suit against a fellow athlete, the injured participant must show that the other's conduct constituted a deliberate, willful, wanton, or reckless disregard for the safety of others.

In addition to assumption of risk, the defendant may have other defenses, such as contributory negligence. Section 7.4A–9 *supra* discusses assumption of risk, contributory negligence, and various other potential defenses against personal injury suits by injured participants.

B. Injured Spectator

Spectators who voluntarily attend an athletic contest assume the obvious and inherent risks incidental to good faith and non-negligent competition in that sport. See discussion of assumption of risk for spectators in § 7.4B *supra*. Spectators do not assume the risk of being intentionally harmed. Nor do they assume the risk of injury due to an athlete's negligence.

The athlete who deliberately injures a spectator is liable for the intentional harm caused. *See, e.g., Atlanta Baseball Co. v. Lawrence,* 38 Ga.App. 497, 144 S.E. 351 (1928) (baseball player enters stands and attacks spectator who had been heckling him). Athletes are likewise expected to exercise reasonable care for the safety of spectators and bystanders. To the extent that reasonable care is not taken, an athlete may be found negligent. It is not necessary for the athlete's conduct to reach the level of a willful, wanton, or reckess act; ordinary negligence is sufficient to establish liability for injuries to a bystander. *See, e.g., Osborne v. Sprowls,* 84 Ill.2d 390, 50 Ill.Dec. 645, 419 N.E.2d 913 (1981) (negligence rather than a willful and wanton standard was correct measure of tort liability for a participant who injured a bystander during game of catch).

7.9 LIABILITY OF DOCTORS AND RELATED MEDICAL PERSONNEL

Physicians, trainers, and related medical personnel may be liable for injuries arising out of the treatment of an athlete. Although the duty of owners, operators and those in control of a sport or recreational activity to provide medical care to injured spectators and participants is a closely related subject, it is not covered in this section.

A. Malpractice

Because of their special skills and training, doctors, trainers, and physical therapists are held to a higher standard of care in the treatment of the sick and injured. These medical professionals are not judged by the traditional reasonable person standard of care. Instead, they are required to have and exercise all of the skills and care ordinarily exercised by one practicing in their profession in the diagnosis and treatment of patients. Stated otherwise, the standard for these professionals is the care commonly exercised by others in their profession, whereas the ordinary reasonable man standard is only a minimum of care under the circumstances. *See* Restatement, Second, Torts § 289 comment m (1965).

If a physician, therapist, or athletic trainer holds himself out as a sports medicine specialist, a still higher standard of care will apply. Medical professionals who claim to be specialists must employ the reasonable skill and knowledge common to others in that specialty rather than the profession in general. Because they are held to a higher standard of care in the diagnosis and treatment of injured athletes, sports medicine specialist may be liable for malpractice when a general practitioner rendering the identical treatment will not be liable.

The medical professional should be particularly careful to disclose all of the alternative treatments as well as the prognosis for each treatment with an injured athlete as a patient. Whether the treatment involves surgery, medication, or therapy, the medical professional has the duty to disclose the alternatives to the recommended treatment and the risks associated with each alternative. This duty was recently reviewed in *Wilson v. Vancouver Hockey Club*, 5 D.L.R.4th 282 (1983), a Canadian case brought by a professional hockey player.

Wilson sued the Victoria Hockey Club, his employer, contending that his professional career had been shortened because of the team doctor's failure to diagnose and promptly treat a cancerous mole on his left arm. The physician apparently suspected that the mole might be cancerous, but advised the athlete that it could be taken care of after the season ended. This delay resulted in an expansion of the tumor which required more radical surgery. The doctor was not responsible for the cancer, but Wilson alleged that had he been informed of the cancer and promptly treated, he would have spent considerably less time recovering from surgery. Wilson's major claim was for the income lost because of the extended recovery period.

The Canadian court concluded that the team physician was negligent for not immediately advising Wilson of both the suspected cancer, and of the risks involved in waiting to be treated until after the end of hockey season. But despite the doctor's negligence, Wilson was not entitled to any damages for loss of income.

Damages were not awarded because Wilson had been waived by every team in the National Hockey League before it was known that he had cancer. The doctor's negligence was not, therefore, the proximate cause of Wilson's loss of income. His professional career would have ended at the conclusion of that season regardless of the cancer surgery.

Wilson is an interesting case because it frames both the duty to disclose and the concept of causation. The law requires that a patient give informed consent to treatment. Consent is informed when the patient is advised of all the available alternatives and the prognosis for each. If the medical professional does not advise the injured athlete of treatment options, that professional is negligent if a reasonable person in the patient's position would not have gone ahead with the treatment had there been proper disclosure. However, Wilson also makes clear that damages are not automatically awarded to the patient merely because there was no informed consent to treatment. The patient is entitled to damages only if the patient can show that harm was in fact caused because proper warning had not been given.

The patient's right to choose establishes the parameters of a medical professional's duty to disclose. Every adult with a sound mind has the right to decide what shall be done to their own body. To aid a patient in exercising this right, a doctor has the duty to give the patient the information the patient needs. A doctor does this by making a reasonable disclosure of the alternatives to the proposed therapy, along with any dangers inherently and potentially involved. *See, e.g., Canterbury v. Spence,* 464 F.2d 772 (D.C.Cir. 1972) (jury question as to whether one percent chance of paralysis from surgery gave rise to a duty to disclose). The disclosure should be in nontechnical terms to insure that it is comprehended by the patient. An otherwise reasonable disclosure of treatment and attendant risks may be defective if given when the patient is medicated and cannot understand the explanation.

This duty to disclose is most troublesome for medical professionals when there is a conflict between the interests of the athlete and the team. A team physician or trainer may be placed in the untenable position of having to elect a treatment procedure based upon the immediate needs of the team rather than the long term interests of the athlete. Loss of a key athlete to injuries can be devastating to a team's performance, thus there is often considerable pressure to quickly return the athlete to competition.

Through modern medical treatment, severely injured athletes can continue to perform, often at the risk of further injury and lasting disability. The choice to play injured rather than sit out the remainder of the season to fully recover is the athlete's choice, not that of the team, coach, or medical professional. Care should be taken by the doctor to thoroughly explain each option to the athlete and the reasonable risks in playing injured as opposed to not playing. If the athlete is a minor, the options must be explained to the parents, for it is their consent which must be obtained. Under no circumstances should the physician, trainer or therapist choose for the patient, nor should they fail to advise of any reasonable treatment alternative.

B. Breach of Warranty

A physician should exercise caution not to speak too assuringly of a particular procedure or expected treatment result. If the doctor's comments go beyond mere pretreatment reassurances, they may be construed as an express warranty, in which case the doctor will be liable if the promised results are not achieved. The basis for the doctor's liability is in contract rather than tort.

This type of suit has one significant advantage over a medical malpractice case. Because it is a contract action, the patient does not have to prove any negligence on the part of the doctor. All that the patient has to show is that the physician promised certain results from the treatment, the patient relied upon the doctor's assurances and underwent the prescribed procedure, and the results were not as promised. Lack of negligence is not a defense to a breach of warranty case. The crucial issue is whether or not the promise was made and relied upon.

Words such as "I guarantee" or "I promise" will almost certainly create a physician's warranty, but these are not the only instances in which an express warranty is created. In *Scarzella v. Saxon,* 436 A.2d 358 (D.C.App.1981) a urologist's assurances that a surgical procedure would be "safe" and without complications were found to be expressed warranties. Consequently, when the patient did develop serious complications, the warranties were breached and the doctor was liable under a breach of contract theory. A warranty is created when the physician's pretreatment statements clearly and unmistakenly gave the patient a positive assurance that a particular result will be achieved or harm avoided.

C. Disclosure of Patient's Medical Information

A final potential source of tort liability for doctors has to do with the disclosure of medical information. Doctors and their patients enjoy a fiduciary relationship. This requires that physicians not disclose information of a confidential nature regarding their patient's condition or treatment. Colleges and professional teams may inquire about the athlete's medical condition, but the doctor is not permitted to disclose this information without his or her patient's consent. (Paragraph eight of the standard NFL player contract, *infra* at § 10.4, requires the athlete to make a full and complete disclosure to the team of his physical and mental condition.) The unauthorized disclosure of a patient's medical data or other confidential communication exposes the physician to tort liability for any resulting harm. *See Hammonds v. Aetna Casualty & Surety Co.,* 243 F.Supp. 793 (N.D.Ohio 1965) (patient is entitled to legal recourse for breach of fiduciary duty regarding confidentiality of medical information).

Furthermore, even when the doctor is authorized to disclose information on an injured athlete's physical condition, care should be taken to give an accurate nonmisleading opinion. If the physician gives an inaccurate or misleading opinion and some third party, such as a professional team, reasonably relies upon that opinion to the team's subsequent detriment, the doctor may be responsible for the resulting harm.

D. Vicarious Liability

Vicarious liability is addressed in § 7.2D *supra,* but brief mention should be made here of the possibility of imputing a doctor's malpractice to the team or school that employs him. If the medical professional is in fact an employee or agent, negligence can be charged to the employer. *See, e.g., Robitaille v. Vancouver Hockey Club, Ltd.,* 124 D.L.R.3d 228 (1981) (National Hockey League club was vicariously liable for negligence of team doctor in treating player with spinal injury). When the athlete is covered by workmen's compensation, however, he or she cannot sue either the employee doctor or the team.

7.10 LIABILITY OF MANUFACTURERS AND COMMERCIAL SUPPLIERS OF ATHLETIC EQUIPMENT

The liability of coaches, owners, and other gratuitous suppliers of athletic equipment was addressed in §§ 7.4A–3 and 7.7B–3 *supra.* Section 3.6A, *supra,* discussed equipment suppliers' liability under state consumer protection laws. This section concerns the tort liability of manufacturers and commercial suppliers of sports equipment for personal injury or property damage caused by their products.

The team "manufacturer" includes not only those in the business of producing athletic equipment, but also any one who sells athletic products under their own name. Products are commonly manufactured by one business entity and sold under the name of another. Both manufacturer and seller are treated under tort law as the manufacturer of that particular product. Sometimes athletic equipment is comprised of component parts. Producers of component parts are considered manufacturers along with the businesses that assemble the various parts into a final piece of athletic equipment.

"Commercial suppliers" are in the business of supplying athletic equipment for a fee. Commercial suppliers are the merchants and stores that sell sporting goods. Lessors of recreational equipment, such as ski rental shops, are normally held to the same tort law standards as sellers.

There are three potential theories for imposing liability upon persons who make, sell, or lease athletic equipment. These theories are: negligence, strict liability, and warranty. The first two are tort theories; the latter involves a breach of contract. A manufacturer or commercial supplier can be liable for injuries caused by equipment under all or any number of these theories.

A. Negligence

As previously mentioned, *supra* § 7.2A–1, negligence is defined as doing something that an ordinary prudent person would not have done under similar circumstances, or failing to do something that an ordinary prudent person would have done under similar circumstances. People and businesses who manufacture athletic equipment must use reasonable care in the design and construction of their product. Reasonable care means not only designing and manufacturing a product that is reasonably safe for its intended uses, but it must also be safe for any foreseeable misuse.

In addition to the care required in designing and making athletic equipment, manufacturers are expected to test their products for hidden defects and to warn equipment users of any dangers. A failure to conduct reasonable tests or to warn of latent defects constitutes negligence even when the product otherwise meets the design and manufacturing standards established by law.

Recently, there has been a sharp increase in litigation involving sports injuries and the makers of protective headgear. Helmet manufacturers employ considerable skill and care in designing and making a safe product, and helmets are extensively tested. Yet despite all of this care, it is not unusual for an athlete to suffer serious head injury while wearing protective headgear. The manufacturer is liable for these injuries if it failed to warn users of the potential dangers inherent in the product.

If a manufacturer knows or should know of potential harm to a user because of the nature of the product, an adequate warning of such dangers must be given. To be effective, the warning must be adequate to perform its intended function of risk reduction. Thus, a product warning should (1) specify the particular risk presented; (2) be consistent with how the product is used; (3) provide the reasons for the warnings; and (4) be presented in such a manner that it can be reasonably expected to reach foreseeable users of the dangerous product. A warning which does not meet all of these criteria may be inadequate. *See, e.g., Pell v. Victor J. Andrew High School,* 123 Ill.App.3d 423, 78 Ill.Dec. 739, 462 N.E.2d 858 (1984) (general warning that "misuse and abuse" of mini-trampoline was dangerous, was not adequate to warn novice gymnast of the serious risk of spinal cord injuries involved in using this particular piece of equipment without either spotters or safety harness.) But there are circumstances that do not require a manufacturer to warn.

A warning is not required when the danger is obvious or when the user already knows of the product's hazardous propensity. Helmet manufacturers, for instance, have been found negligent for failing to warn a high school athlete that his headgear would not prevent all brain injuries, *see Rawlings Sporting Goods Co. v. Daniels,* 619 S.W.2d 435 (Tex.1981); but nonnegligent for not giving a similar warning to an adult hockey player with over twenty-five years of experience playing the sport. *See Durkee v. Cooper of Canada, Ltd.,* 99 Mich.App. 693, 298 N.W.2d 620 (1980). The distinction between these two cases is that in one case the athlete either recognized or should have recognized the helmet's limitations; if the athlete is aware of the danger the manufacturer has no duty to warn.

A high school athlete who is given equipment and encouraged to participate in a contact sport is less likely to appreciate the fact that a helmet will not fully prevent serious injury than the adult who has years of experience and selects the equipment personally. In the *Rawlings Sporting Goods* case, a failure to warn was the proximate cause of the boy's brain damage because had he known of the danger, he would not have made head-to-head contact with the other player. The failure to warn in *Durkee* was regarded as inconsequential since the adult plaintiff already knew or should have known of the risks involved in wearing a particular type of hockey headgear. When the athlete is aware of the danger, the manufacturer's failure to warn cannot be a proximate cause of the injuries.

Merchants in the business of selling athletic equipment are not ordinarily liable for the negligent design, manufacture, and testing of a product, although they are responsible for injuries to a user when the merchant knows or has reason to know that the equipment is unreasonably dangerous for its intended use. Athletic equipment is considered unreasonably dangerous when it poses a foreseeable risk of serious injury and the danger is such that the user will not likely discover it. A supplier of athletic equipment is negligent when reasonable care is not exercised in selling gear which the supplier knew or should have known was dangerous for its intended uses. *See* Restatement, Second, Torts § 388 (1965).

Lessors of athletic equipment have the same general duty as sellers with several additional responsibilities. Lessors are expected to use reasonable care to inspect and maintain their equipment in a condition safe for its intended uses. A lessor must exercise reasonable care to discover any hidden danger which poses an unreasonable risk of injury to others, and to either correct or warn users of such dangers. *See, e.g., Ducas v. Prince,* 336 Mass. 555, 146 N.E.2d 677 (1957) (operator of roller skating rink was liable for personal injuries sustained by a patron to whom he had knowingly furnished skates with age weakened laces).

It is important to note that the breach of duty gives rise to liability under a negligence theory, not the fact that a particular piece of sports equipment caused the injury. However, when negligence is established, the plaintiff can recover for personal injury, death, and economic loss, such as any lost profits which he or she sustained.

The traditional defenses and limitations upon recovery in negligence actions apply to suits against manufacturers and commercial suppliers. Participants assume the risk of injury or may be contributorily negligent when they knowingly use defective equipment. The chance of equipment-induced injuries may be an inherent danger in some sports and thus preclude recovery. *See, e.g., James v. Hillerich & Bradsby Co.,* 299 S.W.2d 92 (Ky.1957) (the risk of being struck and injured by a broken bat is among the dangers common to and assumed by participants in baseball and softball).

B. Strict Liability

Strict liability is literally liability without fault. The policy behind this tort theory was previously discussed in § 7.2A–2 *supra.* Manufacturers and commercial suppliers of athletic equipment can be held strictly liable for the physical harm their products cause.

Strict liability in tort applies to those in the business of making or selling a product that is unreasonably dangerous because of a defect. Lessors of athletic equipment are treated the same as sellers. Strict liability in tort does not apply to coaches, athletic directors, schools, and others who gratuitously furnish equipment because they are not part of the manufacturing and marketing chain. *See, e.g., Hemphill v. Sayers,* 552 F.Supp. 685 (S.D.Ill.1982) (dismissing strict liability action against athletic director, coach and trainer, but indicating that if properly pleaded, suit might stand against manufacturer of defective equipment).

Strict liability will not apply when the equipment has been substantially changed after leaving the defendant's custody and control. Liability is premised upon the fact that the defendant placed a defective and unreasonably dangerous product in the stream of commerce. There is no need to show lack of care or other fault on the part of a defendant who sells a product which is both defective and unreasonably dangerous to consumers. Strict liability exists because of public policy: in marketing a product for use and consumption by the general public, the seller should stand behind that product and assume, as a cost of doing business, the responsibility for anyone injured by his or her defective product. *See* Restatement, Second, Torts § 402A comment c (1965).

Athletic equipment is defective when it is not reasonably safe for its normal and intended uses. The equipment can be defective due to an unsafe design, the manner in which it is manufactured, or the failure to warn of a latent hazard. Equipment is considered "unreasonably dangerous" when the defective condition makes it more dangerous than that contemplated by the ordinary person possessing the knowledge common in that community about both the equipment's characteristics and the particular purposes for which it is used. If the ordinary person would recognize the open and obvious danger of playing hockey with a particular style of helmet, that headgear is neither defective nor unreasonably dangerous.

Under strict liability the focus is upon defects which a reasonable user would not contemplate. This focus is clearly demonstrated by comparing the results in *Garrett v. Nissen Corp.*, 84 N.M. 16, 498 P.2d 1359 (1972) with *Pell v. Victor J. Andrew High School*, 123 Ill.App.3d 423, 78 Ill.Dec. 739, 462 N.E.2d 858 (1984). Both cases involved paralyzing spinal injuries to high school gymnasts sustained in trampoline accidents. Each athlete sued the trampoline manufacturer claming the equipment was defective and unreasonably dangerous but in only one case, *Pell*, did the plaintiff prevail.

In *Garrett* the injured boy was a high school senior and former medalist in the New Mexico State Gymnastics Meet. Garrett was performing a one-and-three-quarter front flip on the high school's trampoline when he landed on his head. Although he came down on the jumping surface of the trampoline, Garrett struck the mat with sufficient force to break his neck, causing permanent paralysis.

Garrett sued the trampoline manufacturer under a strict liability tort theory, contending that the manufacturer was liable because it had marketed the trampoline in a dangerously defective condition. The trampoline's alleged defect consisted of not having a conspicuous sign warning would-be users about the possibility of paralyzing spinal cord injury if they landed on their heads. The trial court summarily dismissed the case and the Supreme Court affirmed because in *Garrett* there was no duty to warn about an open and obvious danger of which the young man was fully aware.

In *Pell*, on the other hand, the Illinois Court of Appeals affirmed a $3,400,000 judgment against the manufacturer of a mini-trampoline ("mini-tramp"). The mini-tramp was purchased for use by high school athletes, including the plaintiff, a 16 year-old sophomore and beginner gymnast. It consisted of a 37-inch square metal frame with adjustable legs; across the frame was stretched a "bed" of polypropylene upon which the user jumped. Mini-tramps differed from regular trampolines in that they are not used for repetitive bouncing, but as a vaulting board. The athlete runs to and jumps on the mini-tramp, and is propelled onto a floor mat with considerably more force and velocity than a vaulting board.

Pell was attempting a somersault from the mini-tramp when she experienced a sharp pain in her knee. Due to this pain she was unable to complete her somersault. She landed on the mat, severing her spine. Like Garrett, Pell sued the manufacturer, claiming the mini-tramp was defective and unreasonably dangerous because it did not adequately warn users of the risk of spinal injuries if somersaults were attempted without the use of a safety harness or spotter.

The distinction between *Garrett* and *Pell* lies in the ability of the injured athletes to perceive and comprehend the danger to which they were exposed by using the equipment. Garrett was an experienced gymnast who was familiar with the trampoline, and he either knew or should have recognized the obvious dangers involved in landing head first on the jumping surface. If Garrett was aware of the danger, the equipment was neither defective nor unreasonably dangerous because of the absence of a warning. If the trampoline was not defective or unreasonably dangerous, the athlete had no basis to recover under strict liability in tort.

Conversely, the danger Pell faced was not as open and obvious. The mini-tramp is apparently a very dangerous piece of equipment and this danger was compounded by the athlete's inexperience. Had Pell been an experienced athlete and fully aware of the dangers involved, the results in that case may have been different, just as *Garrett* may have turned out differently had the injured boy been a beginning gymnast instead of a seasoned athlete.

Contributory negligence is not usually a defense to strict liability. The manufacturer or commercial supplier can, however, raise assumption of risk as a defense. *See* Restatement, Second, Torts § 402A comment n (1965). Misuse of the equipment is also a defense. *See, e.g., Genteman v. Saunders Archery Co.,* 42 Ill.App.3d 294, 355 N.E.2d 647 (1976) (archer's intentional disregard of instructions for attachment and use of bow string silencer precluded his recovering for an eye injury). Another possible defense lies in statutes of repose, which an increasing number of states have enacted. These laws restrict the time for bringing product liability actions, and many reduce or eliminate liability for the merchant who sold the defective injury producing equipment. See *supra* § 7.3F for a discussion of statutes of repose.

C. Warranty Liability

Breach of warranty is a viable and effective cause of action for many injuries caused by athletic equipment. The basis for warranty liability is a breach of contract. A warranty is simply a guarantee the seller makes to the purchaser of a product. If the product does not live up to what was promised, the warranty is broken and the seller is liable under contract law for the resulting harm.

Warranty liability is covered by the Uniform Commercial Code ("UCC"). Article 2 of the UCC covers warranties and has been enacted with slight variations by every state except Louisiana. Warranties are either express or implied by law. It is not necessary for the seller of sports equipment to use the words "guarantee" or "warrant" for a warranty to be created.

1. Express Warranty

Express warranties are created by the statements or conduct of the manufacturer or seller. A seller is generally not liable for the express warranties made by the manufacturer. Persons renting athletic equipment can also make express warranties. When the transaction is gratuitous rather than commercial, tort liability may exist for negligent misrepresentation, but no express warranty exists. An express warranty cannot exist in the absence of a valid contract, and there is no contract when the equipment is gratuitously supplied.

A commercial supplier of equipment creates an express warranty with any "affirmation of fact or promise" made to the buyer about the goods that becomes part of the basis of the bargain between them. Promises become a part of the basis of the bargain when they are made prior to the purchase and are relied upon by the buyer. Express warranties can be created by a description of the equipment, or by showing the buyer a sample or model of what the buyer is to receive. *See* Uniform Commercial Code § 2–313 (1962).

The test is not whether the seller intended to make an express warranty. A warranty exists if a reasonable person would have taken the seller's comments and actions to be a promise or affirmation of fact regarding the performance, characteristics, or suitability of the equipment. A photograph of athletic equipment can be an express warranty if the purchaser sees the picture and buys the items assuming that it will conform to the illustration. *See, e.g., Rinkmasters v. City of Utica,* 75 Misc.2d 941, 348 N.Y.S.2d 940 (1973) (offering ice resurfacing machine for sale through illustrated catalogue without advising purchasers that the equipment did not conform to the illustration constituted an express warranty which was breached when the nonconforming item was shipped to the buyer).

In *Hauter v. Zogarts,* 14 Cal.3d 104, 534 P.2d 377, 120 Cal. Rptr. 681 (1975), the phrase "Completely Safe Ball Will Not Hit Player" on the carton containing a practice aid for golfers was found to be an express warranty. This warranty was breached when a young boy was struck in the head and seriously injured while using the device. The manufacturer was liable for the boy's injuries.

2. Implied Warranty

Implied warranties are created by law. They automatically come into being under certain circumstances. It is not necessary that the manufacturer or commercial supplier of athletic equipment take affirmative steps to create an implied warranty. The UCC provides for two implied warranties that may give rise to liability for equipment-caused injuries. Those are merchantability and fitness for particular purpose.

(a) Merchantability

An implied warranty of merchantability exists when the commercial supplier is a merchant. *See* Uniform Commercial Code § 2–314 (1962). "Merchant" is defined as any person or business entity who deals in that particular item of equipment or otherwise creates the impression of having knowledge or skill peculiar of that equipment. One may also be a merchant by employing someone who either regularly deals in the equipment or claims to have special knowledge about it. *See Id.* at § 2–104. If the equipment supplier is not a merchant, the implied warranty of merchantability does not exist.

A merchant who sells or leases athletic equipment is warranting that the goods are fit for the ordinary purposes for which they are intended to be used. This implied warranty likewise includes the guarantee that the equipment will conform to any promise or affirmation of fact on the label.

(b) Fitness for Particular Purpose

Creation of an implied warranty of fitness for particular purpose does not require the presence of a merchant, but it does require a sale or lease of the equipment. An implied warranty of fitness comes into existence when the manufacturer or commercial supplier knows why the buyer needs the equipment and realizes that the buyer is relying upon the supplier to select the proper equipment to meet those needs. When an implied warranty of fitness exists, the equipment supplier is guaranteeing that the equipment will meet the buyer's particular needs. *See* Uniform Commercial Code § 2–315 (1962).

Equipment may be fit for its ordinary uses so it does not violate the implied warranty of merchantability, yet does breach the warranty of fitness because the buyer's particular needs are not met. A classic case of equipment fit for its ordinary uses but not for the buyer's particular purposes is *Filler v. Rayex Corporation*, 435 F.2d 336 (7th Cir. 1970). *Filler* also serves as a good example of the interrelationship between contract and tort theories for recovering for injuries caused by defective equipment.

Filler was a sixteen year-old high school baseball player who lost an eye during practice. The boy was wearing flip-down sunglasses which were shattered by a flyball, driving sharp splinters of glass into his right eye. These sunglasses had been manufactured by Rayex Corporation.

Rayex ran the following advertisement for its "baseball" sunglasses:

PLAY BALL!

and *Flip* for Instant Eye Protection with

RAYEX

Baseball

SUNGLASSES

Professional

FLIP–SPECS

Id. at 337. Filler's coach saw this ad, and in reliance upon it, purchased six pair of glasses for use by outfielders and second basemen. The coach gave Filler the pair of Rayex glasses he was wearing at the time of the injury, but the boy did not bring suit against either the coach or school district.

The coach and school district were probably not sued because they were not liable under the facts in that case. As his employer, the school district would have been vicariously liable for the coach's torts, but if the coach was not liable, neither was the school district employer. The coach had furnished the glasses to the boy because he had *reasonably* assumed from the ad that the glasses could be safely worn while playing baseball. Since he was not negligent nor engaged in the business of selling the glasses, the coach could not be subject to tort liability under either negligence or strict liability theories.

There was likewise no apparent basis for a breach of express or implied warranty action against the coach because: (1) the coach had let Filler use the glasses and had not leased or sold them to Filler, (2) the coach made no promise or affirmation of fact regarding the Rayex sunglasses, and (3) the coach was not a merchant. Filler, however, sued the manufacturer Rayex under negligence, strict liability, and warranty theories, and prevailed on each one.

By advertising its product as baseball sunglasses, Rayex had created an implied warranty of fitness for particular purpose. That purpose was to wear the glasses while playing baseball. Rayex glasses were obviously not fit for their particular purpose because they lacked shatter-proof lenses. Rayex sunglasses were fit for the ordinary purposes for which sunglasses are used—that is, to protect eyes from sunlight. Consequently, had the glasses been advertised as regular sunglasses, there would have been no implied warranty to breach.

Rayex was found negligent because it knew the sunglasses shattered readily, did not adequately test its sunglasses, and did not warn users of the danger of serious eye injury from wearing the glasses in baseball games. Rayex was also found liable under strict liability. Strict liability existed because Rayex was engaged in the business of manufacturing and marketing sunglasses with an unreasonably dangerous defect: lenses which shattered. Rayex glasses were further defective and unreasonably dangerous because they lacked an adequate warning.

Anyone engaged in the business of selling a product who, by advertising or labels, misrepresents a material fact concerning the character or quality of the product is strictly liable for the physical harm caused to consumers who rely upon the misstatement. It is not necessary that the factual misrepresentation be intentionally or negligently made; strict liability exists if the misstatement is material and the injured consumer purchased the product because of it. *See* Restatement, Second, Torts § 402B (1965).

When Rayex advertised its glasses as baseball sunglasses and stated that they provided "instant eye protection," it was making a misrepresentation of material fact. The glasses were not baseball sunglasses nor did they provide instant eye protection. This misleading advertisement was material and was relied upon by Filler's coach who testified that he would not have purchased the glasses but for the assurances conveyed by the advertisement. Rayex may very well have been strictly liable for the boy's injuries because of this misleading sales ad alone.

The advertisement might similarly have created an express warranty. If a reasonable person would have concluded that Rayex was promising purchasers that its sunglasses could be safely worn while playing baseball, then an express warranty was created. This express warranty was breached when the glasses shattered, causing the loss of the boy's eye.

Filler clearly illustrates that tort and warranty theories can be routinely combined in defective equipment cases, and that there are certain advantages in suing under warranty rather than tort theories. In a breach of warranty case the plaintiff need show only the existence of a warranty and the equipment's failure to meet that warranty. A negligence action requires proof of a lack of due care, and a strict liability action applies only to unreasonably dangerous defects. A plaintiff can recover for breach of warranty when the manufacturer is not negligent and the equipment is not defective. Warranty actions also permit the injured party to recover for lost profits and other economic loss. Economic loss is not generally recoverable under either negligence or strict liability without some additional injury to the plaintiff or the plaintiff's property.

3. *Defenses*

The plaintiff in a breach of warranty suit need not be concerned with either contributory negligence or assumption of risk as defenses. The common defenses and limitations on liability asserted against a breach of warranty claim are existence of a disclaimer, misuse, lack of notice, lack of privity, and statutes of limitation and repose.

(a) *Disclaimers*

Implied warranties may be disclaimed. The implied warranty of merchantability may be disclaimed simply by stating that "there is no implied warranty of merchantability." If the disclaimer is in writing it must be conspicuous, and any disclaimer made after the equipment has been purchased is ineffective. Some courts, however, have held that merely stating there are no implied warranties is not sufficient to disclaim the implied warranty of merchantability. The disclaimer must use the term "merchantability," or general exculpatory clauses such as sold "as is" or "with all faults" to satisfy these courts. An implied warranty of merchantability may also be disclaimed by offering the buyer an opportunity to inspect the equipment before purchase. If the buyer is given the right to inspect, then regardless of whether or not the right is exercised, there is no implied warranty of merchantability covering any defect that was discovered or should have been discovered by inspecting. *See* Uniform Commercial Code § 2–316 (1962).

It is not necessary to use the words "fitness for particular purpose" to disclaim this implied warranty. It is sufficient to state that there are no implied warranties if the disclaimer is in writing and conspicuous. The implied warranties of fitness for particular purpose may also be disclaimed by general exculpatory language or by giving the buyer an opportunity to inspect.

Disclaimers are not generally effective against express warranties. Once made, it is difficult if not impossible to disclaim or modify an express warranty.

(b) Misuse

Misuse is a defense to breach of warranty. When the plaintiff used the equipment in an abnormal manner not intended by the seller misuse has occurred. Misuse may consist of not following the seller's instructions regarding use and maintenance of the equipment. Modifying the equipment may also constitute misuse, but misuse is not a defense when it is reasonably foreseeable.

(c) Notice

The UCC requires the buyer to give notice to the seller within a reasonable time after the buyer discovers or should have discovered the breach of warranty. Failure to give this notice supposedly bars the buyer "from any remedy." *See id.* at § 2–607. Some courts have interpreted this requirement to prevent the buyer from suing when timely notification is not given, while other courts are reluctant to foreclose a breach of warranty suit for lack of notice when physical injuries are involved. *See, e.g., Bengford v. Carlem Corp.,* 156 N.W.2d 855 (Iowa 1968) (failure to give notice did not bar breach of warranty claim for injuries caused by allegedly defective farm machinery).

(d) Privity

Lack of privity is a troublesome defense. Since warranty liability is founded in contract law, some states permit only a party to the contract or one in privity with that party to sue for breach of warranty. In these jurisdictions, the concept of privity has been expanded to include the equipment purchaser, members of the purchaser's family, and guests in the purchaser's household: innocent bystanders, employees, and others injured by the equipment cannot sue for breach of warranty. *See, e.g., Hemphill v. Sayers,* 552 F.Supp. 685 (S.D. Ill. 1982) (because the university and not the athlete had purchased the helmet, the injured football player lacked privity and could not sue the helmet manufacturer for breach of implied warranty). Other states do not limit the right to sue for breach of warranty to the purchaser, the purchaser's family, and the purchaser's guests. These jurisdictions permit suits by anyone who may reasonably be expected to use, consume, or be affected by the product. *See, e.g., Filler v. Rayex Corporation,* 435 F.2d 336 (7th Cir. 1970) (although the sunglasses had been bought by the coach, high school ball player injured while using the glasses successfully sued manufacturer under breach of warranty theory).

(e) Statutes of Limitation and Repose

The statute of limitation for a breach of contract involving athletic equipment is normally four years after the cause of action accrues. A cause of action for breach of warranty accrues when delivery of the equipment is tendered to the buyer. In most instances a breach of warranty suit must be brought within four years of the purchase unless the seller explicitly extends the warranty beyond that time period. *See* Uniform Commercial Code § 2–725 (1962). It is therefore possible that a user may be injured more than four years after the equipment was purchased, and thus the breach of warranty suit would be banned by the statute of limitation.

An increasing number of states have statutes of repose which further hinder breach of warranty suits for injuries caused by equipment. Statutes of repose tend to force the injured party to look to the equipment manufacturer, who is frequently located out-of-state. This relieves local retailers of liability under both strict liability and implied warranty theories. For a more detailed discussion of statutes of limitation and statutes of repose, *see*, respectively, §§ 7.3E and 7.3F *supra*.

7.11 RISK MANAGEMENT

A coach or school administrator cannot prevent sports related injuries. Nor can owners, operators, or managers of athletic facilities avoid being sued by a spectator who has suffered an injury on the premise. Yet there are procedures that may be employed to reduce the likelihood of being sued and having to pay a large money judgment to a seriously injured plaintiff. Many of these are common sense procedures that can be implemented without the aid of lawyers or other professionals.

School administrators and others working with children in sports must hire competent personnel. Children must be given adequate training and supervision to participate in a sports activity, and those in charge must likewise take care to obey any laws or regulations implemented for the participants' safety. If a sports activity involves equipment, care must be taken to insure that participants have the proper equipment. Supervisors must establish a reasonable inspection and maintenance schedule for both equipment and athletic facilities.

To minimize the financial losses associated with law suits, liability insurance should be purchased. Workmen's compensation coverage might also be purchased. Colleges and universities would be prudent to consider workmen's compensation coverage for their athletes. Often, the workmen's compensation premium will be substantially less than premiums the institution pays for insurance coverage for its athletic activities.

Finally, assets may be shielded by incorporating. The law views a corporation as a person, responsible for its own wrongs and those of its employees. If a corporation is properly created and operated, the stockholders normally have no liability for either the torts or contracts of the corporation. Thus, rather than conducting an athletic event itself, an institution may form a corporation and conduct the sports event through that entity.

The corporation hires its employees and leases any equipment or facilities from the institution. That way, if someone were injured and sued, his or her only recourse would be against the corporation. A plaintiff could not reach either the institution or its assets. *See, e.g., Klinsky v. Hanson Van Winkle Munning Co.,* 38 N.J. Super. 439, 119 A.2d 166 (1955) (employer's use of separate corporation to conduct employee recreational activities shielded him from suit by plaintiff injured by a bat that slipped from the batter's hands).

Chapter Eight

WORKMEN'S COMPENSATION

Workmen's compensation statutes are state laws established to compensate workers or their families for job-related injuries, diseases, or death. If covered by workmen's compensation ("workmen's comp"), an injured employee is entitled to benefits for job related injury or illness regardless of fault. Workmen's comp is in fact an insurance plan, whereby those employees killed or injured on the job, or their families, receive payment for medical expenses, lost income, and disability. Workmen's compensation benefits do not, as a general rule, cover casual employees or those hired to perform some service not in the usual course of the employer's trade or business.

The benefits paid under a particular workmen's compensation system are set by the state legislature, and the amounts of compensation vary from state to state as do the workmen's comp statutes themselves. All state workmen's comp laws are similar in one important respect: the compensation provided is usually an *exclusive remedy* for both the employee and the family insofar as the employer's liability is concerned.

When workmen's comp coverage exists, neither the injured employee nor his family may bring a tort action against the employer or co-workers. In some jurisdictions an injured employee may sue his employer and co-workers for intentional torts. The injured employee may also maintain tort actions against third parties, but in most states the employer and fellow workers enjoy absolute immunity for any injury they may have caused. The injured employee or their family, if he or she is killed, are paid their designated benefits irrespective of fault. An employee is not entitled to benefits for self-inflicted harm, nor will the employee be compensated for nonjob-related injury, disease, or death. In

274

deciding whether a particular injury was willfuly self-inflicted or nonjob-related, courts tend to favor granting coverage. *See e.g., Bird v. Lake Hopatcong Country Club,* 119 N.J.L. 415, 197 A. 282 (1938) (injuries sustained by caddy in fall from apple tree on golf course were incurred within the course of his employment because he had climbed tree at the direction of a superior).

Workmen's compensation is funded by the employer. Some states require the employer to purchase an insurance policy on employees, and large employers are often permitted to self-insure by setting up contingency funds to cover claims. Still other states have a state fund to which employers are required to pay a yearly premium. The rate or premium an employer pays for each employee depends upon the risk factor assigned a particular vocation. The more dangerous the employment or greater the likelihood of injury, the higher the rate charged.

Workmen's comp coverage is mandatory for most employers. Unless otherwise exempt, an employer must provide workmen's comp coverage for employees. Charitable nonprofit organizations are among the employers normally exempt from providing workmen's comp coverage. However, even exempt employers are generally given the option of obtaining workmen's compensation coverage if they choose to do so.

Failure of the employer to obtain mandatory coverage does not deprive an injured employee of the right to claim workmen's comp benefits. Instead, the employee is often given a choice of remedies. If the employee has a tort action against the employer, a tort suit can be brought to recover damages from the employer. If the injury was the result of an unavoidable accident or the employer was not negligent no tort action will lie, but the injured employee can still proceed with a workmen's compensation claim. The employer personally pays the benefits in this case, rather than the state fund or an insurance company. The employer is also sanctioned with a fine or penalty for not obtaining the mandatory coverage.

Workmen's compensation can be a blessing as well as a burden to an injured employee. The employee is automatically entitled to benefits even when the injuries are caused solely by the employee's own negligence. The disadvantage of workmen's comp coverage is that the benefits paid to an injured employee usually fall far short of what one could expect a jury to award in a successful tort action. The employee injured as a result of employer negligence loses under workmen's compensation by not having recourse to a suit in tort, while the employee injured solely by the employee's own carelessness benefits because the injuries are paid for regardless of fault. This benefit-burden dichotomy is frequently encountered in sports injury cases.

8.1 EMPLOYER SPONSORED RECREATIONAL ACTIVITIES

Injuries sustained in employer-sponsored recreational activities such as softball leagues, bowling teams, and fishing and hunting trips have been declared to be job-related and thus compensable. *See, e.g., Zuckerman v. Board of Education, Central High School District No. 3,* 35 A.D.2d 757, 314 N.Y.S.2d 814 (1970) (coverage extended to coach injured in a college scholarship benefit basketball game sponsored by the employer school district). Employer-sponsored recreational activities qualify for workmen's compensation coverage when they take place on the job site during working hours; or when they are controlled and dominated by the employer who furnishes uniforms, league fees, equipment, and encourages employees to participate; or when the employer receives some direct benefit such as advertisement or better customer relations. *See generally* 1A A. Larson, *Larson's Workmen's Compensation Law* §§ 22.00 to 22.35 (1985) (containing a comprehensive treatment of workmen's comp coverage for employer sponsored recreational activities).

8.2 COACHES, TEACHERS, AND OTHER ATHLETIC PERSONNEL

Coaches, physical education teachers, team managers, stadium attendants, trainers, and similar athletic personnel are employees. If they are injured in a job-related incident their usual remedy is to apply for workmen's compensation benefits. *See, e.g., Trent v. Employers Liability Assurance Corp.,* 178 So.2d 470 (La.Ct.App.1965) (widow of high school football coach fatally injured in automobile accident, while on route to scout another team, qualified for workmen's comp benefits because her husband was killed in course and scope of his employment).

8.3 PROFESSIONAL ATHLETES

A few states exempt professional athletes from mandatory workmen's comp coverage. Other states have restricted benefits to accidental injuries, precluding athletes injured in contact sports (where injuries are not caused by accident) from receiving benefits. Absent such restrictions, professional athletes may qualify for workmen's comp if they are an employee, but will not qualify if they are an independent contractor. An independent contractor is not eligible for workmen's compensation benefits. The distinction between an employee and an independent contractor is not always clear. When a dispute arises over whether an athlete is an employee or independent contractor, the control the alleged employer can exercise over the details of the athlete's performance is what will determine the athlete's status.

Professional athletes under the direction and authority of a coach or team manager have been found to be employees, whereas the solo performer retained for a single event is probably an independent contractor. *Compare Gambrell v. Kansas City Chiefs Football Club, Inc.,* 562 S.W.2d 163 (Mo.1978) (workmen's comp covered professional football player's preseason injuries) *with Clark v. Industrial Commission,* 54 Ill.2d 311, 297 N.E.2d 154 (1973) (jockey declared to be an independent contractor because horse owner did not possess sufficient control over details of race to make him an employee).

In deciding the question of employee versus independent contractor, the industrial commission or state agency administering the workmen's comp law will consider the following factors to determine the extent of control the employer has over the athlete: (1) the extent of control the employer can exercise over the details of the athlete's performance; (2) whether the performance is rendered under the employer's supervision or that of the agent, or whether the athlete performs without supervision; (3) whether supplies and equipment are furnished by the employer; (4) whether the one hired performs the same service for others, or is employed by one team, owner, or promoter; (5) the manner in which the athlete is paid and whether he or she can be fired.

Under this analysis, the more control the employer exercises over the athlete's performance, the more likely the athlete is an employee. Additionally, the more the athlete's performance is supervised, the more like an employee the athlete is. The third factor courts consider concerns the supply of equipment. If an athlete furnishes the necessary equipment, the athlete is probably an independent contractor. On the other hand, if the employer supplies the equipment, the athlete is probably an employee. The number of employers also influences the status of an athlete. The more individuals an athlete works for, the more likely he or she is an independent contractor. Finally, the athlete's status is influenced by the manner in which he or she is paid, and whether the athlete can be fired. Employees are paid on a regular basis whereas an independent contractor is apt to be paid by the job or event and does not have a long term association with the employer. Employees are likewise subject to an employer's unqualified right to fire them while independent contractors can only be discharged for unsatisfactory performance.

No single factor is dispositive on the question of employer-independent contractor status. The factors are only evidence of the right to control. Whether the evidence is sufficient to establish the existence of an employer-employee relationship is a matter for the administering agency or court to decide.

8.4 REFEREES AND TRAINERS

School districts, universities, leagues, or team owners will occasionally try to avoid maintaining workmen's comp coverage on umpires, referees, or trainers by designating them as independent contractors. Employment contracts may even be drafted in such a way that the person hired purports to be an independent contractor. These practices alone will not make an employee an independent contractor, nor will this tactic prevent the person hired in this manner from obtaining workmen's comp benefits. The status of a referee or any one else as an employee or an independent contractor does not depend on any single fact, but is determined from all the circumstances surrounding the contractual relationship.

The "right to control" the details of another's performance is the essential test, and the existence of that right is determined by looking for the evidence of control previously discussed. In *Ford v. Bonner County School District*, 101 Idaho 320, 612 P.2d 557 (1980), the Idaho Supreme Court upheld the industrial commission's determination that a high school football referee was an employee of the school district, and as such was entitled to workmen's comp benefits for injuries sustained while officiating. The referee was an employee because the school district compensated him, could fire him for any reason, and determined the time and place where his officiating duties were to be performed.

8.5 COLLEGE AND UNIVERSITY ATHLETES

A more troubling question is whether a college athlete is an employee of the school, and thus entitled to workmen's compensation coverage. When the athlete is a walk-on, receiving nothing in the form of scholarship moneys or other aid linked to participation in sports, the student is not considered an employee. However, the student who receives some form of compensation for athletic activities has occasionally been considered an employee and thus entitled to workmen's comp benefits for his or her sports injuries.

But courts have differed in their opinions in these latter cases. Colorado's supreme court upheld payment of workmen's comp benefits to an injured college football player in the case of *University of Denver v. Nemeth,* 127 Colo. 385, 257 P.2d 423 (1953). A similar result was reached by a California court in *Van Horn v. Industrial Accident Commission,* 219 Cal.App.2d 457, 33 Cal.Rptr. 169 (1963), which approved payment of death benefits to the widow and minor children of an athlete killed in a plane crash while returning home from a game.

In *Nemeth* the athlete had a campus job and received free meals. The deceased ball player in *Van Horn* had been getting a $50 per month scholarship plus rent money from a fund administered by the coach. The courts in *Nemeth* and *Van Horn* felt that because the continued receipt of a job, free meals or money was conditioned upon the athlete's participation in football, a contract to play football had been created. Once this employment contract was established, workmen's comp coverage existed for those employees (*i.e.,* athletes) injured or killed during the course of their employment.

The pivotal issue is the existence of an employment contract between the athlete and the college whereby the student athlete is paid to participate. Without this contractual relationship the athlete is not covered by workmen's comp. Lack of a contractual relationship has been a theory other courts have relied on to deny benefits. In *Coleman v. Western Michigan University,* 125 Mich.App. 35, 336 N.W.2d 224 (1983) the Michigan Court of Appeals acknowledged that an injured football player's scholarship was a payment of wages, but refused to allow workmen's compensation benefits for a disabling injury incurred during practice. Benefits were denied because the court felt football was not an integral part of the university's function; hence the athlete was employed but not in the institution's usual trade or business.

Indiana's supreme court also denied benefits to a scholarship athlete because no employment relationship existed in *Rensing v. Indiana State University Board of Trustees,* 444 N.E.2d 1170 (Ind.1983). Rensing was a scholarship football player who was rendered a quadriplegic by an injury incurred during spring practice. The *Rensing* court reasoned that although football was an important part of the university's business of educating students, scholarship moneys were not wages for playing football since payment of wages would violate the NCAA rules against professionalism. If Rensing was not receiving wages, no employment contract existed.

Notwithstanding similar facts, the courts in *Coleman* and *Rensing* applied inconsistent reasoning to find no employer-employee relationship between the respective athletes and their colleges. The *Coleman* court acknowledged that scholarship benefits are in fact wages, but workmen's comp was denied because football was not the university's usual or customary business. The court in *Rensing* indicated that college athletics are in fact an integral part of the business of educating students, but a scholarship did not constitute payment for participation in college sports. In light of these inconsistencies, it remains to be seen whether other states will be persuaded by either opinion.

Chapter Nine

CRIMINAL LIABILITY

Criminal law may relate to sports in a number of different ways. Certain activities are unlawful, and participants who engage in such activities may be charged with a crime. Gambling and player drug use are examples of particular activities that carry criminal sanctions. Few persons would protest the arrest and prosecution of players who engage in these illegal acts.

Another area of criminal law that has application to sports is the regulation of spectator conduct. Spectator violence is increasing. This violent conduct is illegal, and the criminal justice system operates against unlawful conduct by sports fans.

A third and final aspect of the impact of criminal law upon sports relates to violence by and among participants. Unlike the other intrusions of criminal law into sports related conduct, there is little consensus among spectators, player, lawyers, or courts about applying penal sanctions to participant violence.

9.1 CRIMINAL PROSECUTION

Some sports are violent by nature. Both absorbing and dishing out punishment are qualities considered important by coaches and fans alike. A team's notoriety and success may depend upon the aggressiveness of its athletes. Participants who engaged in these sports have necessarily consented to a certain level of violence. The question becomes, however, whether the player violence and brutality has exceeded an acceptable level at some point during the game.

Legal scholars, judges, and lawyers generally agree that if the player's conduct was within the bounds of what one would reasonably foresee as a hazard of the game, the violent act is authorized. Since it is authorized, the act will not expose the perpetrator to criminal liability, even if serious injury or death to another athlete resulted from the actions. Conduct within the rules of the particular sport is clearly authorized and consented to by all who voluntarily play the game. Participants are also considered to have consented to violations of the rules that are reasonably expected and not the result of an intentional act that has no reasonable relation to the sports activity. So long as the athlete is acting in a competitive manner consistent with the objectives of the game, harm producing conduct is not likely to result in criminal charges. *See* Weistart and Lowell, *The Law of Sports*, at 185–86.

While much sports violence is privileged either because it was consented to, or it constitutes legitimate self-defense against the actions of another, athletes can commit criminal acts during the course of play. Neither sports nor athletes enjoy any exemption from prosecution for these criminal acts, yet few criminal actions involving participants are brought in the United States.

Prosecutors are undoubtedly reluctant to bring these sports violence cases to trial because they are difficult to win. Defenses such as self-defense and consent make conviction of an accused athlete in a contact sport like hockey or football very difficult to achieve. Some states have even enacted laws which exempt certain sports related conduct from prosecution. *See, e.g.,* N.D. Cent. Code 12.1–17–08(b) (1976) (establishing a defense from prosecution for conduct and injury which are reasonably foreseeable hazards of joint participation in a lawful athletic contest or competitive sport). There is, in addition, a reluctance on the part of jurors to find athletes guilty of acts that are so prevalent in modern sports. This, however, may change if Congress or state legislatures enact criminal statutes specifically directed at participant violence. *See, e.g.,* H.R. 7903, 96th Cong., 2d Sess. (1980) (although never enacted into law, this Bill would have made it a federal crime for a professional athlete to knowingly use "excessive physical force" against other participants).

In contrast, Canadian courts (at least with respect to professional hockey) have implemented prosecution as a means of deterring sports violence. Prosecutions are generally reserved for the "unprovoked savage attacks in which serious injury results," but are apparently difficult cases to prove. *See, e.g., Regina v. Green*, 16 D.L.R.3d 137, 143 (Ontario Prov. Ct. 1970) (verdict of acquittal for NHL player charged with criminal assault). Given the difficulty in using criminal laws as a deterrence, athletes, team owners, and the sports establishment should probably look elsewhere for a means of reducing violence in sports.

9.2 ALTERNATIVE METHODS OF DETERRING SPORTS VIOLENCE

One way of reducing the level of violence in sports is to enact and enforce rules for participant safety. Game officials should act quickly to sanction violators with penalties or ejection. For persistent violations or serious infractions, suspension of an athlete for a portion of the season may be necessary. However, since many teams depend upon the violent behavior of their athletes to draw media coverage and fan support, it is not likely that the professional associations will promote these methods.

A better means of eliminating the gratuitous violence in sports is to permit the injured athlete to sue for damages. This method is the one apparently favored by American courts. Such suits are typically brought against both the athlete who inflicted the harm, and the team or association for which the athlete played. *See, e.g., Hackbart v. Cincinnati Bengals, Inc.*, 601 F.2d 516 (10th Cir. 1979) (recognizing professional football player's right to sue opposing player and team for injuries inflicted upon him by the latter's intentional and reckless conduct). Exposure to civil liability for injuries to other participants may encourage team owners as well as athletes to curtail much of the unnecessary sports violence.

Chapter Ten

APPENDIX

The materials contained in this appendix relate to professional sports and they are intended to supplement chapters 5 and 6, dealing with agents, collective bargaining and contract negotiations. Reproduced herein are a code of ethics for representatives of professional athletes, and California's athlete agent statute, plus the 1982 NFL collective bargaining agreement, player-agent agreement and player contract which, along with the text, will hopefully give the reader a fairly complete picture of the professional sports contracting process. Professional football agreements were selected for inclusion in this book for the simple reasons that there was not room to present similar documents from all professional team sports, the NFL materials were readily available, and the matters addressed in these standard agreements are generally typical of those which concern all professional athletes and team owners.

10.1 ASSOCIATION OF REPRESENTATIVES OF PROFESSIONAL ATHLETES' (ARPA) CODE OF ETHICS

CANON ONE

A Representative shall maintain the highest degree of integrity and competence in representing the professional athlete.

Rule 1–101   Representing Clients with Competence & Integrity

(A) A Representative shall not:

(1) Violate a rule of conduct of this Code,

(2) Use another to circumvent a rule of this Code,

(3) Engage in illegal conduct involving a felony or conduct involving moral turpitude,

(4) Engage in conduct involving dishonesty, fraud, deceit, or misrepresentation,

(5) Engage in conduct prejudicial to the reasonable conduct of professional athletics,

(6) Engage in conduct which adversely reflects on his fitness.

Rule 1–102 Information Regarding a Violation of this Code

(A) A Representative possessing information which is unprivileged as a matter of law and not protected by Rule 4–101 of this Code concerning a violation of Rule 1–101 shall report such information to the Committee on Discipline of the Association of Representatives of Professional Athletes immediately.

(B) A Representative shall be available to testify or produce a statement under oath as to the nature, source and details of the information described in Rule 1–102(A).

Rule 1–103 Refusing to Accept a Client

(A) A Representative shall refrain from accepting the representation of a professional athlete when

(1) The Representative does not possess the competence through training by education or experience in a particular area,

(2) The Representative's representation of the athlete will create differing or unresolvable conflict of interest with an existing client or with an existing financial enterprise,

(3) The Representative has differing interests with those of his prospective client.

(B) A Representative must disclose in writing in advance of his representation of a professional athlete the nature and degree of his involvement in any matter in which he is recommending, suggesting, or advising that the athlete invest.

Rule 1–104 General

(A) A Representative shall not knowingly give aide to or cooperate in any way with another in conduct which would violate this Code.

(B) A Representative shall act in the best interests of the professional athlete, bearing in mind the high degree of trust and responsibility reposed in him as fiduciary.

(C) A Representative shall become familiar with the Collective Bargaining Agreement, Standard of Uniform Players Contract, Constitution, Bylaws and League Rules or the League and such other relevant documents affecting wages, hours and working conditions of the players in the sport or sports in which he represents professional athletes.

CANON TWO

A Representative shall be dignified in the conduct of his profession.

Rule 2–101 Representative's Letterhead, Stationery, etc.

(A) A Representative shall not compensate or give anything of value to representatives of the print, video or audio media or other communication media in return for professional publicity,

(B) The professional letterhead, business or calling card, stationery, announcements, office signs of a representative and his firm or organization shall be dignified and may;

(1) list the representative's name, firm or organization name, firm members and their position,

(2) list the address of the firm's office or offices, phone number, telex and other such information as may aid the professional athlete in locating the representative,

(3) indicate his membership in ARPA.

(C) A Representative in the operation of his firm may practice under a trade name, partnership corporation or professional association.

(D) The letterhead of the representative shall indicate the name or names of representatives associated with the firm. If the degree of participation by a representative in the firm is less than that of a partner or manager, the nature of such association shall be indicated on the firm's stationery.

Rule 2–102 A Representative engaged in more than one profession or business

(A) A Representative who is engaged both in representation of professional athletes and simultaneously in another profession or business shall clearly distinguish those businesses or professions on his letterhead, office sign, professional card and other public communication.

(B) A Representative, who in addition to his traditional role as a representative, offers to provide services as an investment and/or financial advisor, counselor or director to a professional athlete or in any way assert or maintain control and/or management of the financial affairs of a professional athlete, whether for compensation or not, must be qualified to do so based upon training or experience.

(C) A Representative who assumes the role outlined in Section B of this Rule, shall fully disclose that role in his contract with the professional athlete he represents. Such contract shall provide at least a statement of the services to be provided in connection with investment counseling, the limitations of such services, if any, and the fees to be charged for such services.

(D) A Representative may use or permit the use of, in connection with his name, any earned degree or title.

Rule 2–103 Recommending Employment of the Representative

(A) A Representative shall not compensate in any way or give anything of value or promise to compensate a professional or amateur athlete to recommend or secure the representative's employment in any capacity.

(B) A Representative shall not compensate or give anything of value to any individual as a reward for recommending the representative's employment or for referring an athlete to the representative; except that a representative may pay the customary costs and charges in connection with a Professional Association and with ARPA.

(C) A Representative may receive without the payment of compensation, other than dues, referrals from appropriate referring agencies.

(D) A Representative may employ for compensation, with the consent of his client another representative or other professional to assist him in fulfilling his duties and obligations to a professional athlete he represents.

Rule 2–104 Fees for Service

(A) A Representative shall disclose, in advance of any representation agreement and in writing, the nature of his fees and the services to be performed for the fee.

(B) A Representative shall not enter into an agreement for, charge, or collect an illegal or clearly excessive fee.

(C) A fee is clearly excessive when, after a review of the facts, an individual within the industry of reasonable prudence would be left with the firm conviction that the fee is in excess of a reasonable fee for the work performed.

(D) Among the factors relevant in determining whether a fee is reasonable are:

(1) The time, labor, expenses involved;

(2) The degree of expertise required and the level of expertise of the representative;

(3) The usual and customary charge in the industry for the services performed;

(4) The impact of the services to be performed on the workload of the representative;

(5) The relationship between the fee and the length of the athlete's contract.

(E) In determining his fee, the Representative shall consider the relationship between the fee and foreseeable length of the athlete's employment with the athletic team and shall make every reasonable effort not to inflict serious hardship on the athlete.

(F) A Representative may employ one of the following methods in establishing his fee:

(1) Fixed fee

(2) Percentage fee

(3) Contingent fee

(G) A Representative shall never solicit nor accept any compensation for services rendered in connection with the negotiation of a player contract or in connection with any other services to a professional athlete from a professional athletic team, club or club representative either directly or indirectly.

(1) Prior disclosure of such compensation shall not result in a waiver of the prohibition set forth in 2–104(G).

(2) The prohibition set forth in 2–104(G) may not be waived by prior agreement or by subsequent contract.

Rule 2–105   Financial Payments

(A) A Representative shall not offer, promise or provide financial payments, support or consideration of any kind to an amateur athlete, his family members, athletic coach, director, school official or school with the intent to influence those persons or organizations into recommending that representative for employment by a professional athlete.

(B) The provisions contained in 2–105(A) may not be waived in advance or by subsequent conduct.

CANON THREE

A Representative shall maintain management responsibility for his firm.

Rule 3–101   A Representative working with a non-Representative

(A) A Representative shall not share fees with a non-Representative except:

(1) A Representative may, with the prior consent of the professional athlete he represents, retain the services of another professional or business entity on behalf of the athlete.

(2) All charges in connection with such work shall be billed to the athlete directly or, at least, must be separately listed on the representative's bill for services.

Rule 3–102   A Representative and the Player Contract

(A) A Representative shall not negotiate or agree to, on behalf of an athlete, any provision in a player contract which directly or indirectly violates or circumvents an operative collective bargaining agreement.

(B) ALL Representatives shall have a written contract with their clients which fully discloses all fees, duties and responsibilities. Such contract shall fully disclose all matters in which the representative will receive a financial benefit.

(C) Any dispute arising out of a matter other than a dispute over fee shall be resolved by·binding arbitration before an impartial arbitration panel set up for the particular sport in accordance with the rules of the American Arbitration Association.

(D) The supervision and administration of the binding arbitration shall be conducted by ARPA.

CANON FOUR

A Representative shall preserve the confidence of his client.

Rule 4–101   Maintaining the confidences of the client

(A) A Representative shall not knowingly reveal information of any sort given to him by a client in the course of their professional relationship and which the client reasonably expects to be kept confidential.

(B) A Representative shall not use such confidential information to the direct or indirect disadvantage, harm, or damage of the client.

(C) A Representative shall not use such confidential information for his own advantage unless the client consents in advance after full disclosure by the representative.

Rule 4–102   Confidential information defined

(A) Confidential information refers to information gained in the course of the professional relationship between a representative and a professional athlete which the athlete has requested to be held confidential or which the representative knows or should know would be embarrassing or detrimental to the athlete if released.

Rule 4–103   Representative's Employees

(A) A Representative may reveal:

(1) Confidential information with the written consent of the client after full disclosure ·by the representative.

(2) Confidential information when required by law or directed by a tribunal.

(3) Confidential information concerning illegal conduct past, present or future on the part of the athlete, except where such information is protected by the attorney/client privilege.

CANON FIVE

A Representative shall handle a Client matter competently.

Rule 5–101   A Representative shall not fail to act competently

(A) A Representative shall not handle a matter in the representation of a professional athlete if he knows or should know that he is not competent to handle such a matter.

(B) A Representative shall not handle a matter concerning a professional athlete without proper preparation and shall not neglect a matter entrusted to him by such a client.

Rule 5–102   A Representative shall actively represent the interests of his client

(A) A Representative shall actively represent the interests of the professional athlete he represents.

(B) A Representative shall not knowingly make a public comment containing a false statement to his client's detriment.

(C) A Representative shall not knowingly make false statements concerning professional athletics or a professional athletic team or club.

Rule 5–103   A Representative shall avoid the appearance of impropriety

(A) A Representative shall preserve the identity of all client funds and of property which are given to him by or on behalf of a client.

(1) A Representative shall maintain a separate bank account to retain client funds.

(2) A Representative shall pay any interest earned on such an account to his client wherever practical.

(B) A Representative shall maintain complete records of client funds and property entrusted to the representative's care and shall render a record of such accounts to the client on a regular basis and upon request.

(C) A Representative shall conduct himself in his representation of professional athletes in such a manner as to avoid even the appearance of impropriety.

10.2   CALIFORNIA ATHLETE AGENT STATUTE

Many states do not have specific laws regulating agents for professional athletes, but California does. In fact, California's athlete agency statute is perhaps the most comprehensive legislation of its type among all the states. California's athlete agent statute commences at § 1500 of the California Labor Code, and that law is reproduced in its entirety below. For easier reference, each provision includes the section number assigned it in West's Annotated California Code.

§ 1500. Definitions

The following definitions shall govern the construction of this chapter:

(a) "Person" means any individual, company, corporation, association, partnership, or their agents or employees.

(b) "Athlete agent" means any person who, as an independent contractor, directly or indirectly, recruits or solicits any person to enter into any agent contract or professional sport services contract, or for a fee procures, offers, promises, or attempts to obtain employment for any person with a professional sport team or as a professional athlete.

"Athlete agent" does not include any employee or other representative of a professional sport team, and does not include any member of the State Bar of California when acting as legal counsel for any person.

(c) "Agent contract" means any contract or agreement pursuant to which a person authorizes or empowers an athlete agent to negotiate or solicit on behalf of the person with one or more professional sport teams for the employment of the person by one or more professional sport teams, or to negotiate or solicit on behalf of the person for the employment of the person as a professional athlete.

(d) "Professional sport services contract" means any contract or agreement pursuant to which a person is employed or agrees to render services as a player on a professional sport team or as a professional athlete.

§ 1511. Applications; form; contents; affidavits or certificates of completion

A written application for registration shall be made to the Labor Commissioner on the form prescribed by the commissioner, and shall state all of the following:

(a) The name of the applicant and address of the applicant's residence.

(b) The street and number of the building or place where the business of the athlete agent is to be conducted.

(c) The business or occupation engaged in by the applicant for at least two years immediately preceding the date of application.

(d) The application for registration shall be accompanied by affidavits or certificates of completion of any and all formal training or practical experience in any one of the following specific areas: contracts; contract negotiation; complaint resolution; arbitration or civil resolution of contract disputes. The Labor Commissioner, in evaluating the applicant's qualifications, may consider any other relevant training, education, or experience to satisfy this requirement.

§ 1512. Investigation of applicant and business premises

Upon receipt of an application for a registration, the Labor Commissioner may evaluate and investigate the education, training, experience, and character of the applicant, and may examine the premises designated in the application to verify it to be the principal place of business in which the applicant proposes to conduct business as an athlete agent.

§ 1513. Refusal to grant registration; notice and hearing

The commissioner, upon proper notice and hearing, may refuse to grant a registration. The proceedings shall be conducted in accordance with Chapter 5 (commencing at Section 11500) of Part 1 of Division 3 of Title 2 of the Government Code, and the commissioner shall have all the power granted therein.

§ 1514. Revocation or suspension of registration; reinstatement

If registration of an athlete agent is revoked or suspended, reinstatement of the registration shall be pursuant to the procedures provided by Section 11522 of the Government Code.

§ 1515. Term of registration; renewal; payment of filing fee; branch office registration

A registration shall be valid from July 1 of one year through June 30 of the following year. Renewal shall require the filing of an application for renewal, and a renewal bond. The annual filing fee shall be paid by the athlete agent.

If the applicant or registrant desires, in addition, a branch office registration, he or she shall file an application in accordance with the requirements of the Labor Commissioner.

§ 1515.5. Temporary or provisional registration

Whenever an application for registration or renewal is made, and application processing pursuant to this chapter has not been completed, the Labor Commissioner may, at his or her discretion, issue a temporary or provisional registration valid for a period not exceeding 90 days, and subject, where appropriate, to the automatic and summary revocation by the Labor Commissioner. Otherwise, the conditions for issuance or renewal shall meet the requirements of Section 1511.

§ 1516. Applications for registration or renewal; statement of financially interested persons

All applications for registration or renewal shall state the names and addresses of all persons, except bona fide employees on stated salaries, financially interested either as partners, associates, or profit sharers, in the operation of the business of the athlete agent.

§ 1517. Filing fees; registration fees; fees for branch offices; change of location of athlete agent's office

(a) A filing fee shall be paid to the Labor Commissioner at the time the application for issuance of an athlete agent registration is filed.

(b) In addition to the filing fee required for application for issuance of an athlete agent registration, every athlete agent shall pay to the Labor Commissioner annually at the time registration is obtained or renewed, a registration fee and a fee for each branch office maintained by the athlete agent in this state.

(c) A filing fee shall also be paid to the Labor Commissioner at the time application for consent to the transfer or assignment of an athlete agent registration is made, but no fee shall be required upon the assignment or transfer of a registration.

The location of an athlete agent's office shall not be changed without the written consent of the Labor Commissioner.

§ 1518. Amount of fees

The Labor Commissioner shall set the fees required by Section 1517 in the amount necessary to generate sufficient revenue to cover the costs of administration and enforcement of this chapter.

§ 1519. Surety bond; deposit; amount; certificate of deposit or savings account in lieu of surety bond

(a) An athlete agent shall also deposit with the Labor Commissioner, prior to the issuance or renewal of a registration, a surety bond in the penal sum of twenty-five thousand dollars ($25,000).

(b) For the purposes of this chapter, a certificate of deposit payable to the Labor Commissioner, or a savings account assigned to the Labor Commissioner, shall be considered equivalent to a surety bond, as provided in Section 995.710 of the Code of Civil Procedure, and shall be acceptable to the Labor Commissioner upon such terms and conditions as he or she may prescribe.

§ 1520. Surety bond; payment to state; conditions

(a) The surety bonds shall be payable to the people of the State of California, and shall be conditioned that the person applying for the registration will comply with this chapter and will pay all sums due any

individual or group of individuals when the person or his or her representative or agent has received such sums, and will pay all damages occa-
sioned to any person by reason of intentional or unintentional misstatement, misrepresentation, fraud, deceit, or any unlawful or negligent acts
or commissions or omissions of the registered athlete agent, or his or her
representatives or employees, while acting within the scope of their
employment.

(b) Nothing in this section shall be construed to limit the recovery of
damages to the amount of the surety bond, certificate of deposit, or
savings account.

§ 1521. Suspension of registration; failure to file new bond after notice of cancellation by surety

If any registrant fails to file a new bond with the Labor Commissioner within 30 days after notice of cancellation by the surety of the bond
required under Section 1519, the registration issued to the principal
under the bond is suspended until such time as a new surety bond is filed.
An athlete agent whose registration is suspended pursuant to this section
shall not carry on business as an athlete agent during the period of the
suspension.

§ 1522. Disposition of proceeds from registrations and fines

All moneys collected for registrations and all fines collected for
violations of the provisions of this chapter shall be paid into the State
Treasury and credited to the General Fund.

§ 1523. Contents of registration

Each registration shall contain all of the following:

(a) The name of the registrant.

(b) A designation of the city, street, and number of the place in which
the registrant is authorized to carry on business as an athlete agent.

(c) The number and date of issuance of the registration.

§ 1524. Application of registration

No registration shall apply to any other than the person to whom it is
issued nor any places other than those designated in the registration.

§ 1525. Issuance of certificate of convenience; denomination as estate certificate of convenience

The Labor Commissioner may issue to an eligible person a certificate
of convenience to conduct business as an athlete agent where the person
registered to conduct the athlete agent business has died, or has been
declared incompetent by the judgment of a court of competent jurisdiction, or has had a conservator appointed for his or her estate by a court of

competent jurisdiction. The certificate of convenience may be denominated an estate certificate of convenience.

§ 1526. Eligibility for certificate of convenience; term; renewal

To be eligible for a certificate of convenience, a person shall be any one of the following:

(a) The executor or administrator of the estate of a deceased person registered to conduct the business of an athlete agent.

(b) If no executor or administrator has been appointed, the surviving spouse or heir otherwise entitled to conduct the business of the deceased registrant.

(c) The guardian of the estate of an incompetent person registered as an athlete agent, or the conservator appointed for the conservation of the estate of a person registered to conduct the business of an athlete agent.

The estate certificate of convenience shall continue in force for a period of not to exceed 90 days, and shall be renewable for such period as the Labor Commissioner may deem appropriate, pending the disposal of the athlete agent registration or the procurement of a new registration under the provisions of this chapter.

§ 1527. Revocation or suspension; grounds

The Labor Commissioner may revoke or suspend any registration when any one of the following is shown:

(a) The registrant or his or her representative or employee has violated or failed to comply with any of the provisions of this chapter.

(b) The registrant fails to meet minimum requirements as set by the Labor Commissioner pursuant to subdivision (d) of Section 1511 and Section 1534.

(c) The conditions under which the registration was issued have changed or no longer exist.

§ 1528. Revocation or suspension of registration; hearing

Before revoking or suspending any registration, the Labor Commissioner shall afford the holder of the registration an opportunity to be heard in person or by counsel. The proceedings shall be conducted in accordance with Chapter 5 (commencing at Section 11500) of Part 1 of Division 3 of Title 2 of the Government Code, and the commissioner shall have all the powers granted therein.

§ 1530. Approval of contract forms; contents

Any and all contracts to be utilized as agent contracts shall be on a form approved by the Labor Commissioner. This approval shall not be withheld as to any proposed form of agent contract unless the proposed form of agent contract is unfair, unjust, and oppressive to the person. Each form of agent contract, except under the conditions specified in Section 1544, shall contain an agreement by the agent to refer any controversy between the person and the agent relating to the terms of the agent contract to the Labor Commissioner for adjustment. There shall be printed on the face of the agent contract in prominent type the following: "This athlete agent is registered with the Labor Commissioner of the State of California. Registration does not imply approval by the Labor Commissioner of the terms and conditions of this contract or the competence of the athlete agent."

§ 1530.5. Contents of contract; notice concerning amateur status

(a) The contract shall contain in close proximity to the signature of the athlete a notice in at least 10-point type stating that the athlete may jeopardize his or her standing as an amateur athlete by entering into the contract.

(b) This section shall also apply to any contract negotiated by a member of the State Bar of California which would be an agent contract if negotiated by an athlete agent.

§ 1531. Schedule of fees; filing; changes; limitation of fee of athlete agent; disclosure in contract of services and fees

(a) Every person engaged in the occupation as an athlete agent shall file with the Labor Commissioner a schedule of fees to be charged and collected in the conduct of that occupation. Changes in the schedule may be made from time to time, but no change shall become effective until seven days after the date of filing thereof with the Labor Commissioner.

(b) If a professional sport services contract is negotiated, no athlete agent shall collect a fee in any calendar year which exceeds 10 percent of the total compensation, direct or indirect, and no matter from whom received, the athlete is receiving in that calendar year under the contract. However, an athlete agent may require security that his or her future fees will be paid under the agreement with the athlete.

(c) Every agent contract shall describe the types of services to be performed and a schedule of the fees to be charged under the contract. This subdivision shall also apply to any contract negotiated by a member of the State Bar of California which would be an agent contract if negotiated by an athlete agent.

§ 1531.5. Athlete agent receiving a player's salary; establishment of trust fund

A trust fund shall be established when an athlete agent is the recipient of the player's salary. An athlete agent who receives any payment on behalf of the athlete shall immediately deposit same in a trust fund account maintained by the athlete agent or other recognized depository.

§ 1532. Maintenance of records; false entries

Every athlete agent shall keep records approved by the Labor Commissioner, in which shall be entered all of the following:

(a) The name and address of each person employing the athlete agent.

(b) The amount of fee received from such person.

(c) Other information which the Labor Commissioner requires.

No athlete agent, or his or her representatives or employees, shall make any false entry in any such records. All records required by this section shall be kept for a period of seven years.

§ 1533. Inspection of books, records and papers; copies; reports

All books, records, and other papers kept pursuant to this chapter by any athlete agent shall be open at all reasonable hours to the inspection of the Labor Commissioner and his or her representatives. Every athlete agent shall furnish to the Labor Commissioner upon request a true copy of the books, records, and papers kept pursuant to this chapter, or any portion thereof, and shall make such reports as the Labor Commissioner prescribes.

§ 1534. Rules and regulations

The Labor Commissioner may, in accordance with the provisions of Chapter 3.5 (commencing at Section 11340) of Part 1 of Division 3 of Title 2 of the Government Code, adopt, amend, and repeal such rules and regulations as are reasonably necessary for the purpose of enforcing and administering this chapter and as are not inconsistent with this chapter.

§ 1535. Sale, transfer or gift of interest or right to participate in profits; consent; misdemeanor

No registrant shall sell, transfer, or give away any interest in or the right to participate in the profits of the athlete agent without the written consent of the Labor Commissioner. A violation of this section shall constitute a misdemeanor, and shall be punishable by a fine of not less than five hundred dollars ($500) nor more than five thousand dollars ($5,000), or imprisonment for not more than 90 days, or both.

§ 1535.5. Ownership or financial interest in same sport; prohibition

(a) No athlete agent shall have an ownership or financial interest in any entity which is directly involved in the same sport as a person with whom the athlete agent has entered an agent contract or for whom the athlete agent is attempting to negotiate a professional sports service contract.

(b) This section shall also apply to any member of the State Bar of California when advising athlete clients, when entering contracts which would be an agent contract if negotiated by an athlete agent, and when attempting to negotiate a professional sports service contract for a client.

§ 1535.7. Investment advice; disclosure of any ownership interest

If an athlete agent also advises a client regarding the investment of funds, the athlete agent shall disclose to the client any ownership interest the athlete agent has in any entity regarding which the athlete agent is giving advice to that client.

§ 1536. Unlawful contract terms or conditions; unlawful attempt to fill an order for help to be employed

No athlete agent shall knowingly issue a contract containing any term or condition which, if complied with, would be in violation of law, or attempt to fill an order for help to be employed in violation of law.

§ 1537. False, fraudulent or misleading information, representations, etc.; use of name, address and designation as athlete agent

No athlete agent shall publish or cause to be published any false, fraudulent, or misleading information, representation, notice, or advertisement. All advertisements of an athlete agent by means of cards, circulars, or signs, and in newspapers and other publications, and all letterheads, receipts, and blanks shall be printed and contain the registered name and address of the athlete agent and the words "athlete agent." No athlete agent shall give any false information or make any false promises or representations concerning any employment to any person.

§ 1538. Strikes, lockouts or other labor trouble; notice to person securing employment

No athlete agent shall knowingly secure employment for persons in any place where a strike, lockout, or other labor trouble exists, without notifying the person of those conditions.

§ 1539. Division of fees; agreements with university or educational institution employees; participation in athlete agent's revenues by full-time union employees

(a) No athlete agent shall divide fees with a professional sports league or franchise, or its representative or employee.

(b) No athlete agent shall enter into any agreement whereby the athlete agent offers anything of value, including, but not limited to, the rendition of free or reduced price legal services, to any employee of a university or educational institution in return for the referral of any clients by that employee.

(c) No full-time employee of a union or players association connected with professional sports shall own or participate in any of the revenues of an athlete agent.

(d) This section shall also apply to any member of the State Bar of California.

§ 1540. Repayment of fees and expenses; failure to obtain employment

In the event that an athlete agent collects a fee or expenses from a person for obtaining employment, and the person fails to procure that employment, or the person fails to be paid for that employment, the athlete agent shall, upon demand, repay to the person the fee and expenses so collected. Unless repayment is made within 48 hours after demand therefor, the athlete agent shall pay the person an additional sum equal to the amount of the fee.

§ 1541. Actions against athlete agent; parties; transfer and assignment; jurisdiction

All actions brought in any court against any athlete agent may be brought in the name of the person damaged upon the bond deposited with the state by the athlete agent, and may be transferred and assigned as other claims for damages. The amount of damages claimed by plaintiff, and not the penalty named in the bond, determines the jurisdiction of the court in which the action is brought.

§ 1542. Service upon surety; leaving state with intent to defraud or avoid service

When an athlete agent has departed from the state with intent to defraud creditors or to avoid service of summons in an action brought under this chapter, service shall be made upon the surety of an athlete agent, in accordance with the Code of Civil Procedure. A copy of the summons shall be mailed to the athlete agent at the last known post office address of his or her residence and also at the place where the business of the athlete agent was conducted as shown by the records of the Labor Commissioner. Service is complete as to the athlete agent, after mailing, at the expiration of the time prescribed by the Code of Civil Procedure for service of summons in the particular court in which suit is brought.

§ 1543. Referral of disputes to labor commissioner; appeals; certification without hearing of lack of controversy

In cases of controversy arising under this chapter the parties involved shall refer the matters in dispute to the Labor Commissioner, who shall hear and determine the same, subject to an appeal within 10 days after determination, to the court of competent jurisdiction where the same shall be heard de novo.

The Labor Commissioner may certify without a hearing that there is no controversy within the meaning of this section if he or she has by investigation established that there is no dispute as to the amount of the fee due. Service of the certification shall be made upon all parties concerned by registered or certified mail with return receipt requested and the certification shall become conclusive 10 days after the date of mailing if no objection has been filed with the Labor Commissioner during that period.

§ 1544. Arbitration; validity of contract provisions; procedure

Notwithstanding Section 1543, a provision in a contract providing for the decision by arbitration of any controversy under the contract or as to its existence, validity, construction, performance, nonperformance, breach, operation, continuance, or termination, shall be valid if all of the following occur:

(a) The provision is contained in a contract between an athlete agent and a person for whom the athlete agent under the contract undertakes to endeavor to secure employment.

(b) The provision is inserted in the contract pursuant to any rule, regulation, or contract of a bona fide labor union regulating the relations of its members to an athlete agent.

(c) The contract provides for reasonable notice to the Labor Commissioner of the time and place of all arbitration hearings.

(d) The contract provides that the Labor Commissioner or his or her authorized representative has the right to attend all arbitration hearings.

Except as otherwise provided in this section, any such arbitration shall be governed by the provisions of Title 9 (commencing with Section 1280) of Part 3 of the Code of Civil Procedure.

If there is such an arbitration provision in a contract, the contract need not provide that the athlete agent agrees to refer any controversy between the person and the athlete agent regarding the terms of the contract to the Labor Commissioner for adjustment, and Section 1543 shall not apply to controversies pertaining to the contract.

A provision in a contract providing for the decision by arbitration of any controversy arising under this chapter which does not meet the requirements of this section is not made valid by Section 1281 of the Code of Civil Procedure.

§ 1546. Noncompliance by athlete agent with § 1510; effect on contracts

Any agent contract which is negotiated by any athlete agent who has failed to comply with Section 1510 is void and unenforceable.

§ 1547. Violations of chapter; misdemeanor; punishment

Any person, or agent or officer thereof, who violates any provision of this chapter is guilty of a misdemeanor, punishable by a fine of not less than one thousand dollars ($1,000) or imprisonment for a period of not more than 90 days, or both.

10.3 1982 COLLECTIVE BARGAINING AGREEMENT BETWEEN NATIONAL FOOTBALL LEAGUE PLAYERS ASSOCIATION AND NATIONAL FOOTBALL LEAGUE MANAGEMENT COUNCIL

Printed below is the collective bargaining agreement that was executed between the NFL Players Association and NFL Management Council in 1982. Because of space limitations, some of the less significant appendices to this agreement have been omitted but Appendix M, the NFL Player Contract, is reproduced *infra* at § 10.4.

Table of Contents

PREAMBLE

This Agreement, which is the product of bona fide, arms-length collective bargaining, is made and entered into on the 11th day of December, 1982, in accordance with the provisions of the National Labor Relations Act, as amended, by and between the National Football League Management Council ("Management Council"), which is recognized as the sole and exclusive bargaining representative of present and future employer member clubs of the National Football League, and the National Football League Players Association ("NFLPA"), which is recognized as the sole and exclusive bargaining representative of present and future employee players in the NFL and as set forth in NLRB Certification #18–RC–8308, dated January 22, 1971.

ARTICLE I

Governing Agreement

Section 1. Conflicts. The provisions of this Agreement supersede any conflicting provisions in the Standard Player Contract, the NFL Player Contract, the NFL Constitution and Bylaws, the Bert Bell NFL Player Retirement Plan and Trust Agreement, or any other document affecting terms and conditions of employment of NFL players and all players, clubs, the NFLPA, the NFL, and the Management Council will be bound hereby.

Section 2. Full Force and Effect. Any provisions of the Standard Player Contract, the NFL Player Contract, the NFL Constitution and Bylaws, the Bert Bell NFL Player Retirement Plan and Trust Agreement, or any other document affecting terms and conditions of employment of NFL players, which are not superseded by this Agreement, will remain in full force and effect for the continued duration of this Agreement, and, where applicable, all players, clubs, the NFLPA, the NFL, and the Management Council will be bound thereby. It is recognized that the NFLPA has not participated in the promulgation of the NFL Constitution and Bylaws. However, the provisions of the NFL Constitution and Bylaws will apply to players except where superseded by the provisions of this Agreement.

Section 3. Implementation. The NFLPA and Management Council will use their best efforts to faithfully carry out the terms and conditions of this Agreement and to see that the terms and conditions of this Agreement are carried out in full by players and clubs.

Section 4. Management Rights. The NFL clubs maintain and reserve the right to manage and direct their operations in any manner whatsoever, except as specifically limited by the provisions of this Agreement.

ARTICLE II

Scope of Agreement

Section 1. Scope. This Agreement represents the complete understanding of the parties on all subjects covered herein, and there will be no change in the terms and conditions of this Agreement without mutual consent. Except as otherwise provided in Article XXII, Section 5 on Salaries and Appendix C on Union Security, the NFLPA and the Management Council waive all rights to bargain with one another concerning any subject covered or not covered in this Agreement for the duration of this Agreement; provided, however, that if any proposed change in the NFL Constitution and Bylaws during the term of this Agreement could significantly affect the terms and conditions of employment of NFL players, then the Council will give the NFLPA notice of and negotiate the proposed change in good faith.

Section 2. Arbitration. The question of whether or not the parties engaged in good faith negotiations, or whether any proposed change in the NFL Constitution and Bylaws would violate or render meaningless any provision of this Agreement, may be the subject of a non-injury grievance under Article VII of this Agreement. If the arbitrator finds that either party did not engage in good faith negotiations, or that the proposed change would violate or render meaningless any provision of this Agreement, he may enter an appropriate order, including to cease and desist from implementing or continuing the practice or proposal in question; provided, however, that the arbitrator may not compel either party to this Agreement to agree to anything or require the making of a concession by either party in negotiations.

ARTICLE III

No Strike/Lockout/Suit

Section 1. No Strike/Lockout. Except as otherwise provided in Article XXII, Section 5 on Salaries and Appendix C on Union Security neither the NFLPA nor any of its members will engage in any strike, work stoppage, or other concerted action interfering with the operation of the NFL or any club for the duration of this Agreement, and no club, either individually or in concert with other clubs, will engage in any lockout for the duration of this Agreement. Any claim by the Management Council that the NFLPA has violated this Article III, Section 1, will not be subject to the grievance procedure or the arbitration provisions of this Agreement and the Management Council will have the right to submit such claim directly to the courts.

Section 2. No Suit. The NFLPA agrees that neither it nor any of its members nor any member of its bargaining unit will sue, nor support financially or administratively, nor provide testimony or affidavit in, any suit against the NFL or any club [1] with respect to any claim relating to any aspect of the NFL rules, including, without limitation, the Standard Player Contract, the NFL Player Contract, the NFL Constitution and Bylaws, the college draft, the option clause, the right of first refusal or compensation, the waiver system, the trading of players, tampering, and the maintenance of certain reserve lists; provided, however, that nothing contained in this Section 2 will prevent the NFLPA or any player from

---

1. The NFLPA and its counsel believe this waiver is not lawful and so advised its members before the ratification vote. We do not believe a union can lawfully waive the rights of its members to bring suit, but, absent this clause, the NFLMC said the agreement was not acceptable. More than $60 million in bonus money was threatened, and we were not in a position to strike over the issue. Our legal advice was to include the clause, but to make clear our position that this waiver is not legal.

asserting that any club, acting individually or in concert with other clubs, or the Management Council has breached the terms of this Agreement, the Standard Player Contract, the NFL Player Contract, or the NFL Constitution and Bylaws, and from processing such asserted breach as a non-injury grievance under Article VII of this Agreement. The Management Council agrees that neither it nor any of its member clubs will sue any player with regard to his participation in any NFLPA-sponsored "All-Star" game in 1982.

ARTICLE IV

Union Security

Section 1. Union Security. Every NFL player has the option of joining or not joining the NFLPA; provided, however, that as a condition of employment commencing with the execution of this Agreement and for the duration of this Agreement and wherever and whenever legal: (a) any active player who is or later becomes a member in good standing of the NFLPA must maintain his membership in good standing in the NFLPA; and (b) any active player (including a player in the future) who is not a member in good standing of the NFLPA whose initial employment with an NFL club began or begins subsequent to February 1, 1974 must, on the 30th day following the beginning of his employment or the execution of this Agreement, whichever is later, pay, pursuant to Section 2 below or otherwise to the NFLPA an annual service fee in the same amount as an initiation fee and annual dues required of members of the NFLPA.

Section 2. Check-Off. Commencing with the execution of this Agreement, each club will check-off the initiation fee and annual dues or service charge, as the case may be, in equal weekly or biweekly installments from each pre-season and regular season pay check, beginning with the first pay check after the date of the first pre-season squad cutdown, for each player for whom a current check-off authorization (copy attached hereto as Appendix A and made a part of this Agreement) has been provided to the club. The club will forward the check-off monies to the NFLPA within seven days of the check-off.

Section 3. NFLPA Meetings. The NFLPA will have the right to conduct three meetings on club property each year, provided that the player rep or NFLPA office has given the club at least seven days notice of its desire to hold such a meeting. No meeting will be held at a time which would disrupt a coach's team schedule.

Section 4. Disputes. Any dispute over compliance with, or the interpretation, application or administration of this Article will be processed pursuant to Article VII. Any decision of an outside arbitrator pursuant thereto will constitute full, final and complete disposition of the dispute, and will be binding on the player(s) and club(s) involved and the parties to this Agreement.

Section 5. Other Check-Off. Commencing with the execution of this Agreement, the clubs will be required to honor any request by an individual player for check-off of: (a) Savings deposits in the Professional Athletes Federal Credit Union; (b) Installment payments on any individual player's loan from the Professional Athletes Federal Credit Union; (c) Contributions to the Professional Athletes Youth Foundation. Check-off of contributions and/or payments for the above purposes will be made pursuant to a written authorization signed by the player in the form prescribed in Appendix B, a copy of which is attached hereto and made a part of this Agreement.

Section 6. Procedure for Enforcement. The parties will continue to use the procedure for enforcement of the Union Security Agreement which was attached as Appendix C to the 1977 Collective Bargaining Agreement. Such procedure is attached hereto and incorporated herein by reference and made a part of this Agreement.

ARTICLE V

Player Security

Section 1. No Discrimination. There will be no discrimination in any form against any player by the Management Council, any club, or by the NFLPA because of race, religion, national origin, or activity or lack of activity on behalf of the NFLPA.

Section 2. Personal Appearance. Clubs may make and enforce reasonable rules governing players' appearance on the field and in public places while representing the clubs; provided, however, that no player will be disciplined because of hair length or facial hair.

ARTICLE VI

Club Discipline

Section 1. Maximum Discipline. The following maximum discipline schedule will be applicable for the duration of this Agreement:

Overweight—maximum fine of $25 per lb./per day.

Unexcused late reporting for mandatory off-season training camp, team meeting, practice, transportation, curfew, scheduled appointment with club physician or trainer, or scheduled promotional activity—maximum fine of $100.

Failure to promptly report injury to club physician or trainer—maximum fine of $100.

Losing, damaging or altering club-provided equipment—maximum fine of $100 and replacement cost, if any.

Throwing football into stands—maximum fine of $100.

Unexcused late reporting for or absence from pre-season training camp—maximum fine of $1,000 per day.

Unexcused missed mandatory off-season training camp, team meeting, practice, curfew, bed check, scheduled appointment with club physician or trainer, or scheduled promotional activity—maximum fine of $500.

Unexcused missed team transportation—maximum fine of $500 and transportation expense, if any.

Loss of all or part of playbook, scouting report or game plan—maximum fine of $500.

Ejection from game—maximum fine of $500.

Conduct detrimental to club—maximum fine of an amount equal to one week's salary and/or suspension without pay for a period not to exceed four (4) weeks.

Discipline will be imposed uniformly within a club on all players for the same offense; however, the club may specify the events which create an escalation of the discipline, provided the formula for escalation is uniform in its application.

The club will promptly notify the player of any discipline; notice of any club fine in the $1,000 maximum category and of any "conduct detrimental" fine or suspension will be sent to the NFLPA.

Section 2. Published Lists. All clubs must publish and make available to all players at the commencement of pre-season training camp a complete list of the discipline which can be imposed for designated offenses within the limits set by the maximum schedule referred to in Section 1 above.

Section 3. Uniformity. Discipline will be imposed uniformly within a club on all players for the same offense; however, the club may specify the events which create an escalation of the discipline, provided the formula for escalation is uniform in its application. Any disciplinary action imposed upon a player by the Commissioner pursuant to Article VIII of this Agreement will preclude or supersede disciplinary action by the club for the same act or conduct.

Section 4. Disputes. Any dispute involved in club discipline may be made the subject of a non-injury grievance under Article VII of this Agreement, Non-Injury Grievance.

Section 5. Deductions. Any club fine will be deducted at the rate of no more than $250 from each pay period, if sufficient pay periods remain; or, if less than sufficient pay periods remain, the fine will be deducted in equal installments over the number of remaining pay periods. This will not apply to a suspension.

ARTICLE VII

Non-Injury Grievance

Section 1. Definition. Any dispute (hereinafter referred to as a "grievance") involving the interpretation or application of, or compliance with, any provision of this Agreement, the Standard Player Contract, the NFL Player Contract, and any provision of the NFL Constitution and Bylaws pertaining to terms and conditions of employment of NFL Players, will be resolved exclusively in accordance with the procedure set forth in this Article; provided, however, that any dispute involving Section 1 of Article III, Section 11 of Article VII, Article VIII and Article IX of this Agreement, paragraph 8 of the Standard Player Contract and paragraph 3 of the NFL Player Contract will not be resolved under the procedure of this Article.

Section 2. Initiation. A grievance may be initiated by a player, a club, the Management Council, or the NFLPA. Except as provided otherwise in Article XV, Section 18, a grievance must be initiated within 45 days from the date of the occurrence or non-occurrence upon which the grievance is based, or within 45 days from the date on which the facts of the matter became known or reasonably should have been known to the party initiating the grievance, whichever is later. A player need not be under contract to an NFL club at the time a grievance relating to him arises or at the time such grievance is initiated or processed.

Section 3. Filing. Subject to the provisions of Section 2 above, a player or the NFLPA may initiate a grievance by filing a written notice by certified mail or TELEX with the Management Council and furnishing a copy of such notice to the club(s) involved; and a club or the Management Council may initiate a grievance by filing written notice by certified mail or TELEX with the NFLPA and furnishing a copy of such notice to the player(s) involved. The notice will set forth the specifics of the alleged action or inaction giving rise to the grievance. If a grievance is filed by a player without the involvement of the NFLPA, the Management Council will promptly send copies of the grievance and the answer to the NFLPA. The party to whom a non-injury grievance has been presented will answer in writing by certified mail or TELEX within seven (7) days of receipt of the grievance. The answer will set forth admissions or denials as to the facts alleged in the grievance. If the answer denies the grievance, the specific grounds for denial will be set forth. The answering party will provide a copy of the answer to the player(s) or club(s) involved and the NFLPA or NFLMC as may be applicable.

Section 4. Joint Fact Finding. Within ten days of the receipt of an answer, representatives of the NFLPA and the Management Council will meet in the appropriate team city to mutually determine the relevant facts of the grievance.

Section 5. Joint Fact Finding Report. The parties to any grievance will cooperate fully with the fact finding process by providing statements, witness identification, and production of relevant documents, all of which will be incorporated in and appended to a written report setting forth the facts not in dispute and, where appropriate, the facts in dispute. The report must be completed within fifteen (15) days after receipt of the answer and copies of the report will be provided to the grievant, the answering party, the NFLPA, the Management Council and the PCRC. The failure of either party to participate in the fact-finding process may be immediately brought to the attention of the Notice Arbitrator who is authorized to issue an order directing prompt participation and cooperation in the fact finding process.

Section 6. Player-Club Relations Committee. If a grievance is not resolved after it has been filed and during the fact-finding process, it along with the answer and the fact-finding report will be referred for disposition to the next mid-month conference of the Player-Club Relations Committee (PCRC), which will consist of one representative appointed by NFLPA and one representative appointed by the Management Council. The PCRC will confer once each midmonth to discuss and consider all pending grievances. Such conference may be had by telephone if both representatives agree, or otherwise in person. Meetings of the PCRC will alternate between Washington and New York. No evidence will be taken during the conference except by mutual consent. Discussions between the PCRC representatives will be privileged. If the PCRC resolves any grievance by mutual agreement between the NFLPA and Management Council representatives, such resolution will be made in writing and will constitute full, final and complete disposition of the grievance and will be binding upon the player(s) and club(s) and the parties to this Agreement.

Section 7. Appeal. If the PCRC has not considered a grievance within 30 days after it has been filed, regardless of the reason, or has failed to resolve a grievance within five days of its conference, either the player(s) or club(s) involved, or the NFLPA, or the Management Council may appeal such grievance by filing a written notice of appeal with the Notice Arbitrator and mailing copies thereof to the party or parties against whom such appeal is taken, and either the NFLPA or the Management Council as may be appropriate. If the grievance involves a suspension of a player by a club, the player or NFLPA will have the option to appeal it immediately upon filing to the Notice Arbitrator and a hearing will be held by an arbitrator designated by the Notice Arbitrator within seven (7) days of the filing of the grievance.

Section 8. Arbitration. The parties to this Agreement have designated Sam Kagel as the Notice Arbitrator. Within 30 days after execution of this Agreement, Mr. Kagel will submit to the parties a list of fifteen qualified and experienced arbitrators. Within 10 days thereafter, representatives of the parties will confer by conference call(s) with Mr.

Kagel for the purpose of selecting three arbitrators from the list who, along with Mr. Kagel, will constitute the non-injury arbitration panel. If the parties are unable to select three arbitrators from the original list, the selection process outlined in this section will continue until three arbitrators are selected. In the event of a vacancy in the position of Notice Arbitrator, the senior arbitrator in terms of affiliation with this Agreement will succeed to the position of Notice Arbitrator, and the resultant vacancy on the panel will be filled according to the procedures of this section as well as any other vacancies occurring on the panel. The Notice Arbitrator will, so as to equalize the caseload of non-injury grievances between himself and the other arbitrators and without prior consultation with the NFLPA or the Management Council, designate himself or one of the other arbitrators to hear each case. Either party to this Agreement may discharge a member of the arbitration panel by serving written notice upon him and the other party to this Agreement between December 1 and 10 of each calendar year, but at no time will such discharges result in no arbitrators remaining on the panel.

Section 9. Hearing. Each arbitrator will designate a minimum of one hearing date each month for use by the parties to this Agreement. Upon being appointed, each arbitrator will, after consultation with the Notice Arbitrator, provide to the NFLPA and the Management Council specified hearing dates for each of the ensuing 12 months, which process will be repeated on an annual basis thereafter. The parties will notify each arbitrator 30 days in advance of which dates the following month are going to be used by the parties. The designated arbitrator will set the hearing on his next reserved date and, after consultation with the parties, designate a convenient place for hearing such grievance. If a grievance is set for hearing and the hearing date is then cancelled by a party within 30 days of the hearing date, the cancellation fee of the arbitrator will be borne by the cancelling party unless the arbitrator determines that the cancellation was for good cause. Should good cause be found, the parties will share any cancellation costs equally. If the arbitrator in question cannot reschedule the hearing within 30 days of the postponed date, the case may be reassigned by the Notice Arbitrator to another panel member who has a hearing date available within the 30 days period. At the hearing, the parties to the grievance and the NFLPA and Management Council will have the right to present, by testimony or otherwise, any evidence relevant to the grievance. All hearings will be transcribed. In cases which require one full hearing day or less, the transcript will be prepared on an expedited, daily copy basis. In such cases, if either party requests post-hearing briefs, the parties will prepare and simultaneously submit briefs to the arbitrator postmarked no later than twenty (20) days after receipt of the transcript. In cases requiring more than one full hearing day, the transcript may be prepared by ordinary means and the post-hearing briefs must be submitted to the arbitrator, postmarked no later than thirty (30) days after receipt of the last day's transcript.

Section 10. **Arbitrator's Decision and Award.** The arbitrator will, if at all possible considering the arbitrator's schedule and other commitments, issue a written decision within 30 days of the submission of briefs. The arbitrator may issue the decision after 30 days have passed from the date of receipt of the last day's transcript regardless of the failure of either party to submit a brief. The decision of the arbitrator will constitute full, final and complete disposition of the grievance and will be binding upon the player(s) and club(s) involved and the parties to this Agreement; provided, however, that the arbitrator will not have the jurisdiction or authority: (a) to add to, subtract from, or alter in any way the provisions of this Agreement or any other applicable document; or (b) to grant any remedy whatsoever other than a money award, an order of reinstatement, suspension without pay, a stay of suspension pending decision, a cease and disist order, a credit or benefit award under the Bert Bell NFL Player Retirement Plan, an order of compliance with a specific term of this Agreement or any other applicable document, or an advisory opinion pursuant to Article XI, Section 9.

Section 11. **Integrity and Public Confidence.** In the event a matter filed as a grievance in accordance with the provisions of Section 3 above gives rise to issues involving the integrity of, or public confidence in, the game of professional football, the Commissioner may, at any stage of its processing, after consultation with the PCRC, order that the matter be withdrawn from such processing and thereafter be processed in accordance with the procedure provided in Article VIII of this Agreement on Commissioner Discipline.

Section 12. **Time Limits.** Each of the time limits set forth in this Article may be extended by mutual written agreement of the parties involved. If any grievance is not processed or resolved in accordance with the prescribed time limits within any step, unless an extension of time has been mutually agreed upon in writing, either the player, the NFLPA, the club or the Management Council, as the case may be, after notifying the other party of its intent in writing, may proceed to the next step.

Section 13. **Representation.** In any hearing provided for in this Article, a player may be accompanied by counsel of his choice and/or a representative of the NFLPA. In any such hearing, a club representative may be accompanied by counsel of his choice and/or a representative of the Management Council.

Section 14. **Costs.** All costs of arbitration, including the fees and expenses of the arbitrator and the transcript costs, will be borne equally between the parties. When the arbitrator grants a money award, it will be paid within ten (10) days. Unless the arbitrator determines otherwise, each party will bear the cost of its own witnesses, counsel, and the like.

ARTICLE VIII

Commissioner Discipline

Section 1. Commissioner Discipline. Notwithstanding anything stated in Article VII of this Agreement, Non-Injury Grievance, all disputes involving a fine or suspension imposed upon a player by the Commissioner for conduct on the playing field, or involving action taken against a player by the Commissioner for conduct detrimental to the integrity of, or public confidence in, the game of professional football, will be processed exclusively as follows: The Commissioner will promptly send written notice of his action to the player, with a copy to the NFLPA. Within 20 days following written notification of the Commissioner's action, the player affected thereby or the NFLPA, with the approval of the player involved, may appeal in writing to the Commissioner. The Commissioner will designate a time and place for hearing, which will be commenced within 10 days following his receipt of the notice of appeal. As soon as practicable following the conclusion of such hearing, the Commissioner will render a written decision, which decision will constitute full, final, and complete disposition of the dispute, and will be binding upon the player(s) and club(s) involved and the parties to this Agreement with respect to that dispute.

Section 2. Time Limits. Each of the time limits set forth in this Article may be extended by mutual agreement of the Commissioner and the player(s) and the club(s) involved.

ARTICLE IX

Injury Grievance

Section 1. Definition. An "injury grievance" is a claim or complaint that, at the time a NFL player's Standard Player Contract or NFL Player Contract was terminated by a club, the player was physically unable to perform the services required of him by that contract because of an injury incurred in the performance of his services under that contract. All time limitations in this Article may be extended by mutual agreement of the parties.

Section 2. Filing. Any NFL player and/or the NFLPA must present an injury grievance in writing to a club, with a copy to the Management Council, within 20 days from the date it became known or should have become known to the player that his contract had been terminated. The grievance will set forth the approximate date of the alleged injury and its general nature. If the player passes the physical examination of the club at the beginning of the pre-season training camp for the year in question, having made full and complete disclosure of his known physical and mental condition when questioned by the club physician during the physical examination, it will be presumed that such player was physically fit to play football on the date he reported.

Section 3. Answer. The club to which an injury grievance has been presented will answer in writing within five days. If the answer contains a denial of the claim, the general grounds for such denial will be set forth. The answer may raise any special defense, including but not limited to the following:

(a) That the player did not pass the physical examination administered by the club physician at the beginning of the pre-season training camp for the year in question. This defense will not be available if the player participated in any team drills following his physical examination or in any pre-season or regular season game; provided, however, that the club physician may require the player to undergo certain exercises or activities, not team drills, to determine whether the player will pass the physical examination;

(b) That the player failed to make full and complete disclosure of his known physical or mental condition when questioned during the physical examination;

(c) That the player's injury occurred prior to the physical examination and the player knowingly executed a waiver or release prior to the physical examination or his commencement of practice for the season in question which specifically pertained to such prior injury;

(d) That the player's injury arose solely from a non-football related cause subsequent to the physical examination;

(e) That subsequent to the physical examination the player suffered no new football-related injury;

(f) That subsequent to the physical examination the player suffered no football-related aggravation of a prior injury reducing his physical capacity below the level existing at the time of his physical examination as contemporaneously recorded by the club physician.

Section 4. Neutral Physician. The player must present himself for examination by a neutral physician within 20 days from the date of the grievance. This time period may be extended by mutual consent if the neutral physician is not available. Neither club nor player may submit any medical records to the neutral physician, nor may the club physician or player's physician communicate with the neutral physician. The player will notify the club of the identity of the neutral physician by whom he is to be examined as soon as possible subsequent to a selection by the player. The neutral physician will not become the treating physician nor will the neutral physician examination involve more than one office visit without the prior approval of both the NFLPA and Management Council.

Section 5. List. The NFLPA and the Management Council will maintain a jointly-approved list of neutral physicians, including at least two orthopedic physicians in each city in which an NFL club is located. The list will be subject to review and modification every 12 months, at which time either party may eliminate any two neutral physicians from the list by written notice to the other party. Each physician should be willing and able to examine NFL players promptly.

Section 6. Appeal. A grievance may be appealed to an arbitrator by filing of written notice of appeal with the chairman of the arbitration panel within 30 days from the date of receipt of the neutral physician's written report. There will be a panel of five (5) arbitrators, whose appointment must be accepted in writing by the NFLPA and the Management Council. The parties have designated Pat Fisher as the chairman of the panel. Either party to this Agreement may discharge a member of the arbitration panel by serving written notice upon the arbitrator and the other party to this Agreement between December 1 and 10 of each year, but at no time shall such discharges result in no arbitrators remaining on the panel.

Section 7. Hearing. Each arbitrator shall designate a minimum of one hearing date each month for use by the parties to this Agreement. Upon being appointed, each arbitrator will, after consultation with the Chairman, provide to the NFLPA and the Management Council specified hearing dates for each of the ensuing 12 months, which process will be repeated on an annual basis thereafter. The parties will notify each arbitrator 30 days in advance of which dates the following month are going to be used by the parties. The designated arbitrator will set the hearing on his or her next reserved date and, after consultation with the parties, designate a convenient place for hearing such grievance. If a grievance is set for hearing and the hearing date is then cancelled by a party within 30 days of the hearing date, the cancellation fee of the arbitrator will be borne by the cancelling party unless the arbitrator determines that the cancellation was for good cause. Should good cause be found, the parties will share any cancellation costs equally. If the arbitrator in question cannot reschedule the hearing within 30 days of the postponed date, the case may be reassigned by the Chairman to another panel member who has a hearing date available within the 30 day period. At the hearing, the parties to the grievance and the NFLPA and Management Council will have the right to present, by testimony or otherwise, any evidence relevant to the grievance. All hearings shall be transcribed. Post-hearing briefs must be submitted to the arbitrator postmarked no later than thirty (30) days after receipt of the last day's transcript. The arbitrator will, if at all possible, considering the arbitrator's schedule and other commitments, issue a written decision within 30 days of the submission of briefs. The arbitrator may issue the decison after 30 days have passed from the date of receipt of the last day's transcript regardless of the failure of either party to submit a brief. His decision will be final and binding; provided, however, that no arbitrator will have the authority to add to, subtract from, or alter in any way any provision of this Agreement or any other applicable document.

Section 8. Miscellaneous. The arbitrator will consider the neutral physician's findings conclusive with regard to the physical condition of the player and the extent of an injury at the time of his examination by the neutral physician. The arbitrator will decide the dispute in light of this finding and such other issues or defenses which may have been properly submitted to him. The club or the Management Council must advise the grievant and the NFLPA in writing no later than seven days before the hearing of any special defense to be raised at the hearing. The arbitrator may award the player payments for medical expenses incurred or which will be incurred in connection with an injury.

Section 9. Expenses. Expenses charged by a neutral physician will be shared equally by the club and the player. All travel expenses incurred by the player in connection with his examination by a neutral physician of his choice will be borne by the player. The parties will share equally in the expense of any arbitration engaged in pursuant to this Article; provided, however, the respective parties will bear the expenses of attendance of their own witnesses.

Section 10. Pension Credit. Any player who receives payment for three or more regular season games during any year as a result of filing an injury grievance or settlement of a potential injury grievance will be credited with one year of Credited Service for the year in which injured under the Bert Bell NFL Player Retirement Plan as determined by the Retirement Board.

Section 11. Payment. If an award is made by the arbitrator, payment will be made within twenty (20) days of the receipt of the award to the player or jointly to the player and the NFLPA provided the player has given written authorization for such joint payment. The time limit for payment may be extended by mutual consent of the parties or by a finding of good cause for the extension by the arbitrator.

ARTICLE X

Injury Protection

Section 1. Qualification. A player qualifying under the following criteria will receive an injury protection benefit in accordance with Section 2 below:

(a) The player must have been physically unable, because of a severe football injury in an NFL game or practice, to participate in all or part of his club's last game of the season of injury, as certified by the club physician following a physical examination after the last game; or the player must have undergone club-authorized surgery in the off-season following the season of injury; and

(b) The player must have undergone whatever reasonable and customary rehabilitation treatment his club required of him during the off-season following the season of injury; and

(c) The player must have failed the pre-season physical examination given by the club physician for the season following the season of injury because of such injury and as a result his club must have terminated his contract for the season following the season of injury. The past understanding of the parties concerning a club releasing a player who otherwise qualifies under (a) and (b) above prior to the pre-season physical examination, will be continued during the term of this Agreement.[2]

Section 2. Benefit. Effective after the execution of this Agreement, a player qualifying under Section 1 above will receive an amount equal to 50% of his contract salary for the season following the season of injury, up to a maximum payment of $65,000, unless he has individually negotiated more injury protection into that contract. A player will receive no amount of any contract covering any season subsequent to the season following the season of injury, except if he has individually negotiated injury protection into that contract. The benefit will be paid to the player in equal weekly installments commencing no later than the date of the first regular season game, which benefit payments will cease if the player signs a contract for that season with another NFL club. A player will not be entitled to such benefit more than once during his playing career in the NFL.

Section 3. Disputes. Any dispute under this Article will be processed under Article VII of this Agreement, Non-Injury Grievance.

ARTICLE XI

Committee on Safety and Welfare

A Joint Committee on Player Safety and Welfare (hereinafter the "Joint Committee") will be established for the purpose of discussing the player safety and welfare aspects of playing equipment, playing surfaces, stadium facilities, playing rules, player-coach relationships, and any other relevant subjects.

2. This understanding is recited in a letter from the Management Council, dated June 29, 1977, which states, ". . . it was agreed that a player who qualifies for 'Injury Protection' under subsections (a) and (b) may be waived prior to being given a pre-season physical examination, but the waiving club would retain 'Injury Protection' liability unless and until the player signed a contract with and passed the physical examination of another NFL club. In other words, a club cannot evade 'Injury Protection' liability by early waiving."

Section 1. Composition. The Joint Committee will consist of six members: three club representatives (plus advisors) and three NFLPA representatives (plus advisors).

Section 2. Meetings. The Joint Committee will hold two regular meetings each year on dates and at sites selected by the Committee. Special meetings may be held at any time and place mutually agreeable to the Committee.

Section 3. Powers. The Joint Committee will not have the power to commit or bind either the NFLPA or the Management Council on any issue.

Section 4. Scope. The Joint Committee may discuss and examine any subject related to player safety and welfare it desires, and any member of the Committee may present for discussion any such subject. Any Committee recommendations will be made only to the NFLPA, the Management Council, the Commissioner of the NFL, or any appropriate committee of the NFL: such recommendation will be given serious and thorough consideration.

Section 5. Consultants. The Joint Committee may employ consultants to assist it in the performance of its functions; the compensation and expenses of any such consultants will be paid in such manner as the Committee decides.

Section 6. Appointments. The respective members of the Joint Committee will be selected and the length of their terms fixed under such rules as the NFLPA and the Management Council separately establish; the original appointees on the Committee will be selected within 30 days following the execution of this Agreement.

Section 7. Initial Tasks. The NFLPA and the Management Council agree that a task for the Joint Committee to undertake promptly upon the execution of this Agreement is a review of all current materials on the player safety aspects of player equipment, playing surfaces and other safety matters, and a determination of whether a moratorium on further installation of artificial turf in NFL stadia is desirable.

Section 8. Competition Committee. Two players appointed by the NFLPA will have the right to attend those portions of the annual meeting of the NFL Competition Committee dealing with playing rules in a non-voting capacity to represent the players' viewpoint on such rules. The player-appointees will receive in advance copies of all agenda and other written materials relating to playing rules provided to other Committee members.

Section 9. Playing Rules. Immediately following the NFL annual meeting, the NFLPA will be given notice of all proposed playing rule changes, either tentatively adopted by the clubs or put over for further consideration at a later league meeting. If the NFLPA believes that the adoption of a playing rule change would adversely affect player safety, the NFLPA may call for a meeting of the Joint Committee within two weeks to discuss such proposed rule change. After such meeting, if the NFLPA continues to believe that the adoption of a playing rule change would adversely affect player safety, the NFLPA may request an advisory decision by one of the arbitrators designated in Article VII of this Agreement. A hearing before such arbitrator must be held within two weeks of the Joint Committee meeting and the arbitrator must render his decision within two weeks of the hearing. No such playing rule change will be made by the clubs until after the arbitrator's advisory decision unless the arbitrator has not rendered his decision within two weeks of the hearing. The arbitrator's decision will be advisory only, not final and binding. Except as so limited, nothing in this section will impair or limit in any way the right of the clubs to make any playing rule change whatsoever.

ARTICLE XII

NFL Player Contract

Section 1. Form. The NFL Player Contract form will be used for all player signings. This form cannot be amended without NFLPA approval. In connection with the NFLPA's exclusive right to represent all players in its bargaining unit in negotiations with NFL clubs under Article XXII, Section 2 of this Agreement on Salaries, it is agreed and understood that: (a) copies of all individual player contracts signed by rookie and veteran players before the date of execution of this Agreement covering the 1982 and future seasons will be provided to the NFLPA within 30 days of the execution of this Agreement; (b) copies of all contracts signed by rookie and veteran players after the date of execution of this Agreement covering the 1982 and future seasons will be provided to the NFLPA within 10 days of their execution; and (c) all information in such contracts will be made available to all clubs by the Management Council.

Section 2. Changes. Notwithstanding Section 1 above, changes may be made in a player's contract or contracts consistent with the provisions of this Agreement and with the provisions of the NFL Constitution and Bylaws not in conflict with this Agreement.

ARTICLE XIII

College Draft

Section 1. Time of Draft. Commencing with the college draft to be held on or about May 1, 1983, and with respect to the college draft to be held on or about May 1 each year thereafter, through at least 1992, the following principles will apply; provided, however, that commencing in 1984 the clubs will have the right during the term of this Agreement to move the date of the draft from on or about May 1 to on or about February 1 of the same year, but no later than six days after the Pro Bowl game or, in the absence of a Pro Bowl game, ten days after the Super Bowl game.

Section 2. Number of Choices. There will be no more than 336 selection choices in any college draft (in the event of NFL expansion, there will be an additional 12 selection choices per expansion club, except in the first year of expansion, when the expansion clubs may be given additional choices). Subject to such maximum, the clubs may determine the number of choices allotted to a club in any given round, so long as such allotment does not diminish the number of choices available for compensation under Article XV of this Agreement or any successor agreement.

Section 3. Exclusive Right. A club which drafts a player will, during the period from the date of such college draft (hereinafter "initial draft") to the date of the next college draft (hereinafter "subsequent draft"), be the only NFL club which may negotiate for or sign a contract with such player. If, within the period between the initial and subsequent draft, such player has not signed a contract with the club which drafted him in the initial draft, such club loses the exclusive right, which it obtained in the initial draft, to negotiate for a contract with the player and the player is then eligible to be drafted by another NFL club in the subsequent draft.

Section 4. Subsequent Draft. A club which, in the subsequent draft drafts a player who (a) was drafted in the initial draft, and (b) did not sign a contract with such first NFL club prior to the subsequent draft, will, during the period from the date of the college draft held in the following year, be the only NFL club which may negotiate for or sign a contract with such player. If such player has not signed a contract within the period between the subsequent draft and the next college draft with the club which drafted him in the subsequent draft, that club loses its exclusive right, which it obtained in the subsequent draft, to negotiate for a contract with the player, and the player is free to sign a contract at any time thereafter with any NFL club, and any NFL club is then free to negotiate for and sign a contract with such player, without any compensation between clubs or first refusal rights of any kind.

Section 5. No Subsequent Draft. If a player is drafted by an NFL club in an initial draft and (a) does not sign a contract with an NFL club prior to the subsequent draft and (b) is not drafted by any NFL club in such subsequent draft, the player is free to sign a contract at any time thereafter with an NFL club, and any NFL club is then free to negotiate for and sign a contract with such player, without any compensation between clubs or first refusal rights of any kind.

Section 6. Other Professional Team. If a player is hereafter drafted by an NFL club in an initial draft and, during the period in which he may sign a contract with only the club which drafted him, plays for a professional football team not in the NFL under a contract that covers all or part of at least the season immediately following said initial draft, then such NFL club will retain the exclusive NFL rights to negotiate for and sign a contract with the player for the period ending four years from the date of the initial draft, following which four-year period the player is free to sign a contract with any NFL club, and any NFL club is free to negotiate for and sign a contract with such player, subject to Section 7 below.

Section 7. Return to NFL. If a player who hereafter signs a contract with a professional football team not in the NFL desires to return to the NFL four or more years following the date of his initial draft, the NFL club which had drafted the player will have no right of compensation under Article XV, but will have a right of first refusal under the applicable terms and conditions of that Article. The returning player will notify the NFLPA and the NFL of his desire to sign a contract with an NFL club, which notice will advise of the date on which he will be free of contractual obligations, if any. Within 30 days of receipt of such notice by the NFL or the date of the availability of such player, whichever is later, the NFL club which had drafted the player must tender a written contract offer to the player in order to retain the right of first refusal under this Section.

Section 8. Pre-1983. A player drafted by an NFL club in 1980, 1981 or 1982 who signed a contract in another professional football league and desires to return to the NFL in 1983 or thereafter will be governed by the provisions set forth in Article XIII, Sections 8 and 9 of the 1977 Agreement.

Section 9. Assignment. In the event that the exclusive right to negotiate for a player or the right of first refusal under Section 7 above is assigned by an NFL club to another NFL club, the NFL club to which such right has been assigned will have the same, but no greater, right to negotiate for such player or to exercise the right of first refusal as is enjoyed by the club assigning such right, and such player will have the same, but no greater, obligation to the NFL club to which such right has been assigned as he had to the club assigning such right.

ARTICLE XIV

Option Clause

Section 1. Vested Players. Any contract or series of contracts signed by a veteran player who has completed the season in which his fourth year or more of Credited Service under the Bert Bell NFL Player Retirement Plan has been earned will not include an option year, unless an option clause has been negotiated for the player for a specific consideration other than compensation for the player's services.

Section 2. Rookies and Non-Vested Players. Any one-year contract signed by a rookie player must include an option year; any other contract or series of contracts signed by a rookie player may include an option year; and any contract or series of contracts signed by a veteran player who has not completed the season in which his fourth year of Credited Service under the Bert Bell NFL Player Retirement Plan has been earned may include an option year.

Section 3. Compensation. The option will be exercised by the club at no less than 110% of the player's salary provided in his contract for the previous year, excluding any signing or reporting bonus. Player will receive 100% of performance bonus provisions where the bonus is earned in the option year.

ARTICLE XV

Right of First Refusal/Compensation

Section 1. Applicability. For players who play out the option in their contracts or whose contracts otherwise expire (hereinafter referred to as "Veteran Free Agents") the following principles will apply; provided, however, that in the event the clubs make a determination during the term of this Agreement to move the date of the draft from on or about May 1 to on or about February 1 of the same year, any compensation under Section 12 of this Article XV will be in the next subsequent college draft.

Section 2. Contract Expiration Date. The expiration date of all player contracts will be February 1. After February 1, any NFL club will be free to negotiate for a contract with a veteran free agent.

Section 3. Offer Sheet. When the NFLPA receives an offer from a new club to sign a contract or contracts, which is acceptable, the NFLPA will on or before April 15 give to the player's old club a completed Offer Sheet substantially in the form of Exhibit A attached hereto, signed by the player and by the chief operating officer of the new club, which will contain the "principal terms" (as defined in Section 7 below) of the new club's offer. Subject to Section 10 below, the player's old club, upon receipt of the Offer Sheet, may exercise its "right of first refusal," which will have the consequences set forth in Section 4 below.

Section 4. First Refusal Exercise Notice. Subject to Section 18 below, if, within seven days from the date it receives an Offer Sheet, the veteran free agent's old club gives to the NFLPA a First Refusal Exercise Notice substantially in the form of Exhibit B attached hereto, such player and his old club will be deemed to have entered into a binding agreement, which will be promptly formalized in an NFL Player Contract(s); containing all the "principal terms" of the Offer Sheet and those terms of the NFL Player Contract(s) not modified by the "principal terms."

Section 5. No First Refusal Exercise Notice. Subject to Sections 6 and 10 below, if, within seven days from the date it receives an Offer Sheet, the veteran free agent's old club does not give the NFLPA a First Refusal Exercise Notice, the player and the new club will be deemed to have entered into a binding agreement, which will be promptly formalized in an NFL Player Contract(s), containing all the "principal terms" of the Offer Sheet, those terms of the NFL Player Contract(s) not modified by the "principal terms," and the non-principal terms offered by the new club.

Section 6. One Offer Sheet. There may be only one Offer Sheet signed by both a club and a veteran free agent outstanding at any one time. An Offer Sheet, before it is given to the veteran free agent's old club, may be revoked or withdrawn only upon the written consent of the new club and the NFLPA. An Offer Sheet, after it is given to a veteran free agent's old club, may be revoked or withdrawn only upon the written consent of the old club, the new club and the NFLPA. In either of such events, any NFL club will be free to negotiate for a contract with such player, subject only to his old club's renewed right of first refusal.

Section 7. Principal Terms. For purposes of this Article, the "principal terms" will include the following: (a) the salary the new club will pay to the veteran free agent and/or his designees, currently and/or as deferred compensation in specified installments on specified dates, in consideration for his services as a football player under the contract or contracts; (b) any signing or reporting bonus the new club will pay to the veteran free agent and/or his designees, currently and/or deferred, and the terms thereof; and (c) any modification of and/or addition to the terms contained in the NFL Player Contract form requested for the veteran free agent and acceptable to the new club, which relate to terms of the player's employment as a football player (which will be evidenced by a copy of the NFL Player Contract form, marked to show changes).

Section 8. Non-Principal Terms. For purposes of this Article, the "principal terms" will not include any of the following: (a) any loan the new club will make to the veteran free agent and/or his designees under the contract or contracts, and the terms thereof and security therefor, if any; (b) any performance bonus the new team will pay to the veteran free agent under the contract or contracts; (c) a description of any property other than money which the new club will provide or make available to the veteran free agent and/or his designees under the contract or contracts; (d) any investment opportunity which the new club will provide or make available to the veteran free agent and/or his designees; (e) any money and/or property the new club will pay, provide or make available to the veteran free agent and/or his designees in consideration for services by him or others; (f) any intangible benefits or advantages that might accrue to the veteran free agent as a consequence of living and playing in the geographic area of the new club; (g) any promise by the new club of a try-out, audition or introduction for the possibility of performing services or earning income other than that as a football player; and (h) any other terms not included within the "principal terms" set forth in Section 7 above.

Section 9. Qualifying Offer. For purposes of Section 10, 11, and 12 of this Article, a "qualifying offer" will include the sum of: (a) the total amount of salary to be paid under the contract or contracts, averaged over the full number of years of the contract or contracts, but no more than five years; and (b) any signing or reporting bonus to be paid under the contract or contracts, prorated over the full number of years of the contract or contracts, but no more than five years.

Section 10. Qualification for First Refusal. Anything above in this Article to the contrary notwithstanding, in order for a veteran free agent's old club to be entitled to a right of first refusal, the old club must have given a "qualifying offer" in writing to the NFLPA on or before February 1, to be represented by an Offer Sheet, in the following amounts: (a) $60,000 ($75,000 in 1985 through 1987) or more if the player has not yet completed the season in which his 3rd year of Credited Service under the Bert Bell NFL Player Retirement Plan has been earned; (b) $70,000 ($85,000 in 1985 through 1987) or more if the player has not yet completed the season in which his 4th year of Credited Service has been earned; (c) an increase of $10,000 for each year of Credited Service thereafter, in accordance with the graphs portrayed in Exhibits C and D attached hereto.

Section 11. Qualification for Compensation. In order for a veteran free agent's old club to be entitled to a right of compensation, the old club must have qualified for a right of first refusal under Section 10 above and the new club must have given a "qualifying offer" in writing to the NFLPA on or before April 15, to be represented by an Offer Sheet, in the following amounts: (a) $80,000 ($100,000 in 1985 through 1987) or more if the player has not yet completed the season in which his 3rd year of Credited Service under the Bert Bell NFL Player Retirement Plan has been earned; (b) $90,000 ($110,000 in 1985 through 1987) or more if the player has not yet completed the season in which his 4th year of Credited Service has been earned; and (c) an increase of $10,000 for each year of Credited Service thereafter, in accordance with the graphs portrayed in Exhibits C and D attached hereto. Anything in Subsections (a) through (c) to the contrary notwithstanding, the "qualifying offer" with respect to veteran free agent quarterbacks will increase by $5,000 for each year of Credited Service if the player has not yet completed the season in which his 8th year of Credited Service has been earned and thereafter.

Section 12. Amount of Compensation. Subject to Section 10 above, if, within seven days from the date it receives an Offer Sheet, a veteran free agent's old club, which is entitled to a right of first refusal or a right of compensation, chooses not to exercise its right of first refusal, then the player and the new club will be deemed to have entered into a binding agreement as provided in Section 5 above, and the player's old club will receive the following compensation: (a) the new club's 3rd round selection choice or a better 3rd round choice obtained by assignment from another NFL club, in the next immediate college draft: (i) if the player has not completed the season in which his 3rd year of Credited Service under the Bert Bell NFL Retirement Plan has been earned and if the "qualifying offer" is $80,000 or more but less than $95,000 ($100,000 and $120,000 in 1985 through 1987); (ii) if the player has not completed the season in which his 4th year of Credited Service has been earned and if the "qualifying offer" is $90,000 or more but less than $105,000 ($110,000 and $130,000 in 1985 through 1987); and (iii) an increase of $10,000 for each year of Credited Service thereafter, in accordance with the graphs portrayed in Exhibits C and D attached hereto; (b) the new club's 2nd round selection choice or a better 2nd round choice obtained by assignment from another NFL club, in the next immediate college draft: (i) if the player has not completed the season in which his 3rd year of Credited Service has been earned and if the "qualifying offer" is $95,000 or more but less than $110,000 ($120,000 and $140,000 in 1985 through 1987); (ii) if player has not completed the season in which his 4th year of Credited Service has been earned and if the "qualifying offer" is $105,000 or more but less than $120,000 ($130,000 and $150,000 in 1985 through 1987); and (iii) an increase of $10,000 for each year of Credited Service thereafter, in accordance with the graphs portrayed in Exhibits C and D attached hereto; (c) the new club's 1st round selection choice or a better 1st round choice obtained by assignment from another NFL club in the next immediate college draft: (i) if the player has not completed the season in which his 3rd year of Credited Service has been earned and if the "qualifying offer" is $110,000 or more but less than $150,000 ($140,000 and $180,000 in 1985 through 1987), (ii) if the player has not completed the season in which his 4th year of Credited Service has been earned and if the "qualifying offer" is $120,000 or more but less then $160,000 ($150,000 and $190,000 in 1985 through 1987), and (iii) an increase of $10,000 for each year of Credited Service thereafter, in accordance with the graphs portrayed in Exhibits C and D attached hereto; (d) the new club's 1st and 3rd round selection choices, or better 1st and 3rd round choices obtained by assignment from other NFL clubs in the next immediate college draft: (i) if the player has not completed the season in which his 3rd year of Credited Service has been earned and if the "qualifying offer" is $150,000 or more but less than $200,000 ($180,000 and $230,000 in 1985 through 1987); (ii) if the player has not completed the season in which his 4th year of Credited Service has been earned and if the "qualifying offer" is $160,000 or more, but less than $210,000 ($190,000 and $240,000 in 1985 through 1987); and (iii) an increase of $10,000 for each year of Credited Service thereafter, in accordance with the graphs portrayed in Exhibits C and D attached hereto; (e) the new club's 1st round and 2nd round selection choices or better 1st and 2nd round choices obtained by assignment from other NFL clubs in the next immediate college drafts: (i) if the player has not completed the season in which his 3rd year of Credited Service has been earned and if the "qualifying offer" is $200,000 or more but less than $250,000 ($230,000 and $280,000 in 1985 through 1987); (ii) if the player has not completed the season in which his 4th year of Credited Service has been earned and if the "qualifying offer" is $210,000 or more but less than $260,000 ($240,000 and $290,000 in 1985 through 1987); and (iii) an increase of $10,000 for each year of Credited Service thereafter, in accordance with the graphs portrayed in Exhibits C and D attached hereto; (f) the new club's 1st round selection choices or better 1st round choices obtained by assignment from other NFL clubs, in the next immediate two college drafts: (i) if the player has not completed the season in which his 3rd year of Credited Service has been earned and if the qualifying offer is $250,000 or more ($280,000 in 1985 through 1987), (ii) if the player has not completed the season in which his 4th year of Credited Service has been earned and if the "qualifying offer" is $260,000 or more ($290,000 in 1985 through 1987); and (iii) an increase of $10,000 for each year of Credited Service thereafter, in accordance with the graphs portrayed in Exhibits C and D attached hereto. Anything in Subsections (a) through (f) to the contrary notwithstanding, the "qualifying offer" with respect to veteran free agent quarterbacks will increase by $5,000 for each year of Credited Service if the player has not yet completed the season in which his 8th year of Credited Service has been earned and thereafter.

Section 13. Absences of Choice. A club not having the future selection choice or choices necessary to provide compensation in the event the veteran free agent's old club chooses to exercise its right of compensation, if any, may not sign an Offer Sheet as provided in Section 3 above.

Section 14. Copies. Within seven days after an Offer Sheet is signed by a player and a new club, that club will cause a copy thereof to be given to the NFL; and within seven days after the giving of a First Refusal Exercise Notice to the veteran free agent, the old club will cause a copy thereof to be given to the NFL.

Section 15. Circulation of Veteran Free Agent List. The NFL will prepare and circulate to all NFL clubs and the NFLPA a list containing the names of all players who will become veteran free agents as of February 1. The list will be circulated between January 1 and February 1 of each year.

Section 16. Notice. Any Offer Sheet, First Refusal Exercise Notice, or other writing required or permitted to be given under this Article will be hand delivered or sent by prepaid certified or registered mail addressed as follows: (a) To any club: addressed to that club at the principal address of such club as then listed on the records of the NFL or at that club's principal office, to the attention of the club president; (b) To the NFL: addressed to the NFL at 410 Park Avenue, New York, New York 10022, to the attention of the Commissioner; (c) To the NFLPA: addressed to the NFLPA at 1300 Connecticut Avenue, N.W., Washington, D.C. 20036, to the attention of the Executive Director; and (d) To a veteran free agent: to his address listed on the Offer Sheet. An Offer Sheet will be deemed given only when actually received by the player's old club. A First Refusal Exercise Notice will be deemed given when sent by the player's old club. Other writings required or permitted to be given under this Article (including a "qualifying offer") will be deemed given when hand delivered or sent by prepaid certified or registered mail addressed as above required.

Section 17. Re-Signing. If no offer to sign a contract or contracts with a new NFL club pursuant to this Article is received by a player, and his old club advises the NFLPA in writing by June 1 that it desires to re-sign him, the player may, at his option within 15 days sign either (a) a contract or contracts with his old club at its last best written offer given on or before February 1 of that year, or (b) a one-year contract (with no option year) with his old club at 110% of the salary provided in his contract for the last preceding year (if the player has just played out the option year, the rate will be 120%). If the player's old club does not advise the NFLPA in writing by June 1 that it desires to re-sign the player, he will be free on June 2 to sign a contract or contracts with any NFL club, and any NFL club will be free to negotiate for and sign a contract or contracts with such player, without any compensation between clubs or first refusal rights of any kind.

Section 18. Extreme Personal Hardship. In the event of alleged extreme personal hardship or an alleged violation of Article V, Section 1, of this Agreement, a veteran free agent may, within seven days after the February 1 expiration date of his contract, unless the condition arises after that date, file a non-injury grievance pursuant to Article VII of this Agreement. If the PCRC is unable to resolve the grievance, and should the outside arbitrator conclude that such extreme personal hardship objectively exists or that there has been a substantive violation of Article V, Section 1, then he may deny to the player's old club its right of first refusal. In the event a club's first refusal rights are denied under this Section because of extreme personal hardship, the club's last written contract offer for the player to the NFLPA will constitute a "qualifying offer" for compensation pursuant to Section 11 of Article XV.

EXHIBIT A

FIRST REFUSAL OFFER SHEET

Name of Player: Date:

Address of Player: Name of New Club:

National Football League Players   Name of Old Club:
Association
1300 Connecticut Avenue, N.W.
Washington, D.C. 20036

Principal Terms of NFL Player Contract or
Contracts With New Club:

(Supply Information on this Sheet or on Attachment)

(a) Salary, including deferred compensation:

(b) Signing or reporting bonus, if any:

(c) Modifications and additions to NFL Player Contract(s):
     [attached marked-up copy of NFL Player Contracts(s)]

Player: New Club:

By _____   By _____
                                           Chief Operating Officer

EXHIBIT B

FIRST REFUSAL EXERCISE NOTICE

Name of Player: Date:

Address of Player: Name of Old Club:

National Football League Players   Name of New Club:
Association
1300 Connecticut Avenue, N.W.
Washington, D.C. 20036

     The undersigned member club of the NFL hereby exercises its Right of First Refusal under the Collective Bargaining Agreement dated _____, so as to create a binding agreement with the player named above containing the "principal terms" set forth in the First Refusal Offer Sheet, a copy of which is attached hereto, and those terms of the NFL Player Contract(s) not modified by such "principal terms."

Old Club

By _____
                  Chief Operating Officer

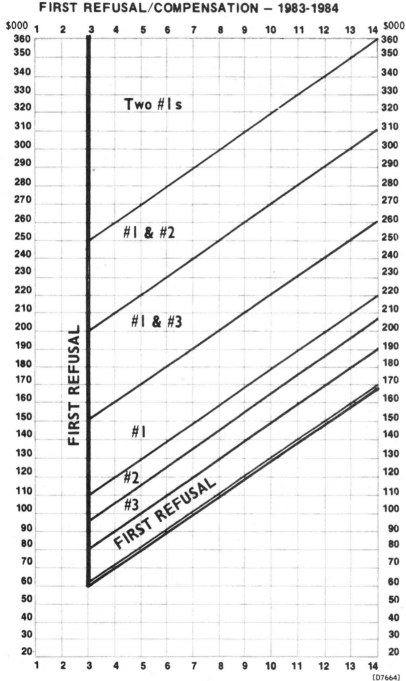

EXHIBIT C

FIRST REFUSAL/COMPENSATION — 1983-1984

[D7664]

EXHIBIT D
FIRST REFUSAL/COMPENSATION — 1985-1986-1987

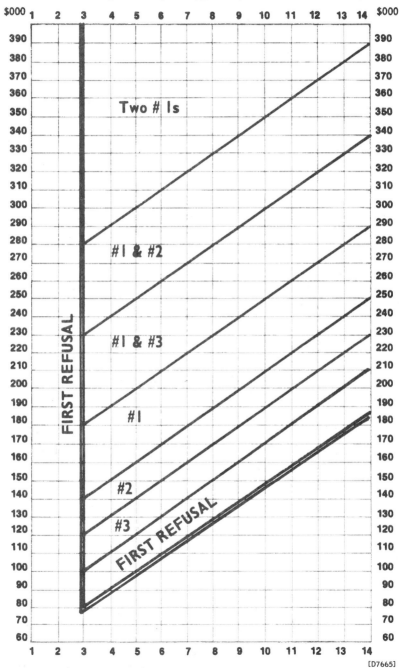

[D7665]

ARTICLE XVI

Waiver System

Section 1. Release. Whenever a player who has completed the season in which his fourth year or more of Credited Service under the provisions of the Bert Bell NFL Player Retirement Plan has been earned is placed on waivers, claimed and would be awarded, the club having requested waivers will immediately advise the player of such fact, provided the waiver request has taken place within the time period of February 1 to the end of the NFL trading period. Within 24 hours after receipt of such information, the player may, at his option, give written notice to the club having requested waivers that he desires to terminate his contract or contracts and obtain his unconditional release. However, should the player fail to give such notice within the 24-hour period, his contract will be awarded to the claiming club in accordance with the rules prescribed in the NFL Constitution and Bylaws. In the event the player requests his unconditional release, the player and the NFLPA will be advised promptly by the NFL which clubs claimed the player.

Section 2. Contact. Coaches or any other persons connected with another NFL club are prohibited from contacting any player placed on waivers until such time as the player is released by the waiving club.

Section 3. Ineligibility. Any NFL player who is declared ineligible to compete in a pre-season, regular season or post-season game because of a breach of waiver procedures and regulations or any other provision of the NFL Constitution and Bylaws by any NFL club by whom he is employed will be paid the salary or other compensation which he would have received if he had not been declared ineligible, which, in any event, will be a minimum of one week's salary and, when applicable, expense payments.

Section 4. Notice of Termination. The Notice of Termination form attached as Exhibit E will be used by all clubs. If possible, the Notice of Termination will be personally delivered to the player prior to his departure from the team. If the Notice of Termination has not been personally delivered to the player prior to his departure from the team, the Notice of Termination will be sent to him by certified mail at his last address on file with the club.

EXHIBIT E

NOTICE OF TERMINATION

_____, _____

TO:_____

You are hereby notified that effective immediately your NFL Player contract(s) with the Club covering the _____ football season(s) has (have) been terminated for the reason(s) checked below:

[ ] You have failed to establish or maintain your excellent physical condition to the satisfaction of the Club physician.

[ ] You have failed to make full and complete disclosure of your physical or mental condition during a physical examination.

[ ] In the judgment of the Club, your skill or performance has been unsatisfactory as compared with that of other players competing for positions on the Club's roster.

[ ] You have engaged in personal conduct which, in the reasonable judgment of the Club, adversely affects or reflects on the Club.

_____

Club

By: _____

ARTICLE XVII

Expansion

Section 1. Veteran Allocation. In the event the clubs make a determination after the execution of this Agreement to expand the number of clubs, it is agreed upon that an expansion allocation of veteran players may be held on the terms decided by the clubs.

Section 2. Future Expansion. Any veteran player selected in any expansion allocation subsequent to the execution of this Agreement will receive a bonus of $6,000 upon making the expansion club's Active List at any time during the club's first regular season.

ARTICLE XVIII

Other Provisions

Section 1. CFL Rule. A player who has practiced and/or played in the CFL may be employed by an NFL club in the same season so long as he is signed by the NFL club on or before July 15 of the year in question.

Section 2. Physically Unable to Perform. Any player placed on Reserve as Physically Unable to Perform under the terms and conditions of the NFL Constitution and Bylaws will be paid at the rate of his full contract salary while on such Reserve. His contract will not be tolled for the period he is on Reserve as PUP except for the option year or, in the absence of an option year, the last year of a player's contract, when the player's contract will be tolled.

Section 3. Non-Football Injury. The contract of a player placed on Reserve as Non-Football Injury or Illness (N–F/I) under the terms and conditions of the NFL Constitution and Bylaws will not be tolled for the period of his failure to perform his services under the contract and will continue to run as if the player were performing, but he will not be entitled to any compensation under his contract during that period. This modification will not apply to the option year of a player's contract or, in the absence of an option year, to the last year of a player's contract.

ARTICLE XIX

Squad Size

Section 1. Active List. For each regular season, the Active List limit will be 45 players per club. This limit may not be reduced by the clubs for the duration of this Agreement; provided, however, that individual clubs may occasionally carry less than 45 players on their Active Lists during the regular season, but at no time less than 40.

Section 2. Pre-Season. The pre-season cutdown dates and active player limits on such dates will be as determined by the clubs. In the event the clubs make a determination during the term of this Agreement that they wish to institute a "down-and-up" once during the pre-season, they may do so, provided that the active player limit may not be reduced below 40 at any time during the pre-season and the Active List limit must return to 45 by the start of the regular season.

Section 3. Inactive List. For the 1982 regular and post season, there will be an Inactive List of 4 players per club. For the 1983, 1984, 1985 or 1986 regular season, the clubs may determine to have an Inactive List limit of any number of players per club. Inactive List players will receive the same benefits and protections as Active List players.

ARTICLE XX

Off-Season Training Camps

Section 1. Number. Each club may hold a maximum of one mandatory off-season training camp for veteran players. If a club hires a new head coach after the end of the regular season, that club may hold two additional voluntary off-season training camps for veteran players. There is no limitation on the number of off-season training camps a club may hold for rookie players.

Section 2. Length. No off-season training camp may exceed three days in length, plus one day for physical examinations. If possible, off-season training camps should be scheduled for weekends and not in conflict with previously scheduled meetings of the NFLPA Board of Reps or the annual NFLPA convention.

Section 3. Expenses. Any veteran player who attends an off-season training camp will receive meal allowances in accordance with Article XXV, Section 1 of this Agreement, plus all travel expenses to and from the camp, plus "per diem" payments at the rate provided in Article XXI, Section 4 of this Agreement. In addition, the club will provide housing at off-season training camps for players coming from out-of-town.

Section 4. Contact. There will be no contact work or use of pads (helmets permitted) at off-season training camps.

Section 5. Injuries. Any player injured in a club's off-season training camp will be protected in the same manner as if injured during the club's pre-season training camp.

ARTICLE XXI

Pre-Season Training Camps

Section 1. Definition. For purposes of this Agreement, a "rookie player" is defined as any player who has not completed one season in which a year of Credited Service under the Bert Bell NFL Player Retirement Plan has been earned, and a "veteran player" is defined as any player who has completed one or more seasons in which a year of Credited Service has been earned under such Plan.

Section 2. Room and Board. All players will receive room and board during the pre-season training camp.

Section 3. Rookie Per Diem. Effective after the execution of this Agreement, a rookie player will receive "per diem" payments at the rate of $375 per week in 1983, $400 per week in 1984, $425 per week in 1985, and $450 per week in 1986, commencing with the first day of pre-season training camp and ending one week prior to the club's first regular season game.

Section 4. Veteran Per Diem. Effective after the execution of this Agreement, a veteran player will receive "per diem" payments at the rate of $425 per week in 1983, $450 per week in 1984, $475 per week in 1985, and $500 per week in 1986, commencing with the first day of pre-season training camp and ending one week prior to the club's first regular season game, and an additional $200 per week in each year of this Agreement commencing with the club's first pre-season game (exclusive of the Canton Hall-of-Fame Game) and ending one week prior to the club's first regular season game (four weeks).

Section 5. Reporting. No veteran player, other than quarterbacks and injured players, will be required to report to a club's official pre-season training camp earlier than 15 days (including one day for physical examinations) prior to its first scheduled pre-season game or July 15, whichever is later. The July 15 date will not apply to clubs participating in the Canton Hall-of-Fame Game.

Section 6. Telephones. Whenever possible, a player will be permitted to have a telephone in his room at pre-season training camp at his own expense.

Section 7. Expenses. Clubs will reimburse all players under contract for reasonable traveling expenses incurred in reaching training camp from the players' residences, upon submission of vouchers. There will be no deductions by the clubs for these payments. Players who are released by club will be reimbursed for their return trips to their residences, upon submission of vouchers.

ARTICLE XXII

Salaries

Section 1. Salaries. Effective after the execution of this Agreement, the salary of a rookie player will be not less than $20,000 and the salary of any player who makes a club's Active List at any time during the regular season will be not less than the following:

Length of Service	1982	1983	1984	1985	1986
Rookie	$ 30,000	$ 40,000	$ 40,000	$ 50,000	$ 50,000
2nd Year	40,000	50,000	50,000	60,000	60,000
3rd Year	50,000	60,000	60,000	70,000	70,000
4th Year	60,000	70,000	70,000	80,000	80,000
5th Year	70,000	80,000	80,000	90,000	90,000
6th Year	80,000	90,000	90,000	100,000	100,000
7th Year	90,000	100,000	100,000	110,000	110,000
8th Year	100,000	110,000	110,000	120,000	120,000
9th Year	110,000	120,000	120,000	130,000	130,000
10th Year	120,000	130,000	130,000	140,000	140,000
11th Year	130,000	140,000	140,000	150,000	150,000
12th Year	140,000	150,000	150,000	160,000	160,000
13th Year	150,000	160,000	160,000	170,000	170,000
14th Year	160,000	170,000	170,000	180,000	180,000
15th Year	170,000	180,000	180,000	190,000	190,000
16th Year	180,000	190,000	190,000	200,000	200,000
17th Year	190,000	200,000	200,000	200,000	200,000
18th Year & Above	200,000	200,000	200,000	200,000	200,000

For purposes of this Article, a player's salary under any contract in existence at the time of execution of this Agreement will include the amount of any signing or reporting bonus, prorated over the full number of years of the contract or contracts executed on the same date (including any option year). A player's salary under any contract executed after the time of execution of this Agreement will not include the prorated amount of any signing or reporting bonus. No other type of incentive bonus will be included at any time in the computation of a player's salary under this

Article. The length of service of a player will be determined by crediting one year of service for each year the player has been on the Active List of a club for at least three regular season games.

Section 2. Other Compensation. A player will be entitled to receive a signing or reporting bonus, additional salary payments, incentive bonuses and such other provisions as may be negotiated between his club (with the assistance of the Management Council) and the NFLPA or its agent. The club and the NFLPA or its agent will negotiate in good faith over such other compensation; provided, however, that a club will not be required to deal with the NFLPA or its agent on a collective or tandem basis for two or more players on that club. Nothing in this Section will be affected by Article II, Section 1 of this Agreement.

Section 3. Arbitration. The question of whether or not the club, the Management Council, the NFLPA or its agent has engaged in good faith negotiations over such other compensation may be the subject of a noninjury grievance under Article VII of this Agreement. If the arbitrator finds that any party did not engage in good faith negotiations, he may enter a cease and desist order; provided, however, that the arbitrator may not compel any party to agree to anything or require the making of a concession by any party in negotiations.

Section 4. Payment. Unless agreed upon otherwise between the club and the player, each player will be paid at the rate of 100% of his salary in equal weekly or bi-weekly installments over the course of the regular season commencing with the first regular season game. Nothing in this Article invalidates or otherwise affects any deferred compensation arrangement or any other method of payment which may have been entered into between a club and a player or which after the execution of this Agreement may be negotiated between a club and the NFLPA or its agent.

Section 5. Re-opener. In the event that the NFL enters into any contract covering any playing season from 1982 through 1986 for the sale of television rights such as, but not limited to, cable, pay cable, satellite, closed circuit broadcasts, or any form of pay television, or in the event that the NFL enters into any new or re-negotiated contract with CBS, NBC or ABC covering any season from 1982 through 1986 and providing for total revenues over and above those contracted for by the NFL as of the date of execution of this Agreement covering the 1982 through 1986 playing seasons, the Management Council will provide immediate written notice of same and information as to the amount of additional revenue to the NFLPA, and, upon receipt of such notice, the NFLPA may re-open this Agreement upon the giving of ten days' written notice to the Management Council. After re-opening, the parties will have an obligation to resume negotiations limited to the issue of player compensation reflecting solely the application of the additional revenue or portion thereof, and both parties will be free to engage in whatever concerted action may be permitted by law in support of their respective positions. This re-opener will not give the NFLPA the right to examine any contract between the NFL and any party; provided, however, that the NFLPA will have the right to choose a senior accountant from any of the "Big Eight" accounting firms who will have the right to examine any such contract to confirm the accuracy of any information regarding any such contract given to the NFLPA by the Management Council in the operation of this Section.

Section 6. Length of Regular Season. The NFL clubs cannot increase the number of regular season games from the standard of sixteen (16) for the duration of this Agreement without providing ninety (90) days notice in writing to the NFLPA and thereafter negotiating with the NFLPA with regard to additional compensation to be paid to players for additional regular season games. If the parties are unable to agree on additional compensation within thirty (30) days after notice has been given, the issue of additional compensation may be submitted by either party to an arbitrator under Article VII of this Agreement for an expedited hearing and a final and binding decision. Notwithstanding the limitations on the arbitrator's powers contained in Article VII, Section 10, the arbitrator will have the full authority to decide the amount of additional compensation to which the players will be entitled. In no event will the regular season be extended for the duration of this Agreement to include more than eighteen (18) games.

ARTICLE XXIII

Money Now

Section 1. Amount. Any player who was on a club's Active, Inactive, Injured Reserve or Physically Unable to Perform list on September 20, 1982 will receive a payment based on the number of Credited Seasons earned under the Bert Bell NFL Player Retirement Plan as of that date in accordance with the following schedule:

Credited Seasons	Amount
None	$10,000
One	20,000
Two	30,000
Three or more	60,000

Section 2. Payment. The amount specified in Section 1 above will be paid to each player who qualifies for such payment on January 3, 1983, or 15 days following the date of execution of this Agreement, whichever occurs later.

Section 3. Game Pay. In consideration of payment of the amounts provided for in this Article, the NFLPA agrees that neither it nor any of its members nor any member of its bargaining unit will file any grievance, suit or any other type of action in any forum claiming that any NFL player is entitled to be paid any salary for the 1982 regular season in excess of the sum arrived at by dividing the yearly salary stated in paragraph 5 of his 1982 NFL Player Contract, or paragraph 3 of his 1982 Standard Player Contract (or 110% of the 1982 paragraph 5 or paragraph 3 salary, as may be the case, if player is in his option year) by 16, and multiplying the dividend by the total number of 1982 regular season games played on the dates of which the player was on a club's Active, Inactive, Injured Reserve or Physically Unable to Perform list. This Section does not apply to injury grievances under Article IX of this Agreement.

ARTICLE XXIV

Severance Pay

Section 1. Amount. Effective November 16, 1982, any player who has earned two (2) or more Credited Seasons under the Bert Bell NFL Player Retirement Plan and leaves the National Football League, will be entitled to receive from the last NFL club to which he was under contract a severance payment in accordance with the following schedule:

Credited Seasons	Last NFL Season 1982, 1983 or 1984	Last NFL Season 1985 or 1986
Two	$ 5,000	$ 10,000
Three	20,000	30,000
Four	60,000	70,000
Five	70,000	80,000
Six	80,000	90,000
Seven	90,000	100,000
Eight	100,000	110,000
Nine	110,000	120,000
Ten	120,000	130,000
Eleven	130,000	140,000
Twelve or more	140,000	150,000

For the 1982 season only, a player who was on any club's Active, Inactive, Injured Reserve or Physically Unable to Perform list on the dates of a club's first two regular season games will be deemed to have earned a Credited Season for purposes of this Article only and for no other purpose, including pension plan purposes.

Section 2. Payment. The foregoing severance payment will be paid to the player immediately following the third game of the NFL regular season next following the player's leaving the National Football League or any other professional football league, whichever occurs later. The amount of the severance payment will be prorated among all clubs to which a player was under contract during his NFL career, except in the case of a player who left the NFL prior to September 20, 1982 and returns to a club after the execution of this Agreement, in which case the player will be entitled to only one-half of his accrued severance benefit and the club to which the player returns will be responsible for one-quarter of his accrued severance benefit as well as any full severance benefit earned following his return. A player may not qualify for more than one severance payment under this provision.

ARTICLE XXV

Meal Allowance

Section 1. Reimbursement. Effective after the execution of this Agreement, a player will be reimbursed for meals not furnished by his club on travel days during the pre-season, regular season and post-season as follows: 1982 through 1984—Breakfast $7.00; Lunch $8.00; Dinner $20.00; 1985 and 1986—Breakfast $8.00; Lunch $9.00; Dinner $21.00.

Section 2. Travel Day. Each travel day will commence at the time a team leaves its home city and will terminate at the time the team arrives back at its home city. If a team is travelling for a day game and leaves its home city after 2:00 P.M. on the day prior to the game, players will receive dinner money if the team does not eat dinner together. When the pre-game meal on a travel day is after 9:00 A.M., players will receive breakfast money.

ARTICLE XXVI

Days Off

Section 1. Rate. All players will be permitted days-off at least at the rate of four days per month as determined by the clubs, commencing with the first pre-season game and continuing until the last regular season or post-season game played by the respective clubs.

Section 2. Requirements. During the 24-hour period constituting a day-off, any injured player may be required to undergo medical treatment and quarterbacks may be required to attend coaches meetings.

ARTICLE XXVII

Moving and Travel Expenses

Section 1. Qualification. Effective after the execution of this Agreement, a player qualifying under either of the following categories will receive reimbursement for moving expenses, upon presentation of vouchers, in accordance with Section 2 below:

(a) Any veteran player who is traded, claimed, assigned in an expansion allocation or a member of a club which relocates to a different home city, and before the first regular season game of the subsequent season, takes up permanent residence in the city of the club to which he is traded or assigned, by which he is claimed or which relocates to a different home city;　or

(b) Any rookie player who is traded or claimed after the start of the regular season, subsequently makes the Active List of the club to which he is traded or by which he is claimed, and takes up permanent residence in the city of the club to which he is traded or by which he is claimed before the first regular season game of the subsequent season.

Section 2. Moving Expenses. A player who qualifies for reimbursement pursuant to Section 1 above will receive, immediately upon presentation of vouchers, reimbursement of his actual, ordinary and reasonable moving expenses, including travel expenses for player and his immediate family, provided he has notified his club prior to the move of at least two estimates of the cost of the move and his club approves one of the estimates, in writing, which approval will not be unreasonably withheld.

Section 3. Travel Expenses. Effective after the execution of this Agreement, any veteran player who is traded or claimed at any time during the calendar year or any rookie player who is traded or claimed after the start of the regular season and subsequently makes the Active List of the club to which he is traded or by which he is claimed will receive, upon presentation of vouchers: (a) first class round trip air fare for his wife or the equivalent in cash if she makes the trip by another mode of transportation;　(b) a sum not to exceed two months' rent on living quarters in the home city from which the player is traded or by which he is waived, provided, however, that such payment shall be made only if and to the extent that the player is legally obligated to such rent and such payment shall not exceed $1,000; and (c) the room cost of seven days' stay at a hotel of the club's choice in the new team city for the player.

Section 4. Transportation. Each player who is traded or claimed during the pre-season or regular season will report to the club to which he is traded or by which he is claimed by the fastest available means of transportation.　Any veteran player who is traded or claimed during the pre-season or regular season or any rookie player who is traded or claimed after the start of the regular season will receive first class air fare.　All other players will be furnished coach air fare.

ARTICLE XXVIII

Post-Season Play

Section 1. System. Beginning with the post-season following the 1982 regular season, a four-tiered ("wild card" game, division playoff game, conference championship game and Super Bowl game) play-off system will be continued throughout the term of this Agreement.

Section 2. Compensation. Effective after the execution of this Agreement, a player who qualifies will receive the following amount for each post-season game played:

Wild Card Game	$6,000
Division Playoff Game	$10,000
Conference Championship Game	$18,000
Super Bowl Game	$18,000 (Losing Team)
	$36,000 (Winning Team)

Section 3. Wild Card Game; Division Play-off Game. A player who is on the Active List, Inactive List, or Injured Reserve List of a club at the time of the game in question will be paid the full amount designated in Section 2 for that game.

Section 4. Conference Championship Game; Super Bowl Game.

(a) A player who at the time of the game in question is and has been on the Active List or Inactive List of a club participating in the game for at least three games (i.e. regular or post-season) will receive the full amount designated in Section 2 for such game.

(b) A player who at the time of the game in question is and has been on the Active List or Inactive List of a club participating in the game for less than three games (i.e. regular or post-season) will receive one-fourth the amount designated in Section 2 for such game.

(c) A player who at the time of the game in question is not on the Active List or Inactive List of a club participating in the game but was on the Active or Inactive List for eight or more games (i.e. regular or post-season) will receive the full amount designated in Section 2 for such game provided he is not under contract to another NFL club at the time of the game in question.

(d) A player who at the time of the game in question is not on the Active List or Inactive List of a club participating in the game, but was on the Club's Active List or Inactive List for at least three and not more than seven games (i.e. regular and post-season) will receive one-half the amount designated in Section 2 for such game, provided he is not under contract to another NFL club at the time of the game in question.

(e) A veteran player injured during the regular season and removed from the Active List or Inactive List of a club participating in the game in question for reason of injury will receive the full amount designated in Section 2 for such game provided he is still under contract to the club at the time of the game.

(f) A veteran player who has completed the season in which his fourth year or more of Credited Service under the Bert Bell NFL Player Retirement Plan has been earned, who was injured during the pre-season and removed from the Active List or Inactive List of a club participating in the game in question for reason of injury will receive the full amount designated in Section 2 for such game provided he is still under contract to the club at the time of the game.

(g) A veteran player who has not completed the season in which his fourth year of Credited Service under the Bert Bell NFL Player Retirement Plan has been earned, who was injured during the pre-season and removed from the Active List or Inactive List of a club participating in the game in question for reason of injury will receive one-half the amount designated in Section 2 for such game provided he is still under contract to the club at the time of the game.

Section 5. Payment. Players will be paid under this Article within 15 days after the game in question has been played.

ARTICLE XXIX

Pro Bowl Game

Section 1. Compensation: Effective after the execution of this Agreement, each player on the winning team in the AFC–NFC Pro Bowl game will receive $10,000 and each player on the losing team will receive $5,000.

Section 2. Selection. Pro Bowl game players will be chosen on the basis of two votes per club, one by the coaches and one by the players. The player rep will conduct the balloting of the players in accordance with the same procedure used by the NFL for the coaches. The NFLPA will actively cooperate with the NFL to insure participation in the game and prompt reporting by players selected.

Section 3. Wives. Airplane, hotel and meal allowances will be provided for players' wives who attend the Pro Bowl games.

Section 4. Injury. In the event a player is injured in a Pro Bowl game and as a direct result is unable to perform in any regular season game the immediate following season, the player will be paid by his club the weekly installments of his salary covering the games missed.

Section 5. Payment. Players will be paid for the Pro Bowl game within 15 days after the game is played.

ARTICLE XXX

Retention of Benefits

No financial benefit granted by any club to its players as a group during the life of, but apart from, any previous collective bargaining agreement between the parties may be reduced or eliminated during the term of this Agreement.

ARTICLE XXXI

Players' Rights To Medical Care and Treatment

Section 1. Club Physican: Each club will have a board certified orthopedic surgeon as one of its club physicians. The cost of medical services rendered by Club physicians will be the responsibility of the respective clubs. If a Club physican advises a coach or other Club representative of a player's physical condition which could adversely affect the player's performance or health, the physician will also advise the player.

Section 2. Club Trainers. All full-time head trainers and assistant trainers hired after the date of execution of this Agreement will be certified by the National Athletic Trainers Association. All part-time trainers must work under the direct supervision of a certified trainer.

Section 3. Players' Right to a Second Medical Opinion. A player will have the opportunity to obtain a second medical opinion. As a condition of the responsibility of the Club for the costs of medical services rendered by the physician furnishing the second opinion, the player must (a) consult with the Club physician in advance concerning the other physician; and (b) the Club physician must be furnished promptly with a report concerning the diagnosis, examination and course of treatment recommended by the other physician.

Section 4. Players' Right to a Surgeon of His Choice. A player will have the right to choose the surgeon who will perform surgery provided that: (a) the player will consult with the Club physician as to his recommendation as to the need for, the timing of and who should perform the surgery; and (b) the player will give due consideration to the Club physician's recommendations. Any such surgery will be at Club expense; provided, however, that the Club, the Club physician, the Club trainers and any other representative of the Club will not be responsible for or incur any liability (other than the cost of the surgery) for or relating to the adequacy or competency of such surgery or other related medical services rendered in connection with such surgery.

Section 5. Standard Minimum Pre-Season Physical. Beginning in 1983, each player will undergo a standardized minimum pre-season physical examination, outlined in Appendix D, which will be conducted by the Club physician. If either the Club or the player requests a post-season physical examination, the Club will provide such an examination and player will cooperate in such examination.

Section 6. Chemical Dependency Program. The parties agree that it is the responsibility of everyone in the industry to treat, care for and eliminate chemical dependency problems of players. Accordingly, the parties agree to jointly designate Hazelden Foundation, Center City, Minnesota or its successor if such becomes necessary, to evaluate existing facilities to assure the highest degree of care and treatment and to assure the strictest observance of confidentiality. Any treatment facility which does not meet standards of adequacy will be eliminated and a successor facility in the same metropolitan area chosen solely by Hazelden. Hazelden will be responsible for conducting an ongoing educational program for all players and Club personnel regarding the detection, treatment and after-care of chemically dependent persons. The cost of retaining Hazelden will be paid by the clubs.

Section 7. Testing. The club physician may, upon reasonable cause, direct a player to Hazelden for testing for chemical abuse or dependency problems. There will not be any spot checking for chemical abuse or dependency by the club or club physician.

Section 8. Confidentiality. All medical bills incurred by any player at a local treatment facility will be processed exclusively through Hazelden which will eliminate all information identifying the patient before forwarding the bills to any insurance carrier for payment. Details concerning treatment any player receives will remain confidential within Hazelden and the local chemical dependency facility. After consultation with Hazelden and the player, the facility will advise the club of the player's treatment and such advice will not in and of itself be the basis for any disciplinary action. No information regarding a player's treatment will be publicly disclosed by Hazelden, the facility, or the club.

ARTICLE XXXII

Access To Personnel and Medical Records

Section 1. Personnel Records. Each club will within 7 days after a written request of any player, permit the player to inspect and copy his individual personnel file or any other document which objectively relates to his performance and which in turn relates to any grievance. Each club may, at its discretion, exclude from an individual player's personnel file, coaching and scouting reports, attorney-client privileged material or any other subjective material.

Section 2. Medical Records. Player may examine his medical and trainers' records in the possession of the club or club physician two times each year, once during the pre-season and again after the regular season. Player's personal physician may, upon presentation to the club physician of an authorization signed by the player, inspect the player's medical and trainers' records in consultation with the club physician or have copies of such medical and trainers' records forwarded to him for his exclusive and confidential use in rendering a medical opinion, which records will not be released by the player's personal physician to the player or any other person.

ARTICLE XXXIII

Group Insurance

Section 1. Life. Effective after the execution of this Agreement, group insurance coverage will be increased to $50,000 for a rookie player, and a veteran player's coverage will be increased by $10,000 for each Credited Season under the Bert Bell NFL Player Retirement Plan to a maximum of $100,000.

Section 2. Major Medical. Effective after the execution of this Agreement, the group major medical maximum for a player and his family will be increased to $1,000,000, and, subject to the $25 deductible, 80% of the first $3,000 and 100% of the excess eligible medical expenses for a player will be reimbursed.

Section 3. Dental. Effective after the execution of this Agreement, there will be a 75% increase, not to exceed reasonable and customary charges, in the dental benefit schedule; the dental maximum will be increased to $2,000 per year per person subject to the $25 deductible.

Section 4. Other Benefits. All other group insurance benefits effective during the 1981 season will be continued in effect during the term of this Agreement.

Section 5. Carrier. Following the execution of this Agreement, the parties will jointly shop the group insurance benefits provided for in this Article with insurance carriers, including the current one, and will thereafter jointly select a carrier or carriers to provide such coverage. In order to qualify to be selected under this Article, a carrier must agree in writing as a part of any bid submitted to the parties that it will provide the coverage provided for in this Article at an average annual cost over the four years from September 1, 1983 to August 31, 1987 of no more than $3.8 million per year. In designing and shopping the insurance benefits the parties will provide insurance coverage for vested veteran players who are released after May 1 for a period ending with the first game of the next subsequent regular season.

ARTICLE XXXIV

Retirement Plan

Section 1. Maintenance. The Bert Bell NFL Player Retirement Plan and Trust Agreement (hereinafter referred to as the "Plan" and "Trust") will be continued and maintained in full force and effect during the term of this Agreement.

Section 2. Contributions. Contributions under the Plan will be made in the five Plan Years beginning April 1, 1982, and ending March 31, 1987, in accordance with the following schedule:

Plan Year Begin. April 1	Contributions Subject to § 3	Contributions Subject to § 4	Total Contributions
1982	$1,160,000	$11,340,000	$12,500,000
1983	$1,160,000	$11,340,000	$12,500,000
1984	$1,160,000	$11,340,000	$12,500,000
1985	$1,160,000	$11,340,000	$12,500,000
1986	$1,160,000	$11,340,000	$12,500,000

Contributions will be used exclusively to provide the benefits of the Plan and to pay for its investment management and administration costs. Contributions will be paid into the Trust on or before the last day of each Plan Year, provided that such contributions are allowable as deductions under the applicable provisions of the Internal Revenue Code. Any contribution not received by the Trustee on or before the date it is due will bear interest from the due date to the date of receipt by the Trustee at an annual rate of 6% interest. It will be the duty of the Retirement Board to pursue all available legal remedies in an effort to assure payment of all contributions due under this Agreement. Contributions in future years will be as provided in the Collective Bargaining Agreement effective during such years, subject to Section 3 below.

Section 3. 1974 and 1975. The then-26 clubs guarantee that contributions for the two Plan Years beginning April 1, 1974 and April 1, 1975, respectively, of $5,200,000 and $6,250,000 will be paid at the rate of $515,000 and $645,000, respectively, or a total of $1,160,000 annually to March 31, 1990, provided that such contributions are allowable as deductions under the applicable provisions of the Internal Revenue Code. Any decrease in the number of NFL clubs after the conclusion of the Plan Year ending March 31, 1983, will decrease the above-stated contributions to the Trust in the ratio that the number of clubs at such time bears to 26.

Section 4. Number of Clubs. Any increase or decrease in the number of NFL clubs after the conclusion of the Plan Year ending March 31, 1982, will increase or decrease the contributions to the Trust stated in Section 2 above, less the portions stated in Section 3 above, in the ratio that the number of clubs at such time bears to 28.

Section 5. Obligations. The obligations of the clubs hereunder will apply only to the amount of contributions to be made by the clubs to the Plan. The clubs do not guarantee any benefits under the Plan, except as provided under the applicable law. Furthermore, it is agreed that the determination of the sources of revenue that will be used to satisfy the contribution obligation of the clubs will be exclusively within the control of the clubs.

Section 6. Retirement Board. The parties agree that it is in the best interests of the Plan and the Plan Beneficiaries that the members of the Board be divorced from the collective bargaining process to the extent possible.

Section 7. Actuaries. There shall be co-actuaries to advise the Board, one designated by the NFLPA and the other designated by the Management Council. The interest assumption used under the Plan will be 6% per annum unless otherwise determined by a vote of a majority of voting members of the Board.

Section 8. Amendments. Subject to the limitations of ERISA, the Retirement Board will, by a vote of a majority (four) of the voting members, promptly amend the Plan (subject to the restrictions contained in Article 8.5(A)(B)(C) and (E) of the Plan) to provide the following:

(a) *Benefits.* The Benefit Credit for each Credited Season will be as follows:

Credited Season	Benefit Credit
1965 and prior	60
1966 and 1967	65
1968 and 1969	85
1970	110
1971	115
1972 through 1976	120
1977 through 1981	130
1982 through 1986	150

(b) *Total and Permanent Disability.* Effective with the amendment of the Plan, in the event of Total and Permanent Disability, the benefit will be the benefit earned to the date of disability, subject to a minimum of $4,000 per month if the disability results from a football injury incurred while an active player or $750 per month if the disability results from other than a football injury. In addition, $50 per month for each dependent child will be payable during the period of both types of disability.

(c) *Widow's and Survivor Benefits.* Effective with the amendment of the Plan, in the event of death or remarriage of a widow, present Widow's Benefit payments subject to a minimum of $600 per month will continue to any surviving children until one of the children last reaches age 19 (or, age 23 if in college), or continuously if any child is mentally or physically incapacitated. Players active in the 1982 season and thereafter will be entitled to a minimum Widow's Benefit of $1,500 per month payable for 48 months following the date of death; thereafter, survivor benefits will be payable as stated above.

(d) *Line-of-Duty.* Effective with the amendment of the Plan, the Line-of-Duty Disability Benefit will be subject to a minimum of $500 per month.

(e) *Early Retirement Reduction Factor.* The early retirement reduction factor currently in use under the Plan may not be increased.

(f) *Other Amendments.* The Plan will be amended to set up a Medical Advisory Board to make final determinations whether applicants for disability benefits have qualifying disabilities and will be amended to provide that Retirement Board disputes related to interpretation or application of benefit, eligibility and other administrative provisions of the Plan may be submitted to arbitration under Article VII of this Agreement, upon motion approved by at least three (3) Board members.

Section 9. Conformance. The Plan and Trust will be amended to conform to the provisions of this Agreement and any requirements of ERISA. All other provisions of the Plan and Trust will remain unchanged, unless duly amended by the Retirement Board.

ARTICLE XXXV

Termination Pay

Section 1. Payment. Effective after the execution of this Agreement, any player who has completed the season in which his fourth year or more of Credited Service under the Bert Bell NFL Player Retirement Plan has been earned, and is released from the Active List, Inactive List or Injured Reserve List of his club after the commencement of the regular season schedule, but prior to the Thursday before the eighth regular season game, is entitled to claim and receive, after the end of the regular season schedule, termination pay in an amount equal to the unpaid balance of the initial 50% of his salary, exclusive of deferred compensation, but not less than an amount equal to one week's salary, up to a maximum of $6,000; provided, however, that (a) the player will not be entitled to such termination pay if he has signed a contract with another club for that same season; and (b) a player will not be entitled to such termination pay more than once during his playing career in the NFL.

Section 2. One Week. Any player who otherwise qualifies for terminational pay under Section 1 above, but is released during the regular season after the time he would be entitled to the unpaid balance of the initial 50% of his salary, will receive termination pay in an amount equal to one week's salary, up to a maximum of $6,000.

ARTICLE XXXVI

Workers' Compensation

Section 1. Benefits. In any states where Worker's Compensation coverage is not compulsory, a club will either voluntarily obtain coverage under the compensation laws of that state or otherwise guarantee equivalent benefits to its players. In the event that a player qualifies for benefits under this section, such benefits will be equivalent to those benefits paid under the compensation law of the state in which his club is located.

Section 2. Rejection of Coverage. Nothing herein stated is to be interpreted as preventing a club, which has the legal right to do so, from rejecting coverage under the worker's compensation law of its state. However, if a club elects to reject coverage under the compensation law of its state, it must nevertheless guarantee benefits to its players in the manner previously prescribed in Section 1 above. Moreover, any club may be excluded from those laws if it elects to do so. However, such a club will be obligated to guarantee benefits to its players in the same manner previously prescribed in Section 1 above.

Section 3. Arbitration. In any state where a club (i.e. Miami Dolphins/Florida) has legally elected not to be covered by the worker's compensation laws of that state, the equivalent benefit, if any, to which a player may be entitled under this Article will be determined under the grievance procedure of Article VII of this Agreement.

ARTICLE XXXVII

Miscellaneous

Section 1. Endorsements. No club may arbitrarily refuse to permit a player to endorse a product.

Section 2. Appearances. No club may unreasonably require a player to appear on radio or television.

Section 3. Promotion. The NFLPA will use its best efforts to see that the players cooperate with the clubs and the news media in reasonable promotional activities on behalf of the clubs and the NFL.

Section 4. Deductions. The involuntary deduction of amounts from any compensation due to a player for the purpose of compensating any clubhouse personnel or any other club attache is prohibited.

Section 5. Public Statements. The NFLPA and the Management Council agree that each will use its best efforts to curtail public comments by club personnel or players which express criticism of any club, its coach or its operation and policy, or which tend to cast discredit upon a club, a player or any other person involved in the operation of a club, the NFL, the Management Council, or the NFLPA.

Section 6. Addresses. The Management Council will furnish upon request to the NFLPA whatever address and telephone lists clubs have covering all players who are under contract to the clubs as of October 1 for in-season and January 1 for off-season. The Management Council will not divulge player telephone numbers to the media. As of the first pre-season cutdown date, the Management Council will provide to the NFLPA employment dates for all players who are then under contract to the clubs.

Section 7. NFLPA Tickets. Two complimentary tickets will be made available to the NFLPA to permit attendance at each regularly scheduled League game by authorized NFLPA representatives. The NFLPA will provide a list of authorized persons to the Management Council. The NFLPA must notify the home club of its desire to attend such a game at least three days prior to the date of the game. NFLPA representatives must possess appropriate identification.

Section 8. Player Tickets. Two complimentary tickets will be made available to each player for each home game of his club. Each player will be afforded the opportunity to purchase two tickets for each away game of his club from the best tickets available for public sale immediately prior to the public sale for each game. Whatever practice a club had with respect to providing players the opportunity to purchase tickets to the 1982 Super Bowl game will be continued for the duration of this Agreement.

Section 9. Tests. No psychological or personality tests will be given to any player after he signs his first contract with an NFL club. A player is entitled to review the results of his psychological or personality tests upon request.

Section 10. League Security. A player will have the right, if he so requests, to have an NFLPA representative present during an interview by any representative of NFL security if the player has reasonable basis for believing that Commissioner discipline might result from the interview.

ARTICLE XXXVIII

Duration of Agreement

Section 1. Effective Date. This agreement will be effective as of July 16, 1982, except as specifically provided otherwise in this Agreement.

Section 2. Termination Date. Except as specifically provided otherwise in this Agreement, either the NFLPA or the Management Council may terminate this Agreement on August 31, 1987, or thereafter by giving 60 days prior written notice to the other party. Except as specifically provided otherwise in this Agreement, all the terms and conditions of this Agreement will be continued in full force and effect for a period of 60 days after such notice is given or until the expiration date of this Agreement, whichever occurs later.

Section 3. Termination. If the continued operation of Article XIII or XV of this Collective Bargaining Agreement is effectively enjoined by a court of competent jurisdiction, or if any portion of Article III of this Agreement is effectively held invalid by a court of competent jurisdiction, then this Agreement, at the option of either party hereto, may be terminated upon the giving of written notice of termination. It is understood between the parties that, upon such termination, all rights, duties, obligations, and privileges of the parties provided for hereunder will cease to be effective; provided, however, that employment practices and procedures already followed pursuant to this Agreement and benefits already paid pursuant to this Agreement will be accepted as fully effective and agreed to between the parties for the period preceding such termination.

Section 4. Ratification. This Agreement is subject to ratification by the NFLPA and the Management Council in accordance with their internal procedures before it becomes effective. In the event of failure of ratification by either party, then this Agreement will not become effective and neither party, nor any of its members, will possess or assert any claim whatsoever against the other party because of the failure of ratification of this Agreement.

NATIONAL FOOTBALL LEAGUE NATIONAL FOOTBALL LEAGUE
PLAYERS ASSOCIATION   MANAGEMENT COUNCIL
BY: BY:

Ed Garvey   Jack Donlan
Executive Director   Executive Director

Gene Upshaw   Charles Sullivan
President   Chairman

10.4 NATIONAL FOOTBALL LEAGUE PLAYER CONTRACT

THIS CONTRACT is between _____, hereinafter "Player," and _____, a _____ corporation (limited partnership) (partnership), hereinafter "Club," operating under the name of the _____ as a member of the National Football League, hereinafter "League." In consideration of the promises made by each to the other, Player and Club agree as follows:

1. Term. This contract covers one football season, and will begin on the date of execution or April 1, 19__, whichever is later, and end on April 1, 19__, unless extended, terminated, or renewed as specified elsewhere in this contract.

2. Employment and Services. Club employs Player as a skilled football player. Player accepts such employment. He agrees to give his best efforts and loyalty to the Club, and to conduct himself on and off the field with appropriate recognition of the fact that the success of professional football depends largely on public respect for and approval of those associated with the game. Player will report promptly for and participate fully in Club's official pre-season training camp, all Club meetings and practice sessions, and all pre-season, regular-season and post-season football games scheduled for or by Club. If invited, Player will practice for and play in any all-star football game sponsored by the League.

Player will not participate in any football game not sponsored by the League unless the game is first approved by the League.

3. Other Activities. Without prior written consent of Club, Player will not play football or engage in activities related to football otherwise than for Club or engage in any activity other than football which may involve a significant risk of personal injury. Player represents that he has special, exceptional and unique knowledge, skill, ability, and experience as a football player, the loss of which cannot be estimated with any certainty and cannot be fairly or adequately compensated by damages. Player therefore agrees that Club will have the right, in addition to any other right which Club may possess, to enjoin Player by appropriate proceedings from playing football or engaging in football-related activities other than for Club or from engaging in any activity other than football which may involve a significant risk of personal injury.

4. Publicity. Player grants to Club and League, separately and together, the authority to use his name and picture for publicity and promotional purposes in newspapers, magazines, motion pictures, game programs and roster manuals, broadcasts and telecasts, and all other publicity and advertising media, provided such publicity and promotion does not in itself constitute an endorsement by Player of a commercial product. Player will cooperate with the news media, and will participate upon request in reasonable promotional activities of Club and the League.

5. Compensation. For performance of Player's services and all other promises of Player, Club will pay Player a yearly salary of $_____, payable as provided in Paragraph 6; such earned performance bonuses as may be called for in Paragraph 24 of or any attachment to this contract; Player's necessary traveling expenses from his residence to training camp; Player's reasonable board and lodging expenses during pre-season training and in connection with playing pre-season, regular-season, and post-season football games outside Club's home city; Player's necessary traveling expenses to and from pre-season, regular-season, and post-season football games outside Club's home city; Player's necessary traveling expenses to his residence if this contract is terminated by Club; and such additional compensation, benefits and reimbursement of expenses as may be called for in any collective bargaining agreement in existence during the term of this contract. (For purposes of this contract, a collective bargaining agreement will be deemed to be "in existence" during its stated term or during any period for which the parties to that agreement agree to extend it.)

6. Payment. Unless this contract or any collective bargaining agreement in existence during the term of this contract specifically provides otherwise, Player will be paid as follows: If Player has not previously reported to any NFL club's official pre-season training camp in any year, he will be paid 100% of his yearly salary under this contract in equal weekly or bi-weekly installments over the course of the regular season period, commencing with the first regular season game played by club. If Player has previously reported to any NFL club's official pre-season training camp in any year, he will be paid 10% of his yearly salary under this contract in equal weekly installments over the course of the pre-season period, commencing with the end of the first week of the Club's official pre-season training camp as designated for Player and ending one week prior to the first regular season game played by Club, and 90% of his yearly salary in equal weekly or bi-weekly installments over the course of the regular season period, commencing with the first regular season game played by Club. If this contract is executed or Player is activated after the start of Club's official pre-season training camp, the yearly salary payable to Player will be reduced proportionately and Player will be paid the weekly or bi-weekly portions of his yearly salary becoming due and payable after he is activated. If this contract is terminated after the start of Club's official pre-season training camp, the yearly salary payable to Player will be reduced proportionately and Player will be paid the weekly or bi-weekly portions of his yearly salary having become due and payable up to the time of termination (prorated daily if termination occurs before one week prior to the first regular season game played by Club).

7. Deductions. Any advance made to Player will be repaid to Club, and any properly levied Club fine or Commissioner fine against Player will be paid, in cash on demand or by means of deductions from payments coming due to the Player under this contract, the amount of such deductions to be determined by Club unless this contract specifically provides otherwise.

8. Physical Condition. Player represents to Club that he is and will maintain himself in excellent physical condition. Player will undergo a complete physical examination by the Club physician upon Club request, during which physical examination Player agrees to make full and complete disclosure of any physical or mental condition known to him which might impair his performance under this contract and to respond fully and in good faith when questioned by the Club physician about such condition. If Player fails to establish or maintain his excellent physical condition to the satisfaction of the Club physician, or make the required full and complete disclosure and good faith responses to the Club physician, then Club may terminate this contract.

9. Injury. If Player is injured in the performance of his services under this contract and promptly reports such injury to the Club physician or trainer, then Player will receive such medical and hospital care during the term of this contract as the Club physician may deem necessary, and in accordance with Club's practice, will continue to receive his yearly salary for so long, during the season of injury only and for no subsequent period, as Player is physically unable to perform the services required of him by this contract because of such injury. If Player's injury in the performance of his services under this contract results in his death, the unpaid balance of his yearly salary for the season of injury will be paid to his stated beneficiary or in the absence of a stated beneficiary, to his estate.

10. **Workmen's Compensation.** Any compensation paid to Player under this contract or under any collective bargaining agreement in existence during the term of this contract for a period during which he is entitled to workmen's compensation benefits by reason of temporary total, permanent total, temporary partial, or permanent partial disability will be deemed an advance payment of workmen's compensation benefits due Player, and Club will be entitled to be reimbursed the amount of such payment out of any award of workmen's compensation.

11. **Skill, Performance and Conduct.** Player understands that he is competing with other players for a position on Club's roster within the applicable player limits. If at any time, in the sole judgment of Club, Player's skill or performance has been unsatisfactory as compared with that of other players competing for positions on Club's roster, or if Player has engaged in personal conduct reasonably judged by Club to adversely affect or reflect on Club, then Club may terminate this contract.

12. **Termination.** The rights of termination set forth in this contract will be in addition to any other rights of termination allowed either party by law. Termination will be effective upon the giving of written notice, except that Player's death, other than as a result of injury incurred in the performance of his services under this contract, will automatically terminate this contract. If this contract is terminated by Club and either Player or Club so requests, Player will promptly undergo a complete physical examination by the Club physician.

13. **Injury Grievance.** Unless a collective bargaining agreement in existence at the time of termination of this contract by Club provides otherwise, the following injury grievance procedure will apply: If Player believes that at the time of termination of this contract by Club he was physically unable to perform the services required of him by this contract because of an injury incurred in the performance of his services under this contract, Player may, within a reasonably brief time after examination by the Club physician, submit at his own expense to examination by a physician of his choice. If the opinion of Player's physician with respect to his physical ability to perform the services required of him by this contract is contrary to that of the Club's physician, the dispute will be submitted within a reasonable time to final and binding arbitration by an arbitrator selected by Club and Player or, if they are unable to agree, one selected by the League Commissioner on application by either party.

14. **Rules.** Players will comply with and be bound by all reasonable Club rules and regulations in effect during the term of this contract which are not inconsistent with the provisions of this contract or of any

collective bargaining agreement in existence during the term of this contract. Player's attention is also called to the fact that the League functions with certain rules and procedures expressive of its operation as a joint venture among its member clubs and that these rules and practices may affect Player's relationship to the League and its member clubs independently of the provisions of this contract.

15. **Integrity of Game.** Player recognizes the detriment to the League and professional football that would result from impairment of public confidence in the honest and orderly conduct of NFL games or the integrity and good character of NFL players. Player therefore acknowledges his awareness that if he accepts a bribe or agrees to throw or fix an NFL game; fails to promptly report a bribe offer or an attempt to throw or fix an NFL game; bets on an NFL game; knowingly associates with gamblers or gambling activity; uses or provides other players with stimulants or other drugs for the purpose of attempting to enhance on-field performance; or is guilty of any other form of conduct reasonably judged by the League Commissioner to be detrimental to the League or professional football, the Commissioner will have the right, but only after giving Player the opportunity for a hearing at which he may be represented by counsel of his choice, to fine Player in a reasonable amount; to suspend Player for a period certain or indefinitely; and/or to terminate this contract.

16. **Extension.** If Player becomes a member of the Armed Forces of the United States or any other country, or retires from professional football as an active player, or otherwise fails or refuses to perform his services under this contract, then this contract will be tolled between the date of Player's induction into the Armed Forces, or his retirement, or his failure or refusal to perform, and the later date of his return to professional football. During the period this contract is tolled, Player will not be entitled to any compensation or benefits. On Player's return to professional football, the term of this contract will be extended for a period of time equal to the number of seasons (to the nearest multiple of one) remaining at the time the contract was tolled. The right of renewal, if any, contained in this contract will remain in effect until the end of any such extended term.

17. **Renewal.** Unless this contract specifically provides otherwise, Club may, by sending written notice to Player on or before the April 1 expiration date referred to in Paragraph 1, renew this contract for a period of one year. The terms and conditions for the renewal year will be the same as those provided in this contract for the last preceding year, except that there will be no further right of renewal in Club and, unless this contract specifically provides otherwise, the rate of compensation for the renewal year will be 90% of the rate of compensation provided in this contract for the last preceding year. The phrase "rate of compensation" as used above means yearly salary, including deferred compensation, and

any performance bonus, but excluding any signing or reporting bonus. In order for Player to receive 90% of any performance bonus under this contract he must meet the previously established conditions of that bonus during the renewal year.

18. Assignment. Unless this contract specifically provides otherwise, Club may assign this contract and Player's services under this contract to any successor to Club's franchise or to any other Club in the League. Player will report to the assignee club promptly upon being informed of the assignment of his contract and will faithfully perform his services under this contract. The assignee club will pay Player's necessary traveling expenses in reporting to it and will faithfully perform this contract with Player.

19. Filing. This contract will be valid and binding upon Player and Club immediately upon execution. A copy of this contract, including any attachment to it, will be filed by Club with the League Commissioner within 10 days after execution. The Commissioner will have the right to disapprove this contract on reasonable grounds, including but not limited to an attempt by the parties to abridge or impair the rights of any other club, uncertainty or incompleteness in expression of the parties' respective rights and obligations, or conflict between the terms of this contract and any collective bargaining agreement then in existence. Approval will be automatic unless, within 10 days after receipt of this contract in his office, the Commissioner notifies the parties either of disapproval or of extension of this 10-day period for purposes of investigation or clarification pending his decision. On the receipt of notice of disapproval and termination, both parties will be relieved of their respective rights and obligations under this contract.

20. Disputes. Any dispute between Player and Club involving the interpretation or application of any provision of this contract will be submitted to final and binding arbitration in accordance with the procedure called for in any collective bargaining agreement in existence at the time the event giving rise to any such dispute occurs. If no collective bargaining agreement is in existence at such time, the dispute will be submitted within a reasonable time to the League Commissioner for final and binding arbitration by him, except as provided otherwise in Paragraph 13 of this contract.

21. Notice. Any notice, request approval or consent under this contract will be sufficiently given if in writing and delivered in person or mailed (certified or first class) by one party to the other at the address set forth in this contract or to such other address as the recipient may subsequently have furnished in writing to the sender.

22. Other Agreements. This contract including any attachment to it, sets forth the entire agreement between Player and Club and cannot be modified or supplemented orally. Player and Club represent that no other agreement, oral or written, except as attached to or specifically incorporated in this contract, exists between them. The provisions of this contract will govern the relationship between Player and Club unless there are conflicting provisions in any collective bargaining agreement in existence during the term of this contract, in which case the provisions of the collective bargaining agreement will take precedence over conflicting provisions of this contract relating to the rights or obligations of either party.

23. Law. This contract is made under and shall be governed by the laws of the State of ＿＿＿＿.

24. Special Provisions.

THIS CONTRACT is executed in triplicate this ＿＿＿＿ day of ＿＿＿＿, 19＿. Player acknowledges that before signing this contract he was given the opportunity to seek advice from or be represented by persons of his own selection.

＿＿＿＿＿＿＿＿＿＿＿＿	＿＿＿＿＿＿＿＿＿＿＿＿
PLAYER	CLUB
＿＿＿＿＿＿＿＿＿＿＿＿	＿＿＿＿＿＿＿＿＿＿＿＿
Home Address	By
＿＿＿＿＿＿＿＿＿＿＿＿	＿＿＿＿＿＿＿＿＿＿＿＿
	Club Address
＿＿＿＿＿＿＿＿＿＿＿＿	＿＿＿＿＿＿＿＿＿＿＿＿
Telephone Number	

10.5 STANDARD REPRESENTATION AGREEMENT BETWEEN NATIONAL FOOTBALL LEAGUE PLAYERS ASSOCIATION CONTRACT ADVISOR AND PLAYER

This Agreement is made this ＿＿＿＿ day of ＿＿＿＿, 198＿ by and between ＿＿＿＿＿＿＿＿, hereinafter "Player," and ＿＿＿＿＿＿＿＿
(Name of Player)   (Name of Contract
＿＿＿＿＿＿, hereinafter "Contract Advisor," pursuant to and in accordance
Advisor)
with the NFLPA Regulations Governing Contract Advisors, as adopted May 5, 1983 and amended from time to time thereafter. In consideration of the promises made by each to the other, Player and Contract Advisor agree as follows:

¶ **1. Contract Negotiation Services.** Contract Advisor hereby warrants and represents that he has been duly certified as an NFLPA Contract Advisor * pursuant to the NFLPA Regulations Governing Contract Advisors. Player hereby retains Contract Advisor to represent, advise, counsel, and assist Player in the negotiation, execution, and enforcement of his playing contract(s) in the National Football League. Such services are to be rendered by Contract Advisor pursuant to and in full compliance with the NFLPA Regulations Governing Contract Advisors. Contract Advisor, serving in a fiduciary capacity, shall act in such manner as to protect the best interests of Player and assure effective representation of Player in individual contract negotiations with NFL clubs. Contract Advisor shall not have the authority to bind or commit Player to enter into any contract without actual execution thereof by the Player. (* If Contract Advisor has been granted only a one-year certificate, he or she must inform the player of this fact.)

2. **Contract Advisor's Compensation.** If Contract Advisor succeeds in negotiating an NFL Player Contract or contracts acceptable to Player and signed by Player during the term hereof, Contract Advisor shall be paid a fee equal to the following:

NOTE! Such fee may be less than but may not exceed the maximum fee for Contract Advisors provided in Section 4 of the NFLPA Regulations Governing Contract Advisors, and, in accordance with that Section, such fee shall not be due and payable to Contract Advisor unless and until Player receives the compensation provided for in the player contract(s) negotiated by Contract Advisor.

3. **Expenses.** Player shall reimburse Contract Advisor for all reasonable and necessary communication expenses (i.e., telephone and postage) actually incurred by Player's NFL Contract(s). Player shall also reimburse Contract Advisor for all reasonable and necessary travel expenses actually incurred by Contract Advisor during the term hereof in the negotiation of Player's NFL Contract(s), but only if such expenses and the approximate amounts thereof are approved in advance by Player. Player shall promptly pay all such expenses upon receipt of an itemized, written statement therefore from Contract Advisor.

4. **Disputes.** Any disputes between Player and Contract Advisor involving the interpretation or application of this Agreement or the obligations of the parties hereunder shall be resolved exclusively through the Arbitration Procedures set forth in Section 7 of the NFLPA Regulations Governing Contract Advisors. If Contract Advisor constitutes or represents an "athlete agency" governed by the Labor Code of the State of California, Contract Advisor shall provide reasonable notice to the Labor Committee of the State of California of the time and place of any arbitration hearing to be held under said Arbitration Procedures, and said Labor Commission or his authorized representative shall have the right to attend all arbitration hearings thereunder.

5. **Disclaimer of Liability.** Player and Contract Advisor, by virtue of entry into this Agreement, agree that they are not subject to the control or direction of any other person with respect to the timing, place, manner or fashion in which individual negotiations are to be conducted

(except to the extent that Contract Advisor shall comply with NFLPA Regulations) and that they will save and hold harmless NFLPA, its officers, employees and representatives from any liability whatsoever with respect to their conduct and activities relating to or in connection with such individual negotiations.

6. Term. Except as provided otherwise in this Paragraph, the term of this Agreement shall begin on the date hereof and continue for the term of any player contract or series of contracts negotiated by Contract Advisor on Player's behalf and signed by Player within one year of the date of this Agreement. Player may terminate this Agreement at any time if:

a. Contract Advisor fails to disclose in writing to Player, prior to accepting representation of Player hereunder or continuing to represent Player hereunder, as the case may be, the names and positions of any NFL management personnel whom Contract Advisor has represented or is representing in matters pertaining to their employment by any NFL club; or

b. Contract Advisor substantially fails or refuses to negotiate in good faith on Player's behalf in individual contract negotiations with the NFL club(s) desiring Player's services.

Such termination shall be effective upon the Player's giving written notice to such effect, either personally delivered or sent by prepaid mail to Contract Advisor's business address.

In the event that Contract Advisor fails to negotiate an NFL Player Contract acceptable to Player and signed by him on or before the date which is one year after the date Player signs this Agreement, this Agreement shall automatically terminate as of such later date.

The revocation or suspension of Contract Advisor's Certification as an NFLPA Contract Advisor pursuant to the NFLPA Regulations Governing Contract Advisors shall automatically terminate this Agreement.

In the event that Player has an opportunity to negotiate a new player contract in the NFL at any time prior to the termination of the contract or series of contracts negotiated by Contract Advisor hereunder, Player shall not be obligated to retain Contract Advisor or use Contract Advisor's services for such negotiation, and Contract Advisor shall not be entitled to any fee for such negotiation unless Player retains Contract Advisor through the signing of a new Representation Agreement.

7. Filing. A copy of this Agreement shall be filed by Contract Advisor with the NFLPA within ten days of execution. Any deviation, deletion, or addition in this form shall not be valid until and unless approved by the NFLPA. Approval shall be automatic unless, within ten days after receipt of this Agreement by the NFLPA, the NFLPA notifies the parties either of disapproval or of extension of this ten-day period for investigation or clarification.

8. Entire Agreement; Governing Law. This Agreement, along with the NFLPA Regulations Governing Contract Advisors, governs the relationship between the parties hereto and can not be modified or supplemented orally. This Agreement supercedes all prior agreements between the parties on the same subject matter.

This Agreement shall be interpreted in accordance with the laws of the State of _____.

EXAMINE THIS CONTRACT CAREFULLY
BEFORE SIGNING IT

IN WITNESS WHEREOF, the parties hereto have hereunder signed their names as hereinafter set forth.

_____

Contract Advisor

_____

Player   Date

_____

Parent or Guardian if Player is
under 21 years of age

*

Index

RESTITUTION, 42–43

RESTRAINT OF TRADE
Amateur athletes, 51–52
Boycotts, 47
Clayton Act, 48–49
Disciplinary rules, 60
Draft system, 61
Eligibility rules, 59
Facilities, 54
Horizontal division of markets, 47
Labor law exemption, 52
League expansion, 58
League franchise, 54
Media coverage, 57
Mergers, 58
Monopoly, 48
NCAA rules, 7, 31
Per se violations, 47
Price fixing, 47
Reserve and option clauses, 55
Rule of reason, 46–47
Rules of sports associations, 60
Rules of competition, 59
Team movement approval rules, 54
Team ownership rules, 62
Tying contracts, 47, 59

RISK MANAGEMENT, 272

ROZELLE RULE, 55

RULE OF REASON TEST, 46–47

RULES
Generally, 6, 10, 32
Age, 35, 98
Alienage, 97
"Amateur" standing, 7
Conference and league, 6, 10
Drug use and testing, 23
Enforcement, 28
Financial aid, 15
Five-year rule, 20
Four-year rule, 21, 34
Full-time student, 20
Good academic standing, 22
Good conduct, 37
Grades, 16, 34
Hardship, 25, 36
Longevity, 35, 98
Marriage, 96
Personal appearance, 37, 82
Physical impairment, 36
Public-private schools, 79, 99
Recruitment, 11

†